AnnualRecipes
2011

INCLUDING PILLSBURY BAKE-OFF® CONTEST WINNERS

Pillsbury Annual Recipes 2011

Our recipes have been tested in the Pillsbury Kitchens and meet our standards of easy preparation, reliability and great taste.

For more great recipes, visit pillsbury.com

Copyright © 2011 General Mills, Inc.
Minneapolis, Minnesota

PUBLISHED BY
Taste of Home Books
Reiman Media Group, LLC
5400 S. 60th St., Greendale WI 53129
www.tasteofhome.com

Printed in U.S.A.

International Standard Book Number (10):
0-89821-835-7
International Standard Book Number (13):
978-0-89821-835-0
International Standard Serial Number:
1930-7349

CREDITS
General Mills, Inc.
EDITORIAL DIRECTOR: Jeff Nowak
PUBLISHING MANAGER: Christine Gray
COOKBOOK EDITOR: Grace Wells
DIGITAL ASSETS MANAGER: Carrie Jacobson
PRODUCTION MANAGER: Michelle Tufts
RECIPE DEVELOPMENT AND TESTING: Pillsbury Test Kitchens
PHOTOGRAPHY: General Mills Photography Studio

Reiman Media Group, LLC
EDITOR IN CHIEF: Catherine Cassidy
VICE PRESIDENT, EXECUTIVE EDITOR/BOOKS: Heidi Reuter Lloyd
CREATIVE DIRECTOR: Howard Greenberg
SENIOR EDITOR/BOOKS: Mark Hagen
EDITOR: Krista Lanphier
ART DIRECTOR: Gretchen Trautman
CONTENT PRODUCTION SUPERVISOR: Julie Wagner
LAYOUT DESIGNERS: Kathy Crawford, Nancy Novak,
   Emma Acevedo
GRAPHIC DESIGN ASSOCIATE: Juli Schnuck
PROOFREADERS: Vicki Jensen, Linne Bruskewitz
PREMEDIA SUPERVISOR: Scott Berger
ADMINISTRATIVE ASSISTANT: Barb Czysz

NORTH AMERICAN CHIEF MARKETING OFFICER: Lisa Karpinski
VICE PRESIDENT/BOOK MARKETING: Dan Fink
CREATIVE DIRECTOR/CREATIVE MARKETING: James Palmen

Reader's Digest Association, Inc.
PRESIDENT AND CHIEF EXECUTIVE OFFICER: Mary G. Berner
PRESIDENT, NORTH AMERICAN AFFINITIES: Suzanne M. Grimes

COVER PHOTOGRAPHY: Taste of Home Photo Studio
   PHOTOGRAPHER: Jim Wieland
   FOOD STYLIST: Kathryn Conrad
   SET STYLIST: Jennifer Bradley Vent

FRONT COVER PHOTOGRAPHS:
Tuscan Sausage and Bean Stew, Pg. 242;
Balsamic-Glazed Chicken Breasts, Pg. 173;
Sautéed Sugar Snap Peas, Peppers and Onions,
Pg. 98; Cranberry Ribbon Cheesecake, Pg. 284;
Pizza-Stuffed Peppers, Pg. 235.

PAGE 5 PHOTOGRAPHS:
Onion and Oregano Beef Pot Roast, Pg. 227;
Apple-Walnut Salad with Cranberry Vinaigrette,
Pg. 96; Oatmeal Raisin Cheesecake Crumble,
Pg. 337; Sesame-Chicken Pot Stickers, Pg. 44.

BACK COVER PHOTOGRAPHS:
Asian Pot Roast, Pg. 222; Spiced Chai, Pg. 48;
Mocha Mousse Puffs, Pg. 322; Sweet Potatoes
with Cinnamon Honey, Pg. 285.

contents

"Hundreds of Spectacular Meals for Everyday Cooks Like You!"

introduction

Home cooks just like you have relied on Pillsbury for over 130 years to make dinner time special. That's why we're excited to offer you the sixth edition in this popular line of cookbooks. *Pillsbury Annual Recipes 2011* has over 400 recipes and tips to help you quickly prepare easy, family-friendly dishes that are bursting with homemade flavor.

Every recipe in this beautiful cookbook comes from a 2010 Pillsbury Classic® Cookbook and offers simple instructions. And to make your cooking adventures even easier, many of the dishes rely on everyday ingredients and kitchen staples you likely have on hand. In addition, each recipe includes a gorgeous color photo and step-by-step directions so that even beginning cooks can serve up success.

Best of all, the recipes have been tested and approved by the experts at the Pillsbury Test Kitchens, so you'll easily win thumbs-up approval from your gang. To locate the recipes you need, simply consider the 13 chapters jam-packed with scrumptious selections.

For example, turn to the Breakfast & Brunch chapter for morning sensations such as Savory and Sweet Breakfast Biscuit Sliders (p. 20). And for elegant bites or sippers for your next casual get-together, try the Razzle-Dazzle Beef Bites (p. 38) and Pomegranate Spiced Tea (p. 42) in the Appetizers & Beverages chapter.

It's easy to put a home-cooked dinner on the table, thanks to Beefy Main Dishes, Chicken & Turkey Entrees and Pork, Seafood & More. You'll find delicious meals in these chapters,

such as Cheeseburger Pot Pie (p. 142) or Pepperoni Pizza Chicken (p. 162). For lighter fare and yummy pairings, try the Soups & Sandwiches or the Sides, Salads & Breads chapters featuring tasty recipes such as Spiced Apple-Squash Soup (p. 63) and Quick and Easy Onion Rolls (p. 118).

We've also created the Budget Recipes chapter, so busy cooks can create scrumptious, low-cost meals, such as Three Cheese-Sausage Lasagna (p. 210). And for traditional American dishes, try Family Favorites, which includes such classic recipes as Sweet and Tangy Brisket (p. 252) and Hot Fudge Brownie Dessert (p. 272).

If you want to keep things simple, give supper a jump-start with ready-when-you-get-home Caramelized Onion Beef Stew (p. 228) and Chicken Cacciatore (p. 241) in the Slow Cooker Specialties chapter.

The Holiday Extravaganza section is brimming with fun Halloween, Thanksgiving and Christmas ideas perfect for special celebrations. Thrill your guests with slices of Apple-Sage Brined Turkey Breast (p. 286), Pumpkin-Ginger Pie with Gingersnap Streusel (p. 293) and more!

Don't forget the sweets! Everyone will save room when you whip up delights from the Cookies & Bars and Decadent Desserts chapters. Indulge in Fudgy Chocolate Chip-Toffee Bars (p. 303) and Cherry-Nut-Crescent Crisp (p. 342).

It's all here for you in *Pillsbury Annual Recipes 2011*. And there's more! Read on...

AT-A-GLANCE ICONS

If you're like most family cooks, you have less time than ever to spend in the kitchen. You need to find the recipes right for you, and fast!

Maybe you're most interested in dishes that are especially fuss-free to prepare...or are on the healthier side...or were winners from the famous Pillsbury Bake-Off® Contests. To quickly locate these types of dishes, look for the following icons located next to the recipe title:

EASY RECIPE

These dishes use 6 ingredients or less OR have a prep time of 20 minutes or less OR are ready to eat in 30 minutes or less.

LOW-FAT RECIPE

These dishes contain 10 grams of fat or less (main dishes) or 3 grams of fat or less (all other recipes).

PILLSBURY BAKE-OFF® RECIPE

These dishes were judged award-winners in a Pillsbury Bake-Off® Contest.

We've also included "Prep" and "Ready in..." times, so you'll know exactly how long it takes to prepare each dish from start to finish. And to provide even more at-a-glance information, we've featured Nutrition Facts with each and every recipe in the book.

HELPFUL INDEXES

This easy-to-use cookbook is indexed in two convenient ways. Look up any major ingredient in the general index, which starts on page 346, and you'll see a comprehensive list of the recipes in which it is included. For instance, if you would like a main dish made with chicken, turn to "chicken" in the general index to find dozens of flavorful options.

The alphabetical index starts on page 344. Once you've found a few favorite recipes for your family, you can easily find them by title the next time you want to make them.

Or, perhaps you just want to page through and look at all of the taste-tempting photos until you discover a new recipe that's perfect for you. No matter which Pillsbury favorite you choose to serve, it's certain to become a permanent, much-loved part of your kitchen collection!

Breakfast & Brunch

These rise-and-shine delights are
a tasty way to jump-start the day.

BLUEBERRY MUFFIN TOPS
PG. 27

DOUBLE CHOCOLATE-
ORANGE SCONES
PG. 22

JAVA-GLAZED CINNAMON ROLLS
PG. 21

BREAKFAST SKILLET
PG. 19

Pear-Havarti Crêpe Squares

ANDRIA ZEHNTBAUER | PORTLAND, OREGON

BAKE-OFF® CONTEST 44, 2010

PREP TIME: 15 MINUTES (READY IN 45 MINUTES)
SERVINGS: 8

e EASY

1 can (8 oz) Pillsbury® refrigerated crescent dinner rolls (8 rolls)

¾ cup Pillsbury Best® all purpose flour

½ teaspoon vanilla

¾ cup milk

3 Eggland's Best eggs

2 tablespoons Land O Lakes® unsalted or salted butter, melted

Dash salt

1 unpeeled medium pear, cored, thinly sliced

⅓ lb Havarti cheese (4 or 5 slices), torn into quarter-size pieces

2 tablespoons powdered sugar

½ cup Smucker's® seedless red raspberry jam

1) Heat oven to 400°F. Spray 13x9-inch pan with Crisco® original no-stick cooking spray. Unroll crescent dough; press in bottom of pan, pressing perforations to seal. Bake about 8 minutes or until light golden brown.

2) In medium bowl, place flour, vanilla, milk, eggs, melted butter and salt. Using electric hand mixer, beat 20 to 30 seconds or until batter is smooth.

3) Top baked crescent layer with pear slices. Pour batter over top. Place cheese pieces on batter; press some pieces down to cover with batter and leave other pieces uncovered.

4) Bake 20 to 30 minutes longer or until top is light golden brown and edges are golden brown. Sprinkle with powdered sugar. Serve with jam.

Nutrition Information Per Serving	
Calories: 370	
Total Fat	18g
Saturated Fat	9g
Sodium	420mg
Total Carbohydrate	40g
Dietary Fiber	1g
Protein	10g

Country Breakfast Pot Pie

PREP TIME: 25 MINUTES (READY IN 50 MINUTES)
SERVINGS: 6

3 tablespoons vegetable oil

1 bag (20 oz) refrigerated shredded hash browns

1 cup shredded Swiss cheese (4 oz)

8 eggs

1 tablespoon chopped fresh chives

½ teaspoon salt

¼ teaspoon freshly ground pepper

1½ cups cubed cooked ham (8 oz)

1 package (3 oz) cream cheese, cut into small cubes

1 can (10.1 oz) Pillsbury® big & buttery refrigerated crescent dinner rolls (6 rolls)

1) Heat oven to 375°F. Spray 11x7-inch (2-quart) glass baking dish with cooking spray. In 12-inch nonstick skillet, heat 2 tablespoons of the oil over medium-high heat. Spread potatoes in skillet; cook until golden brown on bottom.

2) Drizzle potatoes with 1 tablespoon oil. Cut into quarters; turn sections over. Cook until golden brown. Remove hash browns from skillet; arrange in bottom and around side of casserole. Sprinkle Swiss cheese over potatoes.

3) In bowl, beat eggs. Stir in chives, salt, pepper and ham. Pour into same skillet. Cook and stir over medium heat until partially cooked. Stir in cream cheese; cook and stir until eggs are cooked but moist. Spread over Swiss cheese.

4) Separate dough into 6 triangles. Starting at short side of each triangle, roll up halfway. Arrange over hot egg mixture with tips toward center; do not overlap.

5) Bake 20 to 25 minutes or until crust is golden brown.

Nutrition Information Per Serving	
Calories: 680	From Fat: 340
Total Fat	38g
Saturated Fat	13g
Trans Fat	3g
Cholesterol	345mg
Sodium	750mg
Total Carbohydrate	55g
Dietary Fiber	3g
Sugars	7g
Protein	30g

Peanut Butter Cookie Granola

WANDA RILEY | ROXIE, MISSISSIPPI

BAKE-OFF® CONTEST 44, 2010

PREP TIME: 15 MINUTES (READY IN 1 HOUR 10 MINUTES)
SERVINGS: 22 (1/2 CUP EACH)

e EASY

1 roll (16.5 oz) Pillsbury® refrigerated peanut butter cookies

½ teaspoon ground cinnamon

2½ cups old-fashioned oats

1 cup Fisher® Chef's Naturals® natural sliced almonds

1 cup Fisher® Chef's Naturals® chopped pecans

1 cup flaked coconut

⅓ cup raisins

⅓ cup sweetened dried cranberries

½ cup Hershey's® mini chips semi-sweet chocolate

½ cup Reese's® peanut butter chips

1) Let cookie dough stand at room temperature 10 minutes to soften.

2) Meanwhile, heat oven to 325°F. Line 2 large cookie sheets with sides with nonstick foil or cooking parchment paper. In large bowl, mix cookie dough and cinnamon. Add oats, almonds, pecans, coconut, raisins and cranberries; knead into dough until well blended. Crumble mixture evenly on cookie sheets.

3) Bake both cookie sheets at the same time 17 to 22 minutes, stirring every 5 minutes and rotating cookie sheets halfway through baking, until light golden brown. Cool completely on cookie sheets, about 30 minutes.

4) Break granola into smaller pieces if necessary. In large bowl, mix granola, chocolate chips and peanut butter chips. Store in large resealable food-storage plastic bag, or store in ½-cup amounts in small food-storage bags for ready-to-go snacks. Store up to 3 days.

Nutrition Information Per Serving	
Calories: 250	From Fat: 120
Total Fat	13g
Saturated Fat	3.5g
Trans Fat	.5g
Cholesterol	0mg
Sodium	370mg
Total Carbohydrate	27g
Dietary Fiber	2g
Sugars	13g
Protein	4g

tip

Quick-cooking oats and old-fashioned oats can be used interchangeably, but old-fashioned may give the recipe more texture.

Lazy Maple Crescent Pull-Aparts

MARIE FLAHERTY | DORCHESTER, MASSACHUSETTS

 BAKE-OFF® CONTEST 26, 1975

PREP TIME: 15 MINUTES (READY IN 40 MINUTES)
SERVINGS: 6 (2 ROLLS EACH)

🅔 EASY

¼ cup butter or margarine

¼ cup packed brown sugar

2 tablespoons maple-flavored syrup

¼ cup chopped pecans or walnuts

1 can (8 oz) Pillsbury® refrigerated crescent dinner rolls or 1 can (8 oz) Pillsbury® Crescent Recipe Creations® refrigerated seamless dough sheet

1 tablespoon granulated sugar

½ teaspoon ground cinnamon

Nutrition Information Per Serving	
Calories: 310	From Fat: 170
Total Fat	19g
Saturated Fat	8g
Trans Fat	2.5g
Cholesterol	20mg
Sodium	360mg
Total Carbohydrate	31g
Dietary Fiber	0g
Sugars	16g
Protein	3g

1) Heat oven to 375°F. In ungreased 8- or 9-inch round cake pan, place butter, brown sugar and syrup. Place in oven 2 to 4 minutes or until butter melts. Mix well; sprinkle with pecans.

2) If using crescent rolls: Remove dough from can in 2 rolled sections; do not unroll. Cut each section into 6 slices. If using dough sheet: Remove dough from can, and cut in half; do not unroll. Cut each section into 6 slices. In small bowl, mix granulated sugar and cinnamon; dip both sides of each slice in sugar mixture. Arrange slices over butter mixture in pan; sprinkle with any remaining sugar mixture.

3) Bake 17 to 23 minutes or until golden brown. Cool 1 minute; turn upside down onto heatproof serving plate. Serve warm.

Oatmeal-Fruit Porridge

PREP TIME: 10 MINUTES (READY IN 6 HOURS 10 MINUTES)
SERVINGS: 6 (1/3 CUP EACH)

🅔 EASY

3 cups old-fashioned oats

2 apples, peeled, chopped (about 2 cups)

½ cup sweetened dried cranberries or raisins

6 cups water

2 tablespoons butter or margarine, melted

½ teaspoon ground cinnamon

¼ teaspoon salt

Brown sugar, milk or cream, if desired

Nutrition Information Per Serving	
Calories: 250	From Fat: 60
Total Fat	7g
Saturated Fat	3g
Trans Fat	0g
Cholesterol	10mg
Sodium	230mg
Total Carbohydrate	41g
Dietary Fiber	5g
Sugars	12g
Protein	6g

1) Spray 3½ - to 4-quart slow cooker with cooking spray. In cooker, mix oats, apples, cranberries, water, butter, cinnamon and salt.

2) Cover; cook on Low heat setting 6 to 8 hours. Serve porridge with brown sugar and milk or cream.

Italian Brunch Torta

LORETTA TORRENS | GILBERT, ARIZONA

Pillsbury Bake-Off®

BAKE-OFF® CONTEST 44, 2010

PREP TIME: 20 MINUTES (READY IN 1 HOUR 35 MINUTES)
SERVINGS: 8

🅔 EASY

- 1 box Pillsbury® refrigerated pie crusts, softened as directed on box
- 1 tablespoon Crisco® 100% extra virgin olive oil or pure olive oil
- 2 cloves garlic, sliced
- 1 box (9 oz) Green Giant® frozen chopped spinach, thawed, squeezed to drain
- 1 cup shredded Parmesan cheese
- ¼ lb provolone cheese, thinly sliced
- 4 thin slices Genoa salami (1½ oz)
- 1 jar (15 or 16 oz) roasted red bell peppers, drained, patted dry
- ¾ cup olive tapenade (about 5-oz jar), drained
- ½ lb capicollo ham, thinly sliced
- 3½ oz dry-pack sun-dried tomatoes, coarsely chopped
- 1 Eggland's Best egg, beaten
- ½ teaspoon dried oregano leaves

1) Place cookie sheet in oven (torta will bake on heated cookie sheet). Heat oven to 375°F. Make pie crusts as directed on box for Two-Crust Pie using 9-inch glass pie plate.

2) In 10-inch skillet, heat oil over medium heat. Add garlic; cook 30 seconds, stirring constantly. Stir in spinach until well combined.

3) Spread ½ of spinach mixture in crust-lined plate. Reserve 2 tablespoons of the Parmesan cheese. Layer spinach with provolone cheese, salami, red peppers, tapenade, ham, sun-dried tomatoes, remaining Parmesan cheese and remaining spinach mixture. Top with the second crust; seal the edges and flute.

4) Brush egg on top crust; sprinkle with reserved 2 tablespoons Parmesan cheese and oregano. Cut 4 small slits in the top. Place on cookie sheet in the oven.

5) Bake 50 to 55 minutes, covering edge of crust with strips of foil after 15 to 20 minutes, until golden brown. Cool 20 minutes before serving. If desired, serve torta with fresh fruit on plates lined with romaine lettuce.

Nutrition Information Per Serving	
Calories: 470	From Fat: 260
Total Fat	28g
Saturated Fat	13g
Trans Fat	0g
Cholesterol	65mg
Sodium	1360mg
Total Carbohydrate	36g
Dietary Fiber	3g
Sugars	8g
Protein	18g

Rancheros Crescent Rounds

AMY MURPHY | HUNTERSVILLE, NORTH CAROLINA

 Bake-Off BAKE-OFF® CONTEST 44, 2010

PREP TIME: 15 MINUTES (READY IN 35 MINUTES)
SERVINGS: 16

ⓔ EASY

- 2 cans (8 oz each) Pillsbury® Place 'N Bake® refrigerated crescent rounds (16 rounds) or 2 cans (8 oz each) Pillsbury® refrigerated crescent dinner rolls
- 1 Eggland's Best egg
- 2 tablespoons sour cream
- ¼ teaspoon salt
- ⅛ teaspoon pepper
- ¼ teaspoon chili powder
- ¼ teaspoon red pepper sauce
- ½ cup shredded sharp Cheddar cheese (2 oz)
- ⅓ cup canned black beans, drained, rinsed
- ¼ cup salsa

1) Heat oven to 375°F. If using crescent rounds, remove from package, separate into 16 rounds. If using crescent rolls, remove from package, but do not unroll. Using serrated knife, cut each roll into 8 rounds; carefully separate rounds. Place rounds on ungreased large cookie sheet. Press down center and pinch edge of each round to make indentation (about ¾ inch deep and 2 inches in diameter).

2) In small bowl, beat egg, sour cream, salt, pepper, chili powder, pepper sauce and ¼ cup of the cheese with fork or wire whisk until well blended.

3) Place 1 teaspoon of the beans in each crescent bowl. Spoon 1 teaspoon egg mixture into each bowl (do not fill to top). Sprinkle each with about 1 teaspoon of the remaining cheese.

4) Bake 14 to 18 minutes or until bowls are golden brown and the filling is set. Top each with ½ teaspoon of the salsa.

Nutrition Information Per Serving	
Calories: 130	From Fat: 70
Total Fat	8g
Saturated Fat	3g
Trans Fat	1.5g
Cholesterol	15mg
Sodium	310mg
Total Carbohydrate	12g
Dietary Fiber	0g
Sugars	2g
Protein	3g

Pepperoni Quiche Squares

JULIE HALYAMA | PITTSBURGH, PENNSYLVANIA

 Bake-Off BAKE-OFF® CONTEST 44, 2010

PREP TIME: 20 MINUTES (READY IN 1 HOUR 10 MINUTES)
SERVINGS: 12

e EASY

1 can (8 oz) Pillsbury® Crescent Recipe Creations® refrigerated seamless dough sheet

48 slices (1½-inch size) pepperoni

5 Eggland's Best eggs

1 cup whipping cream

1½ teaspoons Italian seasoning

1 tablespoon Crisco® pure olive oil

½ cup chopped green bell pepper

½ cup chopped onion (about 1 small)

1½ cups shredded mozzarella cheese (6 oz)

¾ cup pizza sauce or pasta sauce, heated, if desired

1) Heat the oven to 300°F. Unroll dough sheet; press dough in bottom of ungreased 13x9-inch pan. Top with 24 slices pepperoni (6 rows by 4 rows).

2) In medium bowl, beat eggs, cream and Italian seasoning with wire whisk until well blended.

3) In 10-inch skillet, heat oil over medium heat. Add bell pepper and onion; cook 4 minutes, stirring occasionally, until crisp-tender. Stir vegetable mixture into egg mixture; pour over pepperoni in pan. Sprinkle with cheese. Layer with remaining 24 slices pepperoni.

4) Bake 35 to 45 minutes or until edges are light golden brown and center is set. Cool 5 minutes. Cut into 12 servings; place on plates. Drizzle 1 tablespoon pizza sauce over each serving.

Nutrition Information Per Serving	
Calories: 270	From Fat: 180
Total Fat	20g
Saturated Fat	9g
Trans Fat	0g
Cholesterol	120mg
Sodium	600mg
Total Carbohydrate	11g
Dietary Fiber	0g
Sugars	3g
Protein	13g

Pecan Cookie Waffles with Honey-Cinnamon Butter

CATHY WIECHERT | MOUND, MINNESOTA

BAKE-OFF® CONTEST 44, 2010

PREP TIME: 35 MINUTES (READY IN 35 MINUTES)
SERVINGS: 6 (TWO 4-INCH-SQUARE WAFFLES EACH)

HONEY-CINNAMON BUTTER
- ½ cup Land O Lakes® unsalted or salted butter, softened
- 3 tablespoons honey
- ½ teaspoon ground cinnamon

WAFFLES
- ¾ cup Fisher® Chef's Naturals® chopped pecans
- 1 roll (16.5 oz) Pillsbury® refrigerated sugar cookies
- 2 Eggland's Best eggs
- 1 teaspoon vanilla
- ½ cup half-and-half

1) In small bowl, beat butter, honey and cinnamon with electric mixer on medium-high speed 1 to 2 minutes or until light and creamy; set aside.

2) In 10-inch skillet, cook pecans over medium heat 5 to 7 minutes, stirring frequently until pecans begin to brown, then stirring constantly until light brown. Remove from skillet to plate to cool.

3) Heat oven to 200°F. Heat waffle maker. (Waffle makers without a nonstick coating may need to be brushed with vegetable oil or sprayed with Crisco® original no-stick cooking spray.)

4) In large bowl, break up cookie dough; add eggs and vanilla. Beat on medium speed about 2 minutes or until smooth. Slowly add half-and-half, beating until batter is smooth and thin. Stir in ½ cup of the pecans.

5) Pour ⅓ cup batter onto each waffle section. (Check manufacturer's directions for recommended amount of batter.) Close lid of waffle maker. Cook about 3 minutes or until waffles are golden brown. Carefully remove waffles to heatproof plate; keep warm in oven. Repeat with remaining batter.

6) To serve, top each waffle with about 1 tablespoon honey-cinnamon butter and sprinkle with 1 teaspoon of the remaining pecans.

Nutrition Information Per Serving	
Calories: 650	From Fat: 380
Total Fat	42g
Saturated Fat	16g
Trans Fat	4.5g
Cholesterol	115mg
Sodium	280mg
Total Carbohydrate	60g
Dietary Fiber	1g
Sugars	40g
Protein	6g

Savory Breakfast Pizza

ADRIENNE DAVIS | HIGHLAND, MARYLAND

Pillsbury Bake-Off®

BAKE-OFF® CONTEST 44, 2010

PREP TIME: 30 MINUTES (READY IN 45 MINUTES)
SERVINGS: 6

1 can (13.8 oz) Pillsbury® refrigerated classic pizza crust

⅓ cup basil pesto

10 slices thick-sliced smoked-style bacon, crisply cooked

5 slices (1/8 inch) provolone cheese, 4½ inches in diameter (3½ oz)

1½ cups diced seeded tomatoes (about 2 medium)

Dash salt

Dash pepper

6 Eggland's Best eggs

1) Heat oven to 425°F. Line large cookie sheet with cooking parchment paper. Unroll pizza crust dough onto cookie sheet; press into 13x10-inch rectangle. Form ½-inch rim on each side.

2) Spread pesto evenly over dough. Place bacon on pesto. Top evenly with cheese. Place about ½ of the tomato on dough along rim on all 4 sides. Place 1 line of tomato lengthwise down center of dough. Add 2 more lines of tomato crosswise on dough to create 6 sections of equal size. Sprinkle center of each section with salt and pepper. Carefully crack open each egg and drop into the center of 1 section.

3) Bake 10 to 13 minutes or until egg whites and yolks are firm, not runny. Cut into 6 squares with sharp knife or pizza cutter.

Nutrition Information Per Serving	
Calories: 440	From Fat: 210
Total Fat	23g
Saturated Fat	7g
Trans Fat	0g
Cholesterol	205mg
Sodium	1120mg
Total Carbohydrate	34g
Dietary Fiber	2g
Sugars	6g
Protein	22g

Muffuletta Quiche Cups

KIM ROLLINGS | DALLAS, TEXAS

 BAKE-OFF® CONTEST 44, 2010

| PREP TIME: | 20 MINUTES (READY IN 45 MINUTES) |
| SERVINGS: | 8 |

€ EASY

1 can (8 oz) Pillsbury® Place 'N Bake® refrigerated crescent rounds (8 rounds) or 1 can (8 oz) Pillsbury® refrigerated crescent dinner rolls

3 tablespoons finely diced ham

3 tablespoons finely diced salami

2 tablespoons finely chopped pimiento-stuffed green olives

½ teaspoon dried oregano leaves

2 Eggland's Best eggs

2 tablespoons half-and-half

⅛ teaspoon red pepper sauce

1 cup shredded provolone cheese (4 oz)

2 teaspoons chopped fresh Italian (flat-leaf) parsley

1) Heat oven to 375°F. Spray 8 regular-size muffin cups (2¾ x 1¼ inches) with Crisco® original no-stick cooking spray.

2) If using crescent rounds, remove from package, separate into 8 rounds. If using crescent rolls, remove from package, but do not unroll. Using serrated knife, cut roll into 8 rounds; carefully separate rounds. Press 1 round on bottom and completely up side of each muffin cup.

3) In small bowl, mix ham, salami, olives and oregano. In another small bowl, beat eggs, half-and-half and pepper sauce with fork until well blended.

4) Spoon about 1 tablespoon cheese into each muffin cup. Top each with about 1 rounded tablespoon ham mixture. Divide egg mixture evenly among muffin cups (about 1 tablespoon each). Top with remaining cheese.

5) Bake 12 to 16 minutes or until filling is set and edges of rolls are golden brown. Cool in pan 5 minutes. Run knife around edge of each quiche to loosen; remove to cooling rack. Garnish with parsley. Serve warm.

Nutrition Information Per Serving	
Calories: 190	From Fat: 110
Total Fat	13g
Saturated Fat	5g
Trans Fat	1.5g
Cholesterol	60mg
Sodium	480mg
Total Carbohydrate	12g
Dietary Fiber	0g
Sugars	3g
Protein	8g

Blueberry-Almond Crème Muffins

CYNTHIA BOWSER | JONESBOROUGH, TENNESSEE

BAKE-OFF® CONTEST 44, 2010

PREP TIME: 30 MINUTES (READY IN 1 HOUR 25 MINUTES)
SERVINGS: 8 MUFFINS

- **4 oz cream cheese** (half of 8-oz package), softened
- **½ cup sugar**
- **¼ teaspoon almond extract**
- **¼ teaspoon vanilla**
- **½ cup Fisher® Chef's Naturals® blanched slivered almonds, finely chopped**
- **1 can (16.3 oz) Pillsbury® Grands!® flaky layers refrigerated buttermilk biscuits (8 biscuits)**
- **3 tablespoons Land O Lakes® unsalted or salted butter, melted**
- **¼ cup Smucker's® blueberry preserves**

1) Heat oven to 350°F. Generously spray 8 regular-size muffin cups (2¾ x 1¼ inches) with Crisco® original no-stick cooking spray.

2) In medium bowl, stir cream cheese, ¼ cup of the sugar, almond extract and vanilla until smooth and creamy; set aside. In medium shallow bowl, mix almonds and remaining ¼ cup sugar.

3) Separate dough into 8 biscuits. Separate 1 biscuit into 3 layers. Brush 1 layer with melted butter. Firmly press layer, butter side down, into almond mixture, coating evenly. Place layer, almond side down, in bottom and up side of muffin cup. Fill with 1 tablespoon cream cheese mixture; spread evenly. Top with second biscuit layer; press edges of layers together. Spoon ½ tablespoon of the preserves onto middle of second layer. Brush third biscuit layer with melted butter; firmly press, butter side down, into almond mixture. Place third layer, almond side up, on second layer; press edge of third layer into edge of second layer.

4) Repeat with remaining biscuits, refrigerating biscuits if the dough becomes too soft to separate. Sprinkle any remaining almond mixture onto tops of biscuits.

5) Bake 17 to 27 minutes or until golden brown. Cool in pan 10 minutes. Remove muffins from pan to cooling rack. Cool 15 minutes before serving.

Nutrition Information Per Serving	
Calories: 400	From Fat: 190
Total Fat	21g
Saturated Fat	8g
Trans Fat	2.5g
Cholesterol	25mg
Sodium	590mg
Total Carbohydrate	47g
Dietary Fiber	1g
Sugars	22g
Protein	5g

Breakfast Skillet

PREP TIME: 30 MINUTES (READY IN 30 MINUTES)
SERVINGS: 4

 EASY

¾ lb bacon, cut into 1-inch pieces

3 cups refrigerated cooked shredded hash brown potatoes (from 20-oz bag)

3 eggs

1 can (4.5 oz) Old El Paso® green chiles, drained

¾ cup shredded Cheddar cheese (3 oz)

1 medium tomato, chopped

Nutrition Information Per Serving	
Calories: 420	From Fat: 190
Total Fat	21g
Saturated Fat	9g
Trans Fat	0g
Cholesterol	210mg
Sodium	890mg
Total Carbohydrate	35g
Dietary Fiber	3g
Sugars	4g
Protein	21g

1) In 10-inch nonstick skillet, cook bacon 5 to 7 minutes over medium heat, stirring occasionally, until crisp. (Drain, reserving 2 tablespoons drippings and bacon in pan.)

2) Add potatoes; spread evenly in skillet. Cook 8 to 10 minutes, stirring occasionally, until brown.

3) In small bowl, beat eggs and chiles with fork or wire whisk. Pour egg mixture evenly over potatoes. Reduce heat to low, cover and cook 8 to 10 minutes or until eggs are firm. Sprinkle with cheese and tomato; cover and cook 2 to 4 minutes or until cheese is melted.

Orange-Coconut Breakfast Rolls

JOAN COSSETTE | COLBERT, WASHINGTON

 Bake-Off   BAKE-OFF® CONTEST 44, 2010

PREP TIME: 10 MINUTES (READY IN 40 MINUTES)
SERVINGS: 8 ROLLS

 EASY

1 teaspoon Crisco® pure canola oil

¾ to 1 cup flaked coconut

1 can (12.4 oz) Pillsbury® refrigerated cinnamon rolls with icing (8 rolls)

8 tablespoons Smucker's® sweet orange marmalade

¼ cup Fisher® Chef's Naturals® natural sliced almonds

½ to 1 teaspoon almond extract

1) Heat oven to 400°F (375°F for dark pan). Grease 9-inch round cake pan with canola oil or spray with Crisco® original no-stick cooking spray.

2) Place coconut in shallow dish. Separate dough into 8 rolls; set icing aside. Roll each cinnamon roll in coconut; press coconut onto all sides of roll to coat generously. Place rolls, cinnamon topping sides up, in pan.

3) Make well in each roll, using back of spoon. Fill each with 1 tablespoon marmalade; sprinkle with almonds.

4) Bake 15 to 20 minutes or until golden brown. Cool 10 minutes. Meanwhile, in small bowl, stir almond extract into icing. Carefully spread icing on warm rolls. Serve warm.

Nutrition Information Per Serving	
Calories: 270	From Fat: 90
Total Fat	10g
Saturated Fat	4g
Trans Fat	2g
Cholesterol	0mg
Sodium	370mg
Total Carbohydrate	41g
Dietary Fiber	1g
Sugars	22g
Protein	3g

Savory and Sweet Breakfast Biscuit Sliders

CHRISTINA VERRELLI | DEVON, PENNSYLVANIA

BAKE-OFF® CONTEST 44, 2010

PREP TIME: 35 MINUTES (READY IN 35 MINUTES)
SERVINGS: 8 SANDWICHES

---

1 lb bulk pork sausage

1 box (9 oz) Green Giant® frozen chopped spinach, thawed, squeezed to drain

⅛ teaspoon freshly ground pepper

⅛ teaspoon garlic powder

⅛ teaspoon onion powder

1 Eggland's Best egg

2 teaspoons water

1 can (16.3 oz) Pillsbury® Grands!® homestyle refrigerated southern style biscuits (8 biscuits)

1 tablespoon Crisco® pure canola oil

¼ cup Smucker's® seedless strawberry jam

3 tablespoons Land O Lakes® unsalted or salted butter, cut into ½-inch pieces

32 cocktail picks, if desired

8 fresh strawberries, quartered, if desired

1) Heat oven to 350°F. In large bowl, mix sausage, spinach, pepper, garlic powder and onion powder. Shape mixture into 8 patties, 3 inches in diameter.

2) In small bowl, beat egg and water with wire whisk or fork until blended. Separate dough into 8 biscuits. On ungreased cookie sheet, place biscuits 2 inches apart; brush with egg mixture. Bake 11 to 15 minutes or until golden brown. Remove from cookie sheet to cooling rack.

3) Meanwhile, heat 12-inch nonstick skillet over medium heat. Add half of the oil and 4 sausage patties; cook 5 to 8 minutes on each side or until pork is no longer pink in center. Remove to paper towel-lined plate; cover with foil to keep warm. Repeat with remaining oil and patties.

4) In small microwave bowl, microwave jam uncovered on High 20 to 30 seconds or until hot and bubbly; stir in butter with wire whisk until melted. Using serrated knife, split biscuits. Spread 2 teaspoons strawberry butter on cut sides of each biscuit. Fill biscuits with patties. If desired, place 4 cocktail picks in each sandwich, one in each quadrant; cut sandwiches into quarters with serrated knife. Garnish with strawberries.

Nutrition Information Per Serving	
Calories: 360	From Fat: 190
Total Fat	21g
Saturated Fat	7g
Trans Fat	3.5g
Cholesterol	55mg
Sodium	810mg
Total Carbohydrate	32g
Dietary Fiber	1g
Sugars	9g
Protein	10g

Java-Glazed Cinnamon Rolls

TAMMY LOVE | DALLAS, NORTH CAROLINA

 Pillsbury Bake-Off®   BAKE-OFF® CONTEST 44, 2010

PREP TIME: 15 MINUTES (READY IN 35 MINUTES)
SERVINGS: 5 ROLLS

℮ EASY

1 can (17.5 oz) Pillsbury® Grands!® refrigerated cinnamon rolls with cream cheese icing (5 rolls)

2 tablespoons milk

¼ teaspoon instant coffee granules or crystals

½ cup Hershey's® premier white baking chips

½ cup Fisher® Chef's Naturals® chopped pecans

tip

To add a touch of flavor to the cinnnamon rolls, try flavored instant coffee granules.

1) Heat oven to 350°F. Spray 9-inch round cake pan with Crisco® original no-stick cooking spray. Place cinnamon rolls in pan; reserve icing. Bake 20 to 25 minutes or until golden brown. Cool slightly.

2) Meanwhile, in small microwavable bowl, microwave 1 tablespoon of the milk uncovered on High about 20 seconds or until hot; stir in coffee granules until completely dissolved. Stir in reserved icing. Microwave uncovered on High 25 seconds. Stir in baking chips and remaining 1 tablespoon milk. Microwave 25 seconds longer; stir until chips are completely melted. (Microwave in additional 10-second increments, if necessary, until chips are melted.)

3) Stir pecans into icing mixture. Pour over rolls. Serve warm.

Nutrition Information Per Serving	
Calories: 520	From Fat: 210
Total Fat	23g
Saturated Fat	8g
Trans Fat	2.5g
Cholesterol	0mg
Sodium	700mg
Total Carbohydrate	70g
Dietary Fiber	2g
Sugars	38g
Protein	6g

Double Chocolate-Orange Scones

MICHELLE GAUER | SPICER, MINNESOTA

BAKE-OFF® CONTEST 44, 2010

PREP TIME: 30 MINUTES (READY IN 1 HOUR 15 MINUTES)
SERVINGS: 12 SCONES

SCONES

- 2 cups Pillsbury Best® all purpose flour
- ½ cup granulated sugar
- ⅓ cup Hershey's® baking cocoa
- 2 teaspoons baking powder
- ½ teaspoon salt
- ⅓ cup cold Land O Lakes® butter, cut into ½-inch pieces
- ¾ cup whipping cream
- ¼ cup Smucker's® sweet orange marmalade
- 1 teaspoon vanilla
- 1 cup Hershey's® mini chips semi-sweet chocolate
- 1 tablespoon raw sugar (turbinado sugar), if desired
- 2 oz Hershey's® semi-sweet baking chocolate or ⅓ cup Hershey's® mini chips semi-sweet chocolate

ORANGE BUTTER

- ½ cup Land O Lakes® butter, softened
- ¼ cup powdered sugar
- 2 tablespoons Smucker's® sweet orange marmalade

1) Heat oven to 375°F. Line large cookie sheet with cooking parchment paper. In large bowl, mix flour, granulated sugar, cocoa, baking powder and salt. Cut in ⅓ cup cold butter, using pastry blender or fork, until mixture looks like coarse crumbs.

2) In small bowl, gently stir cream, ¼ cup marmalade and vanilla until mixed. Make a well in center of crumb mixture; add cream mixture to well. Stir with fork until crumb mixture is moistened and dough is sticky. Gently stir in 1 cup mini chocolate chips. Form dough into a ball.

3) On well floured surface, roll or pat dough into 9-inch round, ¾ inch thick. Using knife dipped in flour, cut round into 12 wedges. Place 1 inch apart on cookie sheet. Sprinkle with raw sugar. Bake 14 to 18 minutes or until edges are set. Remove from cookie sheet to cooling rack. Cool 30 minutes.

4) In small microwavable bowl, microwave baking chocolate uncovered on High 30 seconds until softened; stir until smooth. Drizzle diagonally over scones.

5) In small bowl, beat ½ cup butter and powdered sugar with fork until light and fluffy. Stir in 2 tablespoons marmalade. Serve with scones.

Nutrition Information Per Serving	
Calories: 420	From Fat: 220
Total Fat	25g
Saturated Fat	15g
Trans Fat	.5g
Cholesterol	50mg
Sodium	280mg
Total Carbohydrate	46g
Dietary Fiber	3g
Sugars	24g
Protein	4g

Maple-Bacon Breakfast Rolls

SHERRY ROPER | SAN DIEGO, CALIFORNIA

BAKE-OFF® CONTEST 44, 2010

PREP TIME:	15 MINUTES (READY IN 40 MINUTES)
SERVINGS:	12 ROLLS

🄴 EASY

10 slices precooked bacon

1 can (8 oz) Pillsbury® Crescent Recipe Creations® refrigerated seamless dough sheet

3 tablespoons Land O Lakes® butter, softened

5 tablespoons maple syrup

⅓ cup powdered sugar

1) Heat oven to 375°F. Microwave bacon as directed on package until very crisp. Drain on paper towels. Set aside to cool.

2) Generously spray large cookie sheet (dark cookie sheet not recommended) with Crisco® original no-stick cooking spray, or line with cooking parchment paper. Unroll dough sheet on work surface; press into 12x8-inch rectangle.

3) In small bowl, mix 2 tablespoons of the butter and 2 tablespoons of the syrup with fork or wire whisk until smooth and creamy. Spread mixture evenly over dough, covering to edges. Finely chop bacon; reserve 1 tablespoon for garnish. Spread the remaining bacon evenly over the butter mixture. Starting at the short end, roll up the dough; pinch edge to seal. Wrap roll in plastic wrap; refrigerate 5 minutes to chill so the dough will be easier to cut.

4) Unwrap the roll; place seam side down on cutting board. Using serrated knife, cut roll into 12 (about ¾-inch) slices. Place slices, cut sides up, on cookie sheet.

5) Bake 8 to 13 minutes or until light golden brown. Place waxed paper under cooling rack. Remove rolls from cookie sheet to cooling rack; cool 5 minutes.

6) Meanwhile, in small bowl, mix powdered sugar, remaining 1 tablespoon butter and remaining 3 tablespoons syrup with wire whisk until smooth. Drizzle icing over rolls. Garnish with reserved bacon.

Nutrition Information Per Serving	
Calories: 140	From Fat: 70
Total Fat	7g
Saturated Fat	3.5g
Trans Fat	0g
Cholesterol	10mg
Sodium	230mg
Total Carbohydrate	17g
Dietary Fiber	0g
Sugars	10g
Protein	2g

Crescent Caramel Swirl

LOIS GROVES | GREENWOOD VILLAGE, COLORADO

Pillsbury
Bake-Off

BAKE-OFF® CONTEST 27, 1976

PREP TIME: 20 MINUTES (READY IN 55 MINUTES)
SERVINGS: 12

 EASY

½ cup butter (do not use margarine)

½ cup chopped nuts

¾ cup packed brown sugar

1 tablespoon water

2 cans (8 oz each) Pillsbury®
refrigerated crescent dinner rolls or
2 cans (8 oz each) Pillsbury®
Crescent Recipe Creations®
refrigerated seamless dough sheet

1) Heat oven to 350°F. In 1-quart saucepan, melt butter. Coat bottom and sides of 12-cup fluted tube cake pan with 2 tablespoons of the melted butter; sprinkle pan with 3 tablespoons of the nuts. Add remaining nuts, brown sugar and water to remaining melted butter. Heat to boiling, stirring occasionally. Boil 1 minute, stirring constantly.

2) Remove dough from cans; do not unroll. Cut each long roll into 8 slices. Arrange 8 slices, cut side down, in nut-lined pan; separate layers of each pinwheel slightly. Spoon half of brown sugar mixture over dough. Place remaining 8 dough slices alternately over bottom layer. Spoon remaining brown sugar mixture over slices.

3) Bake 23 to 33 minutes or until deep golden brown. Cool 3 minutes. Turn upside down onto serving platter or waxed paper. Serve warm.

Nutrition Information Per Serving	
Calories: 300	From Fat: 170
Total Fat	19g
Saturated Fat	8g
Trans Fat	2.5g
Cholesterol	20mg
Sodium	350mg
Total Carbohydrate	29g
Dietary Fiber	0g
Sugars	16g
Protein	3g

Cheesy Ham and Apple Cups

LINDA JANKOWICH | LATHAM, NEW YORK

BAKE-OFF® CONTEST 44, 2010

PREP TIME: 20 MINUTES (READY IN 50 MINUTES)
SERVINGS: 10

e EASY

1 can (12 oz) Pillsbury® Grands!® Jr. Golden Layers® refrigerated buttermilk biscuits (10 biscuits)

⅓ cup sour cream

½ teaspoon Dijon mustard

¼ cup Smucker's® apricot preserves

¾ cup finely chopped cooked ham steak or cooked ham

¾ cup finely chopped tart apple

¾ cup shredded sharp white or yellow Cheddar cheese (3 oz)

2 tablespoons finely chopped green onions (2 medium)

1) Heat oven to 375°F. Spray 10 regular-size muffin cups (2¾ x 1¼ inches) with Crisco® original no-stick cooking spray.

2) Separate biscuit dough into 10 biscuits. On waxed paper, press each biscuit into 3-inch round. Press each dough round in muffin cup.

3) In medium bowl, stir sour cream, mustard and preserves until well blended. Stir in ham, apple, cheese and onions until well blended. Divide ham mixture among muffin cups.

4) Bake 18 to 25 minutes or until edges of biscuits are golden brown. Cool in pan 5 minutes. Serve warm.

Nutrition Information Per Serving	
Calories: 200	From Fat: 80
Total Fat	9g
Saturated Fat	4g
Trans Fat	1g
Cholesterol	20mg
Sodium	580mg
Total Carbohydrate	21g
Dietary Fiber	0g
Sugars	7g
Protein	6g

Dutch Apple Breakfast Bake

LINDA BIBBO | CHAGRIN FALLS, OHIO

BAKE-OFF® CONTEST 44, 2010

PREP TIME: 25 MINUTES (READY IN 1 HOUR 25 MINUTES)
SERVINGS: 12

½ cup Land O Lakes® unsalted or salted butter, melted

2 cans (13.9 oz each) Pillsbury® refrigerated orange flavor sweet rolls with icing (8 rolls each)

1 can (21 oz) apple pie filling with more fruit

1 package (8 oz) cream cheese, softened

¾ cup sugar

2 teaspoons grated orange peel

1 teaspoon vanilla

1 Eggland's Best egg

⅔ cup sour cream

½ cup shredded sharp Cheddar cheese (2 oz)

½ cup Pillsbury Best® all purpose flour

½ cup Fisher® Chef's Naturals® natural sliced almonds

½ cup Smucker's® sweet orange marmalade

1½ cups frozen (thawed) whipped topping, if desired

1) Heat oven to 375°F. Pour ¼ cup of the melted butter into ungreased 13x9-inch (3-quart) glass baking dish. Separate dough into 16 rolls; set icing aside. Cut each roll into 6 pieces; arrange the pieces on butter in baking dish.

2) Pour pie filling into medium bowl. Cut apples into small pieces with clean kitchen scissors or knife; spoon filling over roll pieces.

3) In large bowl, beat cream cheese, ½ cup of the sugar, 1 teaspoon of the orange peel and vanilla with electric mixer on medium speed until well blended. Beat in egg and sour cream until well blended. Spoon over apple layer; spread to cover.

4) In small bowl, mix remaining ¼ cup butter, ¼ cup sugar, cheese and flour until mixture looks like coarse crumbs. Stir in almonds. Sprinkle mixture over cream cheese layer.

5) Bake 30 to 40 minutes or until set and topping is golden brown. Cool on cooling rack 20 minutes.

6) In small microwavable bowl, mix contents of 2 icing containers, remaining 1 teaspoon orange peel and marmalade. Microwave uncovered on High 40 seconds; stir.

7) For 12 servings, cut apple bake into 4 rows by 3 rows. Serve with sauce on the side. Garnish each serving with 2 tablespoons whipped topping.

Nutrition Information Per Serving	
Calories: 600	From Fat: 260
Total Fat	29g
Saturated Fat	13g
Trans Fat	2.5g
Cholesterol	65mg
Sodium	580mg
Total Carbohydrate	77g
Dietary Fiber	1g
Sugars	46g
Protein	7g

Blueberry Muffin Tops

SUSAN SPICKO | NEWTON FALLS, OHIO

Pillsbury Bake-Off®

BAKE-OFF® CONTEST 44, 2010

PREP TIME: 20 MINUTES (READY IN 45 MINUTES)
SERVINGS: 28 MUFFIN TOPS

ⓔ EASY

1 roll (16.5 oz) Pillsbury® refrigerated sugar cookies

1¼ cups Pillsbury Best® all purpose flour

¼ cup sugar

2 tablespoons Land O Lakes® butter

½ teaspoon baking powder

¼ teaspoon baking soda

1 package (3 oz) cream cheese, softened

1 Eggland's Best egg

⅓ cup milk

2 to 3 teaspoons grated lemon peel

2 tablespoons lemon juice

1¼ cups fresh or frozen (thawed) blueberries

1) Let the cookie dough stand at room temperature 10 minutes to soften. Meanwhile, heat oven to 350°F. Line 2 cookie sheets with cooking parchment paper. In small bowl, mix ¼ cup of the flour, sugar and butter with a fork until crumbly; set aside to use for the topping. In another small bowl, mix the remaining 1 cup flour, baking powder and baking soda; set aside.

2) In medium bowl, beat dough and cream cheese with electric mixer on medium speed until blended. On low speed, beat in egg, milk, lemon peel and lemon juice until well blended. Stir in flour mixture just until combined (do not overmix; mixture will be a thick batter). Carefully fold in blueberries. (If using thawed berries, rinse and pat dry with paper towel before adding.)

3) Drop batter by heaping tablespoonfuls 1 to 2 inches apart onto cookie sheets, using rubber spatula to scrape batter from tablespoon. Bake 3 minutes; remove from oven. Sprinkle each muffin top with about 1 teaspoon crumb topping; immediately return to oven.

4) Bake 16 to 20 minutes longer or just until edges begin to brown. Cool on cookie sheets 2 to 3 minutes before removing to cooling racks. Serve warm or cool.

Nutrition Information Per Serving	
Calories: 120	From Fat: 45
Total Fat	5g
Saturated Fat	2g
Trans Fat	1g
Cholesterol	15mg
Sodium	95mg
Total Carbohydrate	18g
Dietary Fiber	0g
Sugars	9g
Protein	1g

Orange-Kissed Breakfast Bread Pudding

KRISTI STRONG | WEST JORDAN, UTAH

Bake-Off® CONTEST 44, 2010

PREP TIME: 20 MINUTES (READY IN 2 HOURS)
SERVINGS 9

e EASY

- 2 cans (13.9 oz each) Pillsbury® refrigerated orange flavor sweet rolls with icing (16 rolls)
- 2 cups half-and-half
- 2 Eggland's Best whole eggs
- 2 Eggland's Best egg yolks
- ½ cup sugar
- ¾ cup Fisher® Chef's Naturals® walnut halves and pieces, coarsely chopped
- ¼ cup half-and-half
- ¼ cup Land O Lakes® butter
- 1 teaspoon vanilla

1) Heat oven to 400°F. Spray large cookie sheet with Crisco® original no-stick cooking spray. On cookie sheet, place rolls 1 inch apart. Reserve icing. Bake 8 to 10 minutes or until golden brown. Remove from cookie sheet to cooling rack. Cool completely, about 10 minutes.

2) Reduce oven temperature to 350°F. Spray 8-inch square pan with cooking spray. Using serrated knife, cut rolls into ½- to 1-inch pieces; set aside.

3) In large bowl, mix 2 cups half-and-half, whole eggs, egg yolks, sugar and walnuts until well blended. Gently stir in roll pieces. Spread in pan.

4) Bake at 350°F 50 to 55 minutes or until toothpick inserted in center comes clean and top is deep golden brown. Cool 30 minutes.

5) Meanwhile, in 1-quart saucepan, heat icing (from both containers), ¼ cup half-and-half and butter over low heat, stirring occasionally, until butter is melted. Stir in vanilla.

6) Cut warm bread pudding into 9 servings. Drizzle with sauce.

Nutrition Information Per Serving	
Calories: 550	From Fat: 270
Total Fat	30g
Saturated Fat	11g
Trans Fat	3g
Cholesterol	115mg
Sodium	710mg
Total Carbohydrate	61g
Dietary Fiber	0g
Sugars	32g
Protein	9g

Pesto-Quinoa-Spinach Quiche

KATIE ERBECK | CINCINNATI, OHIO

BAKE-OFF® CONTEST 44, 2010

| PREP TIME: | 20 MINUTES (READY IN 1 HOUR 5 MINUTES) |
| SERVINGS: | 8 |

€ EASY

1 Pillsbury® refrigerated pie crust, softened as directed on box

4 oz provolone cheese, shredded (1 cup)

1 cup water

½ cup uncooked quinoa, rinsed, well drained

¼ cup basil pesto

¼ cup Fisher® Chef's Naturals® pine nuts, toasted

1 box (9 oz) Green Giant® frozen chopped spinach, thawed and squeezed to drain

1¼ cups grated Parmesan cheese

4 Eggland's Best eggs

1½ cups half-and-half

¼ teaspoon salt

⅛ teaspoon pepper

2 tablespoons thinly sliced fresh basil leaves, if desired

1) Heat oven to 425°F. Place pie crust in 9½-inch deep-dish glass pie plate as directed on box for One-Crust Filled Pie; flute edge. Bake 5 minutes. Remove from oven. Sprinkle provolone cheese over partially baked crust. Reduce oven temperature to 350°F.

2) Meanwhile, in 2-quart saucepan, heat water to boiling over high heat. Stir in quinoa; reduce heat to low. Cover; simmer 12 to 15 minutes or until water is absorbed. Remove from heat. Fluff with fork. Stir in pesto, pine nuts, spinach and 1 cup of the Parmesan cheese.

3) In large bowl, beat eggs, half-and-half, salt and pepper with wire whisk until well blended. Gently fold quinoa mixture into eggs. Pour filling into crust. Sprinkle with remaining ¼ cup Parmesan cheese.

4) Bake at 350°F 30 to 35 minutes longer or until knife inserted in center comes out clean and edge of crust is golden brown. Sprinkle with basil. Let stand 10 minutes before serving.

Nutrition Information Per Serving	
Calories: 430	From Fat: 260
Total Fat	29g
Saturated Fat	12g
Trans Fat	0g
Cholesterol	130mg
Sodium	710mg
Total Carbohydrate	24g
Dietary Fiber	2g
Sugars	3g
Protein	17g

SHRIMP AND VEGGIE APPETIZER PIZZA
PG. 43

Appetizers &Beverages

Entertaining has never been easier with these tantalizing bites and yummy sippers.

CAPRESE PESTO MARGHERITA
STACKERS
PG. 39

SPICED CHAI
PG. 48

MINI GREEK TURKEY BURGERS
WITH CUCUMBER SAUCE
PG. 54

Pecan-Sweet Potato Appetizers

JULEE CUNNINGHAM | EVERETT, WASHINGTON

Pillsbury Bake-Off

BAKE-OFF® CONTEST 44, 2010

PREP TIME: 45 MINUTES (READY IN 1 HOUR 10 MINUTES)
SERVINGS: 8 APPETIZERS

- 1 small sweet potato (5 to 6 oz)
- 2 tablespoons sugar
- 1 tablespoon water
- ¼ teaspoon ground red pepper (cayenne)
- ½ cup Fisher® Chef's Naturals® chopped pecans
- 1 tablespoon Crisco® 100% extra virgin olive oil or pure olive oil
- ¾ cup thinly sliced red onion (about 3 oz)
- 2 tablespoons Smucker's® apricot preserves
- 1 can (8 oz) Pillsbury® refrigerated garlic butter crescent dinner rolls (8 rolls)
- ½ cup crumbled blue cheese (2 oz)

1) Heat oven to 350°F. Line cookie sheet with cooking parchment paper. Pierce potato with fork; place on microwavable paper towel in center of microwave. Microwave 3 to 4 minutes, turning once, until tender. Cover; let stand 10 minutes. Peel potato and cut crosswise into 8 (½-inch) slices. (Refrigerate any remaining potato for another use.)

2) Meanwhile, in 1-quart saucepan, heat sugar, water and red pepper to boiling over medium heat, stirring occasionally. Boil and stir 2 minutes. Remove from heat; gently stir in pecans until coated. Spread pecans on cookie sheet. Bake 8 to 12 minutes or until golden brown. Remove from cookie sheet; cool completely.

3) Meanwhile, in 10-inch skillet, heat oil, onion and preserves over medium heat 5 to 8 minutes, stirring occasionally, until onion is tender. Remove from heat.

4) Unroll crescent dough; separate into 4 rectangles. Firmly press perforations to seal. Cut each rectangle in half crosswise; press each piece into 4-inch square.

5) On each dough square, place 1 potato slice, 1 rounded teaspoon onion mixture, 2 teaspoons cheese and 1 tablespoon pecans. Bring up 4 corners of dough over filling to center and twist at top. Place on ungreased cookie sheet.

6) Bake 12 to 18 minutes or until golden brown. Remove from cookie sheet to cooling rack and cool 5 minutes. Serve warm.

Nutrition Information Per Serving	
Calories: 190	From Fat: 110
Total Fat	12g
Saturated Fat	3g
Trans Fat	1g
Cholesterol	5mg
Sodium	240mg
Total Carbohydrate	18g
Dietary Fiber	1g
Sugars	9g
Protein	3g

Rachel Meatball Poppers

BETSY CHAN | BLOOMINGTON, MINNESOTA

Bake-Off® BAKE-OFF® CONTEST 44, 2010

PREP TIME: 25 MINUTES (READY IN 50 MINUTES)
SERVINGS: 24 POPPERS

12 refrigerated or frozen (thawed) cooked turkey meatballs (from 24-oz bag)

1 cup well-drained sauerkraut (squeeze to drain)

½ cup shredded Swiss cheese (2 oz)

⅓ cup shredded Parmesan cheese (2 oz)

2 tablespoons Thousand Island dressing

⅛ teaspoon salt

2 teaspoons caraway seed

2 cans (8 oz each) Pillsbury® refrigerated crescent dinner rolls (16 rolls)

1 Eggland's Best egg, well beaten

1) Heat oven to 350°F. Lightly spray 24 regular-size muffin cups (2¾x1¼ inches) with Crisco® original no-stick cooking spray.

2) Cut each meatball in half; set aside. In small bowl, mix sauerkraut, cheeses, dressing, salt and 1 teaspoon of the caraway seed until well blended.

3) Unroll both cans of crescent dough; separate into 8 rectangles. Firmly press perforations to seal. Cut each rectangle into 3 equal pieces. Press each piece into 4x2-inch rectangle. Gently press 1 rectangle on bottom and up side of each muffin cup, leaving both ends hanging over the side of the cup.

4) Place 1 meatball half, flat side down, in center of each cup. Spoon 2 rounded teaspoons sauerkraut mixture onto each meatball. Bring up ends of dough over filling; pinch tops to seal, leaving 2 small openings on sides to vent steam. Brush egg over dough. Sprinkle with remaining 1 teaspoon caraway seed.

5) Bake 12 to 18 minutes or until golden brown. Immediately remove from pan to cooling rack; cool 5 minutes. Serve warm.

Nutrition Information Per Serving	
Calories: 130	From Fat: 70
Total Fat	7g
Saturated Fat	2.5g
Trans Fat	1g
Cholesterol	25mg
Sodium	360mg
Total Carbohydrate	10g
Dietary Fiber	0g
Sugars	2g
Protein	6g

Cranberry-Mango Chutney

PREP TIME: 30 MINUTES (READY IN 30 MINUTES)
SERVINGS: 8 (1/4 CUP EACH)

 EASY   LOW FAT

1 bag (12 oz) fresh cranberries

1 medium mango, peeled and diced

½ cup sugar

2 tablespoons cider vinegar

1 teaspoon pumpkin pie spice

¼ teaspoon salt

⅛ teaspoon crushed red pepper flakes

Nutrition Information Per Serving	
Calories: 90	From Fat: 0
Total Fat	0g
Saturated Fat	0g
Trans Fat	0g
Cholesterol	0mg
Sodium	75mg
Total Carbohydrate	22g
Dietary Fiber	2g
Sugars	18g
Protein	0g

1) In nonreactive 2-quart saucepan, stir together all ingredients. Heat to boiling over high heat, stirring occasionally. Reduce heat to medium-low.

2) Cook 20 to 25 minutes, stirring occasionally, until cranberries pop and sauce thickens slightly. Pour into serving bowl; cover and refrigerate until ready to serve.

Cheesy BLT Mini Sandwiches

PREP TIME: 35 MINUTES (READY IN 35 MINUTES)
SERVINGS: 12 APPETIZERS

1 can (8 oz) Pillsbury® Crescent Recipe Creations® refrigerated seamless dough sheet

½ cup Cheddar-Monterey Jack cheese blend (2 oz)

8 slices bacon, crisply cooked, crumbled (½ cup)

2 tablespoons chopped green onions (2 medium)

⅓ cup mayonnaise or salad dressing

½ cup shredded lettuce

8 cherry tomatoes, sliced

Nutrition Information Per Serving	
Calories: 150	From Fat: 100
Total Fat	11g
Saturated Fat	3.5g
Trans Fat	0g
Cholesterol	10mg
Sodium	290mg
Total Carbohydrate	9g
Dietary Fiber	0g
Sugars	2g
Protein	3g

1) Heat oven to 375°F. Unroll dough on work surface; press into 12x8-inch rectangle. Cut into 24 squares; place on ungreased cookie sheets. Bake 8 to 10 minutes or until deep golden brown. Remove to cooling rack.

2) Meanwhile, in small bowl, mix cheese, bacon, onions and mayonnaise. Place slightly less than 1 tablespoon lettuce on bottoms of 12 crescent squares. Top each with 1 heaping tablespoon bacon mixture and 2 slices tomato. Top with remaining crescent squares.

Tapenade Flatbread Appetizers

STEPHANIE SAWYER | VIRGINIA BEACH, VIRGINIA

Bake-Off® BAKE-OFF® CONTEST 44, 2010

PREP TIME: 30 MINUTES (READY IN 50 MINUTES)
SERVINGS: 24 APPETIZERS

1 cup pitted ripe olives

1 cup pimiento-stuffed green olives

4 cloves garlic, chopped

2 tablespoons capers

½ cup Italian (flat-leaf) parsley

1 teaspoon dried oregano leaves

¼ cup Crisco® 100% extra virgin olive oil or pure olive oil

1 can (11 oz) Pillsbury® refrigerated thin pizza crust

1 cup grated Parmesan cheese

⅔ cup crumbled chèvre (goat) cheese (4 oz)

½ cup chopped drained roasted red bell peppers (from 7-oz jar)

½ cup sliced drained pepperoncini peppers (from 16-oz jar)

1) Heat oven to 400°F. In food processor, place olives, garlic, capers, parsley and oregano. Cover; process with on-and-off pulses until coarsely chopped. With food processor running, pour oil through feed tube; process until well blended.

2) Spray large cookie sheet with Crisco® original no-stick cooking spray. Unroll the pizza crust dough on cookie sheet; press into 15x10-inch rectangle. Bake 7 minutes or until light golden brown.

3) Spread olive tapenade over partially baked crust. Top evenly with cheeses, red peppers and pepperoncini peppers. Bake 8 to 11 minutes longer or until golden brown. Cut into 24 squares. Serve warm or cool.

Nutrition Information Per Serving	
Calories: 120	From Fat: 70
Total Fat	8g
Saturated Fat	2.5g
Trans Fat	0g
Cholesterol	10mg
Sodium	330mg
Total Carbohydrate	8g
Dietary Fiber	0g
Sugars	1g
Protein	4g

Beans and Tomato Bruschetta

PREP TIME: 20 MINUTES (READY IN 20 MINUTES)
SERVINGS: 8

 EASY

8 slices (½ inch thick) Italian bread

3 tablespoons olive or vegetable oil

3 cloves garlic, finely chopped

½ teaspoon crushed red pepper flakes

20 fresh basil leaves

⅓ cup drained sun-dried tomatoes in oil, cut into ¼-inch slices

1 can (19 oz) Progresso® cannellini beans, drained

½ teaspoon salt

½ cup coarsely shredded mozzarella cheese (2 oz)

1) Heat oven to 400°F. Place bread on cookie sheet. Brush top sides of bread with 1 tablespoon of the oil. Bake 12 to 15 minutes or until golden brown. Remove from oven; set aside.

2) Meanwhile, in 10-inch nonstick skillet, cook garlic in remaining 2 tablespoons oil over medium heat, stirring occasionally, until lightly browned. Stir in red pepper flakes; cook 10 seconds. Carefully place basil leaves in skillet; cook until leaves are wilted and beginning to crisp. Stir in tomatoes, beans and salt. Remove from heat.

3) Arrange toasted bread on serving platter. Top each piece with some of the tomato-bean mixture, then with cheese. Serve warm.

Nutrition Information Per Serving	
Calories: 170	
Total Fat	8g
Saturated Fat	2g
Sodium	400mg
Total Carbohydrate	18g
Dietary Fiber	3g
Protein	7g

Crab Cakes Chiarello

PREP TIME: 35 MINUTES (READY IN 1 HOUR 5 MINUTES)
SERVING: 18 CRAB CAKES

1½ cups Progresso® panko crispy bread crumbs

1 cup mayonnaise or salad dressing

2 tablespoons chopped fresh parsley

1 tablespoon finely chopped chives

1 tablespoon lemon juice

2 teaspoons Dijon mustard

⅛ teaspoon freshly ground pepper

2 drops red pepper sauce

2 egg yolks

3 cans (6 to 6½ oz each) lump crabmeat, well drained

1 cup Progresso® panko crispy bread crumbs

2 tablespoons butter, melted

1½ teaspoons seafood seasoning (from 6-oz container)

1) Heat oven to 425°F. In medium bowl, mix 1½ cups bread crumbs, the mayonnaise, parsley, chives, lemon juice, mustard, pepper, pepper sauce and egg yolks. Using rubber spatula, gently fold in crabmeat, keeping pieces as large as possible.

2) Shape mixture by ¼ cupfuls into 18 patties, 2½ inches in diameter.

3) In medium bowl, mix remaining ingredients. Dip crab cakes into crumb mixture, coating both sides. Place in 2 ungreased 15x10-inch pans with sides.

4) Bake both pans on separate oven racks 12 to 15 minutes, turning patties once after 6 minutes, until golden brown. Serve warm.

Nutrition Information Per Serving	
Calories: 190	From Fat: 120
Total Fat	13g
Saturated Fat	2.5g
Trans Fat	0g
Cholesterol	50mg
Sodium	250mg
Total Carbohydrate	11g
Dietary Fiber	0g
Sugars	0g
Protein	6g

tip

To easily cut fresh parsley, place in a small glass container and snip the sprigs with kitchen shears.

Razzle-Dazzle Beef Bites

SHARON MOBLEY | AUSTIN, TEXAS

BAKE-OFF® CONTEST 44, 2010

PREP TIME: 20 MINUTES (READY IN 40 MINUTES)
SERVINGS: 16 APPETIZERS

🅔 EASY

1 can (8 oz) Pillsbury® Place 'N Bake® refrigerated crescent rounds (8 rounds) or 1 can (8 oz) Pillsbury® refrigerated crescent dinner rolls

1 package (3 oz) cream cheese, softened

½ teaspoon lemon-pepper seasoning

½ cup Smucker's® red raspberry preserves

1 tablespoon prepared horseradish

1 teaspoon Dijon mustard

3 oz shaved cooked roast beef (from deli)

1 tablespoon chopped fresh parsley

1) Heat oven to 375°F. If using crescent rounds, remove from package, but do not separate rounds. If using crescent rolls, remove from package, but do not unroll. Using serrated knife, cut roll evenly into 16 rounds; carefully separate rounds. Place 1 round in bottom of each of 16 ungreased regular-size muffin cups. Bake 8 to 10 minutes or until golden brown.

2) Immediately press back of rounded teaspoon into center of each baked round to make indentation. Remove rounds from muffin cups to cooling rack; cool 10 minutes.

3) Meanwhile, in small bowl, mix cream cheese and lemon-pepper seasoning. In another small bowl, mix preserves, horseradish and mustard.

4) Spread 1 teaspoon cream cheese mixture into each round; top with ½ teaspoon preserves mixture. Divide beef evenly among rounds; top each with 1 rounded teaspoon preserves mixture. Sprinkle with parsley.

Nutrition Information Per Serving	
Calories: 110	From Fat: 45
Total Fat	5g
Saturated Fat	2g
Trans Fat	1g
Cholesterol	10mg
Sodium	200mg
Total Carbohydrate	13g
Dietary Fiber	0g
Sugars	0g
Protein	2g

Caprese Pesto Margherita Stackers

JULIE BECKWITH | CRETE, ILLINOIS

Bake-Off®   BAKE-OFF® CONTEST 44, 2010

PREP TIME: 30 MINUTES (READY IN 55 MINUTES)
SERVINGS: 24 APPETIZERS

1 container (8 oz) fresh mozzarella ciliegine cheese (24 cherry-size balls)

1 can (11 oz) Pillsbury® refrigerated original breadsticks (12 breadsticks)

3 tablespoons basil pesto

1 tablespoon Crisco® 100% extra virgin olive oil or pure olive oil

2 tablespoons grated Parmesan cheese

24 frilled toothpicks

24 grape tomatoes

24 fresh basil leaves

1) Heat oven to 375°F. Spray 24 mini muffin cups with Crisco® original no-stick cooking spray. Drain cheese balls; pat dry with paper towels.

2) On work surface, unroll dough; separate into 12 breadsticks. Cut each breadstick in half crosswise; press each half into 3x2-inch rectangle.

3) Spread rounded ¼ teaspoon of the pesto lengthwise down center of each dough rectangle. Place 1 cheese ball on each rectangle. Carefully stretch dough around cheese; pinch edges to seal completely. Place seam sides down in muffin cups. Brush with oil; sprinkle with Parmesan cheese.

4) Bake 14 to 20 minutes or until deep golden brown. Cool in pan 5 minutes. Remove from pan. With each toothpick, spear one tomato and a basil leaf; insert into cheese ball. Serve warm.

Nutrition Information Per Serving	
Calories: 80	From Fat: 40
Total Fat	4.5g
Saturated Fat	2g
Trans Fat	0g
Cholesterol	5mg
Sodium	160mg
Total Carbohydrate	7g
Dietary Fiber	0g
Sugars	1g
Protein	4g

Southwest Mini Crescent Burritos

SHARON SHELTON | RAYTOWN, MISSOURI

Pillsbury Bake-Off®   BAKE-OFF® CONTEST 44, 2010

PREP TIME: 25 MINUTES (READY IN 55 MINUTES)
SERVINGS: 12 MINI BURRITOS

1 box (9 oz) Green Giant® frozen chopped spinach, thawed, squeezed to drain

1 cup shredded cooked chicken breast

½ cup canned black beans, drained, rinsed

½ cup Green Giant® Valley Fresh Steamers™ Niblets® frozen corn

1 cup shredded pepper Jack cheese (4 oz)

1 package (1 oz) taco seasoning mix

2 cans (8 oz each) Pillsbury® refrigerated garlic butter crescent dinner rolls (16 rolls)

1 Eggland's Best egg white, beaten

¾ cup sour cream

¾ cup salsa

1) Heat oven to 375°F. In large bowl, mix spinach, chicken, beans, corn, cheese and taco seasoning mix; set aside.

2) Unroll 1 can of crescent dough; press perforations to seal. Press or roll into 13x9-inch rectangle. Cut rectangle in half lengthwise, then cut crosswise into thirds to make 6 squares.

3) Spoon about ¼ cup spinach mixture onto center of each square. Bring up one side of dough over filling and roll up, folding in sides as you roll. Pinch seam to seal. On ungreased cookie sheet, place rolls seam sides down and 2 inches apart. Repeat with second can of dough and remaining spinach mixture. Brush the rolls with egg white.

4) Bake 14 to 18 minutes or until the edges are golden brown. Cool 10 minutes. Serve warm with the sour cream and salsa.

Nutrition Information Per Serving	
Calories: 160	From Fat: 130
Total Fat	12g
Saturated Fat	4g
Trans Fat	2g
Cholesterol	40mg
Sodium	200mg
Total Carbohydrate	10g
Dietary Fiber	0g
Sugars	4g
Protein	2g

Salmon Pecan-Crusted Tartlets

EVELYN HENDERSON | ROSEVILLE, CALIFORNIA

BAKE-OFF® CONTEST 44, 2010

PREP TIME:	30 MINUTES (READY IN 1 HOUR)
SERVINGS:	20 TARTLETS

1 can (6 oz) premium skinless boneless pink salmon, drained

¼ cup finely chopped dill pickle

1 tablespoon finely chopped onion

⅓ cup mayonnaise or salad dressing

½ cup shredded mild Cheddar cheese (2 oz)

1 tablespoon lemon juice

½ teaspoon dried dill weed

1 box Pillsbury® refrigerated pie crusts, softened as directed on box

⅓ cup Fisher® Chef's Naturals® Pecan Cookie Pieces or Fisher® Chef's Naturals® chopped pecans, finely chopped

1 package (3 oz) cream cheese, softened

1 dill weed sprig

2 lemon wedges

1) In large bowl, mix salmon, pickle, onion, mayonnaise, cheese, lemon juice and ½ teaspoon dill weed. Refrigerate.

2) Heat oven to 400°F. On work surface, unroll 1 pie crust. Sprinkle half of the pecans over crust; gently press into crust. Cut with 3-inch round cookie cutter into 10 rounds. In ungreased nonstick mini muffin pan, gently press each round, pecan side down, on bottom and up side of muffin cup, folding edge under and rounding to shape. Repeat with remaining crust.

3) Spoon 1 teaspoon of the cream cheese into bottom of each cup. Spoon 1 rounded tablespoon salmon mixture on cream cheese in each cup.

4) Bake 12 to 18 minutes or until crust is golden brown. Cool in pan on cooling rack 5 minutes. Remove from pan to serving platter; cool 5 minutes. Garnish with dill weed sprig and lemon wedges. Serve warm.

Nutrition Information Per Serving	
Calories: 160	From Fat: 110
Total Fat	12g
Saturated Fat	4g
Trans Fat	0g
Cholesterol	15mg
Sodium	200mg
Total Carbohydrate	10g
Dietary Fiber	0g
Sugars	0g
Protein	2g

tip

When juicing a fresh lemon by hand, cut it in half at an angle so the juice flows out faster and easier.

Gorgonzola and Hazelnut-Stuffed Mushrooms

PREP TIME: 30 MINUTES (READY IN 50 MINUTES)
SERVINGS: ABOUT 35 MUSHROOMS

LOW FAT

1 lb fresh whole mushrooms

⅓ cup crumbled Gorgonzola cheese

¼ cup Progresso® Italian style bread crumbs

¼ cup chopped hazelnuts (filberts)

¼ cup finely chopped red bell pepper

4 medium green onions, chopped (¼ cup)

½ teaspoon salt

Nutrition Information Per Serving	
Calories: 15	From Fat: 10
Total Fat	1g
Saturated Fat	0g
Trans Fat	0g
Cholesterol	0mg
Sodium	65mg
Total Carbohydrate	1g
Dietary Fiber	0g
Sugars	0g
Protein	1g

1) Heat oven to 350°F. Remove the stems from the mushroom caps; reserve caps. Finely chop enough stems to measure about ½ cup. Discard remaining stems.

2) In small bowl, mix chopped mushroom stems and remaining ingredients until well blended. Spoon into the mushroom caps, mounding slightly. Place in ungreased 15x10x1-inch pan. Bake 15 to 20 minutes or until hot. Serve warm.

Pomegranate Spiced Tea

PREP TIME: 5 MINUTES (READY IN 4 HOURS 5 MINUTES)
SERVINGS: 10 (1 CUP EACH)

 EASY   LOW FAT

8 cups cold water

1 bottle (16 oz) pomegranate juice

¾ cup sugar

2 cinnamon sticks

2 teaspoons whole allspice

½ teaspoon whole cloves

6 tea bags black tea (about 2 tablespoons loose tea)

Nutrition Information Per Serving	
Calories: 30	From Fat: 0
Total Fat	0g
Saturated Fat	0g
Trans Fat	0g
Cholesterol	0mg
Sodium	10mg
Total Carbohydrate	7g
Dietary Fiber	0g
Sugars	5g
Protein	0g

1) In 4- to 5-quart slow cooker, stir together all ingredients except tea. Cut paper label from tea bags. Tie strings of bags together to keep bags attached; place in cooker.

2) Cover; cook on High heat setting 4 hours. Remove tea bags; remove spices with small strainer.

Shrimp and Veggie Appetizer Pizza

PREP TIME: 35 MINUTES (READY IN 1 HOUR 25 MINUTES)
SERVINGS: 32 APPETIZERS

2 cans (8 oz each) Pillsbury® refrigerated reduced fat or regular crescent dinner rolls

8 oz spinach dip (1 cup)

4 oz fresh snow pea pods (1 cup), cut into 1-inch pieces

1 cup cherry tomatoes or grape tomatoes, halved

½ cup julienne (matchstick-cut) jicama (1 x ¼ x ¼ inch)

7 oz cooked deveined peeled salad shrimp, thawed if frozen, tail shells removed

2 tablespoons finely chopped fresh basil leaves

1) Heat oven to 375°F. Grease or spray 15x10x1-inch pan. Unroll both cans of dough; separate into 4 long rectangles. On pan, place 3 rectangles lengthwise, beginning at short end of pan. Place remaining rectangle across other short end of pan, to fill pan with dough. Press the dough in bottom and up the sides to form a crust, firmly pressing the perforations to seal.

2) Bake 13 to 17 minutes or until golden brown. Cool completely, about 30 minutes.

3) Spread spinach dip over cooled crust. Arrange peas, tomatoes, jicama and shrimp over dip. Gently press into dip. Sprinkle with basil.

4) Serve immediately, or cover and refrigerate up to 2 hours before serving. To serve, cut into 8 rows by 4 rows into squares.

Nutrition Information Per Serving	
Calories: 80	From Fat: 35
Total Fat	4g
Saturated Fat	1.5g
Trans Fat	0g
Cholesterol	15mg
Sodium	170mg
Total Carbohydrate	7g
Dietary Fiber	0g
Sugars	2g
Protein	3g

Sesame-Chicken Pot Stickers

DONNA WILKINSON | LAKESIDE, CALIFORNIA

BAKE-OFF® CONTEST 44, 2010

PREP TIME: 55 MINUTES (READY IN 55 MINUTES)
SERVINGS: 16 POT STICKERS

POT STICKERS

¼ cup Jif® creamy peanut butter

1 Eggland's Best egg

1 teaspoon onion powder

1 teaspoon toasted sesame oil

1 teaspoon soy sauce

½ cup shredded carrot

2 green onions, thinly sliced
(2 tablespoons)

¾ teaspoon black pepper

1 lb ground chicken or turkey

1 can (16.3 oz) Pillsbury® Grands!®
flaky layers refrigerated original
biscuits (8 biscuits)

2 tablespoons Crisco® pure
vegetable oil

4 tablespoons Land O Lakes® unsalted
or salted butter

1 cup chicken broth

2 teaspoons sesame seed

SAUCE

¼ cup Smucker's® seedless red
raspberry jam

¼ cup Smucker's® apricot preserves

½ teaspoon crushed red pepper flakes

Thinly sliced green onion tops for
garnish

1) In medium bowl, mix peanut butter, egg, onion powder, sesame oil, soy sauce, carrot, 2 green onions and black pepper until well blended. Stir in chicken until well blended.

2) Separate biscuit dough into 8 biscuits; separate each evenly into 2 layers, making 16 biscuit rounds. Press each into 4-inch round. Place 1 heaping tablespoon chicken mixture on center of each dough round. Fold up dough over filling, pinching edges together to form a standing seam along top of each pot sticker. Place 8 pot stickers on cookie sheet; cover and refrigerate.

3) In 12-inch nonstick skillet with straight sides, heat 1 tablespoon of the oil and 2 tablespoons of the butter over medium-low heat until mixture is bubbly. Add remaining 8 pot stickers, seam sides up; cook 2 to 5 minutes or until bottoms are light golden brown. Remove skillet from heat; slowly add ½ cup broth (be careful—spattering may occur). Sprinkle with 1 teaspoon sesame seed. Immediately cover and return to heat; cook 10 minutes; do not uncover. Turn off heat; let stand covered 5 to 7 minutes or until all liquid is absorbed and chicken is no longer pink. Remove from skillet; cover tightly. Repeat with remaining pot stickers.

4) Meanwhile, in a 1-quart saucepan, heat jam, preserves and red pepper flakes over medium heat 3 to 5 minutes, stirring occasionally, until jam and preserves are melted and mixture is boiling. Remove from heat; strain sauce.

5) Place pot stickers on serving plate. Drizzle with sauce. Garnish with green onion tops. Serve warm.

Nutrition Information Per Serving	
Calories: 230	From Fat: 120
Total Fat	13g
Saturated Fat	4g
Trans Fat	1g
Cholesterol	35mg
Sodium	390mg
Total Carbohydrate	21g
Dietary Fiber	0g
Sugars	8g
Protein	7g

Herb Chicken Sliders with Raspberry Mustard

LAUREEN PITTMAN | RIVERSIDE, CALIFORNIA

BAKE-OFF® CONTEST 44, 2010

Pillsbury
Bake-Off®

PREP TIME: 30 MINUTES (READY IN 55 MINUTES)
SERVINGS: 10

1 Eggland's Best egg

1 teaspoon water

1 can (11 oz) Pillsbury® refrigerated crusty French loaf

½ cup Smucker's® seedless red raspberry jam

2 tablespoons Dijon mustard

2 teaspoons whole-grain Dijon mustard, if desired

1¼ lb ground chicken or turkey

4 medium green onions, chopped (¼ cup)

2 tablespoons chopped fresh Italian (flat-leaf) parsley

1 teaspoon dried tarragon leaves

½ teaspoon granulated garlic or garlic powder

1 tablespoon Crisco® pure canola oil

1 bag (5 oz) mixed baby salad greens

1 medium tomato, thinly sliced

1) Heat oven to 350°F. Spray 10 regular-size muffin cups with Crisco® original no-stick cooking spray. In small bowl, beat egg and water until well blended. Cut loaf of dough crosswise into 10 slices for buns. Place each slice, cut side up, in muffin cup; brush with egg mixture. Bake 16 to 22 minutes or until tops are golden brown. Remove from pan to cooling rack; cool 5 minutes.

2) Meanwhile, in small bowl, beat jam and mustards with fork or wire whisk until smooth; set aside.

3) In medium bowl, mix chicken, green onions, parsley, tarragon and garlic. Shape the mixture into 10 patties, about ½ inch thick. In 12-inch nonstick skillet, heat the oil over medium-high heat. Add the patties; cook 3 to 5 minutes on each side, turning once, until a thermometer inserted into center reads 165°F.

4) Cut each bun in half horizontally. Spoon 1 teaspoon raspberry mustard on cut sides of each bun. Place bottoms of buns on large serving platter; top each with burger, small amount of salad greens and top of bun. Garnish platter with salad greens and tomato slices. Serve with remaining raspberry mustard.

Nutrition Information Per Serving	
Calories: 210	From Fat: 60
Total Fat	6g
Saturated Fat	1.5g
Trans Fat	0g
Cholesterol	50mg
Sodium	290mg
Total Carbohydrate	27g
Dietary Fiber	0g
Sugars	10g
Protein	10g

Fig and Blue Cheese Appetizer Tarts

NADINE CLARK | QUAKERTOWN, PENNSYLVANIA

Bake-Off®   BAKE-OFF® CONTEST 44, 2010

PREP TIME: 30 MINUTES (READY IN 1 HOUR)
SERVINGS: 16 TARTS

3 oz ⅓-less-fat cream cheese (Neufchâtel from 8-oz package), softened

⅔ cup crumbled blue cheese (3 oz)

¼ cup Smucker's® sweet orange marmalade

2 tablespoons balsamic vinegar

16 dried Mission figs, coarsely chopped (1 cup)

1 can (10.1 oz) Pillsbury® big & flaky refrigerated crescent dinner rolls (6 rolls)

½ cup Fisher® Chef's Naturals® chopped pecans

1) Heat oven to 350°F. In small bowl, mix cream cheese and blue cheese with fork until well blended; set aside.

2) In 1-quart saucepan, stir marmalade and vinegar over low heat until mixed; stir in figs. Cook over low heat 5 to 7 minutes, stirring occasionally, until figs are softened. Remove from heat.

3) Remove crescent dough from package, but do not unroll. Cut roll of dough into 16 slices. On 2 ungreased cookie sheets, place slices 2 inches apart. Press center of each slice to make indentation, 1½ inches in diameter.

4) Place 1 heaping teaspoon cheese mixture into each well. Top cheese with about 1 tablespoon fig mixture and 1½ teaspoon pecans.

5) Bake 15 to 19 minutes or until golden brown. Remove from cookie sheets to cooling rack and cool 10 minutes. Serve warm.

Nutrition Information Per Serving	
Calories: 160	From Fat: 80
Total Fat	9g
Saturated Fat	3g
Trans Fat	1g
Cholesterol	10mg
Sodium	230mg
Total Carbohydrate	18g
Dietary Fiber	1g
Sugars	9g
Protein	3g

Game-Day Spinach Pull-Apart

AMANDA SOTO | PHILADELPHIA , PENNSYLVANIA

BAKE-OFF® CONTEST 44, 2010

PREP TIME: 35 MINUTES (READY IN 1 HOUR 30 MINUTES)
SERVINGS: 16

3 tablespoons Land O Lakes® butter, melted

1½ teaspoons garlic salt

1 package (8 oz) cream cheese, softened

¼ cup mayonnaise or salad dressing

¼ cup grated Parmesan cheese

½ cup shredded mozzarella cheese (2 oz)

1 box (9 oz) Green Giant® frozen chopped spinach, thawed, squeezed to drain and finely chopped

½ teaspoon dried basil leaves, if desired

¼ teaspoon pepper

2 cans (8 oz each) Pillsbury® refrigerated garlic butter crescent dinner rolls (16 rolls)

1 cup marinara sauce, heated, if desired

1) Heat oven to 350°F. Spray 12-cup fluted tube cake pan with Crisco® original no-stick cooking spray. In small bowl, mix butter and ½ teaspoon of the garlic salt; set aside.

2) In medium bowl, mix cream cheese, mayonnaise, Parmesan cheese, mozzarella cheese, spinach, basil, pepper and remaining 1 teaspoon garlic salt until blended; set aside.

3) Unroll the crescent dough; separate into 16 triangles. Cut each triangle in half lengthwise to make total of 32 small triangles. Stretch or press 1 triangle slightly, being careful not to tear it. Spoon 1 tablespoon spinach mixture onto center of triangle; pull dough around mixture into a ball. Press edges to seal. Repeat with remaining triangles.

4) Roll each ball in butter mixture; layer in pan. Bake 35 to 40 minutes or until golden brown. Cool 5 minutes. Place heatproof serving plate upside down over pan; turn plate and pan over. Remove pan. Cool 10 minutes longer. Serve warm with marinara sauce.

Nutrition Information Per Serving	
Calories: 220	From Fat: 150
Total Fat	17g
Saturated Fat	8g
Trans Fat	2g
Cholesterol	25mg
Sodium	480mg
Total Carbohydrate	12g
Dietary Fiber	0g
Sugars	1g
Protein	5g

Spiced Chai

PREP TIME: 10 MINUTES (READY IN 3 HOURS 25 MINUTES)
SERVINGS: 8 (1 CUP EACH)

 EASY

2 teaspoons cardamom pods

6 tea bags black tea (about 2 tablespoons loose tea)

4 cups cold water

4 cups whole milk

2 teaspoons whole allspice

1 teaspoon whole cloves

½ teaspoon whole black peppercorns

2 cinnamon sticks, broken in half

1 piece (1 inch) peeled gingerroot

1 cup vanilla-flavored syrup or honey

1) With rolling pin or mortar and pestle, crack open cardamom pods to release seeds. Place pods and seeds in a 4- to 5-quart slow cooker.

2) Cut paper label from strings on tea bags; tie strings of bags to keep attached and place in cooker. Add remaining ingredients except syrup.

3) Cover and cook on High heat setting for 3 hours.

4) Remove tea bags. Stir syrup into chai. Cover; cook 10 to 15 minutes longer or until thoroughly heated. Carefully ladle the chai into cups, avoiding whole spices.

Nutrition Information Per Serving	
Calories: 150	From Fat: 35
Total Fat	4g
Saturated Fat	2.5g
Trans Fat	0g
Cholesterol	10mg
Sodium	55mg
Total Carbohydrate	24g
Dietary Fiber	0g
Sugars	25g
Protein	4g

Parmesan Crostini with Spinach-Pesto Spread

JOAN DUCKWORTH | LEE'S SUMMIT, MISSOURI

BAKE-OFF® CONTEST 44, 2010

PREP TIME: 20 MINUTES (READY IN 50 MINUTES)
SERVINGS: 48

 EASY

1 box (9 oz) Green Giant® frozen chopped spinach

4 oz cream cheese (half of 8-oz package), softened

½ cup sour cream

2 tablespoons basil pesto

1 teaspoon balsamic vinegar

¼ teaspoon salt

¼ teaspoon white or black pepper

½ cup grated Parmesan cheese

1 tablespoon finely chopped garlic

1 can (11 oz) Pillsbury® refrigerated crusty French loaf

¼ cup Crisco® pure olive oil

1) Heat oven to 375°F. Spray 2 large cookie sheets with Crisco® original no-stick cooking spray.

2) Cook spinach in microwave as directed on box. Drain spinach; cool 5 minutes. Carefully squeeze spinach with paper towels to drain completely.

3) In food processor, place spinach, cream cheese, sour cream, pesto, vinegar, salt and pepper. Cover; process until well blended. Cover; refrigerate while preparing crostini.

4) In small bowl, mix cheese and garlic; set aside. Place loaf of dough on cutting board. Using sharp serrated knife, cut dough into ¼-inch slices; place ½ inch apart on cookie sheets. Press slices with fingers into 2-inch rounds. Brush rounds with 2 tablespoons of the oil; sprinkle with half of the cheese mixture.

5) Bake 5 minutes. Remove from oven; turn crostini. Brush with remaining 2 tablespoons oil; sprinkle with remaining cheese mixture. Bake 5 to 10 minutes longer or until golden brown and crisp. Remove from cookie sheets to cooling racks; cool 5 minutes. Serve warm with spinach-pesto spread.

Nutrition Information Per Serving	
Calories: 50	From Fat: 30
Total Fat	3.5g
Saturated Fat	1.5g
Trans Fat	0g
Cholesterol	5mg
Sodium	80mg
Total Carbohydrate	3g
Dietary Fiber	0g
Sugars	0g
Protein	1g

Curry-Mustard Glazed Meatballs

PREP TIME: 10 MINUTES (READY IN 4 HOURS 10 MINUTES)
SERVINGS: 40

e EASY

1 jar (12 oz) pineapple preserves

1 jar (8 oz) Dijon mustard

1 can (8 oz) pineapple tidbits in juice, undrained

½ cup packed dark brown sugar

1 teaspoon curry powder

2½ lb frozen cooked Italian-style meatballs (80 meatballs)

Nutrition Information Per Serving	
Calories: 130	From Fat: 45
Total Fat	7g
Saturated Fat	2g
Trans Fat	0g
Cholesterol	30mg
Sodium	300mg
Total Carbohydrate	13g
Dietary Fiber	0g
Sugars	8g
Protein	6g

1) In 1-quart saucepan, mix all ingredients except meatballs; heat to boiling. Spray 2½- to 3-quart slow cooker with cooking spray. In cooker, place meatballs. Stir in preserves mixture. Cover; cook on High heat setting for 4 hours, stirring twice.

2) Just before serving, stir to coat the meatballs with sauce. Serve with toothpicks. Meatballs can be held on Low heat setting, uncovered, for up to 2 hours.

Pepperoni Pizza Snacks

PREP TIME: 25 MINUTES (READY IN 50 MINUTES)
SERVINGS: 20 SNACKS

e EASY   **f** LOW FAT

1 box (10.6 oz) Pillsbury® refrigerated Italian breadsticks (any flavor)

20 slices pepperoni (about 1½ oz)

20 cubes (½ inch) mozzarella cheese (2½ oz)

1 cup pizza sauce, heated

Nutrition Information Per Serving	
Calories: 70	From Fat: 30
Total Fat	3g
Saturated Fat	1g
Trans Fat	0g
Cholesterol	0mg
Sodium	250mg
Total Carbohydrate	7g
Dietary Fiber	0g
Sugars	1g
Protein	3g

1) Heat oven to 375°F. Spray 8- or 9-inch square pan with cooking spray. Remove dough from can. Unroll the dough and separate into strips. Cut each strip in half crosswise to make 20 pieces. Press each piece to form 2½-inch square.

2) Top each square with 1 slice of pepperoni and 1 cheese cube. Wrap dough around filling to completely cover; firmly press edges to seal.

3) Place spread mixture from breadstick package in small microwavable bowl. Microwave on High 10 to 20 seconds or until melted. Dip each filled dough snack in melted spread mixture. Place seam side down with sides touching in pan. Drizzle with any remaining spread mixture.

4) Bake 15 to 22 minutes or until golden brown. Cool 3 minutes; remove from pan. Serve warm snacks with warm pizza sauce.

Chile and Cheese Empanaditas

PREP TIME: 25 MINUTES (READY IN 45 MINUTES)
SERVINGS: 16 APPETIZERS

 EASY

1 cup shredded pepper Jack cheese (4 oz)

⅓ cup Old El Paso® chopped green chiles (from 4.5-oz can)

1 box (15 oz) Pillsbury® refrigerated pie crusts, softened according to package directions

1 egg, beaten

1 cup sour cream

1) Heat oven to 400°F. Spray cookie sheet with cooking spray. In small bowl, mix cheese and chiles.

2) With 3¼-inch round cutter, cut each pie crust into 8 rounds. Spoon cheese mixture evenly onto half of each dough round. Brush the edge of crust rounds with beaten egg. Fold crust rounds in half; press edges with fork to seal. Place on cookie sheet. Brush tops with egg. Prick top of each with fork to allow steam to escape.

3) Bake 12 to 16 minutes or until golden brown. Serve warm with sour cream.

Nutrition Information Per Serving	
Calories: 180	From Fat: 110
Total Fat	12g
Saturated Fat	6g
Trans Fat	0g
Cholesterol	35mg
Sodium	180mg
Total Carbohydrate	14g
Dietary Fiber	0g
Sugars	0g
Protein	2g

"Empanar" is Spanish for "to bake in pastry." These bite-size snacks are the perfect starter for a Mexican meal.

Mexican Appetizer Cups

JERI SCRANTON-SKYBERG | BOX ELDER, SOUTH DAKOTA

Pillsbury Bake-Off®

BAKE-OFF® CONTEST 44, 2010

PREP TIME: 40 MINUTES (READY IN 1 HOUR 40 MINUTES)
SERVINGS: 60 APPETIZERS

1 box (9 oz) Green Giant® frozen chopped spinach, thawed, squeezed to drain

1 can (10 oz) diced tomatoes with green chiles, undrained

1 package (8 oz) cream cheese, softened

1 cup sour cream

½ teaspoon taco seasoning mix (from 1-oz package)

40 to 45 nacho cheese-flavored tortilla chips

2 cans (12 oz each) Pillsbury® Grands!® Jr. Golden Layers® refrigerated buttermilk biscuits (20 biscuits)

1 cup finely shredded Mexican cheese blend (4 oz)

1) Heat oven to 375°F. Spray 30 mini muffin cups with Crisco® original no-stick cooking spray. In large bowl, mix spinach, tomatoes, cream cheese, sour cream and taco seasoning mix; set aside.

2) Place about 20 of the tortilla chips in gallon-size resealable food-storage plastic bag; seal bag. Using rolling pin, finely crush to measure ½ cup. Stir crushed chips into spinach mixture.

3) Separate 1 can of dough into 10 biscuits; separate each biscuit into 3 layers. Place 1 layer in each of 30 muffin cups; using floured fingers, press dough on bottom and up side of each cup.

4) Fill each cup with about 1 tablespoon spinach mixture. Refrigerate remaining spinach mixture. Sprinkle filling in each cup with about 1 teaspoon cheese. Bake 9 to 14 minutes or until edges of biscuits are golden brown. Cool in pan 5 minutes; remove from pan to cooling rack. Cool 5 minutes longer. Repeat with remaining biscuits, filling and cheese, cooling pans between batches.

5) To serve, break each of the remaining 20 to 25 tortilla chips into 3 triangular pieces. Insert 1 triangle into each cup. Serve warm.

Nutrition Information Per Serving	
Calories: 70	From Fat: 40
Total Fat	4.5g
Saturated Fat	2g
Trans Fat	0g
Cholesterol	10mg
Sodium	170mg
Total Carbohydrate	6g
Dietary Fiber	6g
Sugars	1g
Protein	1g

Spinach Arancini

PREP TIME: 1 HOUR 30 MINUTES (READY IN 3 HOURS)
SERVINGS: 24 APPETIZERS

2 tablespoons extra-virgin olive oil

1 small onion, finely chopped

2 cloves garlic, finely chopped

¾ cup uncooked Arborio rice

½ cup dry white wine

2 cups Progresso® reduced-sodium chicken broth (from 32-oz carton), heated

Freshly ground pepper to taste

1 cup chopped fresh spinach leaves

1 tablespoon butter

½ cup grated Parmigiano-Reggiano cheese

4 oz mozzarella cheese, cut into 24 (½-inch) cubes

½ cup all-purpose flour

1½ cups Progresso® Italian style panko crispy bread crumbs

1 egg

1 tablespoon water

Vegetable oil for frying

1) Line cookie sheet with cooking parchment paper. In 3-quart saucepan, heat olive oil over medium-high heat. Add onion; cook about 1 minute, stirring frequently. Add garlic; cook and stir 5 minutes. Reduce heat to medium. Stir in rice and wine; cook 5 to 10 minutes, stirring frequently, until liquid is absorbed. Add 1 cup broth; cook about 10 minutes, stirring occasionally, until broth is absorbed. Add remaining 1 cup broth; cook about 10 minutes, stirring occasionally, until broth is absorbed.

2) Season with pepper. Stir in spinach, butter and Parmigiano-Reggiano cheese. Spread onto cookie sheet. Cover with plastic wrap; refrigerate at least 1 hour 30 minutes or until firm. (Mixture can be refrigerated overnight.)

3) On cookie sheet, shape rice mixture into 12x8-inch rectangle. Cut into 6 rows by 4 rows to make 24 squares. Place 1 mozzarella cheese cube in center of each square; shape rice around cheese cubes to make balls.

4) Place flour and bread crumbs in separate bowls. In another bowl, beat egg and water until blended. Coat each ball with flour, then dip into egg mixture and coat with bread crumbs. Place coated balls on unlined cookie sheet; refrigerate 30 minutes.

5) Line platter or shallow pan with paper towels. In 4-quart Dutch oven, heat about 2 inches vegetable oil to 350°F. Fry 8 balls at a time 3 to 4 minutes, turning once, until golden brown. With slotted spoon, remove balls from Dutch oven to towel-lined platter to drain. Serve hot.

Nutrition Information Per Serving	
Calories: 130	From Fat: 60
Total Fat	7g
Saturated Fat	2g
Trans Fat	0g
Cholesterol	15mg
Sodium	220mg
Total Carbohydrate	12g
Dietary Fiber	0g
Sugars	0g
Protein	4g

Mini Greek Turkey Burgers with Cucumber Sauce

RENEE HERRINGTON | MURPHY, TEXAS

BAKE-OFF® CONTEST 44, 2010

PREP TIME: 35 MINUTES (READY IN 35 MINUTES)
SERVINGS: 6

1 can (11 oz) Pillsbury® refrigerated crusty French loaf

8 oz fat-free plain Greek yogurt or regular yogurt (¾ cup)

¼ cup finely diced peeled cucumber

¼ teaspoon dried dill weed

¼ teaspoon lemon juice

Dash salt

Dash pepper

1 lb lean ground turkey

2 small cloves garlic, finely chopped

¼ cup finely diced red onion

¼ cup finely chopped fresh Italian (flat-leaf) parsley

1 teaspoon seasoned salt

1 teaspoon cracked black pepper

¼ teaspoon salt

1 tablespoon Crisco® 100% extra virgin olive oil or pure olive oil

1 block (6 oz) reduced-fat feta cheese, cut into 6 (2 x 1½ x ½-inch thick) pieces

6 lettuce leaves

1) Heat oven to 350°F. Spray cookie sheet with Crisco® original no-stick cooking spray. Cut loaf of dough crosswise into 6 pieces to make buns. Place buns, seam sides down and 2 inches apart, on cookie sheet. Cut 2 (½-inch-deep) slashes in top of each bun. Bake 19 to 22 minutes or until golden brown.

2) Meanwhile, in small bowl, mix yogurt, cucumber, dill weed, lemon juice and dash of salt and pepper; refrigerate.

3) In medium bowl, mix turkey, garlic, onion, parsley, seasoned salt, 1 teaspoon pepper, ¼ teaspoon salt and 1 teaspoon of the oil. Shape mixture into 12 patties, about 3 inches in diameter. Place one piece of cheese on each of 6 patties; top with remaining patties. Pinch edges to seal well.

4) In 12-inch nonstick skillet, heat remaining 2 teaspoons oil over medium heat. Add patties; cook 5 minutes on each side. Increase heat to medium-high; cook 3 minutes each side or until burgers have dark brown, caramelized appearance and thermometer inserted in center of turkey (not cheese) reads 165°F.

5) Cut buns horizontally in half. Place 1 tablespoon yogurt sauce on bottom of each bun; top with lettuce leaf, burger and top of bun. Secure each sandwich with toothpick; serve with remaining sauce. If desired, serve with Green Giant® frozen green beans & almonds, prepared as directed on the box.

Nutrition Information Per Serving	
Calories: 340	From Fat: 100
Total Fat	11g
Saturated Fat	3.5g
Trans Fat	0g
Cholesterol	60mg
Sodium	1090mg
Total Carbohydrate	32g
Dietary Fiber	0g
Sugars	9g
Protein	28g

Asian-Spiced Cashew-Chicken Piadinis

BRETT YOUMANS | READING, PENNSYLVANIA BAKE-OFF® CONTEST 44, 2010

PREP TIME: 25 MINUTES (READY IN 55 MINUTES)
SERVINGS: 12 PIADINIS

1 package (6 oz) refrigerated grilled chicken breast strips or 6 oz cooked chicken breast, finely chopped

⅓ cup chopped green onions (about 5 medium)

¼ cup chopped Fisher® cashews, halves and pieces

2 tablespoons teriyaki sauce

1 tablespoon toasted sesame oil

1 tablespoon lime juice

2 teaspoons finely chopped garlic

2 teaspoons grated gingerroot

2 cups coleslaw mix (shredded cabbage and carrots)

⅓ cup loosely packed, chopped fresh cilantro

1 can (11 oz) Pillsbury® refrigerated thin pizza crust

1 Eggland's Best egg

1 teaspoon water

1 tablespoon chopped fresh cilantro, if desired

1) Heat oven to 400°F. Line large cookie sheet with cooking parchment paper or spray with Crisco® original no-stick cooking spray.

2) In 12-inch nonstick skillet, cook chopped chicken, onions, cashews, teriyaki sauce, sesame oil, lime juice, garlic and gingerroot over medium-high heat 2 to 3 minutes, stirring occasionally, until thoroughly heated. Stir in coleslaw mix; cook about 2 minutes or until vegetables are crisp-tender. Stir in ⅓ cup cilantro. Cool completely, about 15 minutes.

3) Unroll pizza crust dough. Starting at center, press dough into 16x12-inch rectangle. Cut rectangle into 12 (4-inch) squares (3 rows lengthwise and 4 rows crosswise).

4) Working with 1 dough square at a time, spoon slightly less than ¼ cup chicken mixture onto center. Fold 1 corner of square over filling; bring opposite corner over first corner, tucking under roll to seal. Leave other ends open. Place on cookie sheet. In small bowl, beat egg and water until well blended; lightly brush over piadinis.

5) Bake 9 to 11 minutes or until golden brown. Remove from cookie sheets to cooling racks. Garnish each piadini with ¼ teaspoon chopped cilantro. Serve warm.

Nutrition Information Per Serving	
Calories: 130	From Fat: 45
Total Fat	5g
Saturated Fat	4g
Trans Fat	0g
Cholesterol	25mg
Sodium	340mg
Total Carbohydrate	15g
Dietary Fiber	4g
Sugars	2g
Protein	6g

Asian Fondue

PREP TIME: 15 MINUTES (READY IN 15 MINUTES)
SERVINGS: 8

 EASY

1 lb boneless skinless chicken breasts, cut into ¼-inch strips

1 lb boneless beef top sirloin steak, cut into ¼-inch strips

1 medium zucchini, cut into ½-inch slices

1 medium red bell pepper, cut into 1-inch cubes

½ lb snow pea pods, strings removed, cut crosswise in half

5¼ cups Progresso® chicken broth (from two 32-oz cartons)

2 tablespoons soy sauce

2 or 3 thin slices gingerroot

2 cloves garlic, thinly sliced

¾ cup peanut sauce

½ cup sweet-and-sour sauce

1) On a serving plate, arrange the chicken, beef, zucchini, bell pepper and pea pods.

2) In 2-quart saucepan, mix broth, soy sauce, gingerroot and garlic. Heat to boiling. Pour into fondue pot; keep warm over heat. (Or follow manufacturer's directions to heat in fondue pot.)

3) Spear chicken, beef and vegetables on fondue forks and cook in broth mixture until chicken is no longer pink center, beef is desired doneness and vegetables are crisp-tender. Let small pieces of food remain in broth. Serve chicken, beef and vegetables with peanut sauce and sweet-and-sour sauce.

Nutrition Information Per Serving	
Calories: 280	From Fat: 10
Total Fat	10g
Saturated Fat	2.5g
Trans Fat	0g
Cholesterol	70mg
Sodium	950mg
Total Carbohydrate	14g
Dietary Fiber	2g
Sugars	10g
Protein	33g

Buffalo Chicken Crescent Puffs

BETH DURNELL | COLUMBUS, OHIO

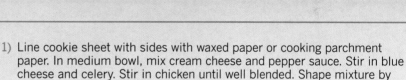

BAKE-OFF® CONTEST 44, 2010

PREP TIME: 25 MINUTES (READY IN 1 HOUR 10 MINUTES)
SERVINGS: 32 PUFFS

12 oz cream cheese (from two 8-oz packages), softened

2 tablespoons Louisiana hot sauce or other red pepper sauce

⅓ cup crumbled blue cheese (1½ oz)

¼ cup finely chopped celery

1 cup finely chopped cooked chicken breast

2 cans (8 oz each) Pillsbury® Place 'N Bake® refrigerated crescent rounds (16 rounds) or 2 cans (8 oz each) Pillsbury® refrigerated crescent dinner rolls

⅓ cup Land O Lakes® unsalted or salted butter, melted

1 cup plain or chicken-flavored panko-style bread crumbs

1) Line cookie sheet with sides with waxed paper or cooking parchment paper. In medium bowl, mix cream cheese and pepper sauce. Stir in blue cheese and celery. Stir in chicken until well blended. Shape mixture by tablespoonfuls into 32 (1½-inch) balls; place on cookie sheet. Refrigerate 20 minutes.

2) Meanwhile, heat oven to 350°F. If using crescent rounds, remove from package, but do not separate rounds. If using crescent rolls, remove from package, but do not unroll. Using serrated knife, cut each roll evenly into 16 rounds; carefully separate rounds. Press each round to 3 inches in diameter. Place chilled chicken mixture ball on center of each dough round; shape dough around ball to cover completely.

3) In shallow dish, place melted butter. In another shallow dish, place bread crumbs. Dip dough balls into butter, then roll in bread crumbs. Place 2 inches apart on large ungreased cookie sheet. Bake 17 to 22 minutes or until golden brown. Cool 5 minutes. Serve warm.

Nutrition Information Per Serving	
Calories: 130	From Fat: 90
Total Fat	10g
Saturated Fat	5g
Trans Fat	1g
Cholesterol	20mg
Sodium	210mg
Total Carbohydrate	8g
Dietary Fiber	0g
Sugars	1g
Protein	3g

Candied Bacon and Apple Canapés

STEPHANIE LEMUS | WESTLAKE VILLAGE, CALIFORNIA

BAKE-OFF® CONTEST 44, 2010

PREP TIME:	1 HOUR (READY IN 1 HOUR)
SERVINGS:	40 CANAPÉS

1 box Pillsbury® refrigerated pie crusts, softened as directed on box

1 Eggland's Best egg

1 tablespoon water

1 tablespoon sea salt

⅓ cup packed dark or light brown sugar

½ teaspoon ground red pepper (cayenne)

20 thin slices center-cut bacon (about 12 oz)

½ cup water

1 teaspoon granulated sugar

1 tablespoon lemon juice

2 small Granny Smith apples

4 oz cream cheese (half of 8-oz package), softened

1¼ cups crumbled blue cheese (6 oz)

1) Heat oven to 400°F. Line large cookie sheets with cooking parchment paper. Unroll pie crusts on work surface. Using 2¼-inch round cookie cutter, cut 20 rounds from each crust, rerolling dough if necessary. Place on cookie sheet; prick each round twice with fork. In small bowl, beat egg and 1 tablespoon water until well blended; brush on rounds. Sprinkle with sea salt. Bake 7 to 10 minutes or until golden brown and crisp. Cool while preparing bacon.

2) Line 15x10x1-inch pan with cooking parchment paper. In small bowl, mix brown sugar and red pepper. Place bacon with sides touching in pan; sprinkle with brown sugar mixture. Bake 10 to 15 minutes or until sugar is hot and bubbly. Remove bacon from pan to a plate; let stand 10 to 15 minutes or until cool enough to handle. Using sharp knife, cut each bacon slice into 4 pieces.

3) Meanwhile, in small bowl, mix ½ cup water, granulated sugar and lemon juice until sugar is dissolved. Cut each unpeeled apple into 20 (2 x ¼-inch) slices; place in water mixture and refrigerate.

4) In another small bowl, mix cream cheese and blue cheese with wooden spoon, leaving small pieces of blue cheese visible. Spoon mixture into pastry bag fitted with ¾-inch tip; pipe onto each cracker. Drain apple slices; pat dry. For each cracker, place 1 apple slice between 2 bacon pieces; press at an angle into cheese mixture.

Nutrition Information Per Serving	
Calories: 90	From Fat: 50
Total Fat	6g
Saturated Fat	2.5g
Trans Fat	0g
Cholesterol	15mg
Sodium	370mg
Total Carbohydrate	8g
Dietary Fiber	0g
Sugars	3g
Protein	2g

Bacon-Chile Rellenos

PREP TIME: 25 MINUTES (READY IN 40 MINUTES)
SERVINGS: 16

4 jalapeño chiles
(about 3 inches long)

⅓ cup Boursin cheese with garlic
and herbs (from 5.2-oz container)

8 slices packaged precooked bacon
(from 2.2-oz package), halved

1 can (8 oz) Pillsbury® refrigerated
crescent dinner rolls

½ cup Old El Paso® thick 'n chunky
salsa, if desired

Nutrition Information Per Serving	
Calories: 90	From Fat: 50
Total Fat	6g
Saturated Fat	2.5g
Trans Fat	1g
Cholesterol	10mg
Sodium	210mg
Total Carbohydrate	6g
Dietary Fiber	0g
Sugars	1g
Protein	3g

1) Heat oven to 375°F. Carefully remove stems from chiles; cut each in half lengthwise and again horizontally to make 4 pieces. Remove and discard seeds. Spoon about 1 teaspoon cheese into each chile quarter. Wrap half slice of bacon around each.

2) On cutting board, unroll dough; separate dough into 8 triangles. From center of longest side to opposite point, cut each triangle in half, making 16 triangles. Place chile, cheese side down, on dough triangle. Fold 1 point of triangle over filling; fold 2 remaining points over first point. Place on ungreased cookie sheet.

3) Bake 12 to 15 minutes or until golden brown. Immediately remove from cookie sheet. Serve with salsa.

White Cranberry Spiced Wine

PREP TIME: 10 MINUTES (READY IN 3 HOURS 10 MINUTES)
SERVINGS: 14 (1/2 CUP EACH)

 EASY

1 bottle (750 ml) white wine (such as Riesling or Pinot Grigio)

1 can (12 oz) frozen orange juice concentrate, thawed

3 cups white cranberry juice

½ cup sugar

¼ cup crystallized ginger slices

1 teaspoon ground nutmeg

1 seedless orange, sliced

6 cinnamon sticks (2 to 3 inch)

Nutrition Information Per Serving	
Calories: 160	From Fat: 0
Total Fat	0g
Saturated Fat	0g
Trans Fat	0g
Cholesterol	0mg
Sodium	5mg
Total Carbohydrate	28g
Dietary Fiber	1g
Sugars	26g
Protein	1g

1) In 3½- to 4-quart slow cooker, mix all ingredients. Cover; cook on Low heat setting 3 to 4 hours.

2) Remove cinnamon sticks with slotted spoon. To serve, have guests ladle hot wine into cups.

Soups & Sandwiches

Hearty soups and savory sandwiches make
for a quick, robust meal any day of the week!

CLAM CHOWDER WITH
ARTICHOKES
PG. 66

TURKEY CLUB SANDWICH RING
WITH AVOCADO AIOLI
PG. 62

CHICKEN CREOLE SOUP
PG. 86

HERBED CHICKEN
AND CHEESE PANINI
PG. 88

Turkey Club Sandwich Ring with Avocado Aioli

HEATHER HALONIE | WEBSTER, WISCONSIN

PREP TIME: 20 MINUTES (READY IN 55 MINUTES)
SERVINGS: 8

🅔 EASY

- 2 cans (11 oz each) Pillsbury® refrigerated crusty French loaf
- 1 Eggland's Best egg
- 1 teaspoon dried oregano leaves
- 1 tablespoon shredded Parmesan cheese
- 1½ cups shredded lettuce
- ¼ cup chopped red onion
- 2 medium plum (Roma) tomatoes, chopped
- ¼ cup Crisco® 100% extra virgin olive oil or pure olive oil
- 1½ tablespoons red wine vinegar
- ½ teaspoon crushed red pepper flakes
- ⅓ cup mayonnaise or salad dressing
- 2 cloves garlic, finely chopped
- ½ avocado, pitted, peeled and chopped
- 8 oz thinly sliced cooked turkey (from deli)
- 8 slices (¾ oz each) provolone cheese, halved
- 8 slices bacon, halved, crisply cooked

1) Heat oven to 350°F. Spray large cookie sheet with Crisco® original no-stick cooking spray, or line with cooking parchment paper. Place both loaves of dough, seam sides down, on cookie sheet. Join ends of loaves to form 11-inch ring; pinch ends together firmly to seal. Using sharp or serrated knife, cut 12 diagonal slashes (½ inch deep) on top of dough.

2) In small bowl, beat egg and ½ teaspoon of the oregano with fork; brush generously over dough. Sprinkle dough with Parmesan cheese. Bake 26 to 30 minutes or until deep golden brown. Cool on cookie sheet 20 minutes.

3) Meanwhile, in medium bowl, mix lettuce, onion, tomatoes, oil, vinegar, red pepper flakes and remaining ½ teaspoon oregano. Refrigerate about 20 minutes to blend flavors and slightly wilt lettuce.

4) In food processor, cover and process mayonnaise, garlic and avocado until smooth.

5) Cut bread ring in half horizontally. Press inside of top and bottom of ring to flatten bread slightly for fillings. Place lettuce mixture in bottom of ring. Top with turkey, provolone cheese and bacon. Spread avocado mixture in top of ring; place on bottom ring. Cut into 8 sections to serve.

Nutrition Information Per Serving	
Calories: 500	From Fat: 120
Total Fat	28g
Saturated Fat	8g
Trans Fat	0g
Cholesterol	65mg
Sodium	1230mg
Total Carbohydrate	40g
Dietary Fiber	1g
Sugars	5g
Protein	21g

Spiced Apple-Squash Soup

PREP TIME: 25 MINUTES (READY IN 8 HOURS 25 MINUTES)
SERVINGS: 8 (1 CUP EACH)

LOW FAT

8 cups cubed peeled butternut squash (about 3 lb)

2 large apples, peeled, chopped (about 3 cups)

¼ cup finely chopped onion (about 1 small)

1 carton (32 oz) Progresso® chicken broth (4 cups)

1 cup apple juice

½ teaspoon salt

½ teaspoon ground cinnamon

¼ teaspoon ground nutmeg

¼ teaspoon ground ginger

½ cup whipping cream

2 tablespoons chopped fresh parsley

1) Spray 4- to 5-quart slow cooker with cooking spray. In cooker, mix all ingredients except whipping cream and parsley.

2) Cover; cook on Low heat setting for 8 to 10 hours.

3) Blend soup in cooker with immersion blender, or blend soup in batches in blender container on low speed and return to cooker. Stir in whipping cream. Sprinkle each serving with chopped parsley.

Nutrition Information Per Serving	
Calories: 160	From Fat: 45
Total Fat	5g
Saturated Fat	3g
Trans Fat	0g
Cholesterol	15mg
Sodium	580mg
Total Carbohydrate	26g
Dietary Fiber	2g
Sugars	15g
Protein	3g

Easy Mulligatawny Soup

PREP TIME: 15 MINUTES (READY IN 6 HOURS 35 MINUTES)
SERVINGS: 6 (1-1/3 CUPS EACH)

 EASY   LOW FAT

1 package (20 oz) boneless skinless chicken thighs

2 cups chopped onions

1 medium stalk celery, chopped (½ cup)

2 medium carrots, chopped (1 cup)

4 teaspoons curry powder

1 teaspoon ground ginger

¼ teaspoon crushed red pepper flakes

1 tablespoon lemon juice

1 carton (32 oz) Progresso® chicken broth (4 cups)

1½ cups Green Giant® Valley Fresh Steamers™ frozen mixed vegetables, thawed, drained

⅓ cup uncooked instant white rice

½ teaspoon salt, if desired

1) Spray 3½- to 4-quart slow cooker with cooking spray. In cooker, mix all ingredients except mixed vegetables, rice and salt.

2) Cover; cook on Low heat setting for 6 to 8 hours.

3) Break chicken into bite-size pieces by pulling apart with 2 forks. Stir in mixed vegetables and rice. Increase heat setting to High. Cover; cook 20 minutes longer or until rice is tender. Season with ½ teaspoon salt.

Nutrition Information Per Serving	
Calories: 230	From Fat: 70
Total Fat	8g
Saturated Fat	2.5g
Trans Fat	0g
Cholesterol	60mg
Sodium	650mg
Total Carbohydrate	15g
Dietary Fiber	3g
Sugars	5g
Protein	23g

Chicken and Gnocchi Soup

PREP TIME: 15 MINUTES (READY IN 8 HOURS 45 MINUTES)
SERVINGS: 6 (1-1/2 CUPS EACH)

 EASY

1¼ lb boneless skinless chicken thighs, cut into ¾-inch pieces

1 cup julienne carrots (1½ x ¼ x ¼-inch pieces)

½ cup chopped celery (1 medium stalk)

½ cup chopped onion (1 medium)

1 teaspoon dried thyme leaves

1 carton (32 oz) Progresso® chicken broth (4 cups)

1 can (10¾ oz) condensed cream of mushroom with roasted garlic soup

1 package (16 oz) gnocchi (not frozen)

1 package (9 oz) Green Giant® frozen baby sweet peas, thawed

1) In 10-inch nonstick skillet, cook chicken 5 to 7 minutes, stirring frequently, until browned and no longer pink in the center.

2) Spray 3- to 4-quart slow cooker with cooking spray. In cooker, mix chicken and remaining ingredients except gnocchi and peas.

3) Cover; cook on Low heat setting for 8 to 10 hours.

4) Increase heat setting to High. Stir in gnocchi and peas. Cover; cook about 30 minutes longer or until gnocchi and peas are tender.

Nutrition Information Per Serving	
Calories: 390	From Fat: 110
Total Fat	12g
Saturated Fat	3.5g
Trans Fat	0g
Cholesterol	60mg
Sodium	1390mg
Total Carbohydrate	43g
Dietary Fiber	4g
Sugars	5g
Protein	28g

tip

Regular cream of mushroom or cream of chicken soup will work in this recipe, but the roasted garlic variety really adds a lot of flavor.

Beef-Barley Soup

PREP TIME: 10 MINUTES (READY IN 8 HOURS 20 MINUTES)
SERVINGS: 6 (1-1/3 CUPS EACH)

 EASY

1½ lb beef stew meat

2 medium carrots, sliced (1 cup)

1 medium onion, chopped (½ cup)

1 cup sliced fresh mushrooms

½ cup uncooked pearl barley

5¼ cups Progresso® beef flavored broth (from two 32-oz cartons)

2 dried bay leaves

1 cup Green Giant® Valley Fresh Steamers™ frozen baby sweet peas

Nutrition Information Per Serving	
Calories: 350	From Fat: 120
Total Fat	13g
Saturated Fat	5g
Trans Fat	.5g
Sodium	1110mg
Total Carbohydrate	23g
Dietary Fiber	4g
Sugars	4g
Protein	35g

1) Spray 4- to 5-quart slow cooker with cooking spray. Mix all ingredients except peas in cooker.

2) Cover; cook on Low heat setting 8 to 9 hours. About 10 minutes before serving, stir in peas. Increase heat setting to High. Cover; cook about 10 minutes or until peas are thoroughly cooked. Remove bay leaves.

Clam Chowder with Artichokes

PREP TIME: 15 MINUTES (READY IN 15 MINUTES)
SERVINGS: 4 (1-1/2 CUPS EACH)

 EASY

1 can (14 oz) Progresso® artichoke hearts

1 jar (4.5 oz) Green Giant® sliced mushrooms

2 cans (18.5 oz each) Progresso® traditional New England clam chowder

½ cup chopped red bell pepper

½ cup water

Dash salt

Dash pepper

Nutrition Information Per Serving	
Calories: 270	From Fat: 100
Total Fat	11g
Saturated Fat	3g
Trans Fat	0g
Cholesterol	35mg
Sodium	1350mg
Total Carbohydrate	34g
Dietary Fiber	10g
Sugars	4g
Protein	8g

1) Drain and quarter artichokes. Drain mushrooms. In 3-quart saucepan, mix all ingredients except salt and pepper. Cook over medium heat, stirring occasionally, until thoroughly heated. Stir in salt and pepper to taste.

Country Chicken Sandwiches with Maple-Mustard Spread

PREP TIME: 15 MINUTES (READY IN 15 MINUTES)
SERVINGS: 4

 EASY

3 tablespoons mayonnaise or salad dressing

2 tablespoons country-style Dijon mustard

2 tablespoons real maple syrup

1 small shallot, finely chopped (about 3 tablespoons)

8 slices rustic bread

4 slices (1 oz each) Swiss cheese

2 cups sliced deli rotisserie chicken (from 2- to 2½-lb chicken)

1 medium ripe avocado, pitted, peeled and sliced

1) In small bowl, mix mayonnaise, mustard, maple syrup and shallot. Spread on all 8 slices of bread.

2) Top 4 slices of bread with cheese, chicken and avocado. Top with remaining bread slices.

Nutrition Information Per Serving	
Calories: 460	From Fat: 200
Total Fat	23g
Saturated Fat	5g
Trans Fat	0.5g
Cholesterol	70mg
Sodium	660mg
Total Carbohydrate	37g
Dietary Fiber	4g
Sugars	9g
Protein	26g

Avocados are often sold when underripe. Plan ahead for this recipe; if your avocado doesn't yield to gentle pressure from your finger, leave it on your countertop for a few days to completely ripen.

Turkey, Squash and Pasta Soup

PREP TIME: 20 MINUTES (READY IN 40 MINUTES)
SERVINGS: 6 (1-1/2 CUPS EACH)

 EASY   LOW FAT

1 tablespoon olive or vegetable oil

2 medium stalks celery, coarsely chopped (1 cup)

1 medium onion, coarsely chopped (½ cup)

1 teaspoon dried sage leaves

6 cups Progresso® reduced-sodium chicken broth (from two 32-oz cartons)

2½ cups ½-inch pieces cooked turkey (12 oz)

1½ cups uncooked tricolor rotini pasta

1½ cups ¾-inch cubes peeled butternut squash (about ½ medium squash)

⅛ teaspoon pepper

1) In 4½- to 5-quart Dutch oven, heat oil over medium-high heat. Add celery, onion and sage; cook 5 to 6 minutes, stirring frequently, until onion is softened.

2) Stir in remaining ingredients. Heat to boiling; reduce heat to medium. Cover; cook 10 to 12 minutes, stirring occasionally, until pasta and squash are tender.

Nutrition Information Per Serving	
Calories: 270	From Fat: 120
Total Fat	8g
Saturated Fat	2g
Trans Fat	0g
Cholesterol	50mg
Sodium	1180mg
Total Carbohydrate	24g
Dietary Fiber	2g
Sugars	2g
Protein	25g

Lentil Soup

PREP TIME: 15 MINUTES (READY IN 8 HOURS 15 MINUTES)
SERVINGS: 8 (1-1/2 CUP EACH)

 e EASY   **lf** LOW FAT

1 lb smoked ham shanks

2 cartons (32 oz each) Progresso® chicken broth (8 cups)

1 package (16 oz) dried lentils (2¼ cups), sorted, rinsed

4 medium stalks celery, chopped (2 cups)

4 medium carrots, chopped (2 cups)

3 tablespoons chopped fresh parsley

3 cloves garlic, finely chopped

2 cups shredded fresh spinach

1) Spray 5- to 6-quart slow cooker with cooking spray. Mix all ingredients except spinach in cooker.

2) Cover; cook on Low heat setting 8 to 9 hours.

3) Remove ham from cooker; place on cutting board. Pull meat from bones, using 2 forks; discard bones and skin. Stir ham and spinach into soup. Stir well before serving.

Nutrition Information Per Serving	
Calories: 280	From Fat: 30
Total Fat	3.5g
Saturated Fat	1g
Trans Fat	0g
Cholesterol	20mg
Sodium	920mg
Total Carbohydrate	37g
Dietary Fiber	10g
Sugars	4g
Protein	25g

Cheesy Potato Soup

PREP TIME: 25 MINUTES (READY IN 6 HOURS 55 MINUTES)
SERVINGS: 6 (1-2/3 CUPS EACH)

4 slices bacon

1½ cups chopped onion

5 cups diced peeled russet potatoes (about 5 medium)

1 medium stalk celery, chopped (½ cup)

1 carton (32 oz) Progresso® chicken broth (4 cups)

½ teaspoon salt

¼ teaspoon pepper

½ cup all-purpose flour

1½ cups half-and-half

1 bag (8 oz) shredded American and Cheddar cheese blend (2 cups)

1) In 12-inch skillet, cook bacon over medium heat, turning occasionally, until browned and crispy. Remove from skillet, reserving fat in skillet. Drain bacon on paper towel, then refrigerate. In same skillet, cook onion in bacon fat over medium heat 4 to 5 minutes, stirring frequently, until tender.

2) Spray 3½- to 4-quart slow cooker with cooking spray. In cooker, mix onion, potatoes, celery, broth, salt and pepper.

3) Cover; cook on Low heat setting 6 to 7 hours.

4) In small bowl, beat flour and half-and-half with wire whisk until well blended; stir into soup. Increase heat setting to High. Cover; cook about 30 minutes longer or until thickened. Stir in cheese until well melted. Crumble bacon; sprinkle over soup.

Nutrition Information Per Serving	
Calories: 420	From Fat: 120
Total Fat	21g
Saturated Fat	13g
Trans Fat	.5g
Cholesterol	65mg
Sodium	1490mg
Total Carbohydrate	39g
Dietary Fiber	3g
Sugars	7g
Protein	17g

Roast Beef and Gorgonzola Hoagies

MELISSA STADLER | GILBERT, ARIZONA

BAKE-OFF® CONTEST 44, 2010

PREP TIME: 35 MINUTES (READY IN 35 MINUTES)
SERVINGS: 6 SANDWICHES

2 cans (11 oz each) Pillsbury®
  refrigerated crusty French loaf

¼ cup Crisco® pure canola oil

2 tablespoons Land O Lakes® butter

1 medium onion, thinly sliced
  (about 1 cup)

1 can (14 oz) beef broth

1½ lb cooked roast beef (from deli),
  thinly sliced

1 cup mayonnaise or salad dressing

2 chipotle chiles in adobo sauce
  (from 7-oz can), diced

1 tablespoon lime juice

½ teaspoon pepper

1 cup crumbled Gorgonzola cheese
  (4 oz)

1) Heat oven to 350°F. Spray large cookie sheet with Crisco® original no-stick cooking spray. Place both loaves of dough, seam sides down and 3 inches apart, on a large cookie sheet. Using sharp knife, cut 4 or 5 diagonal slashes (½ inch deep) on top of each loaf. Bake 22 to 26 minutes or until golden brown.

2) Meanwhile, in 12-inch skillet, heat oil and butter over medium heat. Add onion; cook 15 to 18 minutes, stirring occasionally, until tender. Stir in broth and beef; cook 4 minutes. Remove from heat.

3) In small bowl, mix mayonnaise, chipotle chiles, lime juice and pepper. When bread is done baking, set oven control to broil. Cut each loaf in half horizontally, cutting to but not completely through one long side; place cut sides up on cookie sheet. Spread ½ cup mayonnaise mixture over cut sides of each loaf. Using slotted spoon, remove beef and onion from broth mixture, reserving broth mixture. Top each loaf with half of the beef and onion; top with cheese.

4) Broil with tops 6 inches from heat 2 to 3 minutes or until bread is lightly toasted. Cut each sandwich into 3 pieces. If desired, skim fat from broth mixture and serve broth with sandwiches for dipping.

Nutrition Information Per Serving	
Calories: 800	From Fat: 450
Total Fat	50g
Saturated Fat	10g
Trans Fat	0g
Cholesterol	85mg
Sodium	2370mg
Total Carbohydrate	54g
Dietary Fiber	0g
Sugars	7g
Protein	33g

Vegetarian Black and White Bean Chili

 EASY   LOW FAT

1 tablespoon vegetable oil

1 large onion, chopped (1 cup)

4 cloves garlic, finely chopped
(2 teaspoons)

1 can (15.5 oz) great northern beans,
drained, rinsed

1 can (15 oz) Progresso® black beans,
drained, rinsed

2 cans (14.5 oz each) fire-roasted
crushed tomatoes, undrained

1 can (11 oz) Green Giant® Mexicorn®
whole kernel corn with red and
green peppers

1 can (4 oz) Old El Paso® chopped
green chiles, undrained

1 can (14 oz) vegetable broth

1 tablespoon chili powder

1 teaspoon ground cumin

½ teaspoon salt

Sour cream, if desired

1) In 4-quart saucepan, heat oil over
medium-high heat. Add onion and
garlic; cook 2 minutes, stirring
frequently, until tender.

2) Stir in remaining ingredients except sour
cream. Heat to boiling. Reduce heat to
low; cover and simmer 30 minutes,
stirring occasionally. Top each serving
with sour cream.

Nutrition Information Per Serving	
Calories: 260	From Fat: 30
Total Fat	3.5g
Saturated Fat	0.5g
Trans Fat	0g
Cholesterol	0mg
Sodium	1260mg
Total Carbohydrate	47g
Dietary Fiber	13g
Sugars	8g
Protein	10g

tip

Stir in cornmeal to
thicken the chili
slightly. Or simply
cook longer on low
heat; this will not only
thicken the chili but
blend the flavors.

Southwestern Pork Soup

PREP TIME: 25 MINUTES (READY IN 35 MINUTES)
SERVINGS: 5 (1-1/4 CUPS EACH)

2 teaspoons vegetable oil

1 lb boneless pork loin, trimmed of fat, cut into ½-inch cubes

4 medium green onions, sliced (¼ cup)

1 small jalapeño chile, seeded, finely chopped

1 clove garlic, finely chopped

3½ cups Progresso® reduced-sodium chicken broth (from 32-oz carton)

2 cans (15 to 16 oz each) great northern beans, drained, rinsed

½ cup loosely packed chopped fresh cilantro

¼ cup loosely packed chopped fresh parsley

Nutrition Information Per Serving	
Calories: 400	From Fat: 90
Total Fat	11g
Saturated Fat	3g
Trans Fat	0g
Cholesterol	60mg
Sodium	380mg
Total Carbohydrate	45g
Dietary Fiber	11g
Sugars	1g
Protein	40g

1) In 3-quart nonstick saucepan, heat oil over medium-high heat. Add pork; cook 3 to 5 minutes, stirring occasionally, until browned. Add onions, chile and garlic; cook and stir 1 minute.

2) Add broth and beans. Heat to boiling. Reduce heat; cover and simmer about 10 minutes or until pork is no longer pink in center. Stir in cilantro and parsley; cook until heated through.

Hearty Ham and Vegetable Soup

PREP TIME: 20 MINUTES (READY IN 20 MINUTES)
SERVINGS: 4 (1-1/4 CUPS EACH)

 EASY　　 LOW FAT

1 can (19 oz) Progresso® vegetable classics hearty tomato soup

1 can (15 or 16 oz) pork and beans in tomato sauce

1 cup diced cooked ham

1 cup Green Giant® Valley Fresh Steamers™ frozen mixed vegetables

Nutrition Information Per Serving	
Calories: 250	From Fat: 45
Total Fat	4.5g
Saturated Fat	1g
Trans Fat	0g
Cholesterol	25mg
Sodium	1520mg
Total Carbohydrate	38g
Dietary Fiber	9g
Sugars	14g
Protein	15g

1) In 2-quart saucepan, stir together all ingredients. Heat to boiling over medium-high heat.

2) Reduce heat to medium-low; simmer uncovered 10 minutes, stirring occasionally, until vegetables are tender.

Tangy Asian Chicken and Coleslaw Rolls

EMILY SCHUERMANN | NORMAN, OKLAHOMA   BAKE-OFF® CONTEST 44, 2010

Pillsbury Bake-Off®

PREP TIME: 25 MINUTES (READY IN 50 MINUTES)
SERVINGS: 8 SANDWICHES

2 cans (11 oz each) Pillsbury®
  refrigerated crusty French loaf

1 cup Fisher® Chef's Naturals® natural
  sliced almonds

½ cup Smucker's® apricot preserves

¼ cup chopped fresh chives

¼ cup rice wine vinegar or rice vinegar

2½ tablespoons Crisco® pure
  vegetable oil

1 teaspoon kosher (coarse) salt

½ teaspoon freshly ground pepper

1 red or green jalapeño chile, seeded,
  finely chopped

3 cups cold shredded deli rotisserie
  chicken (from 2-lb chicken)

1 bag (8 oz or 4 cups) coleslaw mix
  (shredded cabbage and carrots)

1) Heat oven to 375°F. Spray large cookie sheet with Crisco® original no-stick cooking spray. Cut each loaf of dough crosswise into 4 pieces to make rolls. Place rolls, seam side down and 2 inches apart on cookie sheet. Bake 12 to 16 minutes or until golden brown. Remove from cookie sheet to cooling rack; cool completely.

2) While oven is warm, toast almonds in ungreased shallow pan 3 to 4 minutes, stirring occasionally, until slightly golden.

3) Meanwhile, in small bowl, beat remaining ingredients except chicken and coleslaw with wire whisk.

4) In medium bowl, mix chicken, coleslaw and almonds. Add apricot vinaigrette; mix thoroughly.

5) Cut each roll horizontally almost to other side. Fill each roll with ½ cup coleslaw mixture. Serve immediately.

Nutrition Information Per Serving	
Calories: 490	From Fat: 170
Total Fat	18g
Saturated Fat	3g
Trans Fat	0g
Cholesterol	45mg
Sodium	890mg
Total Carbohydrate	55g
Dietary Fiber	3g
Sugars	14g
Protein	24g

Summer Chicken Soup with Biscuit Dumplings

PREP TIME: 35 MINUTES (READY IN 50 MINUTES)
SERVINGS: 6 (1-1/2 CUPS EACH)

SOUP

- 1 tablespoon vegetable oil
- 1 medium onion, chopped (½ cup)
- 2 cloves garlic, finely chopped
- 1 carton (32 oz) Progresso® chicken broth
- 12 baby-cut carrots, cut in half lengthwise
- 4 cups shredded cooked chicken
- 1 medium zucchini, cubed
- 1 medium yellow squash, cubed
- 1 box (9 oz) Green Giant® Simply Steam® frozen baby sweet peas, thawed
- ½ teaspoon salt
- ¼ teaspoon pepper
- ¼ cup chopped fresh dill weed

DUMPLINGS

- 1 can (10.2 oz) Pillsbury® Grands!® flaky layers refrigerated biscuits (5 biscuits)
- ¼ cup chopped fresh parsley

1) In 4-quart saucepan, heat oil over medium-high heat. Cook and stir onion and garlic in oil about 2 minutes or until onions are tender.

2) Add chicken broth; heat to boiling. Add carrots; reduce heat to medium. Cook about 5 minutes or until carrots are tender. Add remaining soup ingredients; increase heat to high. Heat to boiling. Reduce heat to medium-high. Cover; cook 2 to 3 minutes or until vegetables are crisp-tender.

3) Cut biscuits into fourths. Dip one side of each biscuit piece in parsley. Drop biscuits, parsley side up, onto hot soup. Reduce heat to medium. Cover; cook 10 to 15 minutes or until the dumplings are no longer doughy in the center.

Nutrition Information Per Serving	
Calories: 400	From Fat: 130
Total Fat	14g
Saturated Fat	3g
Trans Fat	3g
Cholesterol	75mg
Sodium	1340mg
Total Carbohydrate	32g
Dietary Fiber	3g
Sugars	9g
Protein	36g

Easy Italian Wedding Soup

| PREP TIME: | 15 MINUTES (READY IN 15 MINUTES) |
| SERVINGS: | 4 (1-1/2 CUPS EACH) |

 EASY　　**LOW FAT**

3½ cups Progresso® reduced-sodium chicken broth (from 32-oz carton)

1 cup water

1 cup uncooked medium shell pasta (4 oz)

16 frozen cooked meatballs

2 cups fresh spinach leaves, finely shredded

1 can (8 oz) pizza sauce

Nutrition Information Per Serving	
Calories: 300	From Fat: 70
Total Fat	8g
Saturated Fat	2.5g
Trans Fat	0g
Cholesterol	60mg
Sodium	920mg
Total Carbohydrate	37g
Dietary Fiber	3g
Sugars	6g
Protein	20g

1) In 3-quart saucepan, heat broth and water to boiling. Add pasta and meatballs; return to boiling. Cook 7 to 9 minutes or until pasta is almost tender. Do not drain.

2) Add spinach and pizza sauce; cook 1 to 2 minutes longer or until thoroughly heated. If desired, sprinkle individual servings with grated Parmesan cheese.

Chicken Mole Chili

| PREP TIME: | 30 MINUTES (READY IN 30 MINUTES) |
| SERVINGS: | 5 (1-1/2 CUPS EACH) |

 EASY　　**LOW FAT**

1 tablespoon vegetable oil

1 large onion, chopped (1 cup)

2 cups Progresso® chicken broth (from 32-oz carton)

1 jar (16 oz) Old El Paso® thick 'n chunky salsa

2 cans (15 oz each) pinto beans, drained, rinsed

1 can (4.5 oz) Old El Paso® chopped green chiles, undrained

1 package (1.25 oz) chili seasoning mix

1 oz bittersweet baking chocolate, grated

⅛ teaspoon ground cinnamon

2 cups shredded cooked chicken

Chopped green onions, if desired

Nutrition Information Per Serving	
Calories: 390	From Fat: 80
Total Fat	9g
Saturated Fat	3g
Trans Fat	0g
Cholesterol	45mg
Sodium	1600mg
Total Carbohydrate	47g
Dietary Fiber	13g
Sugars	6g
Protein	30g

1) In 4-quart saucepan, heat oil over medium-high heat. Cook onion in oil for 2 minutes, stirring frequently, until tender.

2) Add remaining ingredients except chicken and green onions; heat to boiling, stirring occasionally. Reduce heat to low; cover and simmer 10 to 15 minutes to blend flavors.

3) Stir in chicken; cook 2 to 3 minutes or until chicken is hot. Top each serving with green onions.

Spicy Cashew-Chicken Bundles

PREP TIME: 20 MINUTES (READY IN 40 MINUTES)   EASY
SERVINGS: 4 SANDWICHES

1½ cups chopped cooked chicken

¼ cup finely shredded carrot

3 tablespoons sliced green onions
(3 medium)

3 tablespoons chopped cashews

½ teaspoon grated gingerroot or
¼ teaspoon ground ginger

¼ teaspoon crushed red pepper flakes

¼ cup hoisin sauce

1 can (8 oz) Pillsbury® refrigerated
crescent dinner rolls

Additional sliced green onions, if
desired

1) Heat oven to 375°F. In medium bowl, mix all ingredients except dough and
additional sliced green onions; set aside.

2) On ungreased large cookie sheet, unroll dough; separate into 4 rectangles.
Press each into 7x4½-inch rectangle, firmly pressing perforations to seal.

3) Spoon about ½ cup chicken mixture onto one end of each rectangle. Fold
dough in half over filling; firmly press edges with fork to seal. With fork,
prick top of each to allow steam to escape.

4) Bake 13 to 18 minutes or until deep golden brown. Immediately remove
from cookie sheet. Garnish with additional sliced green onions.
Serve warm.

Nutrition Information Per Serving	
Calories: 380	From Fat: 170
Total Fat	19g
Saturated Fat	6g
Trans Fat	3g
Cholesterol	45mg
Sodium	750mg
Total Carbohydrate	32g
Dietary Fiber	1g
Sugars	6g
Protein	20g

Buffalo-Blue Cheese Chicken Burgers

PREP TIME: 35 MINUTES (READY IN 35 MINUTES)
SERVINGS: 6

1¾ lb ground chicken

¼ cup Buffalo wing sauce

½ teaspoon salt

1 to 3 drops red pepper sauce

6 burger buns, split

6 leaves green leaf lettuce

¼ cup refrigerated chunky blue cheese dressing

¼ cup crumbled blue cheese

1) Heat gas or charcoal grill. Carefully brush oil on grill rack. In large bowl, mix chicken, wing sauce, salt and pepper sauce.

2) Shape mixture into six ½-inch patties, each about 4 inches in diameter. Place on grill over medium heat. Cover grill; cook 10 to 12 minutes or until thermometer inserted in center of patty reads 165°F.

3) Place buns on grill, cut sides down. Cover grill; cook 1 to 2 minutes or until toasted. Place lettuce and patty on bottom of each bun. In small bowl, stir together dressing and blue cheese. Top patties with dressing mixture and tops of buns.

Nutrition Information Per Serving	
Calories: 330	From Fat: 150
Total Fat	17g
Saturated Fat	4.5g
Trans Fat	0g
Cholesterol	85mg
Sodium	890mg
Total Carbohydrate	23g
Dietary Fiber	1g
Sugars	4g
Protein	22g

Thai-Style Chicken Curry Soup

PREP TIME: 15 MINUTES (READY IN 15 MINUTES)
SERVINGS: 4 (1-1/2 CUPS EACH)

 EASY   LOW FAT

1 carton (32 oz) Progresso® chicken broth (4 cups)

3 tablespoons packed brown sugar

2 tablespoons soy sauce

2 tablespoons rice vinegar

2 teaspoons curry powder

1 small red bell pepper, coarsely chopped (½ cup)

1 small jalapeño chile, seeded, finely chopped (1 tablespoon)

2 cups chopped deli rotisserie chicken (from 2- to 2½-lb chicken)

2 tablespoons chopped fresh cilantro, if desired

1) In 3-quart saucepan, mix all ingredients except chicken and cilantro. Heat to boiling over medium-high heat. Reduce heat to medium. Simmer uncovered 3 to 5 minutes or until bell pepper is crisp-tender.

2) Stir in chicken. Cook 1 to 2 minutes or until chicken is hot. Just before serving, add cilantro.

Nutrition Information Per Serving	
Calories: 210	From Fat: 120
Total Fat	7g
Saturated Fat	2g
Trans Fat	0g
Cholesterol	60mg
Sodium	1770mg
Total Carbohydrate	14g
Dietary Fiber	0g
Sugars	11g
Protein	25g

tip

If you like your food to be spicy, add an additional tablespoon of finely chopped jalapeño to the soup.

Chicken and Spinach Tortellini Soup

PREP TIME: 20 MINUTES (READY IN 35 MINUTES)
SERVINGS: 5 (1-1/2 CUPS EACH)

 EASY

1 tablespoon olive or vegetable oil

⅓ cup chopped green onions
(about 5 medium)

⅓ cup julienne carrots
(1½ x ¼ x ¼ inch)

1 teaspoon finely chopped garlic

6 cups Progresso® chicken broth
(from two 32-oz cartons)

2 cups shredded deli rotisserie
chicken (from 2- to 2½-lb chicken)

1 cup frozen small cheese-filled
tortellini

¼ teaspoon ground nutmeg, if desired

⅛ teaspoon pepper

3 cups chopped fresh spinach

1) In 4½- to 5-quart Dutch oven, heat oil over medium-high heat. Cook onions, carrots and garlic in oil 3 to 4 minutes, stirring frequently, until onions are softened.

2) Stir in broth and chicken. Heat to boiling. Stir in tortellini; reduce heat to medium. Cover; cook 3 to 5 minutes or until tortellini are tender.

3) Stir in nutmeg, pepper and spinach. Cover; cook 2 to 3 minutes or until spinach is hot.

Nutrition Information Per Serving	
Calories: 240	From Fat: 100
Total Fat	11g
Saturated Fat	3g
Trans Fat	0g
Cholesterol	80mg
Sodium	1540mg
Total Carbohydrate	10g
Dietary Fiber	1g
Sugars	1g
Protein	25g

Chicken Tortilla Soup

PREP TIME: 35 MINUTES (READY IN 35 MINUTES)
SERVINGS: 6 (1 CUP EACH)

1 carton (32 oz) Progresso® chicken broth (4 cups)

1 cup Old El Paso® thick 'n chunky salsa

2 cups shredded deli rotisserie chicken (from 2- to 2½-lb chicken)

¾ cup crushed tortilla chips

1 medium avocado, pitted, peeled and chopped

1½ cups shredded Monterey Jack cheese (6 oz)

2 tablespoons chopped fresh cilantro

Lime wedges, if desired

1) In 3-quart saucepan, heat broth, salsa and chicken to boiling over medium-high heat, stirring occasionally.

2) Meanwhile, divide crushed chips among 6 serving bowls. Spoon hot soup over chips, then top with avocado, cheese and cilantro. Serve with lime wedges.

Nutrition Information Per Serving	
Calories: 330	From Fat: 180
Total Fat	20g
Saturated Fat	8g
Trans Fat	0g
Cholesterol	65mg
Sodium	1390mg
Total Carbohydrate	13g
Dietary Fiber	2g
Sugars	2g
Protein	24g

North Woods Wild Rice Soup

PREP TIME: 20 MINUTES (READY IN 6 HOURS 40 MINUTES)
SERVINGS: 6

e EASY   ff LOW FAT

2 teaspoons vegetable oil

1 medium onion, chopped

2 medium stalks celery, diced (1 cup)

2 medium carrots, diced

1 cup diced smoked turkey (6 oz)

½ cup uncooked wild rice

1 teaspoon dried tarragon leaves

¼ teaspoon pepper

3½ cups Progresso® chicken broth (from 32-oz carton)

1 cup Green Giant® Valley Fresh Steamers™ frozen sweet peas, thawed

1 can (12 oz) evaporated fat-free milk

⅓ cup all-purpose flour

2 tablespoons dry sherry, if desired

1) In 10-inch skillet, heat oil over medium heat. Add onion; cook about 4 minutes, stirring occasionally, until tender.

2) Spray 3½- to 4-quart slow cooker with cooking spray. Place onion, celery, carrots, turkey, wild rice, tarragon and pepper in cooker. Pour broth over top.

3) Cover and cook on Low heat setting 6 to 8 hours, stirring in peas for last 15 minutes of cooking.

4) In small bowl, mix milk and flour; stir into soup. Cover; cook about 20 minutes or until thickened. Stir in sherry before serving.

Nutrition Information Per Serving	
Calories: 230	From Fat: 20
Total Fat	2.5g
Saturated Fat	0g
Trans Fat	0g
Cholesterol	0mg
Sodium	630mg
Total Carbohydrate	32g
Dietary Fiber	3g
Sugars	11g
Protein	19g

Creamy Asparagus Soup

PREP TIME: 35 MINUTES (READY IN 35 MINUTES)
SERVINGS: 6 (1 CUP EACH)

¼ cup butter or margarine

½ cup chopped onion (1 medium)

½ cup chopped celery

2 tablespoons all-purpose flour

2½ cups Progresso® chicken broth (from 32-oz carton)

2 cans (15 oz each) Green Giant® extra long tender green asparagus spears, drained

1 cup half-and-half

Nutrition Information Per Serving	
Calories: 170	From Fat: 120
Total Fat	13g
Saturated Fat	8g
Trans Fat	0g
Cholesterol	35mg
Sodium	680mg
Total Carbohydrate	8g
Dietary Fiber	2g
Sugars	4g
Protein	5g

1) In 3-quart saucepan, melt butter over medium heat. Add onion and celery; cook 4 to 5 minutes, stirring frequently, until vegetables are crisp-tender. Stir in flour. Cook 1 minute, stirring constantly. Stir in broth. Cook 5 to 7 minutes, stirring constantly, until thoroughly heated.

2) Remove from heat. Stir in asparagus. In food processor or blender, process asparagus mixture until smooth. If necessary, asparagus mixture can be processed in batches. Return to saucepan.

3) Stir in half-and-half. Cook 5 to 8 minutes, stirring occasionally, until slightly thickened and thoroughly heated.

Italian Chicken Club Sandwiches

PREP TIME: 15 MINUTES (READY IN 15 MINUTES)
SERVINGS: 6

ⓔ EASY

½ cup basil pesto

1 tablespoon plus 1 teaspoon balsamic vinegar

6 focaccia breads, each cut horizontally in half

8 oz thinly sliced oven-roasted chicken breast (from deli)

⅓ cup sun-dried tomatoes in oil, drained and thinly sliced

4 oz sliced mozzarella cheese

Nutrition Information Per Serving	
Calories: 660	From Fat: 280
Total Fat	31g
Saturated Fat	7g
Trans Fat	0g
Cholesterol	30mg
Sodium	1920mg
Total Carbohydrate	71g
Dietary Fiber	4g
Sugars	3g
Protein	23g

1) In small bowl, mix pesto and balsamic vinegar. Spread mixture on bottom half of each focaccia bread. Top with chicken, tomatoes and mozzarella. Top each with other half of focaccia bread.

Creamy Chicken Noodle Soup with Pesto Drizzle

PREP TIME: 35 MINUTES (READY IN 35 MINUTES)
SERVINGS: 6 (1-1/2 CUPS EACH)

2 tablespoons butter or margarine

2 medium carrots, sliced (1 cup)

2 medium stalks celery, sliced (1 cup)

1 medium onion, chopped (½ cup)

1 carton (32 oz) Progresso® reduced-sodium chicken broth (4 cups)

2½ cups milk

1 box Tuna Helper® creamy broccoli

2 cups cut-up cooked chicken

1 dried bay leaf

2 tablespoons basil pesto

1) In 5-quart Dutch oven or stockpot, melt butter over medium heat. Add carrots, celery and onion; cook about 5 minutes, stirring frequently, until carrots are crisp-tender.

2) Stir in broth, milk, uncooked pasta and sauce mix (from Tuna Helper box), chicken and bay leaf. Heat to boiling. Reduce heat; simmer uncovered 12 to 15 minutes, stirring occasionally, until pasta and vegetables are tender.

3) Remove bay leaf from soup; ladle soup into bowls. Place pesto in small resealable food-storage plastic bag; seal bag. Cut off small corner of bag; drizzle pesto over soup.

Nutrition Information Per Serving	
Calories: 280	From Fat: 130
Total Fat	15g
Saturated Fat	6g
Trans Fat	0g
Cholesterol	60mg
Sodium	660mg
Total Carbohydrate	16g
Dietary Fiber	1g
Sugars	8g
Protein	19g

tip

Use rotisserie chicken for a quick way to get cooked chicken for this soup.

Asian Sesame Sliders

CHARLOTTE GILTNER | MESA, ARIZONA

Bake-Off BAKE-OFF® CONTEST 44, 2010

PREP TIME: 35 MINUTES (READY IN 35 MINUTES)
SERVINGS: 8 SANDWICHES

1½ lb lean (at least 80%) ground beef

1 cup fresh bean sprouts

½ cup finely chopped celery

½ cup finely chopped fresh mushrooms

¼ cup finely chopped green onions (4 medium)

2 tablespoons soy sauce

1 tablespoon sesame oil

1 teaspoon finely chopped garlic

½ teaspoon pepper

3 tablespoons Crisco® pure vegetable oil

¼ cup sesame seeds

1 can (16.3 oz) Pillsbury® Grands!® homestyle refrigerated buttermilk biscuits (8 biscuits)

1 cup mayonnaise or salad dressing

1 tablespoon wasabi paste (Japanese horseradish)

1½ cups finely shredded Chinese (napa) cabbage

1) Heat oven to 350°F. In large bowl, mix beef, bean sprouts, celery, mushrooms, onions, soy sauce, sesame oil, garlic and pepper. Shape mixture into 8 patties, 3½ inches in diameter.

2) Reserve 1 teaspoon of the vegetable oil. Heat 12-inch nonstick skillet over medium-high heat; add remaining vegetable oil to cover bottom of skillet. Add patties; cook about 5 minutes on each side or until meat thermometer inserted in center reads 160°F.

3) Meanwhile, place sesame seed in shallow dish. Separate dough into 8 biscuits. Brush reserved 1 teaspoon vegetable oil over one side of biscuits. Press oiled side of each biscuit into sesame seed; place seed side up on ungreased cookie sheet. Bake as directed on can. In small bowl, mix mayonnaise and wasabi paste.

4) Carefully split biscuits. Spread 1 tablespoon mayonnaise mixture on split sides of each biscuit. Top bottoms of biscuits with patties, cabbage and biscuit tops.

Nutrition Information Per Serving	
Calories: 640	From Fat: 440
Total Fat	49g
Saturated Fat	10g
Trans Fat	4.5g
Cholesterol	65mg
Sodium	1020mg
Total Carbohydrate	29g
Dietary Fiber	1g
Sugars	5g
Protein	21g

Chicken Creole Soup

PREP TIME: 35 MINUTES (READY IN 55 MINUTES)
SERVINGS: 8 (1-1/2 CUPS EACH)

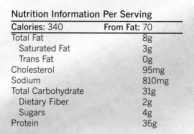 LOW FAT

- 2 tablespoons butter or margarine
- 2 medium onions, coarsely chopped (1 cup)
- 2 medium stalks celery, coarsely chopped (1 cup)
- 1 medium green bell pepper, coarsely chopped (1 cup)
- 2 teaspoons finely chopped garlic
- 2½ lb boneless skinless chicken breasts or thighs, cut into 1-inch pieces
- ¼ cup all-purpose flour
- 2 cans (14.5 oz each) diced tomatoes, undrained
- 1 carton (32 oz) Progresso® reduced-sodium chicken broth (4 cups)
- 2 cups water
- 1 cup uncooked regular long-grain white rice
- 1 teaspoon salt
- ¼ teaspoon ground red pepper (cayenne)
- 2 dried bay leaves

Nutrition Information Per Serving	
Calories: 340	From Fat: 70
Total Fat	8g
Saturated Fat	3g
Trans Fat	0g
Cholesterol	95mg
Sodium	810mg
Total Carbohydrate	31g
Dietary Fiber	2g
Sugars	4g
Protein	36g

1) In 5- to 6-quart Dutch oven, melt butter over medium-high heat. Add onions, celery, bell pepper, garlic and chicken; cook 7 to 9 minutes, stirring frequently, until onion is softened.

2) Stir in the flour. Cook 5 to 6 minutes, stirring constantly, until the flour is light brown.

3) Stir in remaining ingredients. Heat to boiling. Reduce heat to medium-low. Cover; cook 15 to 20 minutes, stirring occasionally, until rice is tender and chicken is no longer pink in center. Remove bay leaves.

Picnic Chicken Loaf

PREP TIME: 15 MINUTES (READY IN 15 MINUTES)
SERVINGS: 4

 EASY

½ loaf soft French bread (from 1-lb, 22-inch loaf)

¼ cup honey mustard

2 tablespoons chopped fresh or 2 teaspoons dried tarragon or basil leaves

2 cups sliced deli rotisserie chicken (from 2- to 2½-lb chicken)

4 oz Brie cheese, sliced

½ Granny Smith apple, unpeeled, thinly sliced

Nutrition Information Per Serving	
Calories: 450	From Fat: 180
Total Fat	20g
Saturated Fat	8g
Trans Fat	0.5g
Cholesterol	95mg
Sodium	810mg
Total Carbohydrate	36g
Dietary Fiber	2g
Sugars	7g
Protein	33g

1) Cut bread horizontally in half; spread inside top and bottom evenly with mustard, and sprinkle with tarragon.

2) Layer chicken, brie and apple over bottom; cover with top.

3) Cut loaf into quarters.

Beef Tortellini Soup

PREP TIME: 20 MINUTES (READY IN 8 HOURS 45 MINUTES)
SERVINGS: 6

 EASY

1 lb beef stew meat

1 large onion, chopped (¾ cup)

1 large carrot, chopped (¾ cup)

1 medium stalk celery, chopped (½ cup)

2 cloves garlic, finely chopped

2 teaspoons sugar

1 can (14.5 oz) diced tomatoes, undrained

2½ cups Progresso® beef flavored broth (from 32-oz carton)

1 teaspoon dried basil leaves

2 cups frozen cheese-filled tortellini

1 cup Green Giant® Valley Fresh Steamers™ frozen cut green beans

Nutrition Information Per Serving	
Calories: 260	From Fat: 100
Total Fat	11g
Saturated Fat	4.5g
Trans Fat	0g
Cholesterol	95mg
Sodium	530mg
Total Carbohydrate	23g
Dietary Fiber	2g
Sugars	6g
Protein	17g

1) Spray 3½- to 4-quart slow cooker with cooking spray. Add beef, onion, carrot, celery, garlic, sugar, tomatoes and broth to cooker in order listed.

2) Cover; cook on Low heat setting 8 to 9 hours. About 25 minutes before serving, stir in the basil, frozen tortellini and green beans. Increase the heat setting to High. Cover and cook about 25 minutes or until the beans are tender.

Herbed Chicken and Cheese Panini

PREP TIME:	25 MINUTES (READY IN 25 MINUTES)
SERVINGS:	2

e EASY

1 tablespoon butter or margarine, softened

1 tablespoon chopped fresh herbs (such as parsley, basil, thyme, oregano)

2 boneless skinless chicken breasts, pounded thin (about ½ lb)

Salt and pepper to taste, if desired

1 tablespoon olive oil

½ cup sliced red onion (about ½ medium onion)

2 (7-inch) pocketless pita breads or flatbreads, each cut in half

4 slices sharp Cheddar cheese (about 1 oz each)

1 medium tomato, thinly sliced

1) In a small bowl, mix the softened butter and chopped fresh herbs until blended; set aside.

2) Season chicken with salt and pepper. In 10-inch nonstick skillet, heat oil over medium-high heat until hot. Cook chicken in oil about 5 minutes, turning occasionally, until no longer pink in center. Remove chicken from skillet; set aside and keep warm. To same skillet, add onion; cook about 3 minutes, stirring occasionally, until tender. Remove onion from skillet, set aside. Reduce heat to medium.

3) Spread generous half teaspoon herbed butter on outside of all of 4 bread halves. Place 2 halves in heated skillet, buttered side down. Top each with 1 slice cheese, 1 chicken breast, half of the onion and sliced tomato, and another slice cheese. Top with remaining pita bread halves.

4) Cook about 2 minutes, pressing down with spatula, until bottom is golden brown. Turn; cook about 2 minutes longer, pressing again with spatula, until cheese is melted. To serve, cut each sandwich in half.

Nutrition Information Per Serving	
Calories: 670	From Fat: 320
Total Fat	36g
Saturated Fat	18g
Trans Fat	1g
Cholesterol	150mg
Sodium	790mg
Total Carbohydrate	39g
Dietary Fiber	2g
Sugars	4g
Protein	47g

Pork and Sweet Potato Chili

PREP TIME: 40 MINUTES (READY IN 40 MINUTES)
SERVINGS: 6 (1-1/3 CUPS EACH)

(f) LOW FAT

1 tablespoon olive oil

1 large onion, chopped (1 cup)

1 lb boneless pork loin, trimmed of fat, cut into ¾-inch cubes

4 teaspoons chili powder

1 cup Progresso® chicken broth (from 32-oz carton)

2 medium sweet potatoes, peeled, cut into ¾-inch cubes (about 3 cups)

1 can (15.5 oz) great northern beans, drained, rinsed

1 can (14.5 oz) diced tomatoes, undrained

1 teaspoon grated orange peel

1 teaspoon salt

½ teaspoon pepper

1) In 4-quart saucepan, heat oil over medium-high heat. Cook onion in oil about 2 minutes, stirring frequently, until tender.

2) Add pork and chili powder; cook and stir about 4 minutes or until pork is no longer pink.

3) Stir in remaining ingredients. Reduce heat to medium-low. Cover and simmer 15 to 20 minutes or until sweet potatoes are tender.

Nutrition Information Per Serving	
Calories: 290	From Fat: 80
Total Fat	9g
Saturated Fat	2.5g
Trans Fat	0g
Cholesterol	45mg
Sodium	890mg
Total Carbohydrate	31g
Dietary Fiber	8g
Sugars	7g
Protein	22g

Asian-Style Turkey Soup

PREP TIME: 15 MINUTES (READY IN 6 HOURS 45 MINUTES)
SERVINGS: 4 (1-1/2 CUPS EACH)

 EASY   LOW FAT

3 green onions

2 teaspoons olive or vegetable oil

1 package (20 oz) turkey breast tenderloins, cut into 1-inch pieces

¾ cup sliced celery (about 2 large stalks)

½ cup diced carrots (about 2 medium)

1 carton (32 oz) Progresso® chicken broth (4 cups)

3 tablespoons stir-fry sauce

½ cup uncooked parboiled (converted) white rice

1) Remove green tops from onions; slice and refrigerate. Chop white parts of onions. In 12-inch skillet, heat oil over medium-high heat. Add turkey and white parts of onions; cook 3 to 4 minutes, stirring occasionally, until turkey is lightly browned on outside.

2) Spray 3½- to 4-quart slow cooker with cooking spray. In cooker, mix turkey mixture, celery and carrots. Stir in broth and stir-fry sauce.

3) Cover; cook on Low heat setting 6 to 7 hours.

4) Stir in rice. Increase heat setting to High. Cover; cook 20 to 30 minutes longer or until rice is tender. Garnish with green onion tops.

Nutrition Information Per Serving	
Calories: 290	
Total Fat	4g
Saturated Fat	1g
Sodium	1320mg
Total Carbohydrate	25g
Dietary Fiber	1g
Protein	39g

Snappy Joes on Texas Toast

DEVON DELANEY | PRINCETON, NEW JERSEY

Pillsbury Bake-Off®   BAKE-OFF® CONTEST 44, 2010

PREP TIME: 35 MINUTES (READY IN 45 MINUTES)
SERVINGS: 6

¼ cup Land O Lakes® butter, softened

2 tablespoons chopped fresh Italian (flat-leaf) parsley

1 clove garlic, finely chopped

¼ cup chopped fresh chives

1 can (11 oz) Pillsbury® refrigerated crusty French loaf

1 tablespoon Crisco® light olive oil

1½ lb extra-lean (at least 90%) ground beef

½ cup pickled jalapeño chiles, drained, chopped and 2 tablespoons liquid reserved

1 teaspoon ancho chili powder or regular chili powder

1 can (8 oz) garlic-and-onion tomato sauce or regular tomato sauce

¼ cup Smucker's® seedless blackberry jam

1 tablespoon Dijon mustard

¼ teaspoon coarse (kosher or sea) salt

¼ teaspoon pepper

½ cup sour cream

1) Heat oven to 350°F. In small bowl, mix butter, parsley, garlic and 2 tablespoons of the chives; set aside.

2) Bake French loaf as directed on can. Cool 5 minutes; cut into 12 (1-inch) slices. Spread butter mixture on one side of each slice.

3) While bread is baking, in 10-inch skillet, heat oil over medium heat. Add beef; cook 8 to 10 minutes, stirring occasionally, until thoroughly cooked; drain. Stir in chiles, reserved chile liquid, chili powder, tomato sauce, jam, mustard, salt and pepper; heat to simmering. Reduce heat to low; cover and cook 5 minutes.

4) For each serving, place 2 bread slices on each plate; top each slice with a heaping 1/4 cup beef mixture, a dollop of sour cream and some of the remaining chives.

Nutrition Information Per Serving	
Calories: 480	From Fat: 220
Total Fat	25g
Saturated Fat	11g
Trans Fat	1g
Cholesterol	100mg
Sodium	790mg
Total Carbohydrate	38g
Dietary Fiber	1g
Sugars	11g
Protein	27g

Super-Tuscan White Bean Soup

PREP TIME: 55 MINUTES (READY IN 55 MINUTES)   **lf** LOW FAT
SERVINGS: 6 (1 CUP EACH)

4   slices bacon, finely chopped

1   medium yellow onion, quartered
    lengthwise

1   medium stalk celery, quartered
    crosswise

1   medium carrot, quartered crosswise

2   cloves garlic, lightly crushed

3   cans (19 oz each) Progresso®
    cannellini beans, drained

1   dried bay leaf

½   cup white wine

1   carton (32 oz) Progresso®
    reduced-sodium chicken broth
    (4 cups)

2   tablespoons olive oil

1   tablespoon finely chopped garlic

¼ to ½ teaspoon crushed red pepper
    flakes

¼   cup lightly packed fresh basil leaves,
    sliced

½   teaspoon gray sea salt

⅛   teaspoon freshly ground pepper

1) In 4-quart saucepan or Dutch oven, cook bacon, onion, celery, carrot and 2 cloves garlic over medium-high heat 5 minutes, stirring occasionally. Reduce heat to medium. Add beans, bay leaf, wine and broth; cover and cook 20 to 25 minutes, stirring occasionally, until vegetables are tender. Remove from heat; cool about 15 minutes.

2) Meanwhile, in 8-inch skillet, heat olive oil over medium-high heat 1 minute. Add 1 tablespoon chopped garlic; cook 3 to 5 minutes, stirring frequently, until garlic begins to brown. Stir in red pepper flakes; cook a few seconds. Stir in basil; cook until basil wilts.

3) Remove bay leaf from bean mixture. Pour mixture into food processor; cover and puree. Return to saucepan; stir in salt and pepper. Simmer over medium heat 5 to 10 minutes, stirring frequently, until thoroughly heated.

4) Ladle soup into individual soup bowls. Top each with basil mixture.

Nutrition Information Per Serving	
Calories: 390	From Fat: 70
Total Fat	8g
Saturated Fat	1.5g
Trans Fat	0g
Cholesterol	5mg
Sodium	1320mg
Total Carbohydrate	55g
Dietary Fiber	13g
Sugars	3g
Protein	24g

Italian Onion Soup

PREP TIME: 35 MINUTES (READY IN 35 MINUTES)
SERVINGS: 4 (1-3/4 CUPS EACH)

2 tablespoons extra-virgin olive oil

1 tablespoon finely chopped garlic

8 cups thinly sliced onions
(about 4 medium)

¼ teaspoon gray salt or sea salt

1 tablespoon finely chopped fresh
or 1 teaspoon dried sage leaves

¼ cup Progresso® balsamic vinegar

1 carton (32 oz) Progresso® beef
flavored broth

4 slices (¾ inch thick) Italian country
bread

1 cup shredded mozzarella cheese
(4 oz)

1) In 12- to 14-inch skillet, heat oil over
medium-high heat. Add garlic; cook and
stir until garlic begins to brown. Stir in
onions and salt. Cook about 7 minutes.
Reduce heat to medium. Cook about
10 minutes longer, stirring occasionally,
until onions are golden brown.

2) Stir in sage and vinegar. Cook 2 to
4 minutes, stirring occasionally, until
liquid has evaporated. Stir in broth.
Simmer over medium heat 10 minutes,
stirring occasionally.

3) Meanwhile, set oven control to broil.
Sprinkle bread with cheese; place on
cookie sheet. Broil with tops 4 to 6
inches from heat until cheese is melted
(watch carefully). Place 1 slice of bread
on each serving of soup.

Nutrition Information Per Serving

Calories: 350	
Total Fat	14g
Saturated Fat	5g
Sodium	1330mg
Total Carbohydrate	44g
Dietary Fiber	5g
Protein	13g

tip

Balsamic vinegar is
made from sweet
white grapes and
aged in wooden
barrels for at least
10 years. You can
substitute cider
vinegar or a mild
red wine vinegar.

GREEN BEANS WITH BACON-WALNUT
VINAIGRETTE
PG. 112

Sides, Salads & Breads

The perfect accompaniment to your meal is just pages away with the delicious recipes in this chapter.

HONEY-MUSTARD GLAZED
CARROTS
PG. 116

ORANGE-CHERRY-ALMOND
PINWHEELS
PG. 108

APPLE-WALNUT SALAD WITH
CRANBERRY VINAIGRETTE
PG. 96

Apple-Walnut Salad with Cranberry Vinaigrette

PREP TIME: 20 MINUTES (READY IN 20 MINUTES)
SERVINGS: 8

 EASY

CRANBERRY VINAIGRETTE

½ cup jellied cranberry sauce (from 14-oz can)

¼ cup olive oil

2 tablespoons sugar

1 tablespoon grated orange peel

2 tablespoons white vinegar

2 tablespoons fresh orange juice

¼ teaspoon salt

SALAD

2 medium apples, cut into bite-size pieces (such as Gala or Braeburn)

3 medium stalks celery, sliced

¾ cup dried sweetened cranberries

8 Bibb lettuce leaves

¾ cup cubed Brie cheese

½ cup chopped walnuts, toasted

1) In blender or food processor, place the vinaigrette ingredients. Cover and blend or process for 15 to 20 seconds or until smooth. Pour into 2-cup liquid measuring cup. Cover and refrigerate up to 2 days. Let stand at room temperature for about 1 hour before serving.

2) In large bowl, stir together apples, celery and cranberries. Divide evenly among 8 lettuce-lined salad plates. Top each salad with cheese and walnuts. Serve with vinaigrette.

Nutrition Information Per Serving	
Calories: 270	From Fat: 140
Total Fat	16g
Saturated Fat	4g
Trans Fat	0g
Cholesterol	15mg
Sodium	180mg
Total Carbohydrate	28g
Dietary Fiber	3g
Sugars	23g
Protein	4g

Pepperoni-Pesto Popovers

LAURA STANKE | MAPLE GROVE, MINNESOTA

 BAKE-OFF® CONTEST 44, 2010

PREP TIME: 15 MINUTES (READY IN 35 MINUTES)
SERVINGS: 6 POPOVERS

 EASY

---

1 tablespoon Crisco® 100% extra virgin olive oil or pure olive oil

1 tablespoon semolina flour or cornmeal

1 can (8 oz) Pillsbury® Crescent Recipe Creations® refrigerated seamless dough sheet

⅛ teaspoon garlic salt

¼ cup basil pesto

18 slices (1½-inch size) pepperoni

½ cup shredded mozzarella cheese (2 oz)

¼ cup grated Parmesan cheese

1) Heat oven to 375°F. In 6-cup popover pan or 6 regular-size muffin cups (2¾ x 1¼ inches), brush ½ teaspoon of the oil over bottom and side of each cup. Sprinkle ½ teaspoon of flour over bottom and side of each cup.

2) Unroll dough sheet on cutting board. Sprinkle with garlic salt; spread with pesto. Top with pepperoni, arranging slices in 6 rows by 3 rows. Sprinkle with cheeses.

3) Using pizza cutter, cut dough in half lengthwise, then cut each half crosswise into thirds to make 6 equal pieces. Starting at short end, roll up each piece; place seam side down in popover cup so center of dough piece is on bottom and ends of dough are facing up (filling will show).

4) Bake 20 to 25 minutes or until tops are golden brown. Using knife or metal spatula, remove popovers from pan. Let cool 5 minutes before serving.

Nutrition Information Per Serving	
Calories: 300	From Fat: 180
Total Fat	20g
Saturated Fat	7g
Trans Fat	0g
Cholesterol	25mg
Sodium	780mg
Total Carbohydrate	19g
Dietary Fiber	0g
Sugars	4g
Protein	11g

Sautéed Sugar Snap Peas, Peppers and Onions

PREP TIME: 15 MINUTES (READY IN 15 MINUTES)
SERVINGS: 6

 EASY

1 bag (12 oz) Green Giant® Valley Fresh Steamers™ frozen sugar snap peas

2 tablespoons olive oil

3 cloves garlic, finely chopped

1 small white onion, cut in half, then cut into wedges

1 small red bell pepper, cut into strips

½ teaspoon salt

¼ teaspoon coarse ground black pepper

⅓ cup orange marmalade

1) Cook peas in microwave as directed on bag; set aside. In a 10-inch skillet, heat the olive oil and garlic over medium-high heat. Stir in onion, bell pepper, salt and pepper. Cook 3 to 4 minutes, stirring frequently, until vegetables are crisp-tender.

2) Stir in cooked peas; cook 1 to 2 minutes longer or until hot. Then stir in marmalade until well mixed.

Nutrition Information Per Serving	
Calories: 130	From Fat: 45
Total Fat	5g
Saturated Fat	0.5g
Trans Fat	0g
Cholesterol	0mg
Sodium	210mg
Total Carbohydrate	19g
Dietary Fiber	2g
Sugars	11g
Protein	2g

Parmesan-Butternut Squash Gratin

PREP TIME: 25 MINUTES (READY IN 1 HOUR 15 MINUTES)
SERVINGS: 6 (1/2 CUP EACH)

1   butternut squash (2½ lb)

¼   cup butter or margarine

2   large cloves garlic, finely chopped

¼   cup Progresso® panko crispy bread crumbs

⅓   cup grated Parmesan cheese

¼   teaspoon salt

⅛   teaspoon pepper

¼   cup chopped fresh parsley

1) Heat oven to 375°F. Spray 13x9-inch (3-quart) glass baking dish with cooking spray. Peel, halve lengthwise and seed squash; cut into ½-inch-thick slices. Arrange with slices overlapping slightly in baking dish.

2) In 2-quart saucepan, melt butter over medium heat. Reduce heat to low. Add garlic; cook 2 to 3 minutes, stirring frequently, until garlic is soft and butter is infused with garlic flavor. Do not let butter brown.

3) In small bowl, mix bread crumbs, cheese and 1 tablespoon of the butter-garlic mixture. Brush squash slices with remaining butter-garlic mixture. Sprinkle with salt, pepper and bread crumb mixture.

4) Bake uncovered 30 to 40 minutes or until squash is tender when pierced with fork. Increase oven temperature to 425°F; bake 5 to 10 minutes longer or until lightly browned. Before serving, sprinkle parsley over top.

Nutrition Information Per Serving	
Calories 180	Total Fat 90
Total Fat	10g
Saturated Fat	6g
Trans Fat	0g
Cholesterol	25mg
Sodium	270mg
Total Carbohydrate	18g
Dietary Fiber	2g
Sugars	6g
Protein	4g

Pear Salads with Creamy Vinaigrette

PREP TIME:	20 MINUTES (READY IN 20 MINUTES)
SERVINGS:	4

 EASY

VINAIGRETTE

- 3 tablespoons olive oil
- 2 tablespoons chopped fresh basil leaves
- 1 tablespoon apple cider vinegar
- 1 tablespoon mayonnaise or salad dressing
- 1 teaspoon finely chopped onion
- ¼ teaspoon salt
- ¼ teaspoon pepper

SALAD

- 6 cups mixed baby greens
- 1 medium pear, thinly sliced
- ⅓ cup fontina cheese, diced

1) In small bowl, mix vinaigrette ingredients with wire whisk.

2) Divide salad ingredients among 4 salad plates. Drizzle with vinaigrette.

Nutrition Information Per Serving

Calories: 210	From Fat: 150
Total Fat	17g
Saturated Fat	4g
Trans Fat	0g
Cholesterol	15mg
Sodium	280mg
Total Carbohydrate	10g
Dietary Fiber	3g
Sugars	6g
Protein	4g

tip

For a main course, serve this salad topped with shredded rotisserie chicken.

Seeded Honey-Mustard Biscuits

PREP TIME: 5 MINUTES (READY IN 25 MINUTES)
SERVINGS: 10 BISCUITS

📧 EASY

2 tablespoons butter, melted

1 tablespoon sweet honey mustard

1 can (7.5 oz) Pillsbury® refrigerated buttermilk biscuits

1 teaspoon sesame seed

¼ teaspoon poppy seed

Nutrition Information Per Serving	
Calories: 80	From Fat: 35
Total Fat	4g
Saturated Fat	1.5g
Trans Fat	0g
Cholesterol	5mg
Sodium	230mg
Total Carbohydrate	10g
Dietary Fiber	0g
Sugars	1g
Protein	1g

1) Heat oven to 375°F. Spray 8-inch round cake pan with cooking spray. In small bowl, mix butter and honey mustard.

2) Separate dough into 10 biscuits. Place in pan. Brush with butter mixture; sprinkle with seeds. Bake 13 to 18 minutes or until golden brown.

Greek Chicken Salad

PREP TIME: 15 MINUTES (READY IN 15 MINUTES)
SERVINGS: 6

📧 EASY

DRESSING

¾ cup Italian dressing

1½ teaspoons dried dill weed

SALAD

12 cups loosely packed torn romaine lettuce

1 deli rotisserie chicken, meat removed from bone, thinly sliced

1 pint (2 cups) cherry tomatoes, halved

1 large cucumber, halved, seeded and sliced

¾ cup pitted kalamata olives

6 thin slices red onion, separated into rings, rinsed under cold water, patted dry

1 package (4 oz) crumbled feta cheese (1 cup)

Nutrition Information Per Serving	
Calories: 130	From Fat: 45
Total Fat	5g
Saturated Fat	0.5g
Trans Fat	0g
Cholesterol	0mg
Sodium	210mg
Total Carbohydrate	19g
Dietary Fiber	2g
Sugars	11g
Protein	2g

1) In small bowl or tightly covered container, mix or shake dressing ingredients.

2) In large bowl, mix lettuce, chicken, tomatoes, cucumber, olives and onion. Drizzle dressing over salad; toss to coat. Arrange salad on serving platter. Sprinkle with cheese.

Persian Date-Filled Cinnamon Roll Muffins

PATRICK MONAHAN | WASHINGTON, DC BAKE-OFF® CONTEST 44, 2010

Bake-Off®

| PREP TIME: | 20 MINUTES (READY IN 50 MINUTES) |
| SERVINGS: | 5 MUFFINS |

⊖ EASY

1 cup pitted dates, finely chopped

⅓ cup Fisher® Chef's Naturals® chopped walnuts

2 teaspoons grated lemon peel

2 teaspoons lemon juice

¼ teaspoon ground cardamom

2 tablespoons packed dark brown sugar

½ teaspoon ground cinnamon

1 can (17.5 oz) Pillsbury® Grands!® refrigerated cinnamon rolls with icing (5 rolls)

2 tablespoons honey

1) Heat oven to 375°F. Generously spray 5 jumbo muffin cups or 5 (6-oz) custard cups with Crisco® original no-stick cooking spray.

2) In medium bowl, mix dates, walnuts, lemon peel, lemon juice and cardamom. In small bowl, mix brown sugar and cinnamon.

3) Separate cinnamon rolls; reserve icing. Using serrated knife, cut each roll horizontally in half. Place bottom of each roll, cut side up, in each muffin cup. Divide date mixture evenly among rolls in muffin cups. Add tops of rolls, cinnamon topping sides up.

4) Spray bottom of large drinking glass with cooking spray; press firmly onto rolls so tops are even with tops of cups. Sprinkle cinnamon-sugar mixture over the tops of rolls; lightly press into dough.

5) Bake 18 to 21 minutes or until tops are golden brown. Meanwhile, in small bowl, mix reserved icing and honey. Place waxed paper under cooling rack. Cool muffins in pan 10 minutes; carefully remove from pan to cooling rack. Drizzle honey icing over muffins. Serve warm.

Nutrition Information Per Serving	
Calories: 510	From Fat: 130
Total Fat	14g
Saturated Fat	2.5g
Trans Fat	2.5g
Cholesterol	0mg
Sodium	650mg
Total Carbohydrate	90g
Dietary Fiber	4g
Sugars	54g
Protein	6g

Sesame-Crouton Asian Chicken Salad

KATIE LONG | SUMMERFIELD, NORTH CAROLINA

BAKE-OFF® CONTEST 44, 2010

| PREP TIME: | 45 MINUTES (READY IN 45 MINUTES) |
| SERVINGS: | 8 (1-1/2 CUPS EACH) |

½ cup sesame seed

¼ cup Land O Lakes® butter, softened

½ cup soy sauce, room temperature

2 teaspoons freshly grated gingerroot

1 can (11 oz) Pillsbury® refrigerated original breadsticks (12 breadsticks)

2½ cups cubed cooked chicken

2½ cups broccoli slaw or shredded broccoli

1 cup chopped cucumber

¾ cup julienne carrots (from 10-oz bag)

½ cup chopped fresh cilantro

¼ cup finely chopped red onion

¼ cup Fisher® cashews, halves and pieces, coarsely chopped

½ cup Crisco® pure olive oil

⅓ cup cider vinegar

½ to 1 teaspoon sesame oil

3 tablespoons sugar

1) In 10-inch skillet, cook sesame seed over medium-high heat 3 to 5 minutes, stirring constantly, until lightly toasted. Remove from skillet to plate to cool.

2) Heat oven to 375°F. In small bowl, beat butter, 1 tablespoon of the soy sauce, 1 teaspoon of the gingerroot and 2 tablespoons of the sesame seed with electric mixer on low speed until blended. Carefully unroll dough into 2 rectangles. On each of 2 ungreased cookie sheets with sides, place 1 rectangle; press into 8x6-inch rectangle. Spread with butter mixture. Using pizza cutter, cut each rectangle lengthwise into 6 breadsticks, then cut each breadstick crosswise into 8 pieces.

3) Bake 8 to 12 minutes, rotating cookie sheets halfway through baking, until crisp. Remove from cookie sheet to cooling rack; cool.

4) Meanwhile, in large bowl, toss chicken, broccoli slaw, cucumber, carrots, cilantro, onion and cashews. In container with tight-fitting lid, shake olive oil, vinegar, sesame oil, sugar and remaining soy sauce, gingerroot and sesame seed until well blended. Just before serving, pour dressing over chicken mixture; toss to coat. Add croutons; stir lightly.

Nutrition Information Per Serving	
Calories: 500	From Fat: 290
Total Fat	32g
Saturated Fat	9g
Trans Fat	0g
Cholesterol	55mg
Sodium	1270mg
Total Carbohydrate	31g
Dietary Fiber	2g
Sugars	9g
Protein	20g

Chicken Salads with Vinaigrette

PREP TIME:	25 MINUTES (READY IN 25 MINUTES)		
SERVINGS:	4		

 EASY

SALADS

- 8 cups torn green leaf lettuce
- 3 cups chopped cooked chicken
- 1 medium red bell pepper, cut into bite-size strips
- 1 cup crumbled chèvre (goat) cheese (about 4 oz)
- ½ cup glazed pecans or walnuts

VINAIGRETTE

- ⅓ cup olive oil
- 2 tablespoons raspberry vinegar
- 2 small shallots, finely chopped (about ¼ cup)
- ½ teaspoon salt
- ⅛ teaspoon pepper

1) Arrange lettuce on 4 salad plates. Top with remaining salad ingredients.

2) In small bowl or tightly covered container, beat with wire whisk or shake vinaigrette ingredients. Just before serving, drizzle vinaigrette over salads.

The cheese in this recipe can easily be changed to suit your own tastes. If you don't care for goat cheese, substitute another crumbled cheese, such as blue cheese or feta.

Nutrition Information Per Serving

Calories: 610	From Fat: 310
Total Fat	35g
Saturated Fat	9g
Trans Fat	0g
Cholesterol	105mg
Sodium	550mg
Total Carbohydrate	34g
Dietary Fiber	2g
Sugars	29g
Protein	40g

Cheesy Vegetable Risotto

PREP TIME: 30 MINUTES (READY IN 30 MINUTES)
SERVINGS: 8 (1/2 CUP EACH)

1 tablespoon butter or margarine

2 tablespoons olive or vegetable oil

1 large onion, chopped (1 cup)

1 clove garlic, finely chopped

1 cup uncooked Arborio rice

1 carton (32 oz) Progresso®
reduced-sodium chicken broth
(4 cups), warmed

1 bag (12 oz) Green Giant® Valley
Fresh Steamers™ frozen broccoli,
carrots, cauliflower & cheese sauce

½ cup shredded Parmesan cheese

2 tablespoons chopped fresh parsley

¼ teaspoon coarse ground pepper

1) In 10-inch nonstick skillet, heat butter and oil over medium-high heat until butter is melted. Add onion and garlic; cook 3 to 4 minutes, stirring frequently, until onion is tender.

2) Stir in rice. Cook, stirring occasionally, until edges of kernels are translucent. Stir in ½ cup of the broth. Cook 2 to 3 minutes, stirring constantly, until broth is absorbed.

3) Reduce heat to medium. Stir in 1½ cups of the broth; cook uncovered about 5 minutes, stirring frequently, until broth is absorbed. Stir in another 1 cup of the broth; cook uncovered about 5 minutes longer, stirring frequently, until broth is absorbed.

4) Stir in remaining 1 cup broth. Cook about 8 minutes, stirring frequently, until the rice is tender and the mixture is creamy.

5) Meanwhile, cook frozen vegetables as directed on bag. Stir vegetables, Parmesan cheese, parsley and pepper into rice mixture.

Nutrition Information Per Serving	
Calories: 200	From Fat: 70
Total Fat	7g
Saturated Fat	2.5g
Trans Fat	0g
Cholesterol	10mg
Sodium	840mg
Total Carbohydrate	26g
Dietary Fiber	1g
Sugars	3g
Protein	7g

Southwestern Bean Combo

PREP TIME: 25 MINUTES (READY IN 25 MINUTES)
SERVINGS: 8

 EASY   LOW FAT

2 slices bacon, cut into ½-inch pieces

¼ cup chopped green bell pepper

1 medium onion, chopped

½ cup Old El Paso® thick 'n chunky mild salsa

½ teaspoon chili powder

1 can (16 oz) baked beans, undrained

1 can (15 oz) spicy chili beans, undrained

Nutrition Information Per Serving	
Calories: 130	From Fat: 15
Total Fat	2g
Saturated Fat	0.5g
Trans Fat	0g
Cholesterol	5mg
Sodium	800mg
Total Carbohydrate	22g
Dietary Fiber	5g
Sugars	6g
Protein	6g

1) In 2-quart saucepan, cook bacon over medium heat until crisp. Remove bacon from saucepan. Drain, reserving 1 tablespoon drippings in saucepan.

2) Add bell pepper and onion to drippings in saucepan. Cook and stir over medium heat 2 to 3 minutes or until crisp-tender.

3) Add bacon and remaining ingredients. Cook over medium heat until mixture just begins to boil, stirring frequently. Reduce heat; simmer 5 to 10 minutes or until hot.

Sun-Dried Tomato Crescents

PAM MARLOWE | MOUNT PLEASANT, SOUTH CAROLINA

 BAKE-OFF® CONTEST 40, 2002

PREP TIME: 15 MINUTES (READY IN 30 MINUTES)
SERVINGS: 8 SNACKS

 EASY

1 can (8 oz) Pillsbury® refrigerated crescent dinner rolls

8 teaspoons sun-dried tomato sauce and spread (from 10-oz jar)

4 teaspoons ricotta cheese

2 tablespoons refrigerated or frozen fat-free egg product, thawed, or 1 egg, beaten

½ to 1 teaspoon poppy seed

Nutrition Information Per Serving	
Calories: 120	From Fat: 60
Total Fat	7g
Saturated Fat	1g
Trans Fat	0g
Cholesterol	0mg
Sodium	280mg
Total Carbohydrate	12g
Dietary Fiber	1g
Sugars	2g
Protein	2g

1) Heat oven to 375°F. Separate dough into 8 triangles. Place 1 teaspoon tomato sauce on short side of each triangle. Top each with ½ teaspoon ricotta cheese.

2) Roll up, starting at short side of triangle and rolling to opposite point. Place, point side down, on ungreased cookie sheet. Curve into crescent shape. Brush tops and sides with egg product; sprinkle with poppy seed.

3) Bake 10 to 13 minutes or until golden brown. Cool about 5 minutes before serving.

Mashed Potato Gratin

PREP TIME: 40 MINUTES (READY IN 1 HOUR 10 MINUTES)
SERVINGS: 9 (1/2 CUP EACH)

Unsalted butter for greasing casserole

2½ cups Progresso® chicken broth (from 32-oz carton)

4 large russet potatoes, peeled, finely chopped (5 cups)

1 teaspoon salt

¼ cup unsalted butter

4 cloves garlic, finely chopped

½ cup grated Parmesan cheese

Salt and pepper to taste, if desired

½ cup Progresso® Italian style panko crispy bread crumbs

1) Heat oven to 375°F. Lightly butter 2-quart casserole. Pour broth into 2-quart saucepan. Add potatoes; stir in 1 teaspoon salt. Heat to boiling. Reduce heat; cover and simmer about 10 minutes, stirring occasionally, until potatoes are tender. Place colander over medium bowl; drain potatoes, reserving broth.

2) Rinse and dry saucepan. In saucepan, cook 2 tablespoons of the butter and the garlic over low heat 2 minutes, stirring occasionally. Return potatoes to saucepan with butter and garlic; mash with potato masher.

3) Add 1 cup of the reserved broth to potatoes; mix until smooth. Stir in remaining 2 tablespoons butter and ¼ cup of the cheese. Adjust seasoning to taste with salt and pepper.

4) Spoon potato mixture into casserole. Top with remaining ¼ cup cheese and the bread crumbs. Bake about 20 minutes or until golden brown.

tip

When you present a meal in interesting, unique serving pieces that reflect your own personality, even the quietest evening at home feels like a special occasion.

Nutrition Information Per Serving	
Calories: 180	
Total Fat	9g
Saturated Fat	4.5g
Sodium	690mg
Total Carbohydrate	21g
Dietary Fiber	1g
Protein	5g

Orange-Cherry-Almond Pinwheels

JOANNE RADEMACHER | BERTHOLD, NORTH DAKOTA

BAKE-OFF® CONTEST 44, 2010

PREP TIME: 20 MINUTES (READY IN 1 HOUR 5 MINUTES)
SERVINGS: 8 ROLLS

e EASY

¼ cup Land O Lakes® unsalted or salted butter, softened

1 tablespoon almond paste

1 Eggland's Best egg

⅛ teaspoon ground nutmeg

1 tablespoon Pillsbury Best® all purpose flour

1 can (8 oz) Pillsbury® Crescent Recipe Creations® refrigerated seamless dough sheet

½ cup dried tart cherries

⅓ cup Hershey's® premier white baking chips

Grated peel of 1 large orange (about 1 tablespoon)

¼ cup plus 1 tablespoon Fisher® Chef's Naturals® natural sliced almonds

½ cup powdered sugar

2 tablespoons whipping cream

⅛ teaspoon almond extract

1) In small bowl, beat butter, almond paste and egg with electric hand mixer until mixture is smooth. Beat in nutmeg and flour.

2) On work surface, unroll dough sheet; press into 14x8-inch rectangle. Spread butter mixture over dough, leaving ½ inch of 1 short end uncovered. Sprinkle cherries, baking chips, 2 teaspoons of the orange peel and ¼ cup almonds over butter mixture to edges of dough; press in lightly.

3) Starting at short end covered with butter mixture, roll up dough. Pinch and press uncovered end into roll to seal. Reshape roll with hands. Wrap roll in waxed paper; refrigerate 30 minutes.

4) Heat oven to 375°F. Lightly spray cookie sheet with Crisco® original no-stick cooking spray, or line with cooking parchment paper. Using serrated knife, cut roll into 8 slices; place cut sides up and 3 inches apart on cookie sheet. Bake 13 to 17 minutes or until golden brown.

5) Meanwhile, in small bowl, mix powdered sugar, cream and almond extract with spoon until smooth; spoon and spread over hot rolls on cookie sheet. Sprinkle with remaining 1 tablespoon almonds and 1 teaspoon orange peel. Remove from cookie sheet to cooling rack. Serve warm or cool.

Nutrition Information Per Serving	
Calories: 300	From Fat: 150
Total Fat	16g
Saturated Fat	8g
Trans Fat	0g
Cholesterol	45mg
Sodium	240mg
Total Carbohydrate	35g
Dietary Fiber	1g
Sugars	22g
Protein	4g

Bourbon Street Muffuletta Braid

JANNINE FISK | MALDEN, MARYLAND

 BAKE-OFF® CONTEST 44, 2010

 EASY

PREP TIME: 20 MINUTES (READY IN 1 HOUR 5 MINUTES)
SERVINGS: 8

½ cup chopped green olives

¼ cup chopped ripe olives

¼ cup drained roasted red bell peppers (from 7-oz jar), diced

2 tablespoons Crisco® 100% extra virgin olive oil or pure olive oil

1 tablespoon red wine vinegar

2 teaspoons capers

½ teaspoon finely chopped garlic

¼ teaspoon salt

2 cans (8 oz each) Pillsbury® Crescent Recipe Creations® refrigerated seamless dough sheet

1 Eggland's Best egg

1 teaspoon water

4 oz thinly sliced ham

2 oz thinly sliced Genoa salami

4 oz thinly sliced provolone cheese

4 oz thinly sliced mortadella (from deli)

1) Heat oven to 350°F. Line large cookie sheet with cooking parchment paper. In medium bowl, mix olives, red peppers, oil, vinegar, capers, garlic and salt; set aside.

2) On large cookie sheet, unroll both dough sheets, placing long sides together to make 15x12-inch rectangle; press edges to seal. In small bowl, beat egg and water until well blended; brush thin layer over dough. Reserve remaining egg mixture.

3) Place ham lengthwise down center of rectangle in 6-inch-wide strip. Layer ham with salami, cheese, olive mixture and mortadella. Using kitchen scissors or sharp knife, make cuts 1 inch apart on each long side of rectangle to within ½ inch of filling. Fold strips of dough diagonally over filling, alternating from side to side and pressing to seal. Brush remaining egg mixture over dough.

4) Bake 25 to 35 minutes or until deep golden brown. Cool on cookie sheet 10 minutes. Cut crosswise into slices. Serve warm.

Nutrition Information Per Serving	
Calories: 390	From Fat: 230
Total Fat	25g
Saturated Fat	9g
Trans Fat	0g
Cholesterol	55mg
Sodium	1300mg
Total Carbohydrate	26g
Dietary Fiber	0g
Sugars	6g
Protein	13g

Featherlight Cheddar-Ranch Puffs

AIMEE HACHIGIAN-GOULD | ULM, MONTANA

Pillsbury Bake-Off BAKE-OFF® CONTEST 44, 2010

PREP TIME:	25 MINUTES (READY IN 1 HOUR)
SERVINGS:	20 PUFFS

1 package (¼ oz) active dry yeast (2½ teaspoons)

¼ cup warm water (105°F to 115°F)

3 cups Pillsbury Best® all purpose unbleached or all purpose flour

1 tablespoon baking powder

¼ teaspoon baking soda

1 teaspoon salt

1 package (1 oz) ranch dressing mix

½ cup cold Land O Lakes® butter

½ cup thinly sliced green onions (8 medium)

2 cups shredded Cheddar cheese (8 oz)

1 lb bacon, cooked, crumbled

1¼ cups buttermilk

1) Heat oven to 400°F. Line cookie sheets with cooking parchment paper; spray paper with Crisco® original no-stick cooking spray. In small bowl, mix yeast and warm water; set aside.

2) In large bowl, mix flour, baking powder, baking soda, salt and dressing mix. Cut in butter, using pastry blender or fork, until mixture looks like coarse crumbs.

3) In small microwavable bowl, place onions. Cover with microwavable plastic wrap, folding back one side to vent; microwave on High 30 seconds. Cool slightly, about 2 minutes.

4) Add cheese and bacon to flour mixture; toss until well coated. Stir in yeast mixture, onions and buttermilk all at once until soft dough forms. Drop dough by ⅓ cupfuls 2 to 3 inches apart onto cookie sheets.

5) Bake 14 to 18 minutes or until puffed and light golden brown. Serve warm with additional butter, if desired.

Nutrition Information Per Serving	
Calories: 200	From Fat: 110
Total Fat	12g
Saturated Fat	7g
Trans Fat	0g
Cholesterol	35mg
Sodium	580mg
Total Carbohydrate	17g
Dietary Fiber	0g
Sugars	1g
Protein	8g

Asian Chicken Salads with Peanuts

PREP TIME: 20 MINUTES (READY IN 20 MINUTES)
SERVINGS: 4

 EASY   LOW FAT

1 lb uncooked chicken breast strips for stir-frying

¾ cup Oriental dressing and marinade

2 teaspoons vegetable oil

3 cups thinly sliced Chinese (napa) cabbage

3 cups fresh baby spinach leaves

¼ cup sliced green onions (4 medium)

2 tablespoons coarsely chopped dry-roasted peanuts

1) In medium bowl, mix chicken and ¼ cup of the dressing; toss to coat. Let stand at room temperature 10 minutes to marinate.

2) In 8-inch nonstick skillet, heat oil over medium-high heat until hot. Remove chicken from marinade with slotted spoon and add to skillet; discard remaining marinade. Cook and stir chicken 4 to 6 minutes or until browned and no longer pink in center. Remove from heat. Add remaining ½ cup dressing; stir to mix.

3) Divide cabbage and spinach among 4 serving plates. Top with chicken mixture. Sprinkle with onions and peanuts. If desired, serve with additional dressing.

Nutrition Information Per Serving	
Calories: 200	From Fat: 80
Total Fat	8g
Saturated Fat	2g
Trans Fat	0g
Cholesterol	70mg
Sodium	600mg
Total Carbohydrate	3g
Dietary Fiber	1g
Sugars	0g
Protein	28g

Green Beans with Bacon-Walnut Vinaigrette

PREP TIME: 25 MINUTES (READY IN 25 MINUTES)
SERVINGS: 4

e EASY **lf** LOW FAT

1 bag (12 oz) Green Giant® Valley Fresh Steamers™ frozen cut green beans

2 slices bacon, cut into ½-inch pieces

½ teaspoon finely chopped garlic

1 tablespoon finely chopped walnuts

2 tablespoons white wine vinegar

2 teaspoons sugar

½ teaspoon seasoned salt

1) Cook beans as directed on bag and set aside.

2) Meanwhile, in 10-inch skillet, cook bacon over medium heat, stirring frequently, until crisp. Stir in garlic and walnuts; cook about 1 minute or until walnuts are lightly browned. Stir in vinegar, sugar and seasoned salt.

3) Stir in cooked beans. Cook 2 to 3 minutes, stirring frequently, until beans are hot.

Nutrition Information Per Serving	
Calories: 70	From Fat: 25
Total Fat	3g
Saturated Fat	0.5g
Trans Fat	0g
Cholesterol	0mg
Sodium	260mg
Total Carbohydrate	8g
Dietary Fiber	2g
Sugars	4g
Protein	3g

tip

This is the perfect side dish for grilled sirloin steak or pork loin chops.

Green Beans with Feta

PREP TIME: 15 MINUTES (READY IN 15 MINUTES)
SERVINGS: 8

 EASY

1 lb fresh green beans, trimmed

2 tablespoons vegetable or olive oil

1 tablespoon tarragon vinegar

2 tablespoons chopped red onion

½ teaspoon salt

¼ teaspoon pepper

1 clove garlic, finely chopped

½ cup crumbled feta cheese (2 oz)

Nutrition Information Per Serving	
Calories: 80	From Fat: 50
Total Fat	5g
Saturated Fat	2g
Trans Fat	0g
Cholesterol	10mg
Sodium	260mg
Total Carbohydrate	5g
Dietary Fiber	2g
Sugars	2g
Protein	2g

1) In 6-quart saucepan, heat 1 inch water and beans to boiling; reduce heat. Simmer uncovered 8 to 10 minutes or until crisp-tender; drain.

2) In large bowl, place beans. Add remaining ingredients except feta cheese; toss to coat. Top with feta cheese; serve warm.

No-Fuss Party Potatoes

PREP TIME: 10 MINUTES (READY IN 3 HOURS 40 MINUTES)
SERVINGS: 12 (1/2 CUP EACH)

 EASY   LOW FAT

1 can (10¾ oz) condensed 98% fat-free cream of mushroom soup

1 container (8 oz) fat-free sour cream

1 can (4.5 oz) Old El Paso® chopped green chiles

1 cup shredded reduced-fat Cheddar cheese (4 oz)

1 bag (32 oz) frozen southern-style diced hash brown potatoes

2½ cups baked nacho-flavored tortilla chips, finely crushed (½ cup)

3 green onions, sliced (⅓ cup)

Nutrition Information Per Serving	
Calories: 200	From Fat: 100
Total Fat	3g
Saturated Fat	6g
Trans Fat	0g
Cholesterol	25mg
Sodium	370mg
Total Carbohydrate	19g
Dietary Fiber	2g
Sugars	2g
Protein	7g

1) In medium bowl, mix soup, sour cream, chiles and cheese.

2) Spray 3½- to 4-quart slow cooker with cooking spray. In cooker, arrange half of the potatoes. Top with half of the sour cream mixture, spreading evenly. Repeat layers.

3) Cover; cook on High heat setting 3½ to 4½ hours.

4) Just before serving, sprinkle chips and onions over top.

Green Bean Bundles

| PREP TIME: | 10 MINUTES (READY IN 20 MINUTES) | | ⓔ EASY |
| SERVINGS: | 4 | | |

TOPPING

¼ cup Progresso® Italian style panko
crispy bread crumbs

Pinch gray salt

Freshly ground black pepper

1 tablespoon finely chopped fresh
parsley

1 teaspoon freshly grated lemon peel

1 tablespoon freshly grated Parmesan
cheese

GREEN BEANS

1 teaspoon salt

¾ lb fresh green beans, trimmed

Unsalted butter for greasing
baking dish

2 tablespoons extra-virgin olive oil

Additional gray salt and freshly
ground black pepper

8 thin slices prosciutto

1) Heat oven to 400°F. In small bowl, mix bread crumbs, gray salt and pepper. Add parsley, lemon peel and cheese; toss well.

2) In 3-quart saucepan, heat 4 cups water and 1 teaspoon salt to boiling. Add green beans. Heat to boiling; reduce heat. Simmer 5 to 6 minutes or until crisp-tender; drain.

3) Butter shallow baking dish. Toss cooled green beans with 2 tablespoons olive oil; sprinkle with additional salt and pepper. Divide green beans into 4 equal bundles. On work surface, arrange 2 slices of the prosciutto so they slightly overlap each other. Top with 1 bundle of green beans and roll up carefully in prosciutto. Place in baking dish. Repeat with remaining prosciutto and green beans. Flatten tops of bundles slightly; sprinkle with topping.

4) Bake about 10 minutes or until thoroughly heated and crisp. Serve immediately.

Nutrition Information Per Serving	
Calories: 180	From Fat: 180
Total Fat	11g
Saturated Fat	2g
Sodium	1180mg
Total Carbohydrate	10g
Dietary Fiber	2g

Garlic Chicken over Baby Spinach with Toasted Pine Nuts

PREP TIME: 20 MINUTES (READY IN 40 MINUTES)
SERVINGS: 4

 EASY

DRESSING

⅓ cup olive oil

¼ cup fresh lemon juice

1 tablespoon honey

½ teaspoon Dijon mustard

¼ teaspoon salt

⅛ teaspoon pepper

CHICKEN AND SPINACH

¼ cup pine nuts

½ cup corn flake crumbs

½ teaspoon garlic powder

1 package (20 oz) boneless skinless chicken thighs, cut into 1-inch pieces

2 tablespoons olive oil

2 shallots, halved and sliced (about ¾ cup)

¾ lb sliced mushrooms (about 4 cups)

3 tablespoons sliced sun-dried tomatoes in oil

8 cups fresh baby spinach leaves

1) In small bowl or tightly covered container, beat with wire whisk or shake dressing ingredients; set aside.

2) Heat 10-inch nonstick skillet over medium heat until hot. Cook pine nuts in skillet about 4 minutes, stirring frequently until nuts begin to brown, then stirring constantly until nuts are light brown; remove and set aside.

3) Meanwhile, in medium bowl, mix corn flake crumbs and garlic powder. Add chicken; toss until evenly coated. Increase heat to medium-high. In same skillet, heat 1 tablespoon of the oil until hot. Cook chicken in oil 8 to 10 minutes, turning occasionally, until no longer pink in center; remove and set aside.

4) In same skillet, heat remaining 1 tablespoon oil until hot. Cook shallots and mushrooms in oil about 7 minutes, stirring occasionally, until golden brown and tender. Stir in sun-dried tomatoes; remove from heat, stir in chicken.

5) To serve, arrange spinach on 4 serving plates; top with chicken mixture. Sprinkle with toasted pine nuts. Serve with dressing.

Nutrition Information Per Serving	
Calories: 690	From Fat: 420
Total Fat	46g
Saturated Fat	9g
Trans Fat	0g
Cholesterol	115mg
Sodium	370mg
Total Carbohydrate	22g
Dietary Fiber	4g
Sugars	9g
Protein	46g

Honey-Mustard Glazed Carrots

PREP TIME: 20 MINUTES (READY IN 20 MINUTES)
SERVINGS: 6 (1/2 CUP EACH)

 EASY   LOW FAT

1 bag (1 lb) ready-to-eat baby-cut carrots

2 tablespoons honey

1 tablespoon olive or canola oil

2 teaspoons Dijon mustard

1 tablespoon fresh chopped parsley

¼ teaspoon salt

⅛ teaspoon pepper

1) In 2-quart saucepan, heat ½ cup water to boiling. Add carrots. Cover; simmer 10 to 15 minutes or until tender. Drain.

2) In medium bowl, mix remaining ingredients. Add carrots; toss lightly to coat.

Nutrition Information Per Serving	
Calories: 80	From Fat: 25
Total Fat	2.5g
Saturated Fat	0g
Trans Fat	0g
Cholesterol	0mg
Sodium	190mg
Total Carbohydrate	13g
Dietary Fiber	2g
Sugars	9g
Protein	0g

tip

If you find pinky-size fresh baby carrots at a farmers' market, just trim and scrub (no need to peel). The cook time may be shorter.

Shredded Thai Chicken Salad

PREP TIME: 15 MINUTES (READY IN 15 MINUTES)
SERVINGS: 4

⊖ EASY

SALAD

- 2 cups shredded deli rotisserie chicken (from 2- to 2½-lb chicken)
- 1 cup julienne (matchstick-cut) carrots
- 1 cup broccoli slaw mix
- 1 large green onion, chopped

DRESSING

- 2 tablespoons creamy peanut butter
- 2 tablespoons rice vinegar
- 1 tablespoon vegetable oil
- 1 tablespoon honey
- 4 teaspoons soy sauce
- ⅛ teaspoon red pepper sauce

  Fresh cilantro, if desired

1) In a large bowl, toss the salad ingredients. In a small bowl, beat dressing ingredients with wire whisk.

2) Just before serving, drizzle dressing over salad; toss until evenly coated. Garnish with cilantro.

Nutrition Information Per Serving	
Calories: 310	From Fat: 150
Total Fat	17g
Saturated Fat	3.5g
Trans Fat	0g
Cholesterol	60mg
Sodium	710mg
Total Carbohydrate	15g
Dietary Fiber	2g
Sugars	11g
Protein	22g

Quick and Easy Onion Rolls

TERRYANN MOORE | OAKLYN, NEW JERSEY

BAKE-OFF® CONTEST 39, 2000

PREP TIME: 20 MINUTES (READY IN 40 MINUTES)
SERVINGS: 12 ROLLS

e EASY

¼ cup finely chopped onion

3 tablespoons chopped pine nuts

3 tablespoons finely chopped sun-dried tomatoes in oil, drained, 1 tablespoon oil reserved

1 tablespoon poppy seed

1 can (11 oz) Pillsbury® refrigerated original breadsticks

¼ cup shredded fresh Parmesan cheese (1 oz)

Nutrition Information Per Serving	
Calories: 110	From Fat: 45
Total Fat	5g
Saturated Fat	1g
Trans Fat	0g
Cholesterol	0mg
Sodium	230mg
Total Carbohydrate	14g
Dietary Fiber	0g
Sugars	2g
Protein	3g

1) Heat oven to 375°F. Grease cookie sheet with shortening. In small skillet, cook and stir onion, pine nuts and tomatoes over medium heat 1 to 2 minutes or until onion is tender and nuts are toasted. Remove from heat. Stir in poppy seed.

2) Unroll dough; separate into 2 sections (6 breadsticks each). Spread onion mixture over dough. Reroll dough sections; pinch edges to seal. Cut each section into 6 rolls.

3) Place rolls cut side up on cookie sheet. Brush with reserved 1 tablespoon tomato oil. Sprinkle with cheese. Bake 13 to 17 minutes or until golden brown. Serve warm.

Leek and Garlic Mashed Potatoes

PREP TIME: 25 MINUTES (READY IN 50 MINUTES)
SERVINGS: 10

3 lb potatoes (about 8 medium), peeled, cut into pieces

2 cups sliced leek with some of green top (about 1 medium)

4 cloves garlic, peeled

¾ teaspoon salt

1 cup Progresso® chicken broth (from 32-oz carton)

¼ cup whipping cream

1 tablespoon butter or margarine

Additional whipping cream, heated, if desired

1 tablespoon chopped fresh chives

Nutrition Information Per Serving	
Calories: 160	From Fat: 30
Total Fat	3.5g
Saturated Fat	2g
Trans Fat	0g
Cholesterol	10mg
Sodium	300mg
Total Carbohydrate	29g
Dietary Fiber	3g
Sugars	1g
Protein	3g

1) In 3-quart saucepan, place potatoes, leek, garlic, salt and broth. Cover and heat to boiling; reduce heat. Simmer covered 20 to 25 minutes or until tender (do not drain). Mash potato mixture on low speed.

2) In 1-quart saucepan, heat ¼ cup whipping cream and the butter over medium heat, stirring occasionally, until butter is melted. Add cream mixture to potato mixture; continue mashing until potatoes are light and fluffy. Add additional heated cream for desired consistency. Stir in chives.

Curried Chicken and Grape Salad

PREP TIME: 30 MINUTES (READY IN 30 MINUTES)
SERVINGS: 5

 EASY

DRESSING

½ cup mayonnaise or salad dressing

2 tablespoons lemon juice

2 to 3 teaspoons curry powder

½ teaspoon salt

¼ teaspoon pepper

SALAD

3 cups diced deli rotisserie chicken
(from 2- to 2½-lb chicken)

1 cup thinly sliced celery

1 cup seedless red grapes, halved

3 tablespoons slivered almonds,
toasted

1) In large bowl, stir dressing ingredients
until well mixed.

2) Fold in chicken, celery and grapes.
Sprinkle with almonds.

Nutrition Information Per Serving	
Calories: 270	From Fat: 120
Total Fat	14g
Saturated Fat	3g
Trans Fat	0g
Cholesterol	80mg
Sodium	860mg
Total Carbohydrate	11g
Dietary Fiber	1g
Sugars	8g
Protein	25g

Broccoli-Bacon Casserole with Cheesy Mustard Sauce

PREP TIME: 25 MINUTES (READY IN 50 MINUTES)
SERVINGS: 16 (1/2 CUP EACH)

 LOW FAT

2 bags (24 oz each) Green Giant® frozen broccoli & three cheese sauce

6 slices bacon, cut into ½-inch pieces

1 small onion, chopped (⅓ cup)

2 teaspoons Dijon mustard

1 cup corn flake crumbs

1 tablespoon butter or margarine, melted

To make ahead, prepare as directed through end of Step 3. Cover and refrigerate up to 24 hours. Bake loosely covered 25 minutes, stirring every 10 minutes. Make and top with crumbs as directed in Step 4. Bake 20 minutes longer.

1) Heat oven to 350°F. Spray 11x7-inch (2-quart) glass baking dish with cooking spray, set aside.

2) Into 4-quart microwavable bowl, pour contents of both bags of broccoli and sauce chips. Cover bowl; microwave on High 15 to 25 minutes, stirring every 5 minutes, until sauce chips are melted and broccoli is thoroughly cooked and tender.

3) Meanwhile, in 10-inch skillet, cook bacon over medium-high heat 7 to 9 minutes, stirring frequently, until bacon is browned. Remove bacon to paper towel-lined plate. Drain all but 1 teaspoon bacon drippings. Decrease heat to medium. In same skillet, cook onion in 1 teaspoon bacon drippings 3 to 4 minutes, stirring frequently, until onion is tender. Stir the bacon, onion and mustard into the broccoli mixture, then spread in a baking dish.

4) In small bowl, stir together corn flake crumbs and melted butter. Sprinkle on broccoli mixture in baking dish.

5) Bake uncovered 25 to 30 minutes or until hot and topping is light golden brown color.

Nutrition Information Per Serving	
Calories: 70	From Fat: 30
Total Fat	3g
Saturated Fat	2.5g
Trans Fat	0g
Cholesterol	5mg
Sodium	430mg
Total Carbohydrate	7g
Dietary Fiber	1g
Sugars	3g
Protein	3g

Corn and Sweet Bean Sauté

PREP TIME:	30 MINUTES (READY IN 30 MINUTES)	EASY
SERVINGS:	6 (ABOUT 1/2 CUP EACH)	

1 bag (12 oz) Green Giant® Valley
   Fresh Steamers™ Niblets® frozen
   corn

1 teaspoon butter or margarine

2 teaspoons canola oil

1 small onion, finely chopped (¼ cup)

1 ½ cups frozen shelled edamame
   (green soybeans)

½ cup Progresso® reduced-sodium
   chicken broth (from 32-oz carton)

¼ teaspoon salt

¼ cup slivered fresh basil leaves

1) In 2-quart saucepan, heat 2 inches of water to boiling. Add corn; reduce heat. Simmer uncovered 5 minutes; drain. Rinse with cold water; drain and set aside.

2) In 10-inch skillet, heat butter and oil over medium-high heat until butter is melted. Add onion; cook 2 to 3 minutes, stirring frequently, until crisp-tender.

3) Stir in the edamame and chicken broth. Heat until boiling and reduce heat. Simmer uncovered about 10 minutes, stirring occasionally, until the edamame are tender.

4) Stir in corn and salt. Cook 4 to 6 minutes, stirring occasionally, until corn is hot. Sprinkle with basil just before serving.

Nutrition Information Per Serving	
Calories: 130	From Fat: 40
Total Fat	4.5g
Saturated Fat	1g
Trans Fat	0g
Cholesterol	0mg
Sodium	150mg
Total Carbohydrate	15g
Dietary Fiber	3g
Sugars	3g
Protein	6g

Lemon-Garlic Broccoli

PREP TIME: 15 MINUTES (READY IN 15 MINUTES)
SERVINGS: 6 (1/2 CUP EACH)

 EASY   LOW FAT

2 bags (12 oz each) Green Giant® Valley Fresh Steamers™ frozen broccoli florets

2 teaspoons olive or canola oil

6 cloves garlic, finely chopped

1 tablespoon grated lemon peel

½ teaspoon salt

⅛ teaspoon pepper

1) Cook broccoli as directed on package; set aside.

2) In 10-inch skillet, heat oil over medium heat. Cook garlic in oil about 1 minute, stirring frequently, until golden brown.

3) Stir in broccoli; cook 1 minute. Stir in lemon peel, salt and pepper.

Nutrition Information Per Serving	
Calories: 50	From Fat: 15
Total Fat	1.5g
Saturated Fat	0g
Trans Fat	0g
Cholesterol	0mg
Sodium	210mg
Total Carbohydrate	7g
Dietary Fiber	3g
Sugars	2g
Protein	3g

tip

This flavorful broccoli dish could easily become a family favorite. Change the taste just a bit by using orange or lime peel instead of the lemon peel.

Grilled Corn on the Cob with Herb Butter

PREP TIME: 40 MINUTES (READY IN 40 MINUTES)
SERVINGS: 4

CORN

4 ears fresh sweet corn,
husks removed, cleaned

HERB BUTTER

¼ cup butter, melted

2 tablespoons chopped fresh basil

1 tablespoon chopped fresh parsley

½ teaspoon garlic salt

Nutrition Information Per Serving	
Calories: 230	From Fat: 120
Total Fat	13g
Saturated Fat	7g
Trans Fat	0g
Cholesterol	30mg
Sodium	200mg
Total Carbohydrate	26g
Dietary Fiber	4g
Sugars	3g
Protein	3g

1) Heat gas or charcoal grill. Cut 4 (18x12-inch) sheets of heavy-duty foil. Place each ear of corn on center of 1 foil sheet. In small bowl, mix herb butter ingredients. Brush or spoon herb butter over surface of each ear. Bring up 2 sides of foil so edges meet. Seal edges, making tight ½-inch fold; fold again, allowing space for heat circulation and expansion.

2) Place wrapped corn on grill over medium heat. Cook 15 to 20 minutes, turning occasionally, until tender. Open foil carefully to allow hot steam to escape. Drizzle corn with any remaining herb butter.

Quick 'n Easy Herb Flatbread

CATHY OLAFSON | COLORADO SPRINGS, COLORADO

Bake-Off   BAKE-OFF® CONTEST 39, 2000

PREP TIME: 10 MINUTES (READY IN 25 MINUTES)
SERVINGS: 9 SERVINGS

e EASY

1 can (13.8 oz) Pillsbury® refrigerated classic pizza crust

1 tablespoon olive or vegetable oil

½ to 1 teaspoon dried basil leaves

½ to 1 teaspoon dried rosemary leaves, crushed

½ teaspoon finely chopped garlic

⅛ teaspoon salt

1 small tomato

¼ cup shredded fresh Parmesan cheese

Nutrition Information Per Serving	
Calories: 140	From Fat: 25
Total Fat	3.5g
Saturated Fat	1g
Trans Fat	0g
Cholesterol	2mg
Sodium	400mg
Total Carbohydrate	21g
Dietary Fiber	0g
Sugars	2g
Protein	4g

1) Heat oven to 425°F. Spray cookie sheet with cooking spray. Unroll dough; place on cookie sheet. Starting at center, press out dough to form 12x8-inch rectangle.

2) In small bowl, mix oil, basil, rosemary and garlic. Brush over dough; sprinkle with salt. Chop tomato; place in shallow bowl. With back of spoon, crush tomato. Spread tomato evenly over dough.

3) Bake 5 to 9 minutes or until edges are light golden brown. Sprinkle cheese evenly over partially baked crust; bake 2 to 3 minutes longer or until edges are golden brown and cheese is melted. Cut into squares. Serve warm.

Beefy Main Dishes

The hearty taste of beef can't be beat when you're looking for a wholesome, home-cooked meal.

TWO-BEAN BURGER CASSEROLE
PG. 136

JUMBO BURGER CUPS
PG. 135

OLD-TIME BEEF AND
VEGETABLE STEW
PG. 133

ITALIAN POT-ROASTED STEAKS
PG. 127

Family Favorite Lasagna

PREP TIME: 20 MINUTES (READY IN 3 HOURS 50 MINUTES)
SERVINGS: 8

 EASY

1 lb lean (at least 80%) ground beef

1 jar (26 to 28 oz) tomato pasta sauce

1 can (8 oz) no-salt-added tomato sauce

½ package (9-oz size) no-boil lasagna noodles (about 8)

1 jar (1 lb) Alfredo pasta sauce

3 cups shredded mozzarella cheese (12 oz)

¼ cup grated Parmesan cheese

1) In 10-inch skillet, cook beef over medium-high heat 5 to 7 minutes, stirring occasionally, until thoroughly cooked; drain.

2) Spray 4- to 5-quart slow cooker with cooking spray. Spread ¾ cup of the tomato pasta sauce in bottom of slow cooker. Stir remaining tomato pasta sauce and tomato sauce into beef.

3) Layer 3 lasagna noodles over sauce in slow cooker, breaking noodles as necessary. Top with ⅓ of the Alfredo pasta sauce, spreading evenly. Sprinkle with 1 cup of the mozzarella cheese. Top with ⅓ of the beef mixture, spreading evenly.

4) Repeat layering twice, using 2 lasagna noodles in last layer. Sprinkle Parmesan cheese over top.

5) Cover; cook on Low heat setting 3 hours 30 minutes to 4 hours 30 minutes. If desired, cut into wedges to serve.

Nutrition Information Per Serving	
Calories: 630	From Fat: 340
Total Fat	37g
Saturated Fat	20g
Cholesterol	115mg
Sodium	970mg
Total Carbohydrate	42g
Dietary Fiber	3g
Protein	31g

Italian Pot-Roasted Steaks

PREP TIME: 25 MINUTES (READY IN 7 HOURS 25 MINUTES)
SERVINGS: 6

(f) LOW FAT

1½ lb beef tip steak, trimmed

3 tablespoons all-purpose flour

1 teaspoon salt

¼ teaspoon pepper

1 tablespoon vegetable oil

1½ cups sliced onions

1 can (14.5 oz) diced tomatoes, undrained

1 teaspoon sugar

1 bag (19 oz) Green Giant® frozen garden vegetable medley

1) Spray 4- to 5-quart slow cooker with cooking spray. Sprinkle both sides of beef with flour, salt and pepper. In 12-inch skillet, heat oil over medium heat until hot. Cook beef in oil 6 to 8 minutes, turning occasionally, until brown on both sides.

2) Place onions in slow cooker. Top with beef and tomatoes; sprinkle with sugar.

3) Cover; cook on Low heat setting 7 to 9 hours or until beef is tender.

4) About 15 minutes before steak is ready to serve, microwave vegetables as directed on bag. Stir into beef mixture.

Nutrition Information Per Serving	
Calories: 280	From Fat: 60
Total Fat	7g
Saturated Fat	2g
Trans Fat	0g
Cholesterol	80mg
Sodium	700mg
Total Carbohydrate	20g
Dietary Fiber	3g
Sugars	6g
Protein	34g

Taco Pan Bread

PREP TIME: 20 MINUTES (READY IN 45 MINUTES)
SERVINGS: 8

 EASY

- 2 lb lean (at least 80%) ground beef
- 1 jar (16 oz) Old El Paso® thick 'n chunky salsa (2 cups)
- 1 package (1 oz) Old El Paso® taco seasoning mix
- 1 can (15 oz) pinto beans or Progresso® black beans, drained, rinsed
- 1 can (3.8 oz) sliced ripe olives, drained
- 1 can (13.8 oz) Pillsbury® refrigerated classic pizza crust
- ½ cup corn chips, crushed
- 1 cup shredded Cheddar cheese (4 oz)
- 2 cups shredded lettuce
- 1 cup diced tomato (1 medium)
- ½ cup sour cream

1) Heat oven to 400°F. In 12-inch skillet, cook beef over medium-high heat 5 to 7 minutes, stirring occasionally, until thoroughly cooked; drain. Stir in salsa and taco seasoning mix. Reduce heat; simmer uncovered 5 minutes.

2) Stir beans and olives into beef mixture. Cook until thoroughly heated and bubbly. Spoon into ungreased 13x9-inch (3-quart) glass baking dish. Unroll dough over filling; sprinkle crushed corn chips over top.

3) Bake 13 to 17 minutes until light golden brown. Sprinkle cheese evenly over chips; let stand 5 minutes to melt cheese. Serve with lettuce, tomato and sour cream.

Nutrition Information Per Serving	
Calories: 530	From Fat: 220
Total Fat	25g
Saturated Fat	10g
Trans Fat	1g
Cholesterol	95mg
Sodium	1470mg
Total Carbohydrate	44g
Dietary Fiber	5g
Sugars	7g
Protein	31g

Bubble Pizza

PREP TIME: 15 MINUTES (READY IN 50 MINUTES)
SERVINGS: 6

 EASY

1 can (11 oz) Pillsbury® refrigerated original breadsticks (12 breadsticks)

1 bag (16 oz) frozen cooked Italian-style meatballs (32 meatballs)

1 can (15 oz) pizza sauce

½ cup chopped pepperoni

2 tablespoons grated Parmesan cheese

2 cups shredded pizza cheese blend (8 oz)

1) Heat oven to 375°F. Spray 11x7-inch (2-quart) glass baking dish with cooking spray. Unroll dough into rectangle; cut rectangle crosswise into 8 strips so each strip has 6 pieces. At perforations, separate dough, or cut if necessary, to make 48 pieces. Arrange ½ of the dough pieces randomly in bottom of baking dish.

2) In large microwavable bowl, place meatballs and pizza sauce. Cover; microwave on Medium-High (70%) 5 to 8 minutes or until sauce is bubbly and meatballs are thawed. Stir in pepperoni. Pour over dough pieces in dish; sprinkle with Parmesan cheese. Arrange the remaining dough pieces over cheese.

3) Bake 16 to 20 minutes or until edges are golden brown and dough pieces are no longer doughy. Sprinkle with pizza cheese blend; bake 4 to 5 minutes longer or until cheese is melted. Let stand 5 to 10 minutes before serving.

Nutrition Information Per Serving	
Calories: 590	From Fat: 320
Total Fat	36g
Saturated Fat	17g
Trans Fat	1g
Cholesterol	80mg
Sodium	1450mg
Total Carbohydrate	37g
Dietary Fiber	2g
Sugars	8g
Protein	29g

Cajun Pot Roast with Maque Choux

PREP TIME: 10 MINUTES (READY IN 8 HOURS 10 MINUTES)
SERVINGS: 6

 EASY LOW FAT

1 boneless beef chuck roast
(2 to 2½ lb)

1 tablespoon Cajun seasoning

1 box (9 oz) Green Giant® Niblets®
frozen corn

½ cup chopped onion

½ cup chopped green bell pepper

1 can (14.5 oz) diced tomatoes,
undrained

⅛ teaspoon pepper

½ teaspoon red pepper sauce

1) Spray 3½- to 4-quart slow cooker with cooking spray. Rub entire surface of beef roast with Cajun seasoning. Place beef in cooker. Top with frozen corn, onion and bell pepper.

2) In small bowl, mix tomatoes, pepper and pepper sauce. Pour over vegetables and beef.

3) Cover; cook on Low heat setting 8 to 10 hours.

4) To serve, cut beef into slices. Remove corn mixture with slotted spoon, and serve with beef.

Nutrition Information Per Serving	
Calories: 210	From Fat: 150
Total Fat	10g
Saturated Fat	6g
Trans Fat	.5g
Cholesterol	80mg
Sodium	420mg
Total Carbohydrate	12g
Dietary Fiber	2g
Sugars	4g
Protein	27g

tip

Maque choux (pronounced "MOCK shoo") means "smothered corn" in Cajun country. This corn is smothered with tomatoes, bell peppers and onions.

Zesty Italian Crescent Casserole

| PREP TIME: | 20 MINUTES (READY IN 45 MINUTES) |
| SERVINGS: | 6 |

 EASY

1 lb lean (at least 80%) ground beef

¼ cup chopped onion

1 cup tomato pasta sauce

1½ cups shredded mozzarella or Monterey Jack cheese (6 oz)

½ cup sour cream

1 can (8 oz) Pillsbury® Crescent Recipe Creations® seamless dough sheet

⅓ cup grated Parmesan cheese

2 tablespoons butter or margarine, melted

1) Heat oven to 375°F. In 10-inch skillet, cook beef and onion over medium heat 8 to 10 minutes, stirring frequently, until beef is thoroughly cooked; drain. Stir in pasta sauce; cook until hot.

2) Meanwhile, in a medium bowl, combine the mozzarella cheese and the sour cream.

3) Pour hot beef mixture into ungreased 9½- or 10-inch glass deep-dish pie plate or 11x7-inch (2-quart) glass baking dish. Spoon cheese mixture over beef mixture.

4) Unroll dough over cheese mixture. In small bowl, mix Parmesan cheese and melted butter. Spread evenly over dough.

5) Bake 18 to 25 minutes or until deep golden brown.

Nutrition Information Per Serving	
Calories: 450	From Fat: 290
Total Fat	29g
Saturated Fat	15g
Trans Fat	0g
Cholesterol	85mg
Sodium	810mg
Total Carbohydrate	22g
Dietary Fiber	0g
Sugars	10g
Protein	28g

Wild West Pizza

PREP TIME: 20 MINUTES (READY IN 35 MINUTES)
SERVINGS: 6

 EASY

1 can (13.8 oz) Pillsbury® refrigerated classic pizza crust

½ lb lean (at least 80%) ground beef

¼ teaspoon salt

⅛ teaspoon pepper

1 can (16 oz) refried beans

1 cup taco sauce or chunky-style salsa

1 can (11 oz) whole kernel corn with red and green peppers, well drained

1 cup shredded Cheddar cheese (4 oz)

2 cups shredded lettuce

1 medium tomato, chopped (¾ cup)

½ cup sliced green onions

1) Heat oven to 400°F. Spray large cookie sheet with cooking spray. Unroll dough; place on cookie sheet. Starting at center, press out dough into 14x12-inch rectangle. Bake 8 to 10 minutes or until edges of crust begin to brown.

2) Meanwhile, in 8-inch skillet, cook ground beef sprinkled with salt and pepper over medium-high heat, stirring frequently, until thoroughly cooked; drain.

3) Spread refried beans evenly over partially baked crust. Spread ½ cup of the taco sauce over beans. Top with ground beef mixture, corn and cheese.

4) Bake 10 to 14 minutes longer or until crust is golden brown and cheese is melted. Top with lettuce, tomato and onions. Cut into squares or wedges; serve with remaining ½ cup taco sauce.

Nutrition Information Per Serving

Calories: 440	From Fat: 130
Total Fat	14g
Saturated Fat	6g
Trans Fat	0g
Cholesterol	50mg
Sodium	1360mg
Total Carbohydrate	56g
Dietary Fiber	6g
Sugars	9g
Protein	23g

Old-Time Beef and Vegetable Stew

PREP TIME: 20 MINUTES (READY IN 20 MINUTES)
SERVINGS: 6

 EASY   LOW FAT

1 tablespoon vegetable oil

1 boneless beef sirloin steak (1 lb), cut into ½-inch cubes

1 bag (1 lb) frozen stew vegetables, thawed, drained

1 can (15 oz) garlic-and-onion or Italian-style tomato sauce

1¾ cups Progresso® beef flavored broth (from 32-oz carton)

2 cans (5½ oz each) spicy eight-vegetable juice

Nutrition Information Per Serving	
Calories: 260	From Fat: 70
Total Fat	8g
Saturated Fat	1.5g
Trans Fat	0g
Cholesterol	50mg
Sodium	800mg
Total Carbohydrate	26g
Dietary Fiber	3g
Sugars	11g
Protein	22g

1) In 12-inch nonstick skillet, heat oil over medium-high heat. Add beef; cook 6 to 8 minutes, stirring occasionally, until brown.

2) Stir in remaining ingredients. Heat to boiling. Reduce heat; cover and simmer 5 minutes, stirring occasionally.

Simple Hamburger Hot Dish

PREP TIME: 25 MINUTES (READY IN 1 HOUR 15 MINUTES)
SERVINGS: 6

3 cups uncooked rotini pasta (8 oz)

1 lb lean (at least 80%) ground beef

1 large onion, chopped (about 1 cup)

1 teaspoon garlic powder

½ teaspoon salt

1 can (14.5 oz) diced tomatoes, undrained

1 can (15 oz) tomato sauce

1 tablespoon sugar

1 cup shredded American-Cheddar cheese blend (4 oz)

Nutrition Information Per Serving	
Calories: 410	From Fat: 140
Total Fat	15g
Saturated Fat	7g
Trans Fat	.5g
Cholesterol	65mg
Sodium	1120mg
Total Carbohydrate	43g
Dietary Fiber	4g
Sugars	9g
Protein	24g

1) Heat oven to 350°F. Cook and drain pasta as directed on package, using minimum cook time. Meanwhile, in 10-inch skillet, cook beef, onion, garlic powder and salt over medium heat 8 to 10 minutes, stirring occasionally, until beef is thoroughly cooked; drain.

2) Stir in tomatoes, tomato sauce, sugar and cooked pasta. Pour into ungreased 8-inch square (2-quart) glass baking dish.

3) Cover dish with foil. Bake 30 to 40 minutes or until bubbly around edges. Sprinkle with cheese; bake uncovered 5 to 10 minutes longer or until cheese is melted.

Crescent Cabbage and Beef Bundles

DEBRA TWICHELL | VALLEY FALLS, KANSAS

BAKE-OFF® CONTEST 31, 1984

PREP TIME: 35 MINUTES (READY IN 55 MINUTES)
SERVINGS: 8

SANDWICHES

    1 lb lean (at least 80%) ground beef

    ⅓ cup chopped onion

    2 cups chopped cabbage

    ½ teaspoon salt

    ¼ teaspoon pepper

    ½ cup shredded Cheddar cheese
      (2 oz)

    2 cans (8 oz each) Pillsbury®
      refrigerated crescent dinner rolls

SAUCE

    ½ cup mayonnaise or salad dressing

    3 tablespoons horseradish sauce

1) Heat oven to 375°F. In a 12-inch skillet, cook the ground beef and onion over medium-high heat, stirring frequently, until beef is thoroughly cooked; drain.

2) Stir in cabbage, salt and pepper. Reduce heat to medium. Cover; cook 10 to 15 minutes, stirring occasionally, until cabbage is crisp-tender. Cool 5 minutes. Stir in cheese.

3) Separate dough into 16 triangles; press or roll each until slightly larger. Spoon about ¼ cup beef mixture onto shortest side of each triangle. Roll up, starting at shortest side of triangle, gently wrapping dough around beef mixture and rolling to opposite point. Pinch edges to seal. Place point side down on ungreased large cookie sheet.

4) Bake 15 to 20 minutes or until golden brown. Meanwhile, in small bowl, mix mayonnaise and horseradish sauce. Serve sauce with sandwiches.

Nutrition Information Per Serving	
Calories: 460	From Fat: 310
Total Fat	32g
Saturated Fat	9g
Trans Fat	0g
Cholesterol	55g
Sodium	760mg
Total Carbohydrate	25g
Dietary Fiber	1g
Sugars	7g
Protein	16g

Jumbo Burger Cups

BRIDGET UHRICH | DOYLESTOWN, PENNSYLVANIA

BAKE-OFF® CONTEST 44, 2010

PREP TIME: 35 MINUTES (READY IN 1 HOUR)
SERVINGS: 8

1½ lb lean (at least 80%) ground beef

½ cup ketchup

⅓ cup dill pickle relish

2 tablespoons yellow mustard

4 oz cream cheese (half of 8-oz package)

1 teaspoon onion powder

½ teaspoon salt

½ teaspoon pepper

1 can (16.3 oz) Pillsbury® Grands!® Flaky Layers Butter Tastin'® refrigerated biscuits (8 biscuits)

1 Eggland's Best egg

1 teaspoon water

2 tablespoons sesame seed

1) Heat oven to 350°F. In 12-inch skillet, cook beef over medium heat 8 to 10 minutes, stirring occasionally, until thoroughly cooked; drain. Stir in ketchup, relish, mustard, cream cheese, onion powder, salt and pepper. Cook about 5 minutes, stirring occasionally, until cheese is melted and mixture is creamy. Reduce heat to low.

2) Separate dough into 8 biscuits. Using serrated knife, split each biscuit in half horizontally. Press 1 biscuit half into about 4-inch round. In ungreased non-stick jumbo muffin pan, press round in bottom and ½ to ¾ of the way up side of muffin cup. Repeat with remaining biscuit halves.

3) Divide beef mixture evenly among biscuits in cups. Top with remaining biscuit halves, stretching slightly to cover beef mixture and slightly pressing the edges to the bottom of the biscuits to seal.

4) In small bowl, beat egg and water until well blended; brush on top of biscuits. Sprinkle with sesame seed.

5) Bake 15 to 20 minutes or until tops are golden brown. Cool in pan 5 minutes before serving.

Nutrition Information Per Serving	
Calories: 440	From Fat: 220
Total Fat	25g
Saturated Fat	9g
Trans Fat	3.5g
Cholesterol	90mg
Sodium	1080mg
Total Carbohydrate	34g
Dietary Fiber	0g
Sugars	11g
Protein	20g

Two-Bean Burger Casserole

PREP TIME: 25 MINUTES (READY IN 45 MINUTES)
SERVINGS: 6

6 slices bacon

1 lb lean (at least 80%) ground beef

1 cup chopped onions (2 medium)

1 can (16 oz) baked beans with bacon and brown sugar, undrained

1 can (15 oz) Progresso® red kidney beans, drained, ¼ cup liquid reserved

¼ cup packed brown sugar

¼ cup ketchup

3 tablespoons white vinegar

1 can (11 oz) Pillsbury® refrigerated original breadsticks (12 breadsticks)

1 tablespoon milk

2 teaspoons sesame seed

1) Heat oven to 400°F. In 12-inch nonstick skillet, cook bacon over medium heat, turning once, until crisp. Drain on paper towels; crumble bacon. Drain drippings from skillet.

2) In skillet, cook beef and onions over medium-high heat, stirring occasionally, until thoroughly cooked; drain. Stir in bacon, baked beans, kidney beans with reserved ¼ cup liquid, brown sugar, ketchup and vinegar. Reduce heat to medium-low; cook until bubbly, stirring occasionally. Pour into ungreased 11x7-inch (2-quart) glass baking dish.

3) Unroll dough; separate into 12 strips. Arrange strips in lattice design over bean mixture, overlapping as necessary to fit. Brush dough with milk; sprinkle with sesame seed.

4) Bake 15 to 20 minutes or until breadsticks are golden brown and filling is bubbly.

Nutrition Information Per Serving	
Calories: 590	From Fat: 170
Total Fat	19g
Saturated Fat	7g
Trans Fat	.5g
Cholesterol	65mg
Sodium	1040mg
Total Carbohydrate	74g
Dietary Fiber	7g
Sugars	29g
Protein	31g

Beef Enchilada Stack

PREP TIME: 20 MINUTES (READY IN 50 MINUTES)
SERVINGS: 6

 EASY

1 lb lean (at least 80%) ground beef

½ cup chopped onion

½ medium green bell pepper, chopped (½ cup)

½ cup Green Giant® Valley Fresh Steamers™ Niblets® frozen corn

1 package (1 oz) Old El Paso® 40% less-sodium taco seasoning mix

1 can (14.5 oz) diced tomatoes in sauce, undrained

1 can (10 oz) Old El Paso® enchilada sauce

9 corn tortillas (6 inch)

2 cups shredded Cheddar cheese (8 oz)

½ cup sour cream

3 medium green onions, sliced (3 tablespoons)

1) Heat oven to 350°F. Spray 9-inch glass pie plate or 9½-inch glass deep-dish pie plate with cooking spray. In 12-inch skillet or 4-quart Dutch oven, cook beef and onion over medium-high heat, stirring occasionally, until thoroughly cooked; drain. Stir in bell pepper, corn, taco seasoning mix, tomatoes and enchilada sauce. Heat to boiling; remove from heat.

2) Spread about ¼ of beef mixture in thin layer in pie plate. Top with 3 tortillas (tortillas will overlap), ¼ of beef mixture and ⅓ of cheese. Repeat layers 2 more times, starting with tortillas and ending with cheese on top. Pie plate will be very full but should not overflow.

3) Bake about 30 minutes or until cheese is melted and lightly browned. Let stand 5 minutes before serving. Top each serving with sour cream and green onions.

Nutrition Information Per Serving	
Calories: 460	From Fat: 240
Total Fat	27g
Saturated Fat	14g
Trans Fat	1g
Cholesterol	100mg
Sodium	910mg
Total Carbohydrate	30g
Dietary Fiber	3g
Sugars	5g
Protein	26g

Philly Cheese Steak Pizza

PREP TIME: 30 MINUTES (READY IN 50 MINUTES)
SERVINGS: 6

1 can (13.8 oz) Pillsbury® refrigerated classic pizza crust

1 tablespoon butter or margarine

1 small green bell pepper, cut into thin strips

1 medium onion, halved, thinly sliced

2 cups finely shredded Cheddar cheese (8 oz)

½ lb cooked roast beef (from deli), diced

3 plum (Roma) tomatoes, sliced

1) Heat oven to 425°F. Grease 12-inch pizza pan with shortening. Unroll dough; place in pan. Starting at center, press out dough to edge of pan, forming ½-inch rim. Bake 8 to 10 minutes or until light golden brown.

2) Meanwhile, in 8-inch skillet, melt butter over medium-high heat. Add bell pepper and onion; cook 3 to 5 minutes, stirring occasionally, until tender.

3) Sprinkle 1 cup of the cheese evenly over partially baked crust. Top with bell pepper mixture, beef, remaining 1 cup cheese and the tomato slices (be sure beef is completely covered with cheese).

4) Bake 12 to 18 minutes longer or until crust is deep golden brown. Cut into wedges to serve.

tip

If you do not have a 12-inch pizza pan, just lay the dough out on a cookie sheet. Press the edges up to form a 1/2-inch rim. Continue as directed.

Nutrition Information Per Serving	
Calories: 500	From Fat: 170
Total Fat	23g
Saturated Fat	10g
Trans Fat	0g
Cholesterol	80mg
Sodium	600mg
Total Carbohydrate	22g
Dietary Fiber	0g
Sugars	6g
Protein	29g

Italian Beef and Ravioli Stew

PREP TIME: 30 MINUTES (READY IN 1 HOUR 40 MINUTES)
SERVINGS: 6 (1-1/3 CUPS EACH)

1 tablespoon olive or vegetable oil

1 medium onion, coarsely chopped
(½ cup)

2 teaspoons finely chopped garlic

2 teaspoons chopped fresh rosemary
leaves

1 medium yellow or green bell pepper,
cut into 2-inch strips

2 lb boneless beef chuck, cut into
1-inch pieces

2 cans (14.5 oz each) diced tomatoes
with balsamic vinegar, basil and
olive oil, undrained

½ cup Progresso® beef flavored broth
(from 32-oz carton) or red wine

1½ cups Green Giant® Valley Fresh
Steamers™ frozen cut green beans

1 package (9 oz) refrigerated
cheese-filled ravioli

1) In 4½- to 5-quart Dutch oven, heat oil over medium-high heat. Add onion, garlic, rosemary and bell pepper; cook 4 to 5 minutes, stirring frequently, until onion is softened. Stir in beef. Cook 6 to 8 minutes, stirring occasionally, until beef is lightly browned.

2) Stir in tomatoes and broth. Heat to boiling. Reduce heat to medium-low; cover and cook 45 to 50 minutes, stirring occasionally, until beef is tender.

3) Stir in frozen green beans and ravioli. Increase heat to medium-high; cook uncovered 8 to 10 minutes, stirring occasionally, until ravioli are tender.

Nutrition Information Per Serving	
Calories: 460	From Fat: 210
Total Fat	23g
Saturated Fat	9g
Trans Fat	.5g
Cholesterol	100mg
Sodium	500mg
Total Carbohydrate	29g
Dietary Fiber	3g
Sugars	8g
Protein	33g

Beef with Broccoli

PREP TIME: 35 MINUTES (READY IN 35 MINUTES)
SERVINGS: 4

2 cups uncooked instant brown rice

1¾ cups water

1 cup Progresso® beef flavored broth (from 32-oz carton)

1 tablespoon cornstarch

2 tablespoons soy sauce

1 teaspoon packed brown sugar

1 tablespoon olive or vegetable oil

1 teaspoon freshly grated gingerroot

1 lb boneless beef round or tip steak, thinly sliced

1 small onion, thinly sliced (½ cup)

Salt and pepper to taste

½ lb fresh broccoli florets and peeled stems, cut into bite-size pieces (about 2 cups)

1) Cook rice in water as directed on package. Meanwhile, in small bowl, mix broth, cornstarch, soy sauce and brown sugar. Stir until cornstarch is dissolved.

2) In 12-inch nonstick skillet, heat oil over medium-high heat. Add gingerroot, beef and onion; sprinkle with salt and pepper. Cook 2 to 4 minutes, stirring occasionally, until beef is brown. Remove beef mixture from skillet; cover to keep warm.

3) Add broth mixture and broccoli to skillet. Heat to boiling; reduce heat. Cook 5 to 10 minutes or until sauce thickens and broccoli is tender. Return beef mixture to skillet; cook until hot, stirring occasionally.

4) Serve the beef with broccoli over warm rice.

Nutrition Information Per Serving	
Calories: 590	From Fat: 100
Total Fat	11g
Saturated Fat	2.5g
Trans Fat	0g
Cholesterol	85mg
Sodium	1030mg
Total Carbohydrate	80g
Dietary Fiber	12g
Sugars	4g
Protein	43g

Crusty-Topped Beef in Beer

PREP TIME: 30 MINUTES (READY IN 2 HOURS 20 MINUTES)
SERVINGS: 8

2 tablespoons olive or vegetable oil

1½ lb boneless beef stew meat, cut into 1-inch pieces

½ teaspoon salt

¼ teaspoon freshly ground pepper

3 medium carrots, sliced (1½ cups)

1 onion, halved, cut into ½-inch-thick wedges (about 3 cups)

3 tablespoons all-purpose flour

3 cups cubed unpeeled potatoes

¼ cup chopped fresh parsley

1 tablespoon packed brown sugar

1 teaspoon beef bouillon granules

1 teaspoon dried thyme leaves

1 can (14.5 oz) diced tomatoes with basil, garlic and oregano, undrained

1 can (12 oz) beer

1 cup small pretzel twists

1 can (12 oz) Pillsbury® Grands!® Jr. Golden Layers® refrigerated buttermilk flaky biscuits (10 biscuits)

2 tablespoons spicy brown mustard

1) Heat oven to 350°F. In 4-quart Dutch oven, heat oil over medium-high heat. Add beef in batches; cook and stir until browned. With slotted spoon, remove beef to bowl; sprinkle with salt and pepper.

2) When all beef is browned and removed from Dutch oven, add carrots and onion to drippings. Cook and stir over medium-high heat 3 to 4 minutes, scraping up browned bits. Sprinkle with flour; stir to mix well. Stir in beef and remaining beef mixture ingredients. Pour into ungreased 13x9-inch (3-quart) glass baking dish.

3) Cover dish with foil. Bake about 1 hour 30 minutes or until beef is tender and sauce is thickened. Remove from oven; stir. Increase oven temperature to 375°F.

4) Place pretzels in 1-gallon food-storage plastic bag; crush with rolling pin to make about ¾ cup. Separate dough into 10 biscuits; cut each into 4 pieces. Brush mustard over dough pieces. Drop handful of dough pieces at a time into bag; shake to coat. Place the biscuit pieces evenly on beef mixture, leaving space between pieces.

5) Bake uncovered 14 to 18 minutes longer or until the biscuits are golden brown.

Nutrition Information Per Serving	
Calories: 420	From Fat: 170
Total Fat	19g
Saturated Fat	5g
Trans Fat	2.5g
Cholesterol	45mg
Sodium	950mg
Total Carbohydrate	42g
Dietary Fiber	3g
Sugars	8g
Protein	20g

Cheeseburger Pot Pie

PREP TIME: 25 MINUTES (READY IN 45 MINUTES)
SERVINGS: 6

1½ lb lean (at least 80%) ground beef

¼ cup chopped onion

¾ cup ketchup

2 tablespoons chopped dill pickle, if desired

⅛ teaspoon pepper

1 cup shredded sharp Cheddar cheese (4 oz)

1 Pillsbury® refrigerated pie crust, softened as directed on box

1) Heat oven to 450°F. In 10-inch skillet, cook beef and onion over medium-high heat, stirring occasionally, until beef is thoroughly cooked; drain. Reduce heat to medium. Stir in ketchup, pickle and pepper; cook 2 to 3 minutes or until thoroughly heated.

2) In ungreased 9-inch glass pie plate, spread beef mixture. Sprinkle with cheese. Unroll pie crust over hot beef mixture. Seal edge and flute. Cut slits in several places in top crust.

3) Bake 13 to 20 minutes or until crust is golden brown and filling is bubbly. During last 10 minutes of baking, cover crust edge with strips of foil to prevent excessive browning.

Nutrition Information Per Serving

Calories: 460	From Fat: 260
Total Fat	28g
Saturated Fat	12g
Trans Fat	1g
Cholesterol	95mg
Sodium	650mg
Total Carbohydrate	26g
Dietary Fiber	0g
Sugars	8g
Protein	25g

Chile Rellenos Bake

PREP TIME: 15 MINUTES (READY IN 1 HOUR 5 MINUTES)
SERVINGS: 4

 EASY

2 cans (4.5 oz each) Old El Paso® chopped green chiles

2 cups shredded 4-cheese Mexican cheese blend (8 oz)

1 can (11 oz) Pillsbury® refrigerated original breadsticks (12 breadsticks)

3 eggs

1 cup half-and-half

½ teaspoon red pepper sauce

2 medium plum (Roma) tomatoes, chopped (about 1 cup)

1) Heat oven to 350°F. Spray 8-inch square (2-quart) glass baking dish with cooking spray; lightly flour. Spread green chiles in bottom of dish; sprinkle with 1 cup of the cheese.

2) Unroll dough; separate into 2 squares. To make 24 short strips, cut each square in half across strips. Shape each short strip into a coil; arrange cut side down over cheese. Top with remaining cheese. In medium bowl, beat eggs, half-and-half and pepper sauce with wire whisk until blended. Pour over dough in dish.

3) Bake 40 to 45 minutes or until edges are golden brown and center is set. Let stand 5 minutes before serving. Top each serving with ¼ cup chopped tomatoes.

Nutrition Information Per Serving	
Calories: 580	From Fat: 290
Total Fat	32g
Saturated Fat	19g
Trans Fat	.5g
Cholesterol	240mg
Sodium	1250mg
Total Carbohydrate	47g
Dietary Fiber	0g
Sugars	12g
Protein	26g

CHICKEN SATAY WITH
CUCUMBER SALAD
PG. 158

Chicken & Turkey Entrees

You can never have enough no-fuss recipes that use popular chicken and turkey as the main ingredient!

DOUBLE BARBECUE
BACON-WRAPPED CHICKEN
PG. 146

INDIAN-STYLE CURRY CHICKEN
PG. 156

RASPBERRY-CHIPOTLE BARBECUE
CHICKEN PIZZA
PG. 165

Double Barbecue Bacon-Wrapped Chicken

PREP TIME: 20 MINUTES (READY IN 35 MINUTES)
SERVINGS: 4

 EASY

WHITE BARBECUE SAUCE

- ¼ cup mayonnaise or salad dressing
- 2 teaspoons lemon juice
- 1 teaspoon cider vinegar
- 2 teaspoons chopped parsley
- ¼ to ½ teaspoon red pepper sauce

BACON-WRAPPED CHICKEN

- 4 boneless skinless chicken breasts
- 8 slices packaged precooked bacon
- 2 teaspoons barbecue seasoning
- ¼ cup barbecue sauce

1) Heat gas or charcoal grill. In small bowl, stir together white barbecue sauce ingredients; cover and refrigerate until serving time.

2) Wrap each chicken breast with 2 slices bacon, stretching bacon to cover as much of the breast as possible; secure ends of bacon to chicken with toothpicks. Sprinkle both sides with barbecue seasoning.

3) Place chicken on grill over medium heat. Cover grill; cook 5 minutes. Brush with 2 tablespoons of the barbecue sauce. Cook 5 to 7 minutes longer or until juice of chicken is clear when center of thickest part is cut (170°F). Turn chicken; brush with remaining barbecue sauce. Serve chicken topped with white barbecue sauce.

Nutrition Information Per Serving	
Calories: 350	From Fat: 190
Total Fat	22g
Saturated Fat	5g
Trans Fat	0g
Cholesterol	95mg
Sodium	920mg
Total Carbohydrate	7g
Dietary Fiber	0g
Sugars	5g
Protein	32g

Asian Barbecued Chicken

PREP TIME: 4 HOURS 10 MINUTES (READY IN 4 HOURS 40 MINUTES)
SERVINGS: 6

1 jar (8 oz) hoisin sauce

¼ cup soy sauce

2 tablespoons Dijon mustard

2 tablespoons lemon juice

2 tablespoons sesame oil

½ teaspoon ground ginger

1 cut-up whole chicken (3 to 3½ lb)

1) In medium bowl, mix hoisin sauce, soy sauce, mustard, lemon juice, sesame oil and ginger. Measure out ½ cup mixture; cover and refrigerate for use in Step 3. Place remaining mixture in large resealable food-storage plastic bag. Add chicken; seal bag and marinate in refrigerator 4 hours.

2) Heat gas or charcoal grill. Remove chicken from marinade, reserve marinade. Place chicken on grill over medium heat. Cover grill; cook 25 to 30 minutes, turning frequently and brushing with marinade from plastic bag, until juice of chicken is clear when thickest piece is cut to bone (170°F for breasts; 180°F for thighs and drumsticks).

3) Before serving, brush chicken with the ½ cup mixture reserved in Step 1.

Nutrition Information Per Serving	
Calories: 370	From Fat: 180
Total Fat	20g
Saturated Fat	4.5g
Trans Fat	0g
Cholesterol	90mg
Sodium	1420mg
Total Carbohydrate	18g
Dietary Fiber	1g
Sugars	3g
Protein	29g

tip

Be sure to turn the chicken frequently as it grills so the heat doesn't char the sugars in the sauce.

Turkey and Wild Rice Casserole

PREP TIME: 25 MINUTES (READY IN 2 HOURS)
SERVINGS: 8 (1-1/3 CUPS EACH)

2½ cups water

1 cup uncooked wild rice

4 cups cut-up cooked turkey

1 bag (12 oz) Green Giant® Valley Fresh Steamers™ frozen mixed vegetables, thawed

1½ cups uncooked instant brown rice

½ teaspoon salt

½ teaspoon dried thyme leaves

1 cup Progresso® chicken broth, heated

3 containers (10 oz each) refrigerated reduced-fat Alfredo pasta sauce

½ cup Progresso® panko crispy bread crumbs

¼ cup finely chopped walnuts

3 tablespoons butter or margarine, melted

1) In 2-quart saucepan, heat water to rolling boil. Stir in wild rice; reduce heat. Cover; simmer 40 to 50 minutes or until rice is tender.

2) Heat oven to 350°F. Spray 3-quart casserole with cooking spray.

3) In large bowl, mix turkey, vegetables, cooked wild rice, uncooked brown rice, salt and thyme. Stir in heated broth and Alfredo sauce. Pour into casserole.

4) In small bowl, mix the bread crumbs, walnuts and butter; sprinkle over the turkey mixture.

5) Bake uncovered about 45 minutes or until hot.

Nutrition Information Per Serving

Calories: 630	From Fat: 220
Total Fat	25g
Saturated Fat	12g
Trans Fat	.5g
Cholesterol	110mg
Sodium	920mg
Total Carbohydrate	65g
Dietary Fiber	8g
Sugars	7g
Protein	36g

Chili-Glazed Chicken

PREP TIME: 30 MINUTES (READY IN 30 MINUTES)
SERVINGS: 4

 EASY

3 tablespoons chili sauce

3 tablespoons soy sauce

1 teaspoon sesame oil

1 teaspoon finely chopped garlic

¼ teaspoon crushed red pepper

8 bone-in, skin-on chicken thighs
(5 to 6 oz each)

¼ teaspoon salt

¼ teaspoon pepper

Nutrition Information Per Serving	
Calories: 380	From Fat: 220
Total Fat	24g
Saturated Fat	6g
Trans Fat	0g
Cholesterol	130mg
Sodium	1120mg
Total Carbohydrate	4g
Dietary Fiber	1g
Sugars	2g
Protein	38g

1) Heat gas or charcoal grill. In small bowl, mix chili sauce, soy sauce, sesame oil, garlic and red pepper.

2) Sprinkle chicken with salt and pepper. Place chicken on grill over medium heat. Cover grill; cook 8 minutes. Turn chicken; brush with chili sauce mixture. Continue turning chicken and brushing with sauce 8 to 10 minutes longer or until juice of chicken is clear when thickest part is cut to bone (180°F).

French Peasant Chicken Stew

PREP TIME: 10 MINUTES (READY IN 35 MINUTES)
SERVINGS: 6 (1-1/3 CUPS EACH)

 EASY LOW FAT

2 cups ready-to-eat baby-cut carrots

1 cup sliced fresh mushrooms (about 3 oz)

4 small red potatoes, cut into quarters

1 jar (12 oz) chicken gravy

1¾ cups Progresso® reduced-sodium chicken broth (from 32-oz carton)

1 teaspoon dried thyme leaves

½ cup Green Giant® Valley Fresh Steamers™ frozen baby sweet peas

1 deli rotisserie chicken (2 to 2½ lb), cut into serving pieces

Nutrition Information Per Serving	
Calories: 290	From Fat: 90
Total Fat	10g
Saturated Fat	2.5g
Trans Fat	0g
Cholesterol	75mg
Sodium	920mg
Total Carbohydrate	22g
Dietary Fiber	4g
Sugars	4g
Protein	28g

1) In 4-quart saucepan, mix all ingredients except peas and chicken. Heat to boiling over medium-high heat. Reduce heat to medium-low. Cover; simmer about 20 minutes or until vegetables are tender.

2) Stir in the peas and chicken. Cover and simmer about 5 minutes or until the peas are tender.

CHICKEN & TURKEY ENTREES 149

Chicken and Cheese Crescent Chimichangas

MARLENE ZEBLECKIS | SALINAS, CALIFORNIA   BAKE-OFF® CONTEST 33, 1988

Bake-Off®

PREP TIME: 20 MINUTES (READY IN 45 MINUTES)
SERVINGS: 8

e EASY

½ cup chopped onion

2 cloves garlic, finely chopped

3 tablespoons vegetable oil

2½ cups shredded cooked chicken

2 cans (8 oz each) Pillsbury®
refrigerated crescent dinner rolls

½ cup picante salsa

2 cups shredded Cheddar cheese
(8 oz)

Sour cream

Salsa

1) Heat oven to 350°F. Grease large cookie sheet. In 10-inch skillet, cook onion and garlic in oil until onion is tender. Add chicken; cook over low heat until hot, stirring occasionally.

2) Separate dough into 8 rectangles; firmly press perforations to seal. Spread about 2 teaspoons of the salsa on each rectangle to within ½ inch of edges. Stir 1 cup of the cheese into chicken mixture. Spoon heaping ⅓ cup chicken mixture onto half of each rectangle. Starting with short side topped with chicken, roll up; pinch ends to seal. Place seam side down on cookie sheet.

3) Bake 16 to 21 minutes or until golden brown. Remove from oven; top each with about 2 tablespoons of the remaining cheese. Bake 1 to 2 minutes longer or until cheese is melted. Serve with sour cream and additional salsa.

Nutrition Information Per Serving	
Calories: 490	From Fat: 290
Total Fat	32g
Saturated Fat	13g
Trans Fat	3.5g
Cholesterol	75mg
Sodium	770mg
Total Carbohydrate	26g
Dietary Fiber	0g
Sugars	6g
Protein	24g

Chicken Souvlaki Pot Pie

PREP TIME: 25 MINUTES (READY IN 1 HOUR)
SERVINGS: 6

2 tablespoons olive or vegetable oil

1¼ lb boneless skinless chicken breasts, cut into bite-size strips

1 medium red onion, chopped (about 1¼ cups)

2 small zucchini, cut in half lengthwise, then cut crosswise into slices (about 2⅓ cups)

2 cloves garlic, finely chopped

2 teaspoons chili powder

1½ teaspoons dried oregano leaves

½ teaspoon salt

1 can (14.5 oz) diced tomatoes, undrained

½ cup plain yogurt

2 tablespoons all-purpose flour

1 Pillsbury® refrigerated pie crust, softened as directed on box

1) Heat oven to 400°F. In 12-inch nonstick skillet, heat 1 tablespoon of the oil over medium-high heat. Add chicken; cook about 8 minutes, stirring occasionally, until no longer pink in center. Remove chicken from skillet.

2) Heat remaining 1 tablespoon oil in skillet. Add onion and zucchini; cook and stir about 6 minutes or until zucchini is crisp-tender. Return chicken to skillet (discard chicken juices). Stir in garlic, chili powder, oregano and salt. Cook and stir 2 minutes. Stir in tomatoes; cook until thoroughly heated. Remove from heat.

3) In small bowl, beat yogurt and flour with wire whisk until blended; stir into chicken mixture. Spoon into ungreased 9-inch glass pie plate.

4) Unroll pie crust over hot chicken mixture. Fold excess crust under and press to form thick crust edge; flute the pie crust edge. Cut slits in several places in crust. Place pie plate on cookie sheet with sides.

5) Bake 25 to 30 minutes or until crust is golden brown (sauce may bubble slightly over crust). Let stand 5 minutes before serving.

Nutrition Information Per Serving	
Calories: 360	From Fat: 160
Total Fat	17g
Saturated Fat	5g
Trans Fat	0g
Cholesterol	65mg
Sodium	510mg
Total Carbohydrate	26g
Dietary Fiber	2g
Sugars	4g
Protein	23g

Mini Chicken Alfredo Pot Pies

PREP TIME: 20 MINUTES (READY IN 50 MINUTES)
SERVINGS: 8

EASY

4 cups chopped cooked chicken

4 cups Green Giant® Valley Fresh Steamers™ frozen mixed vegetables (from two 12-oz bags), thawed, well drained

1 jar (16 oz) Alfredo pasta sauce

½ cup milk

¼ cup grated Parmesan cheese

1 can (8 oz) Pillsbury® refrigerated garlic breadsticks

Nutrition Information Per Serving	
Calories: 520	From Fat: 300
Total Fat	33g
Saturated Fat	16g
Trans Fat	2g
Cholesterol	120mg
Sodium	630mg
Total Carbohydrate	28g
Dietary Fiber	4g
Sugars	6g
Protein	29g

1) Heat oven to 400°F. Place 8 (10-oz) ramekins or custard cups on large cookie sheet with sides. In 3-quart saucepan, heat chicken, thawed vegetables, pasta sauce and milk over medium heat, stirring occasionally, until thoroughly heated. Spoon mixture into ramekins.

2) Sprinkle cheese on plate. Unroll dough. Separate 1 strip at a time and press both sides into cheese. Twist the strip and arrange on top of chicken mixture in ramekin in loose spiral shape, beginning at outside and coiling toward center. Repeat with remaining strips of dough and cheese. Sprinkle any remaining cheese over dough.

3) Bake 15 minutes. Cover ramekins loosely with sheet of foil; bake about 12 minutes longer or until filling is hot and bubbly.

Ultimate Barbecue-Rubbed Chicken

PREP TIME: 20 MINUTES (READY IN 20 MINUTES)
SERVINGS: 4

EASY **LOW FAT**

1 tablespoon packed brown sugar

2 teaspoons smoked Spanish paprika

½ teaspoon ground cumin

¼ teaspoon garlic salt

¼ teaspoon ancho chili powder

4 boneless skinless chicken breasts

½ cup barbecue sauce, warmed

Nutrition Information Per Serving	
Calories: 210	From Fat: 35
Total Fat	4g
Saturated Fat	1g
Trans Fat	0g
Cholesterol	75mg
Sodium	460mg
Total Carbohydrate	17g
Dietary Fiber	0g
Sugars	14g
Protein	27g

1) Heat gas or charcoal grill. In small bowl, mix brown sugar, paprika, cumin, garlic salt and chili powder. Rub both sides of chicken with seasoning mixture.

2) Place chicken on grill over medium heat. Cover grill; cook 8 to 10 minutes, turning once, until juice of chicken is clear when center of thickest part is cut (170°F). Serve chicken with barbecue sauce.

Pesto-Parmesan Crusted Chicken

PREP TIME: 45 MINUTES (READY IN 45 MINUTES)
SERVINGS: 4

LOW FAT

1 tablespoon olive oil

1 teaspoon finely chopped garlic

½ cup Progresso® panko bread crumbs

½ cup basil pesto

3 tablespoons grated Parmesan cheese

4 bone-in skin-on chicken breasts (8.25 oz each)

¼ teaspoon salt

¼ teaspoon pepper

1) Heat gas or charcoal grill. In 10-inch skillet, heat oil over medium-high heat. Cook garlic in oil about 30 seconds, stirring constantly, until fragrant. Add bread crumbs. Cook 2 to 3 minutes, stirring frequently, until toasted. Remove crumb mixture to small bowl. Stir pesto and Parmesan cheese into bowl with crumbs.

2) Loosen skin on chicken to form a pocket, without detaching skin completely. Fill each pocket with pesto mixture. Sprinkle with salt and pepper.

3) Place chicken on grill, skin side down, over medium-low heat. Cover grill; cook 10 minutes, moving occasionally as needed to avoid burning the skin. Turn chicken; spoon any remaining pesto over chicken. Cook 10 to 15 minutes longer or until juice of chicken is clear when thickest part is cut to bone (170°F).

Nutrition Information Per Serving	
Calories: 450	From Fat: 260
Total Fat	29g
Saturated Fat	7g
Trans Fat	0g
Cholesterol	85mg
Sodium	770mg
Total Carbohydrate	12g
Dietary Fiber	1g
Sugars	1g
Protein	33g

Piccata Chicken

| PREP TIME: | 30 MINUTES (READY IN 30 MINUTES) | EASY |
| SERVINGS: | 4 | |

4 boneless skinless chicken breasts

¼ cup all-purpose flour

¼ teaspoon salt

¼ teaspoon white pepper

2 tablespoons vegetable oil

½ cup chicken broth

2 teaspoons Worcestershire sauce

¼ teaspoon dried marjoram leaves

2 tablespoons fresh lemon juice

¼ cup chopped fresh parsley

1) Place 1 chicken breast between 2 pieces of plastic wrap or waxed paper. Working from center, gently pound chicken with flat side of meat mallet or rolling pin until about ¼ inch thick; remove wrap. Repeat with remaining chicken breasts.

2) In shallow bowl, mix flour, salt and pepper. Coat chicken breasts with flour mixture. In 10-inch skillet, heat oil over medium-high heat until hot. Add chicken; cook 3 to 5 minutes on each side or until golden brown on outside and no longer pink in center.

3) Remove chicken from skillet; cover to keep warm. Add broth, Worcestershire sauce and marjoram to skillet; cook and stir 1 to 2 minutes or until hot. Stir in lemon juice and parsley. Serve over chicken.

Nutrition Information Per Serving	
Calories: 240	From Fat: 100
Total Fat	11g
Saturated Fat	2g
Trans Fat	0g
Cholesterol	75mg
Sodium	370mg
Total Carbohydrate	7g
Dietary Fiber	0g
Sugars	0g
Protein	28g

Moroccan-Style Chicken-Crescent Casserole

PREP TIME: 25 MINUTES (READY IN 50 MINUTES)
SERVINGS: 6

1 tablespoon olive or vegetable oil

6 boneless skinless chicken breasts (about 1½ lb), cut into bite-size pieces

½ cup chopped onion

½ cup sliced carrot

1 can (14.5 oz) diced fire-roasted or regular tomatoes, undrained

1 tablespoon tomato paste

3 tablespoons chopped fresh parsley

3 tablespoons chopped fresh cilantro

1½ teaspoons paprika

½ teaspoon salt

½ teaspoon ground cumin

¼ to ½ teaspoon ground cinnamon

⅛ teaspoon ground red pepper (cayenne)

1 can (8 oz) Pillsbury® Crescent Recipe Creations® refrigerated seamless dough sheet

1 egg, beaten

1 tablespoon sliced almonds

1) Heat oven to 375°F. In 12-inch skillet, heat oil over medium-high heat. Add chicken, onion and carrot; cook and stir about 7 minutes or until chicken is browned and no longer pink in center. Stir in tomatoes, tomato paste, parsley, cilantro, paprika, salt, cumin, cinnamon and red pepper. Cook and stir about 5 minutes or until thoroughly heated.

2) Into ungreased 11x7-inch (2-quart) glass baking dish or 9½- or 10-inch deep-dish pie plate, pour hot chicken mixture. Immediately unroll dough over chicken mixture; pinch edges and perforations to seal. Brush dough with beaten egg; sprinkle with almonds.

3) Bake 18 to 25 minutes or until deep golden brown. If desired, garnish with fresh cilantro.

Nutrition Information Per Serving	
Calories: 320	From Fat: 110
Total Fat	13g
Saturated Fat	4g
Trans Fat	0g
Cholesterol	70mg
Sodium	690mg
Total Carbohydrate	23g
Dietary Fiber	2g
Sugars	6g
Protein	29g

Indian-Style Curry Chicken

PREP TIME: 25 MINUTES (READY IN 1 HOUR 5 MINUTES)
SERVINGS: 6

4 cups frozen potatoes O'Brien with onions and peppers (from 28-oz bag), thawed

1 bag (12 oz) Green Giant® Valley Fresh Steamers™ frozen sweet peas, thawed

1 can (14.5 oz) diced tomatoes with green chiles, undrained

4 teaspoons curry powder

½ teaspoon salt

3 tablespoons all-purpose flour

1 teaspoon paprika

1 teaspoon garlic salt

12 chicken drumsticks

1 tablespoon vegetable oil

1) Heat oven to 350°F. Spray 13x9-inch (3-quart) glass baking dish with cooking spray. In large bowl, stir together potatoes, peas, tomatoes, 2 teaspoons of the curry powder and the salt. Spread evenly in baking dish.

2) In large resealable food-storage plastic bag, mix remaining 2 teaspoons curry powder, the flour, paprika and garlic salt; shake to mix. Add drumsticks; seal bag, and shake to coat.

3) In 12-inch skillet, heat oil over medium-high heat. Cook drumsticks in oil 8 to 10 minutes, turning frequently, until skin is brown (cook 6 drumsticks at a time if all don't fit in skillet). Place drumsticks in 2 rows lengthwise over potato mixture, alternating direction of drumsticks to cover potato mixture. Cover tightly with foil.

4) Bake 30 minutes. Remove foil; bake about 10 minutes longer or until juice of chicken is clear when thickest part is cut to bone (180°F).

Nutrition Information Per Serving	
Calories: 510	From Fat: 190
Total Fat	21g
Saturated Fat	5g
Trans Fat	0g
Cholesterol	85mg
Sodium	990mg
Total Carbohydrate	46g
Dietary Fiber	6g
Sugars	8g
Protein	35g

tip Curry powder is actually a blend of ground herbs, spices and seeds. The blend can vary dramatically. The type most often found in grocery stores resembles the blends of southern India. The "Madras" variety will be hotter than the standard variety.

Broiled Buffalo Chicken Pizza

| PREP TIME: | 20 MINUTES (READY IN 30 MINUTES) |
| SERVINGS: | 4 |

 EASY

¼ cup refrigerated ranch-style dip

1 prebaked Italian pizza crust (12 inch)

1½ cups diced cooked chicken

1 cup chopped plum (Roma) tomatoes (about 3 medium)

¼ cup buffalo wing sauce

2 cups shredded Colby-Monterey Jack cheese blend (8 oz)

¼ cup chopped green bell pepper

Nutrition Information Per Serving

Calories: 670	From Fat: 290
Total Fat	32g
Saturated Fat	16g
Trans Fat	1g
Cholesterol	115mg
Sodium	1610mg
Total Carbohydrate	54g
Dietary Fiber	3g
Sugars	3g
Protein	42g

1) Set oven control to broil. Spread dip evenly over pizza crust. Sprinkle with chicken and tomatoes. Drizzle with buffalo wing sauce; sprinkle with cheese and bell pepper. Place pizza on rack in broiler pan.

2) Broil 4 to 6 inches from heat for 6 to 8 minutes or until pizza is golden brown and cheese is melted.

Chicken and Spinach Dip Pizza

| PREP TIME: | 15 MINUTES (READY IN 30 MINUTES) |
| SERVINGS: | 8 |

 EASY

Cornmeal

1 can (13.8 oz) Pillsbury® refrigerated classic pizza crust

1 container (8 oz) refrigerated spinach dip

1 cup chopped cooked chicken

1 large tomato, seeded, chopped (1 cup)

1 cup sliced fresh mushrooms (3 oz)

1½ cups shredded mozzarella cheese (6 oz)

Nutrition Information Per Serving

Calories: 280	From Fat: 120
Total Fat	12g
Saturated Fat	5g
Trans Fat	0g
Cholesterol	35mg
Sodium	680mg
Total Carbohydrate	27g
Dietary Fiber	0g
Sugars	5g
Protein	15g

1) Heat oven to 400°F. Sprinkle cornmeal on 12-inch pizza stone or 12-inch pizza pan. Unroll dough; place on pizza stone or pizza pan. Starting at center, press out dough into 12-inch round or to edge of pan, forming ½-inch rim. Bake 8 minutes.

2) Spread spinach dip over partially baked crust. Top with chicken, tomato and mushrooms. Sprinkle with cheese.

3) Bake 12 to 15 minutes longer or until crust is golden brown and cheese is melted.

Chicken Satay with Cucumber Salad

PREP TIME: 40 MINUTES (READY IN 40 MINUTES)
SERVINGS: 4

CHICKEN SATAY

- ½ cup Asian peanut sauce
- 4 boneless skinless chicken breasts
- ¼ teaspoon salt

CUCUMBER SALAD

- 3 cups thinly sliced peeled seedless cucumbers
- ⅓ cup halved thinly sliced red onion
- 2 tablespoons white vinegar
- 1 teaspoon sugar
- ½ teaspoon salt
- ¼ teaspoon pepper

TOPPINGS

- 2 tablespoons coarsely chopped cocktail peanuts
- 2 tablespoons thinly sliced green onions (2 medium)
- ¾ cup Asian peanut sauce

1) Soak 8 (10-inch) wooden skewers in water 30 minutes. Heat gas or charcoal grill. Place ½ cup peanut sauce in medium bowl; set aside. Cut chicken crosswise into ½-inch thick slices. Thoroughly coat chicken slices with sauce in bowl; sprinkle with ¼ teaspoon salt. Cover and refrigerate 30 minutes.

2) In another medium bowl, stir together the cucumber salad ingredients and set aside.

3) Remove chicken from bowl; discard peanut sauce. On each skewer, thread 4 to 5 chicken slices. Place skewers on grill over medium heat. Cover grill; cook 6 to 8 minutes, turning once, until chicken is no longer pink in center.

4) To serve, divide cucumber salad among 4 serving plates. Top with chicken skewers and toppings.

Nutrition Information Per Serving	
Calories: 430	From Fat: 220
Total Fat	25g
Saturated Fat	5g
Trans Fat	0g
Cholesterol	75mg
Sodium	700mg
Total Carbohydrate	13g
Dietary Fiber	3g
Sugars	7g
Protein	37g

Peanut sauces can be spicy. Check out the ingredients on the label before buying to get an idea of how hot the sauce is.

Chicken and Mushrooms

PREP TIME: 40 MINUTES (READY IN 40 MINUTES)
SERVINGS: 4

1 tablespoon olive oil

4 bone-in chicken thighs
(about 1½ lbs)

Salt and pepper to taste

1 package (8 oz) fresh mushrooms,
sliced

½ teaspoon salt

½ teaspoon pepper

1 package (.81 oz) homestyle gravy
mix

1¼ cups water

Plain mashed potato mix (enough
for 4 servings) and water, milk,
butter and salt called for on potato
mix box

1) In 10-inch nonstick skillet, heat oil over medium-high heat. Add chicken thighs; sprinkle with salt and pepper. Cook about 5 minutes or until browned. Reduce heat to medium; add mushrooms. Cook 8 to 12 minutes, turning occasionally, until mushrooms are tender. Remove chicken and mushrooms from skillet; drain if necessary. Cover to keep warm.

2) To same skillet, add gravy mix and water. Heat to boiling over medium heat, stirring frequently with wire whisk. Stir in cooked chicken and mushrooms. Reduce heat to low; cover and cook 10 to 15 minutes or until sauce is thickened and juice of chicken is clear when thickest part is cut to bone (180°F).

3) Meanwhile, cook potatoes as directed on box. Serve chicken and mushrooms with mashed potatoes.

Nutrition Information Per Serving	
Calories: 440	From Fat: 200
Total Fat	22g
Saturated Fat	8g
Trans Fat	0.5g
Cholesterol	110mg
Sodium	1340mg
Total Carbohydrate	25g
Dietary Fiber	2g
Sugars	2g
Protein	36g

Oregano Chicken Stir-Fry

PREP TIME: 35 MINUTES (READY IN 35 MINUTES)
SERVINGS: 4

2 tablespoons all-purpose flour

½ teaspoon salt

¼ teaspoon pepper

1 lb boneless skinless chicken breasts, cut into 1-inch pieces

2 tablespoons olive oil

1 red onion, cut into wedges (about 1½ cups)

1 yellow bell pepper, seeded and coarsely chopped (about 1¾ cups)

4 oz fresh sugar snap peas (about 1 cup)

2 cloves garlic, finely chopped

½ cup chicken broth

2 tablespoons cider vinegar

1 teaspoon lemon pepper seasoning

2 tablespoons chopped fresh oregano leaves

1) In medium bowl, mix flour, salt and pepper. Add chicken; toss until evenly coated.

2) In 10-inch nonstick skillet, heat 1 tablespoon of the oil over medium-high heat until hot. Cook chicken in oil about 10 minutes, turning occasionally, until brown on outside and no longer pink in center. Remove chicken from skillet and keep warm.

3) In same skillet, heat remaining 1 tablespoon oil until hot. Cook onion, bell pepper and peas in oil about 6 minutes, stirring occasionally, until crisp-tender. Add garlic; cook 30 seconds, stirring constantly. Return chicken to skillet. Stir in broth, vinegar and lemon pepper seasoning. Cook about 1 minute or until hot. Sprinkle with oregano.

tip

If you don't have cider vinegar on hand, try using red wine vinegar, white wine vinegar or even sherry vinegar.

Nutrition Information Per Serving

Calories: 250	From Fat: 100
Total Fat	11g
Saturated Fat	2g
Trans Fat	0g
Cholesterol	70mg
Sodium	580mg
Total Carbohydrate	11g
Dietary Fiber	2g
Sugars	4g
Protein	28g

Sizzling Chicken Fajitas

PREP TIME: 35 MINUTES (READY IN 2 HOURS 35 MINUTES)
SERVINGS: 2

2 teaspoons chili powder

½ teaspoon ground cumin

¼ teaspoon salt

2 cloves garlic, finely chopped

2 tablespoons lime juice

2 boneless skinless chicken breasts, cut into ½-inch strips

1 red or yellow bell pepper, seeded, cut into rings

1 small onion, thinly sliced, separated into rings

4 Old El Paso® flour tortillas for burritos (8 inch from 11-oz package)

1) In medium bowl, mix chili powder, cumin, salt, garlic and lime juice. Add chicken, bell pepper and onion; stir to coat. Cover bowl; refrigerate at least 2 hours to marinate, turning once.

2) Heat gas or charcoal grill. Cut 2 (18x12-inch) sheets of heavy-duty foil. Remove chicken and vegetables from marinade; discard marinade. Place half of chicken and vegetables on center of each sheet. Bring up 2 sides of foil so edges meet. Seal edges, making tight ½-inch fold; fold again, allowing space for heat circulation and expansion. Fold other sides to seal. Cut another sheet of foil; wrap tortillas securely in foil.

3) Place packets on grill over medium heat. Cook chicken and vegetables 10 to 15 minutes or until chicken is no longer pink in center and vegetables are crisp-tender. Cook tortillas 2 to 3 minutes or until warm. Open foil carefully to allow hot steam to escape.

4) Serve each chicken and vegetable packet with 2 tortillas. If desired, top tortillas with shredded lettuce, sour cream, guacamole, shredded cheese and salsa.

5) Oven Directions: Heat oven to 425°F. Marinate chicken and vegetables and prepare packets as directed above; place packets on cookie sheet. Prepare tortilla packet as directed above. Bake chicken and vegetable packets 15 to 20 minutes or until chicken is no longer pink in center and vegetables are crisp-tender. Bake tortillas 3 to 5 minutes or until warm. Serve as directed above.

Nutrition Information Per Serving	
Calories: 450	From Fat: 110
Total Fat	13g
Saturated Fat	3g
Trans Fat	2g
Cholesterol	75mg
Sodium	990mg
Total Carbohydrate	50g
Dietary Fiber	3g
Sugars	5g
Protein	34g

Pepperoni Pizza Chicken

PREP TIME:	10 MINUTES (READY IN 35 MINUTES)	EASY
SERVINGS:	4	

4 boneless skinless chicken breasts

2 oz sliced pepperoni

½ cup shredded mozzarella cheese (about 2 oz)

1 tablespoon olive oil

4 cups water

1 package (7 oz) uncooked elbow macaroni

1 jar (1 lb 8 oz) tomato pasta sauce (any variety)

Chopped fresh basil, if desired

1) Place chicken breasts flat on cutting surface. With knife parallel to cutting surface, cut a lengthwise slit in each chicken breast, forming a pocket, keeping other 3 sides intact. Stuff each chicken breast with pepperoni and mozzarella cheese, pressing the edges of each chicken breast to seal.

2) In 12-inch nonstick skillet, heat oil over medium-high heat. Cook chicken in oil about 9 minutes, turning occasionally, until well browned on both sides. (Chicken pockets will open slightly during cooking.) Remove from skillet and set aside.

3) In same skillet, slowly add water so as not to splatter. Increase heat setting to high. Heat water to boiling. Add macaroni; cook about 3 minutes or until almost tender. Do not drain. Stir in pasta sauce. Heat to boiling. Return chicken to skillet. Reduce heat to medium. Cover and simmer 8 to 10 minutes or until juice of chicken is clear when center of thickest part is cut (170°F). Garnish with basil.

Nutrition Information Per Serving	
Calories: 710	From Fat: 220
Total Fat	24g
Saturated Fat	7g
Trans Fat	0g
Cholesterol	110mg
Sodium	1420mg
Total Carbohydrate	74g
Dietary Fiber	5g
Sugars	18g
Protein	49g

Chutney Pizza with Turkey, Spinach and Gorgonzola

AMY BRNGER | PORTSMOUTH, NEW HAMPSHIRE

BAKE-OFF® CONTEST 43, 2008

PREP TIME: 25 MINUTES (READY IN 40 MINUTES)
SERVINGS: 6

2 tablespoons unsalted or salted butter

2 cloves garlic, finely chopped

1 box (9 oz) Green Giant® frozen chopped spinach, thawed, squeezed to drain

1 can (13.8 oz) Pillsbury® refrigerated classic pizza crust

8 oz uncooked ground turkey breast

¼ teaspoon salt

¼ teaspoon freshly ground pepper

¼ cup mango chutney

¼ cup slivered blanched almonds

1 cup crumbled Gorgonzola cheese (4 oz)

2 green onions, thinly sliced (2 tablespoons)

1) Heat oven to 425°F. Spray 13x9-inch pan with cooking spray.

2) In 10-inch nonstick skillet, melt 1 tablespoon of the butter over low heat. Add garlic; cook, stirring occasionally, until tender. Add spinach. Increase heat to medium; cook 2 to 3 minutes, stirring occasionally, until liquid from the spinach has evaporated and mixture is thoroughly heated. Remove spinach mixture to a bowl.

3) Unroll pizza crust dough in pan; press dough to edges of pan. Bake 7 to 10 minutes or until light golden brown.

4) Meanwhile, add remaining 1 tablespoon butter to skillet; melt over medium heat. Add turkey; cook 4 to 6 minutes, stirring frequently, until no longer pink; drain. Stir in salt and pepper; remove from heat.

5) Cut up large fruit pieces in chutney if necessary. Spread chutney evenly over partially baked crust. Top chutney evenly with turkey and spinach mixture. Sprinkle with almonds and cheese.

6) Bake 10 to 12 minutes longer or until the cheese is melted and crust is golden brown. Immediately sprinkle with onions. To serve, cut with serrated knife.

Nutrition Information Per Serving	
Calories: 450	From Fat: 260
Total Fat	29g
Saturated Fat	7g
Trans Fat	0g
Cholesterol	85mg
Sodium	770mg
Total Carbohydrate	12g
Dietary Fiber	1g
Sugars	1g
Protein	33g

Easy Mexican Chicken Pizza

PREP TIME: 15 MINUTES (READY IN 30 MINUTES)
SERVINGS: 4

 EASY

1 can (13.8 oz) Pillsbury®
refrigerated classic pizza crust

1 cup Old El Paso® Refried Beans,
stirred

½ cup Old El Paso® thick 'n chunky
salsa

1½ cups shredded hot pepper
Monterey Jack cheese (6 oz)

1 package (6 oz) refrigerated
cooked southwestern-flavored
chicken breast strips

¼ cup diced plum (Roma) tomato

Nutrition Information Per Serving	
Calories: 500	From Fat: 140
Total Fat	16g
Saturated Fat	8g
Trans Fat	0g
Cholesterol	65mg
Sodium	1600mg
Total Carbohydrate	61g
Dietary Fiber	4g
Sugars	9g
Protein	30g

1) Heat oven to 425°F. Spray 12- or 14-inch pizza pan with cooking spray.
Unroll dough; place in pan. Starting at center, press out dough to form
12-inch round. Bake about 8 minutes or until crust begins to brown.

2) Spread refried beans evenly over partially baked crust. Spread salsa over
beans. Sprinkle with cheese, chicken and tomato.

3) Bake 9 to 12 minutes longer or until edges of crust are golden brown and
cheese is melted. Cut into wedges to serve.

Arroz con Pollo (Rice with Chicken)

PREP TIME: 45 MINUTES (READY IN 45 MINUTES)
SERVINGS: 4

LOW FAT

1 tablespoon olive or vegetable oil

8 chicken drumsticks (about 2 lb)

1 bag (8 oz) saffron yellow rice

3 cups Progresso® chicken broth
(from 32-oz carton)

1 bag (12 oz) Green Giant® Valley
Fresh Steamers™ frozen mixed
vegetables

Nutrition Information Per Serving	
Calories: 450	From Fat: 70
Total Fat	8g
Saturated Fat	2g
Trans Fat	0g
Cholesterol	95mg
Sodium	740mg
Total Carbohydrate	61g
Dietary Fiber	4g
Sugars	4g
Protein	34g

1) In 12-inch nonstick skillet, heat oil over medium heat. Cook drumsticks in
oil 10 to 15 minutes, turning occasionally, until chicken is well browned on
all sides.

2) Stir in rice, broth and frozen vegetables. Heat to boiling; reduce heat to
medium-low. Cover and cook 25 to 30 minutes, stirring occasionally, until
rice is tender and liquid is absorbed.

Raspberry-Chipotle Barbecue Chicken Pizza

PATRICIA KALB | ALBUQUERQUE, NEW MEXICO

BAKE-OFF® CONTEST 43, 2008

| PREP TIME: | 15 MINUTES (READY IN 35 MINUTES) |
| SERVINGS: | 6 |

🅔 EASY   Ⓕ LOW FAT

1 can (13.8 oz) Pillsbury® refrigerated classic pizza crust

¼ cup red raspberry preserves

¼ cup hickory smoke-flavored barbecue sauce (or other favorite flavor)

2 teaspoons chopped chipotle chiles in adobo sauce (from 7-oz can)

1 package (6 oz) refrigerated grilled chicken breast strips, cubed

½ medium red onion, cut into thin strips

1½ cups shredded mozzarella cheese (6 oz)

¼ cup grated Parmesan cheese

¼ cup chopped fresh cilantro

1) Heat oven to 425°F. Lightly spray 13x9-inch pan with cooking spray. Unroll pizza crust dough in pan; press dough to edges of pan.

2) In small bowl, mix preserves, barbecue sauce and chiles. Spread mixture evenly over dough to within ¼ inch of edges. Top with chicken, onion and cheeses.

3) Bake 12 to 20 minutes or until cheeses are melted and edges are deep golden brown. Sprinkle with cilantro.

Nutrition Information Per Serving

Calories: 370	From Fat: 90
Total Fat	10g
Saturated Fat	5g
Trans Fat	0g
Cholesterol	45mg
Sodium	840mg
Total Carbohydrate	47g
Dietary Fiber	0g
Sugars	15g
Protein	23g

tip

Have extra chiles? Freeze any remaining chipotle chiles with the adobo sauce in small serving-sized containers in the freezer for up to three months.

Harvest Turkey Pot Pie

PREP TIME: 25 MINUTES (READY IN 50 MINUTES)
SERVINGS: 5

1 cup uncooked instant brown rice

1 tablespoon olive or vegetable oil

2 medium stalks celery, sliced
(about 1 cup)

1 large onion, chopped (about 1 cup)

1 large apple, chopped
(about 1½ cups)

3 cups cut-up cooked turkey

1 jar (12 oz) turkey gravy

½ teaspoon salt

½ teaspoon dried sage leaves

1 Pillsbury® refrigerated pie crust,
softened as directed on box

1 can (16 oz) whole berry
cranberry sauce

1) Heat oven to 400°F. Spray 2-quart round casserole with cooking spray. Cook rice as directed on package. Spread rice in bottom and 1 inch up side of casserole.

2) In 12-inch nonstick skillet, heat oil over medium-high heat. Add celery and onion; cook and stir 5 minutes. Stir in apple; cook and stir 3 minutes. Stir in turkey, gravy, salt and sage. Cook and stir about 3 minutes or until thoroughly heated. Spoon turkey mixture over rice in casserole.

3) Unroll pie crust over hot turkey mixture. Fold excess crust under and press to form thick crust edge; flute. Cut slits in several places in crust.

4) Bake about 25 minutes or until crust is golden and filling is bubbly. Serve with cranberry sauce.

Nutrition Information Per Serving	
Calories: 630	From Fat: 180
Total Fat	19g
Saturated Fat	6g
Trans Fat	0g
Cholesterol	75mg
Sodium	900mg
Total Carbohydrate	86g
Dietary Fiber	4g
Sugars	39g
Protein	28g

Summer-Fresh Chicken Tacos

| PREP TIME: | 20 MINUTES (READY IN 40 MINUTES) |
| SERVINGS: | 4 |

 EASY

8 Old El Paso® taco shells

2 tablespoons olive or vegetable oil

1 lb boneless skinless chicken breasts, cut into ¼-inch cubes

1 large onion, chopped (about 1¼ cups)

2 cloves garlic, finely chopped

1 medium jalapeño chili, seeded, finely chopped

½ teaspoon ground cumin

½ teaspoon chili powder

½ teaspoon salt

2 medium tomatoes, chopped (about 1½ cups)

2 cups shredded lettuce

1 cup shredded Cheddar cheese (4 oz)

¼ cup chopped fresh cilantro

1) Heat taco shells as directed on package.

2) Meanwhile, in 10-inch nonstick skillet, heat 1 tablespoon of the oil over medium-high heat until hot. Cook chicken in oil about 6 minutes, stirring occasionally, until no longer pink in center. Remove chicken from skillet, and keep warm.

3) In same skillet, heat remaining 1 tablespoon oil until hot. Cook onion in oil about 4 minutes, stirring occasionally, until tender. Stir in garlic, jalapeño chili, cumin, chili powder and salt. Cook 1 minute, stirring constantly. Return chicken to skillet. Stir in tomatoes. Cook about 2 minutes, stirring occasionally, until hot.

4) To serve, place ¼ cup shredded lettuce in each taco shell; divide chicken mixture among shells. Top with cheese and cilantro.

Nutrition Information Per Serving	
Calories: 460	From Fat: 220
Total Fat	25g
Saturated Fat	9g
Trans Fat	2g
Cholesterol	100mg
Sodium	640mg
Total Carbohydrate	23g
Dietary Fiber	3g
Sugars	5g
Protein	35g

Herbed Chicken Lattice Pot Pie

PREP TIME: 35 MINUTES (READY IN 1 HOUR)
SERVINGS: 6

1 cup uncooked instant white rice

1 cup water

2 tablespoons olive oil

1¼ lb boneless skinless chicken breasts, cut into ¾-inch pieces

1 large red bell pepper, chopped (about 1½ cups)

1 large onion, chopped (about 1 cup)

1 medium zucchini, chopped (about 1 cup)

2 tablespoons savory herb with garlic soup mix (from packet in 2.4-oz box)

¾ cup milk

1 can (8 oz) Pillsbury® Crescent Recipe Creations™ refrigerated seamless dough sheet

1) Heat oven to 375°F. Spray 9-inch glass pie plate with cooking spray. Cook rice in water as directed on package. Pat cooked rice evenly in bottom of pie plate. In 12-inch nonstick skillet, heat 1 tablespoon of the oil over medium-high heat. Add chicken; cook and stir until no longer pink in center. Remove chicken from skillet.

2) Heat remaining 1 tablespoon oil in skillet. Add bell pepper, onion and zucchini; cook and stir until crisp-tender. In small bowl, mix soup mix and milk; stir into vegetable mixture. Heat to boiling over high heat. Remove from heat; stir in chicken (discard chicken juices). Spoon over rice in pie plate.

3) Unroll dough on work surface; cut lengthwise into 8 strips. Arrange 4 strips evenly in same direction over filling. Top with remaining strips in opposite direction. Fold overhanging ends of strips at an angle around edge of pie plate to form rim.

4) Bake about 20 minutes. Let stand 5 minutes before serving.

Nutrition Information Per Serving	
Calories: 390	From Fat: 130
Total Fat	15g
Saturated Fat	4.5g
Trans Fat	0g
Cholesterol	60mg
Sodium	570mg
Total Carbohydrate	38g
Dietary Fiber	2g
Sugars	7g
Protein	26g

Greek Garlic and Herb-Stuffed Chicken Breasts

PREP TIME: 30 MINUTES (READY IN 30 MINUTES)
SERVINGS: 4

 EASY

1 container (4 oz) garlic-and-herbs spreadable cheese

⅓ cup coarsely chopped kalamata olives, patted dry

⅓ cup finely chopped green onions

1½ teaspoons chopped fresh oregano leaves

4 boneless skinless chicken breasts

1 tablespoon olive oil

¼ teaspoon salt

¼ teaspoon pepper

Nutrition Information Per Serving	
Calories: 290	From Fat: 170
Total Fat	18g
Saturated Fat	8g
Trans Fat	0g
Cholesterol	105mg
Sodium	400mg
Total Carbohydrate	2g
Dietary Fiber	0g
Sugars	0g
Protein	29g

1) Heat gas or charcoal grill. In medium bowl, stir together cheese, olives, onions and oregano. Place chicken breasts flat on cutting surface. Cut a lengthwise slit in each chicken breast forming a pocket, keeping other 3 sides intact. Stuff each chicken with cheese mixture; secure with toothpicks. Brush chicken with oil; sprinkle with salt and pepper.

2) Place chicken on grill over medium heat. Cover grill; cook 8 to 10 minutes, turning occasionally, until juice of chicken is clear when center of thickest part is cut (170°F).

White Chicken Pizza with Caramelized Sweet Onions

PREP TIME: 30 MINUTES (READY IN 45 MINUTES)
SERVINGS: 4

2 tablespoons butter or margarine

3 cups halved thinly sliced sweet onions

1 teaspoon sugar

1 teaspoon fresh thyme leaves

2 oz cream cheese

1 package (14 oz) prebaked original Italian pizza crust (12 inch)

⅓ cup refrigerated Alfredo pasta sauce (from 10-oz container)

1 cup shredded deli rotisserie chicken (from 2- to 2½-lb chicken)

Nutrition Information Per Serving	
Calories: 570	From Fat: 260
Total Fat	28g
Saturated Fat	13g
Trans Fat	1g
Cholesterol	80mg
Sodium	770mg
Total Carbohydrate	59g
Dietary Fiber	4g
Sugars	6g
Protein	19g

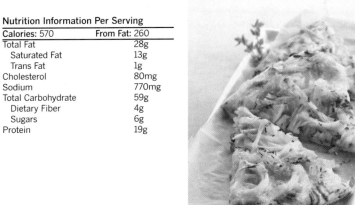

1) In 10-inch skillet, melt butter over medium heat. Cook onions and sugar in butter 20 to 25 minutes, stirring frequently, until deep golden brown and caramelized; stir in thyme leaves.

2) Heat gas or charcoal grill. Spread cream cheese evenly over pizza crust. Top with Alfredo sauce, shredded chicken and onions. Place on grill over medium-low heat. Cover grill; cook 8 to 10 minutes or until hot.

Make-Ahead White Chicken Lasagna

PREP TIME: 40 MINUTES (READY IN 10 HOURS 15 MINUTES)
SERVINGS: 12

1 tablespoon butter or margarine

1 lb boneless skinless chicken breasts, cut into ½-inch pieces

1½ cups coarsely chopped red bell pepper (2 medium)

1 cup finely chopped celery

½ cup chopped onion

2 cloves garlic, finely chopped

1 pint (2 cups) half-and-half

½ cup Progresso® chicken broth

4 oz cream cheese

7 oz Gouda cheese, shredded (about 2 cups)

1 container (12 oz) small-curd cottage cheese

¼ cup fresh basil leaves, cut into thin strips

1 egg, beaten

9 uncooked lasagna noodles

1 package (16 oz) sliced mozzarella cheese

½ cup grated Parmesan cheese

Fresh basil sprigs or chopped basil leaves, if desired

1) Spray 13x9-inch (3-quart) glass baking dish with cooking spray. In 4-quart Dutch oven, melt butter over medium-high heat. Add chicken; cook 3 minutes, stirring occasionally. Stir in bell pepper, celery, onion and garlic; cook about 2 minutes, stirring occasionally, until chicken is no longer pink in center.

2) Reduce heat to low. Add half-and-half, broth and cream cheese; cook and stir until cream cheese is melted. Gradually add Gouda cheese, stirring until cheese is melted. Remove from heat; set aside. In bowl, mix cottage cheese, 1/4 cup fresh basil and the egg until blended.

3) Spread 1 cup chicken mixture in baking dish. Top with 3 noodles, 1½ cups chicken mixture, ½ of the cottage cheese mixture and ½ of the mozzarella cheese. Repeat layers once, starting with noodles. Top with remaining 3 noodles and remaining chicken mixture. Sprinkle with Parmesan cheese. Cover with foil; refrigerate at least 8 hours or overnight.

4) Heat oven to 350°F. Bake lasagna covered 45 minutes. Uncover; bake 30 to 35 minutes longer or until noodles are tender and casserole is bubbly. Cover; let stand 15 minutes before serving. Garnish with fresh basil sprigs.

Nutrition Information Per Serving	
Calories: 440	From Fat: 230
Total Fat	26g
Saturated Fat	15g
Trans Fat	.5g
Cholesterol	115mg
Sodium	640mg
Total Carbohydrate	20g
Dietary Fiber	1g
Sugars	5g
Protein	33g

Pineapple-Chicken Kabob Packets

PREP TIME: 20 MINUTES (READY IN 40 MINUTES)
SERVINGS: 4

 EASY   LOW FAT

⅓ cup pineapple preserves

2 tablespoons packed brown sugar

1 tablespoon soy sauce

¼ teaspoon crushed red pepper

4 boneless skinless chicken breasts, cut into 2-inch cubes (1 lb)

1 medium red bell pepper, cut into 1½-inch cubes

1 medium green bell pepper, cut into 1½-inch cubes

1 cup pineapple chunks

¼ teaspoon salt

1) Heat gas or charcoal grill. In small bowl, stir together pineapple preserves, brown sugar, soy sauce and crushed red pepper.

2) Cut 4 (24x12-inch) sheets of heavy-duty foil. Divide chicken, bell peppers, pineapple chunks and pineapple preserves mixture among foil sheets. Sprinkle with salt. Bring up 2 sides of foil so edges meet. Seal the edges, making a tight ½-inch fold, then fold again, allowing space for heat circulation and expansion. Fold the other sides to seal.

3) Place packets on grill over medium heat. Cover grill; cook 6 minutes. Using tongs, carefully turn packets over, taking care not to puncture foil. Cook 10 to 12 minutes longer or until chicken is no longer pink in center and vegetables are crisp-tender.

Nutrition Information Per Serving	
Calories: 300	From Fat: 35
Total Fat	4g
Saturated Fat	1g
Trans Fat	0g
Cholesterol	70mg
Sodium	450mg
Total Carbohydrate	38g
Dietary Fiber	2g
Sugars	31g
Protein	26g

Chicken Taco Stew in Bread Bowls

PREP TIME: 35 MINUTES (READY IN 35 MINUTES)
SERVINGS: 3

1 can (11 oz) Pillsbury® refrigerated crusty French loaf

1 package (6 oz) refrigerated cooked Southwest-flavor chicken breast strips, coarsely chopped

1 can (15 oz) Progresso® dark red kidney beans, drained, rinsed

1 can (10 oz) diced tomatoes and green chiles, undrained

1 cup Green Giant® Valley Fresh Steamers™ Niblets® frozen corn

1 cup Progresso® chicken broth (from 32-oz carton)

1 tablespoon cornstarch

½ cup shredded Cheddar cheese (2 oz)

1) Heat oven to 350°F. Spray cookie sheet with cooking spray. Cut dough into 3 equal pieces. Shape each into a ball, placing seam at bottom so dough is smooth on top. Place dough balls, seam sides down, on cookie sheet.

2) Bake 18 to 22 minutes or until golden brown. Cool 5 minutes.

3) Meanwhile, in 2-quart saucepan, mix remaining ingredients except cheese. Cook over medium heat, stirring occasionally, until mixture boils and thickens.

4) Cut top off each bread loaf. Lightly press center of bread down to form bowls. Place each bread bowl in individual shallow soup plate. Spoon about 1 cup stew into each bread bowl. Sprinkle with cheese. Place top of each bread bowl next to filled bowl.

Nutrition Information Per Serving	
Calories: 620	From Fat: 110
Total Fat	12g
Saturated Fat	6g
Trans Fat	0g
Cholesterol	45mg
Sodium	1400mg
Total Carbohydrate	90g
Dietary Fiber	9g
Sugars	10g
Protein	36g

Balsamic-Glazed Chicken Breasts

PREP TIME:	35 MINUTES (READY IN 35 MINUTES)	🄵 LOW FAT
SERVINGS:	4	

GLAZE

⅓ cup packed brown sugar

⅓ cup balsamic vinegar

1 teaspoon chopped fresh rosemary leaves

1 teaspoon finely chopped garlic

CHICKEN

4 bone-in skin-on chicken breasts (8 oz each)

½ teaspoon salt

¼ teaspoon pepper

Nutrition Information Per Serving

Calories: 310	From Fat: 80
Total Fat	9g
Saturated Fat	2.5g
Trans Fat	0g
Cholesterol	95mg
Sodium	380mg
Total Carbohydrate	22g
Dietary Fiber	0g
Sugars	21g
Protein	34g

1) Heat gas or charcoal grill. In a small bowl, combine the glaze ingredients and set aside.

2) Sprinkle chicken with salt and pepper. Place chicken on grill, skin side down, over medium heat. Cook 10 minutes. Turn chicken; brush half the glaze evenly over chicken. Continue cooking and brushing with remaining glaze 10 to 12 minutes longer or until juice of chicken is clear when thickest part is cut to bone (170°F).

Lime Chicken

PREP TIME:	10 MINUTES (READY IN 1 HOUR 5 MINUTES)	🄴 EASY
SERVINGS:	4	

1 whole chicken (3 to 3½ lb)

1 teaspoon salt

1 teaspoon ground cumin

½ teaspoon pepper

1 teaspoon garlic powder

¼ cup frozen limeade concentrate (from 12-oz can), thawed

Nutrition Information Per Serving

Calories: 560	From Fat: 270
Total Fat	30g
Saturated Fat	8g
Trans Fat	1g
Cholesterol	195mg
Sodium	770mg
Total Carbohydrate	12g
Dietary Fiber	0g
Sugars	8g
Protein	60g

1) Heat gas or charcoal grill. Remove backbone from chicken; discard. Firmly press whole chicken to flatten. Cut two ½-inch slits through each breast about 1 inch from tip; tuck legs into slits. Fold each wing back behind the neck area.

2) In small bowl, mix salt, cumin, pepper and garlic powder. Rub mixture all over outside of chicken. Place chicken in 13x9-inch disposable foil pan, breast side up. Place pan of chicken on grill over medium-low heat. Cover grill; cook chicken 20 minutes. Turn chicken over; insert ovenproof meat thermometer so tip is in thickest part of inside thigh and does not touch bone. Cook 10 to 15 minutes longer, brushing with limeade last 5 minutes of cook time, until thermometer reads 180°F and legs move easily when lifted or twisted.

3) Remove chicken from grill; cover with foil. Let stand 10 to 15 minutes before serving.

Pork, Seafood & More

For a change of pace, try these entrees
made with fish, pork or meatless ingredients.

CHORIZO AND RICE STEW
PG. 187

ZESTY LIME-FISH TACOS
PG. 182

FOUR CHEESE-VEGGIE LASAGNA
CUPS
PG. 192

NOT-YOUR-MOTHER'S
TUNA POT PIE
PG. 181

Balsamic Roasted Tomato-Spinach-Bacon Pie

ALLISON FOLEY | GREENWICH, CONNECTICUT

BAKE-OFF® CONTEST 44, 2010

PREP TIME: 35 MINUTES (READY IN 1 HOUR 20 MINUTES)
SERVINGS: 8

1 Pillsbury® refrigerated pie crust, softened as directed on box

9 medium plum (Roma) tomatoes, halved lengthwise, seeded

2 cloves garlic, finely chopped

½ teaspoon Italian seasoning

⅛ teaspoon salt

⅛ teaspoon black pepper

2 tablespoons balsamic vinegar

2 tablespoons Crisco® 100% extra virgin olive oil or pure olive oil

3 Eggland's Best eggs

½ cup mascarpone cheese (4 oz), softened

1 box (9 oz) Green Giant® frozen chopped spinach, thawed, squeezed to drain

1 cup grated Parmesan cheese

2 or 3 dashes ground red pepper (cayenne), if desired

¼ teaspoon salt

½ teaspoon black pepper

6 slices bacon, cooked, crumbled

1) Heat oven to 425°F. Place pie crust in 9-inch glass pie plate as directed on box for one-crust filled pie; flute edge. Bake 6 to 8 minutes or until just beginning to brown. Remove from oven.

2) Line 15x10-inch pan (with sides) with foil. Arrange tomatoes, cut sides up, in single layer in pan. Sprinkle tomatoes with garlic, Italian seasoning and 1/8 teaspoon each salt and black pepper. Drizzle with vinegar and oil. Roast 25 to 30 minutes or until tomatoes are very tender. Remove from oven; reduce oven temperature to 375°F.

3) Meanwhile, in medium bowl, beat eggs with wire whisk. Add mascarpone cheese; beat until well blended. Stir in spinach, ½ cup of the Parmesan cheese, red pepper, ¼ teaspoon salt and ½ teaspoon black pepper. Spread mixture evenly in partially baked crust.

4) Arrange tomatoes, overlapping slightly, in single layer on spinach mixture. Sprinkle with remaining ½ cup Parmesan cheese and bacon.

5) Bake at 375°F 25 to 35 minutes, covering edge of crust with strips of foil after 10 to 15 minutes, until the filling is set in center and crust is golden brown. Let stand 10 minutes before serving.

Nutrition Information Per Serving	
Calories: 300	From Fat: 180
Total Fat	20g
Saturated Fat	8g
Trans Fat	0g
Cholesterol	95mg
Sodium	630mg
Total Carbohydrate	17g
Dietary Fiber	1g
Sugars	2g
Protein	11g

Rice and Bean Burrito Pot Pie

PREP TIME: 20 MINUTES (READY IN 1 HOUR 10 MINUTES)
SERVINGS: 6

 EASY

1 tablespoon olive or vegetable oil

1 large onion, chopped (about 1 cup)

2 cloves garlic, finely chopped

1 jalapeño chile, seeded, finely chopped

2 large tomatoes, chopped (about 2 cups)

2 cans (15 oz each) Spanish rice with bell peppers and onions

1 cup shredded Monterey Jack cheese (4 oz)

1 can (15 oz) pinto beans, drained, rinsed

1 can (11 oz) Pillsbury® refrigerated original breadsticks (12 breadsticks)

½ cup sour cream

1) Heat oven to 375°F. Spray 2-quart oval casserole or 11x7-inch (2-quart) glass baking dish with cooking spray. In 10-inch nonstick skillet, heat oil over medium-high heat. Add onion; cook about 5 minutes, stirring occasionally, until golden brown. Stir in garlic and chile; cook 1 minute, stirring constantly. Stir in tomatoes; cook until thoroughly heated. Remove from heat.

2) In medium bowl, mix rice and cheese; spread in bottom and ½ inch up side of casserole. Spread beans evenly over rice mixture. Top with the tomato mixture.

3) Bake uncovered 20 minutes. Remove casserole from oven. Unroll dough; separate into 12 strips. Twist 10 strips; carefully arrange crosswise in single layer over rice and bean mixture. Stretch and twist remaining 2 strips; place lengthwise across other strips of dough.

4) Bake uncovered 20 to 25 minutes longer or until breadsticks are golden brown. Let stand 5 minutes before serving. Serve with sour cream.

Nutrition Information Per Serving	
Calories: 480	From Fat: 140
Total Fat	15g
Saturated Fat	8g
Trans Fat	0g
Cholesterol	30mg
Sodium	730mg
Total Carbohydrate	68g
Dietary Fiber	7g
Sugars	11g
Protein	17g

Chorizo and Pasta

PREP TIME: 25 MINUTES (READY IN 25 MINUTES)
SERVINGS: 5

 EASY

1 lb bulk pork chorizo sausage

1 medium onion, finely chopped (½ cup)

1 can (14.5 oz) organic diced tomatoes with garlic and onion, undrained

1¾ cups Progresso® chicken broth (from 32-oz carton)

5 cups uncooked dumpling egg noodles or wide egg noodles (8 oz)

½ cup water

Nutrition Information Per Serving	
Calories: 600	From Fat: 330
Total Fat	37g
Saturated Fat	14g
Trans Fat	0g
Cholesterol	115mg
Sodium	1560mg
Total Carbohydrate	37g
Dietary Fiber	2g
Sugars	4g
Protein	29g

1) In 12-inch nonstick skillet, cook chorizo and onion over medium-high heat 8 to 10 minutes, stirring frequently, until chorizo is no longer pink and onion is tender.

2) Stir in remaining ingredients. Increase heat to high; heat to boiling. Reduce heat to medium; cover and cook 10 to 15 minutes, stirring occasionally, until noodles are tender and mixture is desired consistency.

Barbecue Pork and Veggie Pizza

PREP TIME: 10 MINUTES (READY IN 35 MINUTES)
SERVINGS: 4

 EASY

1 can (13.8 oz) Pillsbury® refrigerated classic pizza crust or Pillsbury® refrigerated thin pizza crust

1 container (18 oz) refrigerated original barbecue sauce with shredded pork

1½ cups shredded Monterey Jack cheese (6 oz)

½ medium red onion, cut in thin wedges

1 medium green bell pepper, cut into thin bite-size strips

Nutrition Information Per Serving	
Calories: 610	From Fat: 180
Total Fat	20g
Saturated Fat	10g
Trans Fat	0g
Cholesterol	70mg
Sodium	1790mg
Total Carbohydrate	74g
Dietary Fiber	0g
Sugars	28g
Protein	32g

1) Heat oven to 425°F. Spray 12-inch pizza pan with cooking spray. Unroll dough in pan; starting at center, press out dough to edge of pan to form crust. Bake 7 to 9 minutes or until light golden brown.

2) Spoon barbecue sauce with pork over crust. Top with cheese, onion and bell pepper.

3) Bake 10 to 12 minutes longer or until crust is golden brown and cheese is melted.

Spicy Double-Mozzarella Pancetta Pizza

BEE ENGELHART | BLOOMFIELD HILLS, MICHIGAN

PREP TIME: 20 MINUTES (READY IN 35 MINUTES)
SERVINGS: 8

e EASY

1 tablespoon olive oil

2 tablespoons cornmeal

1 can (13.8 oz) Pillsbury® refrigerated classic pizza crust

2 tablespoons grated Asiago cheese

2 tablespoons sesame seed

1 teaspoon garlic powder

1 teaspoon Italian seasoning

½ teaspoon crushed red pepper flakes

8 oz fresh mozzarella cheese, cut into ¼-inch cubes

2 cups shredded mozzarella cheese (8 oz)

¼ cup chopped dry-pack sun-dried tomatoes

4 oz thinly sliced pancetta or smoked ham, chopped (about ½ cup)

1) Heat oven to 425°F. Brush oil on bottom and sides of 15x10x1-inch pan. Sprinkle cornmeal over bottom of pan. Unroll pizza crust dough in pan; press dough to edges of pan.

2) Bake 6 to 8 minutes or until light golden brown. Meanwhile, in small bowl, mix Asiago cheese, sesame seed, garlic powder, Italian seasoning and red pepper flakes.

3) Sprinkle remaining ingredients in order listed over partially baked crust. Sprinkle seasoning blend over toppings.

4) Bake 7 to 11 minutes longer or until the cheese is melted and the crust is golden brown.

Nutrition Information Per Serving	
Calories: 370	From Fat: 170
Total Fat	18g
Saturated Fat	9g
Trans Fat	0g
Cholesterol	40mg
Sodium	890mg
Total Carbohydrate	29g
Dietary Fiber	0g
Sugars	4g
Protein	23g

Veggie-Bacon Squares

PREP TIME: 45 MINUTES (READY IN 1 HOUR 15 MINUTES)
SERVINGS: 6

8 slices thick-sliced bacon, cut into
  1-inch pieces

1 cup whipping cream

2 tablespoons butter, cut into small
  pieces

½ package (3-oz size) cream cheese,
  cut into pieces

¾ cup grated Parmesan cheese

1¼ teaspoons garlic powder

1 can (11 oz) Pillsbury® refrigerated
  thin pizza crust

2 small zucchini (8 oz), cut into
  julienne pieces (1½ x ¼ x ¼ inch)

1 small yellow summer squash
  (4 oz), cut into julienne pieces
  (1½ x ¼ x ¼ inch)

2 cups sliced fresh mushrooms

⅛ teaspoon freshly ground pepper

1 cup halved grape tomatoes

½ cup shredded mozzarella cheese
  (2 oz)

1) Heat oven to 400°F. In skillet, cook bacon over medium heat, stirring occasionally, until crisp. Remove bacon; drain on paper towels. Reserve 3 tablespoons bacon drippings in small bowl; set aside. Discard remaining drippings; wipe skillet clean and set aside.

2) In 1-quart saucepan, mix 2 tablespoons of reserved drippings, the whipping cream, butter and cream cheese. Cook over medium-low heat, stirring frequently with wire whisk, until melted and blended. Stir in Parmesan cheese and 1 teaspoon of the garlic powder until well blended. Keep warm over low heat.

3) Spray 11x7-inch (2-quart) glass baking dish with cooking spray. Unroll dough in baking dish; press in bottom and up sides of dish. Bake 5 minutes. Meanwhile, in reserved skillet, add remaining 1 tablespoon bacon drippings, the zucchini, yellow squash, mushrooms, pepper and remaining ¼ teaspoon garlic powder; toss to coat with drippings. Cook and stir over medium-high heat 3 to 5 minutes or until vegetables are crisp-tender. Stir in bacon.

4) Using slotted spoon, spoon zucchini mixture evenly onto partially baked crust. Pour sauce over vegetables. Top with tomato halves and mozzarella cheese.

5) Bake 16 to 20 minutes or until crust is evenly browned and cheese is melted. Let stand 10 minutes before serving.

Nutrition Information Per Serving	
Calories: 550	From Fat: 310
Total Fat	34g
Saturated Fat	18g
Trans Fat	1g
Cholesterol	100mg
Sodium	1210mg
Total Carbohydrate	38g
Dietary Fiber	2g
Sugars	8g
Protein	22g

Not-Your-Mother's Tuna Pot Pie

PREP TIME: 25 MINUTES (READY IN 50 MINUTES)
SERVINGS: 5

1 cup uncooked ditalini (short tubes) pasta

4 slices bacon

1 large onion, chopped (about 1 cup)

1 teaspoon dried thyme leaves

2 tablespoons all-purpose flour

1 cup Progresso® chicken broth (from 32-oz carton)

⅔ cup milk

2 cups frozen crinkle-cut carrots, thawed, well drained

1 can (12 oz) solid white tuna in water, drained, flaked

1 can (7 oz) Green Giant® Niblets® whole kernel corn, drained

2 tablespoons Dijon mustard

2 slices white bread

2 tablespoons butter or margarine, melted

1) Heat oven to 375°F. Cook pasta as directed on package, using minimum cook time; drain. In 12-inch nonstick skillet, cook bacon over medium-high heat until crisp. Reserving drippings in skillet, remove bacon to drain on paper towels. Crumble bacon; set aside.

2) Add onion and thyme to drippings; cook over medium-high heat, stirring occasionally, until onion is golden brown. Stir in flour; cook 1 minute, stirring constantly. Stir in broth and milk; heat to boiling. Boil, stirring constantly, until thickened. Stir in carrots, tuna, corn, pasta and mustard; heat to boiling. Fold in bacon. Spoon into ungreased 2-quart casserole.

3) In food processor, place bread. Cover; process with on-and-off pulses several times to make bread crumbs. In small bowl, mix bread crumbs and butter. Sprinkle over tuna mixture.

4) Bake uncovered 20 to 25 minutes or until mixture is bubbly and topping is golden brown.

Nutrition Information Per Serving	
Calories: 380	From Fat: 100
Total Fat	11g
Saturated Fat	5g
Trans Fat	0g
Cholesterol	40mg
Sodium	940mg
Total Carbohydrate	43g
Dietary Fiber	4g
Sugars	7g
Protein	27g

Zesty Lime-Fish Tacos

KELLIE WHITE | ST. LOUIS, MISSOURI

BAKE-OFF® CONTEST 44, 2010

PREP TIME: 40 MINUTES (READY IN 40 MINUTES)
SERVINGS: 8

1 lb tilapia fillets (about 4)

½ cup fresh lime juice (2 to 3 limes)

3 cloves garlic, finely chopped

¼ cup Pillsbury Best® all-purpose flour

¼ cup yellow cornmeal

1 can (16.3 oz) Pillsbury® Grands!® homestyle refrigerated buttermilk biscuits (8 biscuits)

6 tablespoons Crisco® pure canola oil

1½ tablespoons chipotle chiles in adobo sauce (from 7-oz can), finely chopped

½ teaspoon salt

¼ teaspoon pepper

½ cup salsa

½ cup sour cream

1½ cups shredded cabbage

Lime wedges if desired

1) Heat oven to 200°F. Cut each fish fillet lengthwise into 4 strips. In shallow glass dish, mix 7 tablespoons of the lime juice and garlic. Add fish; turn to coat. Let stand while preparing biscuits.

2) On work surface, mix flour and cornmeal. Separate dough into 8 biscuits. Press both sides of each biscuit into flour mixture, then press or roll into 6- to 7-inch round.

3) In 12-inch nonstick skillet, heat 1½ tablespoons of the oil over medium heat. Add 2 biscuit rounds; cook about 1 minute on each side or until golden brown and cooked through. Place on cookie sheet; keep warm in oven. Cook remaining rounds, adding 1½ tablespoons oil to skillet for each batch. Wipe skillet clean.

4) Heat same skillet over medium-high heat. Add fish and lime juice mixture, chiles, salt and pepper; cook about 5 minutes, turning fish once, until fish flakes easily with fork.

5) In small bowl, mix the salsa, sour cream and remaining 1 tablespoon of lime juice.

6) Using slotted spoon, remove fish and divide evenly among biscuit rounds. Top each with cabbage and 1 to 2 tablespoons salsa mixture. Fold biscuit rounds in half over filling. Serve with any remaining salsa mixture. Garnish with lime wedges, if desired.

Nutrition Information Per Serving	
Calories: 400	From Fat: 200
Total Fat	22g
Saturated Fat	4.5g
Trans Fat	2g
Cholesterol	40mg
Sodium	860mg
Total Carbohydrate	35g
Dietary Fiber	1g
Sugars	6g
Protein	15g

Asian Vegetable Stir-Fry

PREP TIME:	25 MINUTES (READY IN 25 MINUTES)
SERVINGS:	4

e EASY   **lf** LOW FAT

1 tablespoon olive oil

1 medium onion, chopped (½ cup)

1 medium carrot, sliced (½ cup)

2 cloves garlic, finely chopped

2 cups uncooked instant white rice

2 cups water

1 package (8 oz) sliced fresh mushrooms (3 cups)

1 bag (12 oz) Green Giant® Valley Fresh Steamers™ frozen Asian style medley vegetables in sauce

½ cup stir-fry sauce

⅛ teaspoon red pepper flakes

1) In 12-inch skillet, heat oil over medium heat. Cook onion, carrot and garlic in oil 5 to 7 minutes, stirring occasionally, until slightly tender.

2) Cook rice in water as directed on package; cover to keep warm.

3) Into mixture in skillet, stir mushrooms, frozen vegetables in sauce, stir-fry sauce and pepper flakes; cook 5 to 7 minutes, stirring occasionally, until vegetables are tender. Serve over rice.

Nutrition Information Per Serving	
Calories: 330	From Fat: 50
Total Fat	6g
Saturated Fat	1g
Trans Fat	0g
Cholesterol	0mg
Sodium	1160mg
Total Carbohydrate	62g
Dietary Fiber	4g
Sugars	12g
Protein	7g

This is a good recipe for using up any leftover vegetables you have in your refrigerator, such as celery, broccoli or green bell pepper. Just cut them up and add with the onion and carrots.

Butternut Squash-Pesto Pizza

KAREN STUBER | FULTON, NEW YORK

 BAKE-OFF® CONTEST 44, 2010

PREP TIME: 35 MINUTES (READY IN 50 MINUTES)
SERVINGS: 8

2½ cups diced peeled butternut squash

½ cup chopped onion (about 1 small)

1 tablespoon packed brown sugar

1 teaspoon sea salt or kosher salt

½ teaspoon black pepper

2 tablespoons Crisco® 100% extra virgin olive oil or pure olive oil

1 can (13.8 oz) Pillsbury® refrigerated classic pizza crust

4 oz pancetta, diced

3 tablespoons basil pesto

½ cup chopped drained roasted red bell peppers (from 7-oz jar)

⅓ cup Fisher® Chef's Naturals® chopped walnuts

1 cup shredded Asiago cheese (4 oz)

½ cup crumbled feta cheese (2 oz)

1) Heat oven to 400°F. In medium bowl, mix squash, onion, brown sugar, salt, black pepper and 1½ tablespoons of the oil. Spread mixture in ungreased 13x9-inch (3-quart) glass baking dish. Bake about 20 minutes, stirring occasionally, until squash is tender.

2) Spray large cookie sheet with Crisco® original no-stick cooking spray. Unroll pizza crust dough on cookie sheet into 13x9-inch rectangle. Bake at 400°F for 7 to 10 minutes or until light golden brown.

3) Meanwhile, in 10-inch skillet, heat remaining ½ tablespoon oil over medium heat. Add pancetta; cook 4 minutes, stirring frequently, until lightly browned. Drain.

4) Spread pesto over partially baked crust. Top with squash mixture, pancetta, roasted peppers, walnuts and cheeses. Bake 6 to 8 minutes longer or until the edges are golden brown. Let pizza stand 5 minutes before serving.

Nutrition Information Per Serving	
Calories: 360	From Fat: 180
Total Fat	20g
Saturated Fat	7g
Trans Fat	0g
Cholesterol	30mg
Sodium	1070mg
Total Carbohydrate	33g
Dietary Fiber	2g
Sugars	8g
Protein	12g

Family-Style Paella

1 tablespoon olive oil

1 cup coarsely chopped onions (1 large)

1 cup coarsely chopped green bell pepper (1 medium)

1 lb boneless skinless chicken breasts, cut into 1-inch pieces

½ lb smoked chorizo sausage, cut into ½-inch slices

1 cup uncooked regular long-grain white rice

½ teaspoon salt

½ teaspoon ground turmeric

2 cups chicken broth

½ lb uncooked deveined peeled medium shrimp, tail shells removed

1 cup Green Giant Select® Valley Fresh Steamers™ frozen sweet peas

1 can (14.5 oz) Italian-style stewed tomatoes, undrained

1) In 12-inch nonstick skillet or Dutch oven, heat oil over medium-high heat until hot. Add onions and bell pepper; cook and stir 2 minutes. Add chicken and sausage; cook 8 to 10 minutes, stirring frequently, until chicken and sausage are no longer pink in center.

2) Add rice, salt, turmeric and broth; mix well. Heat to boiling. Reduce heat to medium-low. Cover; cook 20 minutes, stirring occasionally.

3) Add shrimp, peas and tomatoes; stir gently to mix. Cover; cook 8 to 12 minutes longer, stirring occasionally, until shrimp turn pink and liquid is absorbed.

Nutrition Information Per Serving

Calories: 490	From Fat: 180
Total Fat	20g
Saturated Fat	7g
Trans Fat	0g
Cholesterol	135mg
Sodium	1320mg
Total Carbohydrate	39g
Dietary Fiber	2g
Sugars	6g
Protein	38g

Just-in-Time Pork Stew

PREP TIME: 1 HOUR (READY IN 1 HOUR)
SERVINGS: 4 (1-1/2 CUPS EACH)

- 2 cartons (32 oz each) Progresso® reduced-sodium chicken broth (8 cups)
- 1 lb pork tenderloin, trimmed of fat
  Freshly ground pepper
- 4 tablespoons olive oil
- 3 tablespoons all-purpose flour
- 1 cup pearl onions
- 1 cup ½-inch chunks carrots (about 2 medium)
- 1 cup ½-inch chunks peeled turnips (about 6 oz)
- 2 teaspoons fennel seed
- 1 tablespoon unsalted butter
- 1 cup dry red wine
- 1 teaspoon finely chopped fresh rosemary leaves
- 2 cups packed chard leaves, torn or cut into 1-inch pieces
- 1 can (19 oz) Progresso® cannellini beans

1) In 4-quart Dutch oven, cook broth over high heat, about 30 minutes, until reduced by half (about 4 cups). Remove from heat.

2) Meanwhile, cut pork into 1-inch pieces. Season well with pepper. In 12-inch skillet, heat 2 tablespoons of the oil over medium-high heat. Coat pork with 2 tablespoons of the flour; add to skillet, separating so pieces do not touch. Cook 2 minutes (do not move pork pieces until moisture begins to show on tops and pork has browned on one side). Turn pork; brown about 2 minutes longer. Remove pork from skillet to large plate.

3) Return skillet to medium-high heat; add remaining 2 tablespoons oil, the onions, carrots, turnips and fennel. Cook about 10 minutes, stirring occasionally, until vegetables are lightly browned (watch so vegetables do not burn). Add butter; cook 2 minutes longer.

4) Sprinkle remaining tablespoon flour over vegetables in skillet; cook and stir over medium heat 1 minute. Increase the heat to high. Stir in wine; heat to boiling. Cook until wine is reduced by half.

5) Stir in reduced broth; heat to boiling. Reduce heat to low; simmer uncovered 8 minutes. Stir in rosemary and simmer 2 minutes longer. Return pork to skillet. Stir in chard and beans. Cook until thoroughly heated.

Nutrition Information Per Serving	
Calories: 540	From Fat: 190
Total Fat	22g
Saturated Fat	5g
Trans Fat	0g
Cholesterol	55mg
Sodium	1570mg
Total Carbohydrate	43g
Dietary Fiber	9g
Sugars	8g
Protein	40g

tip

Hollow out a 1-lb loaf of crusty bread to use as a serving container. You can also serve the stew over white or brown rice, noodles or soft polenta flavored with roasted winter squash puree.

Grilled Crisp-Crust Pizzas

PREP TIME:	20 MINUTES (READY IN 20 MINUTES)	EASY
SERVINGS:	4 PIZZAS	

4 Old El Paso® flour tortillas (8 inches in diameter)

2 teaspoons olive oil

1½ cups finely shredded Cheddar-Monterey Jack cheese blend (6 oz)

½ cup sliced pimiento-stuffed green olives

½ cup diced tomato, well drained

24 (1-inch) slices pepperoni

1 teaspoon dried oregano leaves

Nutrition Information Per Serving

Calories: 500	From Fat: 310
Total Fat	34g
Saturated Fat	15g
Trans Fat	1g
Cholesterol	75mg
Sodium	1310mg
Total Carbohydrate	27g
Dietary Fiber	3g
Sugars	1g
Protein	21g

1) Heat gas or charcoal grill. Place the tortillas on ungreased cookie sheets. Brush with olive oil. Sprinkle with 1 cup of the cheese. Top evenly with olives, tomato and pepperoni. Sprinkle with remaining ½ cup cheese and the oregano.

2) With broad spatula, carefully slide pizzas onto grill. Cover grill; cook over medium heat 3 to 6 minutes or until cheese is melted and crust is crisp. Slide pizzas back onto cookie sheets.

Chorizo and Rice Stew

PREP TIME:	45 MINUTES (READY IN 45 MINUTES)
SERVINGS:	4 (1-1/4 CUPS EACH)

1 large onion, chopped (1 cup)

8 oz smoked chorizo sausage links, cut into ¼-inch slices (about 2 cups, from a 12-oz package)

1 carton (32 oz) Progresso® chicken broth

1 cup uncooked regular long-grain white rice

1 can (4 oz) Old El Paso® chopped green chiles

1 box (9 oz) Green Giant® Simply Steam® frozen baby sweet peas

Queso fresco cheese, if desired

Nutrition Information Per Serving

Calories: 520	From Fat: 200
Total Fat	22g
Saturated Fat	8g
Trans Fat	0g
Cholesterol	50mg
Sodium	1710mg
Total Carbohydrate	55g
Dietary Fiber	3g
Sugars	6g
Protein	23g

1) In 3-quart saucepan, cook onion and sausage over medium-high heat about 8 minutes or until sausage is brown; drain. Add broth, rice and chiles. Heat to boiling, stirring occasionally.

2) Reduce the heat to low; cover and cook 5 minutes. Stir in the peas; cover and cook 15 to 20 minutes longer or until rice is tender. Top with crumbled queso fresco.

Sausage, Corn and Broccoli Bake

PREP TIME: 15 MINUTES (READY IN 1 HOUR 20 MINUTES)
SERVINGS: 6

 EASY

1 can (8 oz) Pillsbury® refrigerated crescent dinner rolls (8 rolls) or 1 can (8 oz) Pillsbury® Crescent Recipe Creations® refrigerated seamless dough sheet

8 oz spicy or mild bulk pork sausage

2 cups Green Giant® Select® frozen broccoli florets, thawed

3 eggs

1 tablespoon all-purpose flour

1 teaspoon seasoned salt

1 can (14.75 oz) Green Giant® cream style sweet corn

1 cup shredded Cheddar cheese (4 oz)

1) Heat oven to 325°F. Spray 11x7-inch (2-quart) glass baking dish with cooking spray. Unroll dough in baking dish; press on bottom and ½ inch up sides of dish. Press edges and perforations to seal.

2) In 10-inch skillet, cook pork over medium-high heat, stirring occasionally, until no longer pink; drain. Spoon evenly over dough in dish. Top with broccoli. In large bowl, beat eggs, flour and seasoned salt until well blended. Stir in corn. Pour over broccoli; sprinkle with cheese.

3) Cover with foil; bake 30 minutes. Uncover; bake 25 to 35 minutes longer or until knife inserted in center comes out clean.

Nutrition Information Per Serving	
Calories: 400	From Fat: 200
Total Fat	23g
Saturated Fat	9g
Trans Fat	2g
Cholesterol	140mg
Sodium	1010mg
Total Carbohydrate	31g
Dietary Fiber	2g
Sugars	6g
Protein	17g

Veggie Lovers' Pot Pie

PREP TIME: 30 MINUTES (READY IN 55 MINUTES)
SERVINGS: 8

3 tablespoons butter or margarine

1 large russet potato (1 lb), peeled, cut into ½-inch pieces (about 2½ cups)

1 large onion, chopped (about 1 cup)

1 teaspoon dried thyme leaves

½ teaspoon salt

¼ teaspoon pepper

¼ cup all-purpose flour

1 can (14 oz) vegetable broth

1 bag (1 lb) frozen broccoli, cauliflower and carrots, thawed, well drained

¼ cup milk

3 tablespoons grated Parmesan cheese

1 can (8 oz) Pillsbury® refrigerated garlic butter crescent dinner rolls (8 rolls)

1) Heat oven to 375°F. Spray 9- or 10-inch glass deep-dish pie plate with cooking spray. In 12-inch nonstick skillet, melt butter over medium-high heat. Add the potato, onion, thyme, salt and pepper; cook and stir 10 to 12 minutes until potatoes are lightly browned.

2) Sprinkle flour over potato mixture. Cook and stir 1 minute. Stir in broth; heat to boiling. Reduce heat; cover and simmer about 8 minutes, stirring occasionally, until potatoes are almost tender. Remove from heat. Stir in thawed vegetables, milk and cheese. Spoon mixture into pie plate.

3) Separate dough into 8 triangles. Starting at short side of each triangle, roll up triangle halfway. Carefully arrange over the vegetable mixture with tips toward center; do not overlap. Place pie plate on cookie sheet with sides.

4) Bake 20 to 25 minutes or until crust is golden brown.

Nutrition Information Per Serving	
Calories: 230	From Fat: 110
Total Fat	12g
Saturated Fat	5g
Trans Fat	1.5g
Cholesterol	15mg
Sodium	690mg
Total Carbohydrate	25g
Dietary Fiber	3g
Sugars	4g
Protein	5g

Stuffed-Crust Pizza

PREP TIME: 15 MINUTES (READY IN 35 MINUTES)
SERVINGS: 8

 EASY

1 can (13.8 oz) Pillsbury® refrigerated classic pizza crust

7 sticks (1 oz each) string cheese

½ cup pizza sauce

24 slices pepperoni (from 3.5-oz package)

2 cups shredded Italian cheese blend (8 oz)

1) Heat oven to 425°F. Grease 12-inch pizza pan with shortening, or spray with cooking spray.

2) Unroll dough. Place in pan. Starting at center, press out dough with hands to edge of pan, pressing up and extending over sides by at least 1 inch. Place string cheese around inside edge of crust. Fold extended edge of dough over cheese; pinch firmly to seal.

3) Spoon sauce evenly over dough. Top with pepperoni and cheese blend.

4) Bake 12 to 16 minutes or until crust is deep golden brown and cheese in center is melted. Cut into wedges.

Nutrition Information Per Serving	
Calories: 370	From Fat: 180
Total Fat	20g
Saturated Fat	11g
Trans Fat	0g
Cholesterol	60mg
Sodium	1050mg
Total Carbohydrate	27g
Dietary Fiber	0g
Sugars	5g
Protein	20g

Braised Sausage and Beans

PREP TIME: 20 MINUTES (READY IN 20 MINUTES)
SERVINGS: 4

e EASY

1   tablespoon olive or vegetable oil

1   medium onion, chopped (½ cup)

2   cloves garlic, finely chopped

1   box (10 oz) Green Giant® frozen honey glazed carrots

1   package (14 oz) fully cooked kielbasa sausage, cut into 4 pieces, halved lengthwise

2   cans (15.5 oz each) great northern beans, drained, rinsed

½   cup Progresso® chicken broth (from 32-oz carton)

¼   teaspoon dried thyme leaves

1) In 12-inch nonstick skillet, heat oil over medium heat. Add onion, garlic, frozen carrots and sausage; cook 5 to 7 minutes, stirring occasionally, until onion and carrots are tender and sausage is no longer pink.

2) Stir in beans, chicken broth and thyme. Heat to boiling. Cover; reduce heat to medium-low, and cook about 5 minutes or until hot.

Nutrition Information Per Serving	
Calories: 620	From Fat: 300
Total Fat	34g
Saturated Fat	12g
Trans Fat	1.5g
Cholesterol	60mg
Sodium	1710mg
Total Carbohydrate	54g
Dietary Fiber	18g
Sugars	11g
Protein	24g

It's okay to use other types of sausage, such as bratwurst or Italian sausage, in this recipe.

Four Cheese-Veggie Lasagna Cups

CINDY EGERSDORFER | CUYAHOGA FALLS, OHIO

 Bake-Off® BAKE-OFF® CONTEST 44, 2010

PREP TIME: 20 MINUTES (READY IN 1 HOUR 10 MINUTES)
SERVINGS: 6

 EASY

1 can (16.3 oz) Pillsbury® Grands!® flaky layers refrigerated original biscuits (8 biscuits)

1 bag (12 oz) Green Giant® Valley Fresh Steamers™ frozen broccoli, carrots, cauliflower & cheese sauce

¾ cup diced tomatoes with roasted garlic and onion (from 14-oz can)

⅓ cup Italian-style tomato paste (from 6-oz can)

½ teaspoon salt

½ teaspoon finely chopped garlic

½ cup ricotta cheese

1 tablespoon grated Parmesan cheese

½ teaspoon parsley flakes

1¼ cups shredded mozzarella cheese (5 oz)

1) Heat oven to 350°F. Separate dough into 8 biscuits. Separate 2 biscuits into 3 layers each; add 1 layer to each of remaining 6 biscuits. In ungreased jumbo muffin pan, press each biscuit on bottom and up side of muffin cup.

2) Microwave frozen vegetables as directed on bag. Pour vegetables into medium bowl; stir in tomatoes, tomato paste, salt and garlic.

3) In small bowl, mix ricotta cheese, Parmesan cheese and ¼ teaspoon of the parsley. Spoon 1 rounded tablespoon ricotta mixture into each biscuit. Top each with 1 tablespoon mozzarella cheese and rounded ¼ cup vegetable mixture. Sprinkle with remaining mozzarella cheese and parsley.

4) Bake 30 to 35 minutes or until biscuits are golden brown and filling is hot. Cool in pan 5 minutes. Carefully run knife around side of cups to loosen; remove from pan. Cool 10 minutes longer before serving. Serve warm.

Nutrition Information Per Serving	
Calories: 390	From Fat: 160
Total Fat	18g
Saturated Fat	7g
Trans Fat	3g
Cholesterol	20mg
Sodium	1450mg
Total Carbohydrate	43g
Dietary Fiber	2g
Sugars	11g
Protein	15g

Deep-Dish Sausage Patty Pizza

AMY WINTERS | BARTLETT, ILLINOIS

BAKE-OFF® CONTEST 44, 2010

PREP TIME: 35 MINUTES (READY IN 1 HOUR 15 MINUTES)
SERVINGS: 8

SAUCE

- 2 tablespoons Crisco® 100% extra virgin olive oil or pure olive oil
- ¼ cup chopped onion
- 2 teaspoons finely chopped garlic
- 1 can (28 oz) whole tomatoes, drained, ½ cup juice reserved and tomatoes coarsely chopped
- 1 teaspoon dried basil leaves
- 1 dried bay leaf
- ¼ teaspoon salt
- 2 or 3 dashes pepper

PIZZA

- 1 lb bulk sweet Italian pork sausage
- 2 tablespoons Crisco® 100% extra virgin olive oil or pure olive oil
- 1 tablespoon cornmeal
- 1 can (13.8 oz) Pillsbury® refrigerated classic pizza crust
- 4 cups shredded mozzarella cheese (1 lb)
- 2 teaspoons grated Parmesan cheese

1) Heat oven to 400°F. In 2-quart saucepan, heat 2 tablespoons oil over medium-high heat. Add onion and garlic; cook about 4 minutes, stirring constantly, until onion is tender. Stir in tomatoes, basil, bay leaf, salt and pepper. Reduce heat to medium-low. Simmer uncovered 20 minutes, stirring occasionally. Stir in reserved tomato juice. (Sauce should be thick.) Remove and discard bay leaf.

2) Meanwhile, spray 12-inch skillet with Crisco® original no-stick cooking spray. Spread sausage over bottom of skillet into large patty. Cook over medium-high heat 5 to 8 minutes on each side, turning once, until no longer pink in center. (If necessary, cut the sausage patty in half or into quarters to turn.)

3) Coat bottom and side of 12-inch cast-iron skillet or other ovenproof skillet with 1 tablespoon oil; sprinkle with cornmeal. Unroll pizza crust dough in skillet; press on bottom and at least halfway up side. Brush dough with remaining 1 tablespoon oil; prick bottom and sides of dough with fork. Sprinkle mozzarella cheese over dough. Top with sausage patty, keeping patty in one piece.

4) Bake 15 to 18 minutes or until crust is light golden brown. Spread sauce over sausage. Bake 5 to 10 minutes longer or until crust is golden brown. Sprinkle with Parmesan cheese. Let stand 10 minutes before cutting.

Nutrition Information Per Serving	
Calories: 520	From Fat: 280
Total Fat	31g
Saturated Fat	13g
Trans Fat	0g
Cholesterol	55mg
Sodium	1360mg
Total Carbohydrate	33g
Dietary Fiber	2g
Sugars	7g
Protein	27g

Spicy Pork Chimichurri-Style Casserole

PREP TIME: 30 MINUTES (READY IN 1 HOUR 30 MINUTES)
SERVINGS: 5

2 tablespoons olive

2 tablespoons all-purpose flour

1 teaspoon salt

½ teaspoon paprika

¼ teaspoon black pepper

1 pork tenderloin (about 1 lb), cut into ¾-inch cubes

1 large onion, halved, cut into ½ inch-thick wedges

1 lb unpeeled small red potatoes, quartered (2½ cups)

¾ to 1 lb sweet potatoes (about 2 medium), peeled, cut into 1½-inch pieces (3 cups)

1 cup chopped fresh parsley

2 tablespoons chopped fresh oregano leaves

2 tablespoons fresh lime juice

½ teaspoon crushed red pepper flakes

2 cloves garlic, finely chopped

1¾ cups Progresso® chicken broth (from 32-oz carton)

1 can (12 oz) Pillsbury® Grands!® Jr. Golden Layers® refrigerated biscuits (10 biscuits)

¼ cup finely chopped fresh cilantro

1) Heat oven to 350°F. In 3- or 4-quart ovenproof Dutch oven, heat oil over medium-high heat. In large shallow bowl, mix flour, salt, paprika and black pepper. Stir in pork until evenly coated. Add to hot oil; cook and stir until evenly browned. Add remaining ingredients except biscuits and cilantro, including any unused flour mixture; mix well.

2) If handles of Dutch oven are not ovenproof, wrap them in foil. Cover Dutch oven; bake 40 minutes. Remove Dutch oven from oven; increase oven temperature to 375°F.

3) Separate dough into 10 biscuits; arrange on top of hot pork mixture. Bake uncovered 14 to 18 minutes longer or until biscuits are golden brown. Sprinkle with fresh cilantro before serving.

Nutrition Information Per Serving	
Calories: 550	From Fat: 170
Total Fat	19g
Saturated Fat	4g
Trans Fat	3g
Cholesterol	40mg
Sodium	1630mg
Total Carbohydrate	66g
Dietary Fiber	5g
Sugars	11g
Protein	28g

Mediterranean Three-Tomato Tart

CATHERINE HEERS | SIMPSONVILLE, SOUTH CAROLINA

Pillsbury Bake-Off BAKE-OFF® CONTEST 44, 2010

PREP TIME: 25 MINUTES (READY IN 50 MINUTES)
SERVINGS: 6

1 can (13.8 oz) Pillsbury® refrigerated classic pizza crust

2½ tablespoons Crisco® 100% extra virgin olive oil or pure olive oil

½ cup drained sun-dried tomatoes in oil (from 7-oz jar), coarsely chopped

½ teaspoon fresh thyme leaves

12 slices soppressata (dry-cured salami) or regular salami (4 oz)

6 medium regular tomatoes or plum (Roma) tomatoes, cut lengthwise into ¼- to ½-inch slices

¼ teaspoon salt

1 teaspoon chopped fresh oregano leaves

¾ cup shredded Asiago cheese (3 oz)

1 cup grape tomatoes, halved

½ cup pitted kalamata olives, halved

1 cup crumbled feta cheese (4 oz)

⅛ teaspoon freshly ground pepper

2 teaspoons lemon juice

2 tablespoons chopped fresh basil leaves

1) Heat oven to 425°F. Spray large cookie sheet with Crisco® original no-stick cooking spray. Unroll pizza crust dough on cookie sheet; press dough into 14x10-inch rectangle and flute edges.

2) Brush 1 tablespoon of the oil over dough. Press sun-dried tomatoes into dough. Sprinkle with thyme. Bake 7 to 10 minutes or until dough is light golden brown. Reduce oven temperature to 375°F.

3) On partially baked crust, layer ingredients in following order: soppressata (gently press into dough), sliced tomatoes, salt, oregano, Asiago cheese, grape tomatoes, olives, feta cheese and pepper. In small bowl, mix remaining 1½ tablespoons oil and lemon juice; spoon over tart.

4) Bake at 375°F 10 to 12 minutes longer or until thoroughly heated. Sprinkle with basil. Cut into squares.

Nutrition Information Per Serving	
Calories: 430	From Fat: 210
Total Fat	24g
Saturated Fat	9g
Trans Fat	0g
Cholesterol	45mg
Sodium	1270mg
Total Carbohydrate	39g
Dietary Fiber	3g
Sugars	9g
Protein	15g

Tomato Pesto Pizza

PREP TIME: 15 MINUTES (READY IN 25 MINUTES)
SERVINGS: 8

 EASY

1 can (11 oz) Pillsbury® refrigerated thin pizza crust

¼ cup refrigerated basil pesto (from 7-oz container)

2 large plum (Roma) tomatoes, chopped

1 cup shredded Italian cheese blend (4 oz)

2 tablespoons fresh basil leaves, thinly sliced

Nutrition Information Per Serving	
Calories: 210	From Fat: 100
Total Fat	11g
Saturated Fat	4g
Trans Fat	0g
Cholesterol	10mg
Sodium	410mg
Total Carbohydrate	19g
Dietary Fiber	1g
Sugars	3g
Protein	7g

1) Heat oven to 400°F. Spray or grease 15x10-inch or larger dark or nonstick cookie sheet. Unroll dough on cookie sheet; starting at center, press dough into 15x10-inch rectangle.

2) Spread pesto to within ½ inch of edges of dough. Top with tomatoes; sprinkle with cheese.

3) Bake 10 to 12 minutes or until crust edges are golden brown and cheese is melted. Sprinkle with basil.

Italian Sausage and Pepper Stew

PREP TIME: 25 MINUTES (READY IN 25 MINUTES)
SERVINGS: 4 (1 CUP EACH)

 EASY

1 package (19.5 oz) Italian turkey sausage (sweet or hot), casings removed, links cut into 2-inch pieces

1 large red bell pepper, cut into bite-size strips

1 large yellow bell pepper, cut into bite-size strips

1 can (14.5 oz) diced tomatoes, undrained

1 teaspoon dried basil leaves, crushed

8 oz uncooked penne rigate pasta (2½ cups)

Grated Parmesan cheese, if desired

Nutrition Information Per Serving	
Calories: 550	From Fat: 150
Total Fat	16g
Saturated Fat	3.5g
Trans Fat	0.5g
Cholesterol	125mg
Sodium	1070mg
Total Carbohydrate	58g
Dietary Fiber	5g
Sugars	7g
Protein	43g

1) In 6-quart Dutch oven, cook and stir the sausage and bell peppers over medium-high heat for about 8 minutes or until the sausage is no longer pink; drain.

2) Reduce heat to medium-low. Stir in tomatoes and basil; cover and simmer 10 minutes.

3) Meanwhile, cook and drain pasta as directed on package. Serve sausage and peppers over cooked pasta; top with cheese.

Swiss Spinach Strudel

DEVON DELANEY | PRINCETON, NEW JERSEY

Pillsbury
Bake-Off

BAKE-OFF® CONTEST 40, 2002

PREP TIME: 15 MINUTES (READY IN 45 MINUTES)
SERVINGS: 5

e EASY

1 egg

½ cup reduced-fat chives-and-onion cream cheese spread (from 8-oz container)

1 box (9 oz) Green Giant® frozen chopped spinach, thawed, squeezed to drain

1 cup shredded Swiss cheese (4 oz)

¼ teaspoon salt

¼ teaspoon pepper

⅛ to ¼ teaspoon ground nutmeg

⅛ teaspoon red pepper sauce

1 can (8 oz) Pillsbury® refrigerated reduced fat or regular crescent dinner rolls or 1 can (8 oz) Pillsbury® Crescent Recipe Creations® refrigerated seamless dough sheet

¼ cup sliced almonds

Olive oil cooking spray or regular cooking spray

2 tablespoons Italian style bread crumbs

1) Heat oven to 400°F. In large bowl, beat egg. Add cream cheese; blend well. Add spinach, Swiss cheese, salt, pepper, nutmeg and red pepper sauce; mix well.

2) If using crescent rolls: Unroll dough onto ungreased cookie sheet. Press to form 12x8-inch rectangle; firmly press perforations to seal. If using dough sheet: Unroll dough onto ungreased cookie sheet. Press to form 12x8-inch rectangle.

3) Spoon and spread spinach mixture lengthwise on half of dough. Sprinkle with almonds. Fold untopped half of dough over filling; press edges and ends to seal. Spray top of dough with cooking spray. Sprinkle with bread crumbs.

4) Bake 18 to 24 minutes or until deep golden brown. Cool 5 minutes. Cut into crosswise slices.

Nutrition Information Per Serving	
Calories: 300	From Fat: 210
Total Fat	16g
Saturated Fat	10g
Trans Fat	2.5g
Cholesterol	75mg
Sodium	610mg
Total Carbohydrate	30g
Dietary Fiber	2g
Sugars	6g
Protein	15g

GARDEN VEGETABLE LASAGNA
PG. 202

Budget
Recipes

These mouthwatering recipes prove that
delectable meals don't have to break the bank.

PORK CHOPS WITH SAUERKRAUT
PG. 205

CHUNKY TOMATO-BASIL SOUP
PG. 208

MEDITERRANEAN CHICKEN
AND VEGETABLES
PG. 212

Easy Pasta E Fagioli

PREP TIME: 10 MINUTES (READY IN 35 MINUTES)
SERVINGS: 4 (1-1/2 CUPS EACH)

 EASY LOW FAT

1 tablespoon vegetable oil

1 medium onion, chopped (½ cup)

2 cloves garlic, finely chopped

1 can (15 oz) Progresso® cannellini beans, drained, rinsed

1 can (14.5 oz) diced tomatoes

1 carton (32 oz) Progresso® chicken broth

2 tablespoons chopped fresh parsley

1 teaspoon dried basil leaves, crushed

1 cup uncooked elbow macaroni (4 oz)

½ cup shredded Parmesan cheese

1) In 3-quart saucepan, heat oil over medium-high heat. Add onion and garlic; cook and stir 2 minutes. Add remaining ingredients except macaroni and cheese. Heat to boiling. Reduce heat to medium-low; cover and simmer 10 minutes, stirring occasionally.

2) Remove cover; increase heat to high. Heat to boiling. Reduce heat to medium. Add macaroni; cook 10 to 15 minutes or until tender. Sprinkle each serving with cheese.

Nutrition Information Per Serving

Calories: 360	From Fat: 70
Total Fat	8g
Saturated Fat	3g
Trans Fat	0g
Cholesterol	10mg
Sodium	1420mg
Total Carbohydrate	51g
Dietary Fiber	8g
Sugars	6g
Protein	20g

tip

Crushing the dried basil helps to release the oils and enhances the flavor. If you have some basil growing in your garden, use about 1 tablespoon chopped in place of the dried.

Edamame Corn Chowder

| PREP TIME: | 40 MINUTES (READY IN 40 MINUTES) |
| SERVINGS: | 6 (1-1/3 CUPS EACH) |

lf LOW FAT

4 slices bacon, chopped

1 medium onion, chopped (½ cup)

2 tablespoons all-purpose flour

¾ teaspoon salt

¼ teaspoon pepper

4 cups milk

1 bag (12 oz) frozen shelled edamame (green) soybeans

1 can (14.75 oz) Green Giant® cream style sweet corn

1 can (11 oz) Green Giant® Niblets® whole kernel sweet corn

4 cups frozen southern-style diced hash brown potatoes (from 32-oz bag), thawed

Chopped fresh parsley, if desired

1) In 4-quart saucepan, cook bacon over medium heat until crisp. Drain, reserving 1 tablespoon drippings in pan. Cook onion in drippings, stirring frequently, about 2 minutes or until soft.

2) Using wire whisk, stir flour, salt and pepper into onion mixture. Cook over medium-high heat, stirring constantly. Stir in milk. Heat to boiling, stirring constantly. Boil and stir 1 minute.

3) Stir edamame, both cans corn, potatoes and reserved cooked bacon into milk mixture. Heat to boiling. Reduce heat to low; cover and simmer 10 to 15 minutes or until potatoes are tender. Top each serving with parsley.

Nutrition Information Per Serving	
Calories: 420	From Fat: 90
Total Fat	10g
Saturated Fat	3.5g
Trans Fat	0g
Cholesterol	20mg
Sodium	840mg
Total Carbohydrate	64g
Dietary Fiber	8g
Sugars	15g
Protein	19g

Garden Vegetable Lasagna

PREP TIME: 50 MINUTES (READY IN 1 HOUR 55 MINUTES)
SERVINGS: 8

8 uncooked lasagna noodles

1 tablespoon olive oil

1 garlic clove, chopped

3 cups frozen broccoli cuts

1½ cups sliced fresh mushrooms (4 oz)

1 medium bell pepper, coarsely chopped

1 egg

1 container (15 oz) ricotta cheese

1 teaspoon Italian seasoning

1 jar (26 to 28 oz) chunky vegetable tomato pasta sauce

2 cups shredded Italian cheese blend (8 oz)

1) Cook lasagna noodles as directed on package. Drain; place in cold water to cool. Meanwhile, heat oven to 350°F. In 10-inch skillet, heat oil over medium-high heat until hot. Add garlic, broccoli, mushrooms and bell pepper; cook 3 to 4 minutes, stirring frequently, until vegetables are crisp-tender. Remove from heat.

2) In a small bowl, beat the egg. Add ricotta cheese and Italian seasoning; mix well.

3) Drain cooled lasagna noodles. Spread ½ cup of the pasta sauce in an ungreased 13x9-inch (3-quart) glass baking dish. Top with 4 noodles, overlapping as necessary, half of ricotta mixture, half of cooked vegetables, half of remaining pasta sauce (about 2¼ cups) and 1 cup of the shredded cheese. Repeat layers, starting with noodles.

4) Bake 45 to 50 minutes or until hot and bubbly. If cheese is getting too brown, cover baking dish loosely with aluminum foil. Let stand 15 minutes before serving.

Nutrition Information Per Serving	
Calories: 390	From Fat: 130
Total Fat	15g
Saturated Fat	6g
Trans Fat	0g
Cholesterol	60mg
Sodium	750mg
Total Carbohydrate	42g
Dietary Fiber	4g
Sugars	12g
Protein	21g

Buffalo Chicken Casserole

PREP TIME: 25 MINUTES (READY IN 55 MINUTES)
SERVINGS: 4

½ cup uncooked regular long-grain white rice

1 cup water

1 tablespoon olive or vegetable oil

1 lb boneless skinless chicken breasts, cut into thin strips

2 medium stalks celery, thinly sliced (1 cup)

1 can (14.5 oz) stewed tomatoes, undrained

½ cup buffalo wing sauce

¼ cup blue cheese dressing

1) Cook rice in water 20 minutes as directed on package. Meanwhile, heat oven to 350°F. In 12-inch skillet, heat oil over medium-high heat. Add chicken and celery; cook 5 to 7 minutes, stirring frequently, until chicken is no longer pink in center. Remove from heat. Open can of tomatoes; cut up tomatoes in can. Stir tomatoes and wing sauce into chicken mixture.

2) Spray 8-inch square baking dish with cooking spray. Spoon cooked rice into dish. Spread chicken mixture over rice (do not stir).

3) Bake 25 to 30 minutes or until hot in center. Drizzle dressing over top.

Nutrition Information Per Serving	
Calories: 390	From Fat: 160
Total Fat	18g
Saturated Fat	3g
Trans Fat	0g
Cholesterol	75mg
Sodium	1610mg
Total Carbohydrate	29g
Dietary Fiber	1g
Sugars	6g
Protein	28g

Garden Patch Minestrone

PREP TIME: 30 MINUTES (READY IN 30 MINUTES)
SERVINGS: 7 (1-1/2 CUPS EACH)

 EASY   **LOW FAT**

- 2 tablespoons extra-virgin olive oil
- 2 medium carrots, sliced (1 cup)
- 2 medium stalks celery, sliced (1 cup)
- 1 small onion, chopped ($\frac{1}{3}$ cup)
- 2 cloves garlic, finely chopped
- 1 medium zucchini or yellow summer squash, cut in half lengthwise, then cut crosswise into $\frac{1}{4}$-inch pieces
- $\frac{1}{4}$ cup chopped fresh basil leaves
- 1 box Hamburger Helper® beef pasta
- 1 can (15 oz) Progresso® cannellini or dark red kidney beans, drained, rinsed
- 1 can (14.5 oz) diced tomatoes with basil, garlic and oregano, undrained
- 5 cups hot water

1) In 5-quart Dutch oven or stockpot, heat oil over medium heat. Add carrots, celery, onion and garlic; cook about 5 minutes, stirring frequently, until vegetables are almost tender.

2) Stir in zucchini, basil, uncooked pasta and sauce mix (from Hamburger Helper box), beans, tomatoes and hot water. Heat to boiling. Reduce heat; cover and simmer about 10 minutes or until pasta and vegetables are tender.

Nutrition Information Per Serving

Calories: 220	From Fat: 45
Total Fat	4.5g
Saturated Fat	0.5g
Trans Fat	0g
Cholesterol	0mg
Sodium	790mg
Total Carbohydrate	36g
Dietary Fiber	6g
Sugars	5g
Protein	8g

Pork Chops with Sauerkraut

PREP TIME: 35 MINUTES (READY IN 35 MINUTES)
SERVINGS: 4

2 tablespoons olive or vegetable oil

4 bone-in pork loin chops, thin cut (about 1 lb)

1 teaspoon salt

¼ teaspoon pepper

1 lb small red potatoes, cut into ¼-inch wedges

1 can (1 lb) sauerkraut, drained

1 teaspoon parsley flakes

Nutrition Information Per Serving	
Calories: 340	From Fat: 140
Total Fat	13g
Saturated Fat	4g
Trans Fat	0g
Cholesterol	40mg
Sodium	1300mg
Total Carbohydrate	24g
Dietary Fiber	5g
Sugars	1g
Protein	27g

1) In 12-inch nonstick skillet, heat 1 tablespoon of the oil over medium heat. Sprinkle pork with ½ teaspoon of the salt and the pepper; cook pork in oil 5 to 8 minutes, turning once, until brown. Remove pork from skillet; cover to keep warm.

2) In same skillet, heat remaining tablespoon oil. Sprinkle potatoes with remaining ½ teaspoon salt; cook potatoes in oil 7 to 10 minutes, stirring occasionally, until just starting to brown. Add the pork. Stir in sauerkraut and parsley.

3) Cover; cook 7 to 10 minutes or until pork is no longer pink in center and potatoes are tender. Serve pork over sauerkraut.

Southwestern Corn Skillet

PREP TIME: 25 MINUTES (READY IN 25 MINUTES)
SERVINGS: 6

EASY

8 oz uncooked rotini pasta (2⅔ cups)

1 lb lean (at least 80%) ground beef

½ cup chopped onion (1 medium)

1 jar (26 oz) chunky tomato pasta sauce

1 can (11 oz) Green Giant® Southwestern style corn, undrained

½ teaspoon salt

1 cup shredded Cheddar cheese (4 oz)

4 medium green onions, sliced (¼ cup), if desired

Nutrition Information Per Serving	
Calories: 560	From Fat: 180
Total Fat	20g
Saturated Fat	8g
Trans Fat	0.5g
Cholesterol	65mg
Sodium	1100mg
Total Carbohydrate	66g
Dietary Fiber	5g
Sugars	15g
Protein	27g

1) Cook and drain pasta as directed on package. Meanwhile, in 12-inch nonstick skillet, cook beef and onion over medium heat 8 to 10 minutes, stirring occasionally, until beef is thoroughly cooked; drain.

2) Stir in pasta sauce, corn, salt and cooked pasta. Cook until hot. Sprinkle with Cheddar cheese; let stand 2 to 3 minutes or until melted. Sprinkle with green onions.

Tuna Florentine

PREP TIME: 25 MINUTES (READY IN 25 MINUTES)
SERVINGS: 4

e EASY

1 box (8.4 oz) Betty Crocker® Tuna Helper® creamy Parmesan

2 cups water

1⅔ cups milk

3 tablespoons butter or margarine

¼ teaspoon garlic powder

1 can (5 oz) tuna in water, drained

1 box (9 oz) Green Giant® frozen chopped spinach, thawed, squeezed to drain

1 cup cherry tomatoes, halved

1 tablespoon lemon juice

2 tablespoons grated Parmesan cheese

1) In 12-inch skillet, stir together uncooked pasta and sauce mix from Tuna Helper box, water, milk, butter and garlic powder. Heat to boiling over medium heat, stirring occasionally. Stir in tuna, spinach and tomatoes.

2) Reduce heat to medium-low; cover and cook 13 to 15 minutes, stirring occasionally, until pasta is tender. Stir in lemon juice; sprinkle with cheese.

Nutrition Information Per Serving	
Calories: 420	From Fat: 140
Total Fat	15g
Saturated Fat	8g
Trans Fat	1.5g
Cholesterol	40mg
Sodium	1410mg
Total Carbohydrate	50g
Dietary Fiber	4g
Sugars	10g
Protein	21g

Shredded Turkey Gyros

PREP TIME: 20 MINUTES (READY IN 9 HOURS 20 MINUTES)
SERVINGS: 6

 EASY   LOW FAT

2 tablespoons butter or margarine, softened

6 cloves garlic, finely chopped

1 teaspoon salt

1½ teaspoons dried oregano leaves

1 teaspoon red pepper sauce

1½ lb turkey thighs, skin removed

1 medium red onion, halved, sliced (1 cup)

1 cup plain yogurt

1 teaspoon dried dill weed

2 cloves garlic, finely chopped (about 1 teaspoon)

½ small cucumber, unpeeled, finely chopped (½ cup)

6 pita fold breads (without pocket)

¾ cup chopped tomatoes

1) Spray 4-quart slow cooker with cooking spray. In small bowl, mix butter, garlic, ¾ teaspoon of the salt, the oregano and pepper sauce. Rub mixture onto turkey thighs.

2) Place onion in slow cooker; top with turkey thighs. Cover; cook on Low heat setting 7 to 9 hours or until turkey pulls apart easily with fork. Meanwhile, in medium bowl, stir together the yogurt, dill, garlic, cucumber and remaining 1/4 teaspoon salt; cover and refrigerate until serving.

3) Remove turkey from slow cooker; remove from bones. Shred turkey; stir into mixture remaining in slow cooker. Using slotted spoon, divide meat and onion mixture among 6 pita folds. Top with yogurt sauce and tomatoes; pass additional sauce at table.

Nutrition Information Per Serving	
Calories: 320	From Fat: 80
Total Fat	9g
Saturated Fat	4g
Trans Fat	0g
Cholesterol	100mg
Sodium	780mg
Total Carbohydrate	32g
Dietary Fiber	1g
Sugars	4g
Protein	29g

Chunky Tomato-Basil Soup

PREP TIME: 30 MINUTES (READY IN 30 MINUTES)
SERVINGS: 4 (1-1/4 CUPS EACH)

 EASY

2 tablespoons butter or margarine

1 medium onion, chopped (½ cup)

3 small carrots, shredded (1 cup)

2 tablespoons all-purpose flour

1 cup half-and-half

1 jar (26 oz) chunky tomato pasta sauce

1 can (14.5 oz) diced tomatoes, undrained

¼ cup chopped fresh basil leaves

1) In 3-quart saucepan, heat butter over medium-high heat. Add onion and carrots; cook and stir 3 to 4 minutes or until softened. Add flour; cook and stir until moistened. Gradually add half-and-half, cooking and stirring about 2 minutes or until smooth.

2) Stir in remaining ingredients. Cover and cook over medium heat for about 15 minutes, stirring frequently, just until mixture comes to a boil.

3) If desired, top with additional chopped fresh basil leaves.

Nutrition Information Per Serving

Calories: 400	From Fat: 170
Total Fat	19g
Saturated Fat	9g
Trans Fat	0g
Cholesterol	40mg
Sodium	1140mg
Total Carbohydrate	50g
Dietary Fiber	5g
Sugars	26g
Protein	6g

tip

You can use any type of tomato pasta sauce in this recipe that you like. Chunky sauce with vegetables adds wonderful texture to this easy soup.

Vegetable Frittata

PREP TIME: 30 MINUTES (READY IN 1 HOUR)
SERVINGS: 8

lf LOW FAT

6 eggs

2 tablespoons milk

⅓ cup freshly shredded Parmesan cheese

⅛ teaspoon garlic powder

½ teaspoon dried basil leaves

¼ teaspoon salt

¼ teaspoon pepper

6 medium green onions, sliced (6 tablespoons)

2 teaspoons olive or vegetable oil

2 small unpeeled red potatoes, cubed (1 cup)

6 oz fresh spinach, stems removed, leaves torn into bite-size pieces (about 6 cups loosely packed)

5 cherry tomatoes, quartered

1) In medium bowl, beat eggs and milk with wire whisk. Stir in cheese, garlic powder, basil, salt, pepper and onions.

2) In 9- to 10-inch nonstick skillet with sloping sides (omelet or crepe pan), heat oil over medium heat. Cook potatoes in oil about 5 minutes, stirring frequently, until tender. Add spinach; cover and cook 1 to 2 minutes or until spinach is wilted.

3) Reduce heat to low. Spread potatoes and spinach evenly in skillet; top evenly with tomatoes. Pour egg mixture over top. Cover; cook 12 to 15 minutes, lifting edges occasionally to allow uncooked egg mixture to flow to bottom of skillet, until bottom is lightly browned and top is set. Cut into wedges.

Nutrition Information Per Serving

Calories: 110	From Fat: 60
Total Fat	7g
Saturated Fat	2g
Trans Fat	0g
Cholesterol	165mg
Sodium	220mg
Total Carbohydrate	6g
Dietary Fiber	1g
Sugars	2g
Protein	7g

Three Cheese-Sausage Lasagna

PREP TIME: 20 MINUTES (READY IN 1 HOUR 10 MINUTES)
SERVINGS: 6

 EASY

- 1 lb Italian turkey sausage, casings removed
- 1 box Hamburger Helper® lasagna
- 2 cups water
- 1 medium red bell pepper, chopped (1 cup)
- 1 cup sliced fresh mushrooms (3 oz)
- 1 small zucchini, diced (1 cup)
- 1 cup ricotta cheese
- ½ cup shredded mozzarella cheese (2 oz)
- ¼ cup grated Parmesan cheese

1) Heat oven to 375°F. In 10-inch skillet, crumble sausage. Cook over medium-high heat about 8 minutes, stirring frequently, until sausage is no longer pink; drain well.

2) In ungreased 11x7-inch (2-quart) microwavable dish, stir sauce mix (from Hamburger Helper box) and water until blended. Microwave uncovered on High 1 to 2 minutes or until sauce is thickened. Stir in uncooked pasta (from Hamburger Helper box), sausage, bell pepper, mushrooms and zucchini.

3) In small bowl, mix ricotta, mozzarella and Parmesan cheeses. Spoon the cheese mixture evenly over the sausage mixture.

4) Bake uncovered 40 to 50 minutes or until the top is golden brown and sauce is bubbly.

Nutrition Information Per Serving	
Calories: 340	From Fat: 100
Total Fat	12g
Saturated Fat	3.5g
Trans Fat	0g
Cholesterol	80mg
Sodium	1360mg
Total Carbohydrate	28g
Dietary Fiber	1g
Sugars	9g
Protein	31g

Easy Gyro Pizza

PREP TIME:	20 MINUTES (READY IN 35 MINUTES)
SERVINGS:	8

 EASY

1 can (13.8 oz) Pillsbury® refrigerated classic pizza crust

½ lb lean (at least 90%) ground turkey

2 cloves garlic, finely chopped

½ teaspoon dried oregano leaves

¼ teaspoon salt

½ cup sour cream

1½ cups shredded mozzarella cheese (6 oz)

¾ cup coarsely chopped cucumber

1 medium tomato, coarsely chopped

4 thin slices red onion

½ cup crumbled feta cheese

1) Heat oven to 425°F. Spray 13x9-inch pan with cooking spray. Press pizza dough in bottom and slightly up sides of pan to form crust. Bake about 7 minutes or until crust just begins to turn brown on edges.

2) Meanwhile, in 6-inch skillet, cook turkey and garlic over medium-high heat 5 to 7 minutes, stirring occasionally, until turkey is no longer pink. Stir in oregano and salt.

3) Spread sour cream over warm crust. Sprinkle with 1 cup of the mozzarella cheese. Evenly top cheese with cooked turkey. Sprinkle with cucumber and tomato. Separate red onion into rings; arrange over tomato. Sprinkle with remaining ½ cup mozzarella cheese and feta cheese.

4) Bake 13 to 14 minutes or until the edges of crust are golden brown and cheese is melted.

Nutrition Information Per Serving	
Calories: 290	From Fat: 110
Total Fat	12g
Saturated Fat	7g
Trans Fat	0g
Cholesterol	50mg
Sodium	670mg
Total Carbohydrate	27g
Dietary Fiber	1g
Sugars	5g
Protein	17g

Mediterranean Chicken and Vegetables

| PREP TIME: | 50 MINUTES (READY IN 1 HOUR 35 MINUTES) |
| SERVINGS: | 6 |

MARINADE

- ½ cup lemon juice
- 3 tablespoons olive oil
- 2 teaspoons dried rosemary leaves
- ½ teaspoon salt
- ¼ teaspoon pepper
- 8 cloves garlic, chopped

CHICKEN AND VEGETABLES

- 6 chicken thighs (about 2.25 lb)
- 2 large red potatoes, cut into ½-inch pieces
- 2 small zucchini, cut into 1-inch pieces
- 1 medium red bell pepper, cut into 1-inch pieces
- 1 red onion, cut into 1-inch pieces
- Shredded Parmesan cheese, if desired

1) In small bowl or measuring cup, mix marinade ingredients. In large resealable food-storage plastic bag, place chicken thighs. In another large resealable food-storage plastic bag, place potatoes, zucchini, bell pepper and onion. Pour half of the marinade over contents in each bag. Seal bags; turn to coat contents with marinade. Refrigerate at least 30 minutes but no longer than 6 hours, turning bags occasionally.

2) Heat oven to 400°F. Line 15x10x1-inch pan with foil. Place chicken thighs, skin side up, on one side of pan and vegetables on other side of pan. Pour any remaining marinade over chicken and vegetables.

3) Bake 35 to 45 minutes or until vegetables are tender and juice of chicken is clear when thickest part is cut to bone (180°F), spooning juice in pan over chicken and vegetables halfway through bake time. Sprinkle with shredded Parmesan cheese.

Nutrition Information Per Serving	
Calories: 430	From Fat: 200
Total Fat	22g
Saturated Fat	6g
Trans Fat	0g
Cholesterol	85mg
Sodium	380mg
Total Carbohydrate	28g
Dietary Fiber	4g
Sugars	4g
Protein	28g

Italian Pepperoni-Vegetable Quiche

PREP TIME: 20 MINUTES (READY IN 1 HOUR)
SERVINGS: 6

 EASY

1 Pillsbury® refrigerated pie crust, softened as directed on box

1 box (7 oz) Green Giant® Immunity Blend frozen broccoli, carrots and pepper strips in an olive oil seasoning

1½ cups shredded mozzarella cheese (6 oz)

½ cup chopped seeded tomato

½ cup sliced pepperoni, chopped

5 eggs

¾ cup milk

1 teaspoon Italian seasoning

1) Heat oven to 375°F. Place pie crust in ungreased 9-inch glass pie plate as directed on box for One-Crust Filled Pie.

2) Microwave broccoli, carrots and peppers as directed on box. Sprinkle 1 cup of the mozzarella cheese in crust. Top with tomato and pepperoni. Spoon broccoli, carrots and peppers over pepperoni. Sprinkle with remaining ½ cup mozzarella cheese.

3) In small bowl, beat eggs, milk and Italian seasoning. Pour egg mixture over cheese.

4) Bake 35 to 40 minutes or until crust is golden brown and knife inserted near center comes out clean. Cool 5 minutes before serving.

Nutrition Information Per Serving	
Calories: 380	From Fat: 220
Total Fat	25g
Saturated Fat	10g
Trans Fat	0g
Cholesterol	210mg
Sodium	540mg
Total Carbohydrate	23g
Dietary Fiber	1g
Sugars	4g
Protein	16g

tip

One-fourth pound of bulk Italian sausage, cooked and drained, can be used in place of the pepperoni.

Impossibly Easy Chiles Rellenos Pie

PREP TIME: 15 MINUTES (READY IN 45 MINUTES)
SERVINGS: 6

 EASY

2 cans (4 oz each) Old El Paso® whole green chiles, drained

1½ cups shredded Mexican cheese blend (6 oz)

3 eggs

¾ cup original all-purpose baking mix

¼ teaspoon garlic powder

1½ cups milk

¾ cup Old El Paso® thick 'n chunky salsa

Sour cream, if desired

1) Heat oven to 400°F. Spray 9-inch glass pie plate with cooking spray. Slit chiles lengthwise; remove seeds. Arrange chiles in single layer in bottom and up side of pie plate. Sprinkle 1 cup of the cheese over chiles.

2) In medium bowl, beat eggs with wire whisk. Add baking mix, garlic powder and milk; beat until well blended. Pour over cheese.

3) Bake 25 to 30 minutes or until knife inserted in center comes out clean. Sprinkle with remaining ½ cup cheese. Let stand 5 minutes before serving. Serve with salsa and sour cream.

Nutrition Information Per Serving

Calories: 255	From Fat: 135
Total Fat	130g
Saturated Fat	8g
Trans Fat	0g
Cholesterol	140mg
Sodium	740mg
Total Carbohydrate	16g
Dietary Fiber	1g
Sugars	7g
Protein	15g

tip Chiles rellenos are cheese-stuffed poblano chiles coated in egg batter and fried until the outside is crisp and the cheese inside is melted. This recipe adapts the flavors of the much-loved Mexican classic.

Chicken and Vegetable Alfredo

PREP TIME: 15 MINUTES (READY IN 40 MINUTES)
SERVINGS: 6

 EASY

1 bag (19 oz) Green Giant® frozen broccoli & carrots with garlic & herbs

1 cup all-purpose flour

¼ cup grated Parmesan cheese

⅓ cup cold butter or margarine, cut into small pieces

1 egg, slightly beaten

1½ cups cubed cooked chicken

1 jar (16 oz) four-cheese Alfredo pasta sauce

1 can (15.25 oz) Green Giant® whole kernel sweet corn, drained

1) Heat oven to 375°F. In large microwavable bowl, microwave broccoli & carrot mixture as directed on package, using minimum cook time.

2) Meanwhile, in small bowl, mix flour, Parmesan cheese, butter and egg with pastry blender or fork until crumbly. Set aside.

3) To hot vegetables in large bowl, add chicken, pasta sauce and corn. Stir gently to combine. Pour into ungreased 2-quart casserole or 9-inch deep-dish glass pie plate. Sprinkle with crumbly mixture.

4) Bake 20 to 25 minutes or until topping is golden brown.

Nutrition Information Per Serving

Calories: 610	From Fat: 350
Total Fat	39g
Saturated Fat	23g
Trans Fat	1.5g
Cholesterol	170mg
Sodium	830mg
Total Carbohydrate	40g
Dietary Fiber	3g
Sugars	6g
Protein	24g

Chicken Alfredo with Sun-Dried Tomato Cream

PREP TIME: 35 MINUTES (READY IN 35 MINUTES)
SERVINGS: 5

1 tablespoon olive oil

4 boneless skinless chicken breasts (about 1 lb)

1 medium onion, chopped (½ cup)

1 box Chicken Helper® fettuccine Alfredo

1 cup hot water

1 cup half-and-half

¼ cup chopped dry-pack sun-dried tomatoes

¼ cup chopped fresh basil leaves

1) In 10-inch skillet, heat oil over medium-high heat. Add chicken and onion; cook 15 to 18 minutes, stirring onion frequently and turning chicken once, until onion is tender and juice of chicken is clear when center of thickest part is cut (170°F). Remove from heat; cover to keep warm.

2) Meanwhile, fill 2-quart saucepan ⅔ full of water. Heat to boiling. Stir in uncooked pasta (from Chicken Helper box). Gently boil uncovered about 15 minutes, stirring occasionally, until pasta is tender; drain. Set aside.

3) In same saucepan, mix hot water, half-and-half, tomatoes and sauce mix (from Chicken Helper box). Heat to boiling. Reduce heat; cover and simmer 10 minutes, stirring occasionally, until sauce is slightly thickened.

4) Cut chicken into slices. To serve, spoon cooked pasta onto serving plate. Arrange chicken slices and onion over pasta. Top with sauce mixture. Sprinkle with basil.

Nutrition Information Per Serving	
Calories: 350	From Fat: 110
Total Fat	12g
Saturated Fat	4.5g
Trans Fat	0g
Cholesterol	75mg
Sodium	860mg
Total Carbohydrate	33g
Dietary Fiber	2g
Sugars	6g
Protein	27g

Cheesy Biscuit Bean 'n Beef Casserole

PREP TIME:	15 MINUTES (READY IN 35 MINUTES)
SERVINGS:	6

 EASY

½ lb lean (at least 80%) ground beef

½ cup chopped onion

1 can (21 oz) baked beans with bacon and brown sugar sauce, undrained

1 can (16 oz) kidney beans, drained, rinsed

1 can (15.8 oz) great northern beans, drained, rinsed

½ cup barbecue sauce

1 can (10.2 oz) Pillsbury® Grands!® homestyle refrigerated buttermilk biscuits, separated and each cut into 6 pieces

½ cup finely shredded Cheddar cheese (2 oz)

1) Heat oven to 350°F. Spray 11x7-inch (2-quart) glass baking dish with cooking spray.

2) In 12-inch nonstick skillet, cook beef and onion over medium heat 4 to 6 minutes, stirring occasionally, until beef is thoroughly cooked; drain. Stir in baked beans, kidney beans, great northern beans and barbecue sauce. Heat to boiling, stirring occasionally. Pour into baking dish. Immediately top hot mixture with biscuit pieces. Sprinkle with cheese.

3) Bake 18 to 20 minutes or until the biscuits are golden brown and baked through.

Nutrition Information Per Serving	
Calories: 700	From Fat: 180
Total Fat	20g
Saturated Fat	8g
Trans Fat	3g
Cholesterol	45mg
Sodium	1490mg
Total Carbohydrate	96g
Dietary Fiber	14g
Sugars	28g
Protein	34g

Slow Cooker Specialties

Supper is a snap, even on busy days, when your slow cooker simmers up a savory sensation.

ASIAN POT ROAST
PG. 222

CUBAN CHICKEN, BEANS
AND RICE
PG. 220

TACO TURKEY JOES
PG. 233

SAUCY ORANGE-
BARBECUED CHICKEN
PG. 225

Cuban Chicken, Beans and Rice

PREP TIME: 15 MINUTES (READY IN 7 HOURS 30 MINUTES)
SERVINGS: 6

 EASY   LOW FAT

1⅓ cups chopped onion

2 medium stalks celery, chopped (1 cup)

2 cans (15 oz each) small red beans, drained, rinsed

2 cans (15 oz each) tomato sauce

1 tablespoon lime juice

2 teaspoons ground cumin

1 teaspoon salt

1 package (20 oz) boneless skinless chicken thighs (6 thighs)

1 dried bay leaf

1 cup uncooked instant white rice

Chopped fresh cilantro, if desired

Bottled red pepper sauce, if desired

1) Spray 5- to 6-quart slow cooker with cooking spray. In cooker, mix onion, celery, beans, tomato sauce, lime juice, cumin and salt. Add chicken and bay leaf; spoon tomato mixture over chicken.

2) Cover; cook on Low heat setting 7 to 9 hours.

3) Stir in rice, breaking up large pieces of chicken. Increase heat setting to High. Cover; cook 10 to 15 minutes longer or until rice is tender. Remove bay leaf. Sprinkle with cilantro; serve with pepper sauce.

Nutrition Information Per Serving	
Calories: 400	From Fat: 80
Total Fat	9g
Saturated Fat	2.5g
Trans Fat	0g
Cholesterol	60mg
Sodium	1210mg
Total Carbohydrate	48g
Dietary Fiber	10g
Sugars	9g
Protein	32g

Fajita Pulled Pork Sandwiches with Avocado-Onion Slaw

PREP TIME: 25 MINUTES (READY IN 7 HOURS 25 MINUTES)
SERVINGS: 6

1 tablespoon vegetable oil

1 lb boneless pork shoulder roast, trimmed

¾ cup Old El Paso® mild salsa

1 teaspoon chili powder

¾ teaspoon ground cumin

3 tablespoons mayonnaise or salad dressing

1 tablespoon white vinegar

¼ teaspoon salt

1 medium avocado, cubed

½ cup halved and thinly sliced onion

12 small Old El Paso® flour tortillas or Old El Paso® taco shells

¼ cup chopped cilantro

1) Spray 4-quart slow cooker with cooking spray. In 10-inch skillet, heat oil over medium heat. Cook pork in oil 6 to 8 minutes or until brown on both sides. Place pork in slow cooker. Cover; cook on Low heat setting 7 to 8 hours or until pork pulls apart easily with fork.

2) Remove pork from slow cooker; shred pork. Reserve ¼ cup liquid in slow cooker; discard remaining liquid. Stir pork, salsa, chili powder and cumin into liquid in slow cooker.

3) In medium bowl, stir together mayonnaise, vinegar and salt. Gently stir in avocado and onion. To serve, place pork in tortillas; top with avocado-onion slaw and chopped cilantro.

Nutrition Information Per Serving	
Calories: 430	From Fat: 220
Total Fat	25g
Saturated Fat	6g
Trans Fat	1.5g
Cholesterol	50mg
Sodium	770mg
Total Carbohydrate	31g
Dietary Fiber	3g
Sugars	3g
Protein	21g

tip

The avocado-onion slaw adds creaminess as well as crunch, but for those who are not avocado fans, try substituting diced tomato or shredded lettuce in its place.

Asian Pot Roast

PREP TIME: 5 MINUTES (READY IN 6 HOURS 5 MINUTES)
SERVINGS: 8

 EASY LOW FAT

1 boneless beef rump roast
(3 to 4 lb), trimmed of fat

3 green onions

¼ cup honey

¼ cup soy sauce

3 tablespoons rice vinegar

1 teaspoon ground ginger

½ teaspoon salt

½ teaspoon pepper

1) Spray 3½- to 4-quart slow cooker with cooking spray. In cooker, place beef roast. Remove green tops from onions; chop and refrigerate. Chop white parts of onions; sprinkle over beef.

2) In small bowl, mix remaining ingredients; pour over beef.

3) Cover and cook on Low heat setting 6 to 8 hours.

4) Cut beef into slices; place on serving platter. Serve with sauce; garnish with green onion tops.

tip

If desired, substitute teriyaki sauce for soy sauce or substitute 1 small onion, diced, for chopped green onions.

Nutrition Information Per Serving

Calories: 240	From Fat: 45
Total Fat	5g
Saturated Fat	2g
Trans Fat	0g
Cholesterol	90mg
Sodium	640mg
Total Carbohydrate	10g
Dietary Fiber	0g
Sugars	9g
Protein	37g

Pineapple-Pork Tacos

PREP TIME: 20 MINUTES (READY IN 7 HOURS 20 MINUTES)
SERVINGS: 6 (2 TACOS EACH)

 EASY

1 lb boneless pork shoulder roast, trimmed

1 package (1 oz) Old El Paso® taco seasoning mix

1 can (8 oz) pineapple tidbits in juice, drained

2 teaspoons lime juice

1 package (4.6 oz) Old El Paso® taco shells

¾ cup shredded Cheddar cheese (3 oz)

1½ cups shredded lettuce

¾ cup chopped tomato

⅓ cup sour cream

⅓ cup Old El Paso® salsa

1) Spray 3- to 4-quart slow cooker with cooking spray. Place pork in slow cooker; sprinkle with taco seasoning mix. Cover; cook on Low heat setting 7 to 9 hours or until pork pulls apart easily with fork.

2) Remove pork from slow cooker; shred pork. Stir into liquid in slow cooker. Stir in pineapple and lime juice.

3) To serve, divide pork among taco shells (about ¼ cup each), and top with remaining ingredients.

Nutrition Information Per Serving	
Calories: 360	From Fat: 190
Total Fat	21g
Saturated Fat	9g
Trans Fat	2g
Cholesterol	70mg
Sodium	720mg
Total Carbohydrate	22g
Dietary Fiber	1g
Sugars	6g
Protein	21g

Turkey Brats with Potatoes and Sauerkraut

PREP TIME: 5 MINUTES (READY IN 6 HOURS 5 MINUTES)
SERVINGS: 6

 EASY

1½ lb small red potatoes (12 small)

½ teaspoon salt

⅛ teaspoon pepper

1 package (19.5 oz) uncooked turkey bratwurst

1 can (15 or 16 oz) sauerkraut, undrained

½ teaspoon caraway seed

Nutrition Information Per Serving	
Calories: 270	From Fat: 100
Total Fat	11g
Saturated Fat	3g
Trans Fat	0g
Cholesterol	55mg
Sodium	1250mg
Total Carbohydrate	25g
Dietary Fiber	5g
Sugars	3g
Protein	18g

1) Spray 4- to 5-quart slow cooker with cooking spray. Cut potatoes into eighths; place in cooker. Sprinkle with salt and pepper. Place bratwurst on potatoes. Top with sauerkraut. Sprinkle with caraway seed.

2) Cover; cook on Low heat setting 6 to 7 hours. Remove bratwurst, potatoes and sauerkraut from cooker with slotted spoon.

Honey Barbecue Pork Roast with Carrots

PREP TIME: 5 MINUTES (READY IN 6 HOURS 35 MINUTES)
SERVINGS: 6

 EASY

1½ lb boneless pork loin roast or sirloin roast, trimmed of fat

⅓ cup barbecue sauce

2 tablespoons honey

1 tablespoon balsamic vinegar

1 tablespoon soy sauce

½ teaspoon ground ginger

¼ teaspoon pepper

2 boxes (10 oz each) Green Giant® frozen honey glazed carrots, thawed

Nutrition Information Per Serving	
Calories: 300	From Fat: 100
Total Fat	11g
Saturated Fat	4.5g
Trans Fat	0g
Cholesterol	70mg
Sodium	490mg
Total Carbohydrate	24g
Dietary Fiber	2g
Sugars	20g
Protein	26g

1) Spray 3½- to 4-quart slow cooker with cooking spray. In cooker, place pork roast. In 1-cup measuring cup, stir together barbecue sauce, honey, balsamic vinegar, soy sauce, ginger and pepper; pour over pork. Cover; cook on Low heat setting 6 to 7 hours.

2) Place carrots around pork. Increase heat setting to High. Cover; cook about 30 minutes longer or until carrots are crisp-tender. Remove pork from cooker to cutting board with slotted spoon. Cut pork into slices; place on serving platter. Top pork with sauce and carrots.

Saucy Orange-Barbecued Chicken

PREP TIME: 35 MINUTES (READY IN 7 HOURS 35 MINUTES)
SERVINGS: 4

1 tablespoon vegetable oil

2 packages (1.5 lb each) bone-in chicken thighs, skin removed

SAUCE

¾ cup chili sauce

⅓ cup orange marmalade

1 tablespoon packed brown sugar

1 tablespoon Dijon mustard

1 tablespoon red wine vinegar

1 teaspoon Worcestershire sauce

1) Spray 4-quart slow cooker with cooking spray. In 12-inch nonstick skillet, heat oil over medium-high heat. Cook chicken in oil 8 to 10 minutes, turning occasionally, until brown on both sides (cook a few pieces at a time if all don't fit in skillet).

2) Place chicken in slow cooker. Cover; cook on Low heat setting 6 to 7 hours or until chicken is tender. About 30 minutes before serving, in 1-quart saucepan, heat sauce ingredients over medium heat 10 to 15 minutes, stirring occasionally, until thickened.

3) Drain excess liquid from slow cooker. Pour sauce over chicken; cook 10 to 15 minutes longer.

Nutrition Information Per Serving	
Calories: 690	From Fat: 280
Total Fat	31g
Saturated Fat	9g
Trans Fat	0.5g
Cholesterol	210mg
Sodium	990mg
Total Carbohydrate	32g
Dietary Fiber	3g
Sugars	22g
Protein	72g

Chicken-Coconut-Pineapple Curry

PREP TIME: 25 MINUTES (READY IN 6 HOURS 55 MINUTES)
SERVINGS: 6

1¼ lb boneless skinless chicken thighs, cut into 1-inch pieces

2 dark-orange sweet potatoes (1½ lb), peeled, cut into ¾-inch pieces

1 can (14 oz) coconut milk (not cream of coconut)

1 can (8 oz) pineapple chunks, drained

1 can (4.5 oz) Old El Paso® chopped green chiles

½ cup Progresso® chicken broth (from 32-oz carton)

4 teaspoons curry powder

2 teaspoons cornstarch

½ teaspoon salt

1 medium red bell pepper, cut into bite-size strips

4 oz fresh snow pea pods (1 cup), strings removed, cut diagonally in half

1 large firm ripe banana, cut in half lengthwise, then cut crosswise into 1-inch chunks

2 cups uncooked instant white rice

1) Spray 3- to 4-quart slow cooker with cooking spray. In cooker, mix all ingredients except bell pepper, pea pods, banana and rice.

2) Cover; cook on Low heat setting 6 to 7 hours.

3) Stir in bell pepper and pea pods. Cover; cook about 30 minutes longer or until bell pepper and pea pods are crisp-tender. Stir in banana. Meanwhile, cook rice as directed on package. Serve the curry mixture over rice.

Nutrition Information Per Serving	
Calories: 570	From Fat: 200
Total Fat	22g
Saturated Fat	15g
Trans Fat	0g
Cholesterol	60mg
Sodium	460mg
Total Carbohydrate	66g
Dietary Fiber	6g
Sugars	18g
Protein	26g

Onion and Oregano Beef Pot Roast

PREP TIME: 15 MINUTES (READY IN 8 HOURS 15 MINUTES)
SERVINGS: 10

e EASY   **lf** LOW FAT

2 medium onions, each cut
into 8 wedges

1 teaspoon salt

½ teaspoon pepper

2 teaspoons dried oregano leaves

1 tablespoon olive or vegetable oil

1 boneless beef round tip roast (4 lb)

½ cup cold water

3 tablespoons all-purpose flour

Fresh oregano sprigs, if desired

1) Spray 5- to 6-quart slow cooker with cooking spray. In cooker, place onion wedges. Sprinkle with half each of the salt, pepper and oregano. Drizzle with oil.

2) If beef roast comes in netting or is tied, do not remove; place beef on onions. Sprinkle beef with remaining salt, pepper and oregano.

3) Cover; cook on Low heat setting 8 to 9 hours. Remove beef to cutting board; keep warm. Strain onions and cooking liquid into a 2-quart saucepan; reserve onions.

4) In small bowl, stir water and flour until well blended; stir into cooking liquid. Cook over medium heat 3 to 5 minutes, stirring frequently, until gravy is thickened and bubbly.

5) Remove netting from beef if necessary. Cut beef into slices; place on serving platter. Surround beef with onions. Serve with gravy; garnish with fresh oregano.

Nutrition Information Per Serving	
Calories: 300	From Fat: 80
Total Fat	8g
Saturated Fat	8g
Trans Fat	2.5g
Cholesterol	0mg
Sodium	300mg
Total Carbohydrate	4g
Dietary Fiber	0g
Sugars	0g
Protein	51g

Caramelized Onion Beef Stew

PREP TIME: 35 MINUTES (READY IN 8 HOURS 50 MINUTES)
SERVINGS: 6

- 2 tablespoons butter or margarine
- 4 cups halved and thinly sliced sweet onions (about 1½ onions)
- 2 teaspoons sugar
- 2 teaspoons chopped fresh thyme leaves
- 1½ lb beef stew meat
- 1 cup Progresso® beef flavored broth (from 32-oz carton)
- 1 package (.87 oz) onion gravy mix
- 2 cups 1-inch pieces diagonally cut carrots
- 1 cup 1-inch pieces diagonally cut parsnips
- ½ cup Green Giant® Valley Fresh Steamers™ frozen sweet peas

1) Spray 4- to 5-quart slow cooker with cooking spray. In 10-inch skillet, melt butter over medium-low heat. Cook onions and sugar in butter 30 to 35 minutes, stirring frequently, until onions are deep golden brown and caramelized. Stir in thyme and stew meat; place in slow cooker.

2) In medium bowl, mix broth and gravy mix; pour over meat mixture in slow cooker. Top with carrots and parsnips. Cover; cook on Low heat setting 8 to 9 hours or until beef and vegetables are tender.

3) Stir in peas. Cover; cook 10 to 15 minutes longer or until hot.

Nutrition Information Per Serving

Calories: 290	From Fat: 130
Total Fat	15g
Saturated Fat	6g
Trans Fat	0.5g
Cholesterol	60mg
Sodium	450mg
Total Carbohydrate	21g
Dietary Fiber	4g
Sugars	9g
Protein	18g

tip

Substitute mushroom beef gravy mix or brown beef gravy mix for the onion gravy mix, if desired.

Pork Roast with Mushroom-Leek Compote

PREP TIME: 15 MINUTES (READY IN 7 HOURS 20 MINUTES)
SERVINGS: 10

 EASY

2   tablespoons olive or vegetable oil

1   boneless pork loin roast (3 to 4 lb)

3   leeks, cut into 1/2-inch slices

½   teaspoon salt

¼   teaspoon pepper

2   jars (4.5 oz each) Green Giant® sliced mushrooms, undrained

1   package (1.8 oz) leek soup and recipe mix

1) In 12-inch skillet, heat oil over medium-high heat. Add pork; cook 10 to 12 minutes, turning once, until browned on all sides.

2) Spray 5- to 6-quart slow cooker with cooking spray. In cooker, place leeks. Top with pork. Sprinkle with salt and pepper. Cover; cook on Low heat setting 7 to 9 hours.

3) Transfer pork to cutting board; keep warm. Stir mushrooms with liquid and leek soup mix into leeks. Increase heat setting to High. Cover; cook 3 to 5 minutes longer or until compote is thickened. (Stir in additional water for a thinner compote, if desired.)

4) Cut pork into ¼-inch-thick slices and place on a serving platter. Serve with the compote.

Nutrition Information Per Serving	
Calories: 280	From Fat: 120
Total Fat	13g
Saturated Fat	4g
Trans Fat	0g
Cholesterol	85mg
Sodium	730mg
Total Carbohydrate	8g
Dietary Fiber	1g
Sugars	3g
Protein	31g

Greek Chicken Stew

PREP TIME: 25 MINUTES (READY IN 9 HOURS 40 MINUTES)
SERVINGS: 6

lf LOW FAT

- 2 cups baby-cut carrots, halved lengthwise if large
- 1 bag (1 lb) frozen small whole onions
- 6 bone-in chicken thighs (from two 1.5-lb packages), skin removed
- 1 teaspoon ground cinnamon
- ½ teaspoon salt
- ½ teaspoon pepper
- 2 cloves garlic, finely chopped
- 2 cans (14½ oz each) diced tomatoes, undrained
- ⅓ cup tomato paste
- 2 teaspoons grated lemon peel
- ½ teaspoon dried oregano leaves
- ¼ cup chopped parsley

1) Spray 4- to 5-quart slow cooker with cooking spray. Place carrots and onions in slow cooker. Top with chicken thighs. Sprinkle with cinnamon, salt, pepper and garlic; top with tomatoes. Cover; cook on Low heat setting 7 to 9 hours or until vegetables are tender and chicken pulls apart easily with a fork.

2) Remove chicken with slotted spoon; cover to keep warm. Stir tomato paste, lemon peel and oregano into liquid in slow cooker. Cover; cook about 15 minutes longer or until thickened and hot. Meanwhile, remove chicken from bones. Stir chicken into mixture in slow cooker, breaking up larger pieces.

3) To serve, spoon stew in shallow bowls, and top with parsley.

Nutrition Information Per Serving

Calories: 200	From Fat: 50
Total Fat	6g
Saturated Fat	2g
Trans Fat	0g
Cholesterol	45mg
Sodium	580mg
Total Carbohydrate	20g
Dietary Fiber	5g
Sugars	10g
Protein	17g

tip

For added flavor, substitute a flavored diced tomato such as one with roasted garlic or one with added Italian seasoning.

Ham and Lentil Stew

PREP TIME: 20 MINUTES (READY IN 7 HOURS 20 MINUTES)
SERVINGS: 8 (1-1/2 CUPS EACH)

 EASY   LOW FAT

3 cups diced cooked ham

2 cups chopped celery

2 cups chopped carrots

2 cups dried lentils, sorted, rinsed

1 cup chopped onion

6½ cups Progresso® chicken broth
(from two 32-oz cartons)

Nutrition Information Per Serving	
Calories: 280	From Fat: 35
Total Fat	4g
Saturated Fat	1g
Trans Fat	0g
Cholesterol	25mg
Sodium	1260mg
Total Carbohydrate	35g
Dietary Fiber	16g
Sugars	5g
Protein	28g

1) Spray 3½- to 4-quart slow cooker with cooking spray. In cooker, mix all ingredients. Cover; cook on Low heat setting 7 to 9 hours.

Sweet-and-Sour Pork

PREP TIME: 20 MINUTES (READY IN 5 HOURS)
SERVINGS: 4

 EASY

2 tablespoons butter or margarine

1 boneless pork shoulder blade roast (2 lb)

1 jar (10 oz) sweet-and-sour sauce

¼ cup Progresso® chicken broth
(from 32-oz carton)

1 can (20 oz) pineapple chunks in juice, drained

¼ cup cold water

1 tablespoon cornstarch

Nutrition Information Per Serving	
Calories: 680	From Fat: 340
Total Fat	38g
Saturated Fat	14g
Trans Fat	.5g
Cholesterol	170mg
Sodium	440mg
Total Carbohydrate	31g
Dietary Fiber	2g
Sugars	23g
Protein	50g

1) In 10-inch skillet, melt butter over medium heat. Add pork roast; cook 3 to 4 minutes on each side or until browned.

2) Spray 3½- to 4-quart slow cooker with cooking spray. Into cooker, pour sweet-and-sour sauce. Add pork, broth and pineapple. Cover; cook on Low heat setting 4 hours 30 minutes to 5 hours.

3) About 15 minutes before serving, in small bowl, mix water and cornstarch until smooth. Remove pork from cooker; place on cutting board or serving platter. Stir cornstarch mixture into liquid in cooker. Return pork to cooker. Increase heat setting to High. Cover; cook 10 minutes longer or until sauce has slightly thickened. Cut pork into slices; serve with sauce.

Beef-Vegetable Chili

PREP TIME: 20 MINUTES (READY IN 7 HOURS 20 MINUTES)
SERVINGS: 6 (1-1/2 CUPS EACH)

 EASY   LOW FAT

1½ lb boneless beef round steak, cut into ½-inch cubes

1 large onion, coarsely chopped (1 cup)

2 cups Green Giant® Valley Fresh Steamers™ frozen mixed vegetables, thawed

2 cans (14.5 oz each) diced tomatoes with green chiles, undrained

1 can (15 oz) Progresso® black beans, drained, rinsed

1 can (15 oz) Progresso® dark red kidney beans, drained, rinsed

1 package (1 oz) Old El Paso® chili seasoning mix

2 cups water

¾ cup shredded Cheddar cheese (3 oz)

2 tablespoons chopped fresh cilantro

1) Spray 12-inch skillet with cooking spray; heat over medium-high heat. Add beef and onion; cook 7 to 9 minutes, stirring occasionally, until beef is brown; drain.

2) Spray 3½- to 4-quart slow cooker with cooking spray. Mix beef mixture and remaining ingredients except cheese and cilantro in cooker.

3) Cover; cook on Low heat setting 7 to 9 hours. Top individual servings with cheese and cilantro.

Nutrition Information Per Serving	
Calories: 450	From Fat: 90
Total Fat	10g
Saturated Fat	4.5g
Trans Fat	0g
Cholesterol	75mg
Sodium	840mg
Total Carbohydrate	48g
Dietary Fiber	14g
Sugars	8g
Protein	42g

Taco Turkey Joes

PREP TIME: 15 MINUTES (READY IN 4 HOURS 15 MINUTES)
SERVINGS: 16 SANDWICHES

 EASY   LOW FAT

2 teaspoons vegetable oil

2 packages (20 oz each) ground turkey

½ cup chopped onion

1 teaspoon dried minced garlic

½ teaspoon pepper

1 package (1 oz) Old El Paso® taco seasoning mix

1 tablespoon Worcestershire sauce

½ cup cold water

1 cup chili sauce

1 can (8 oz) tomato sauce

16 burger buns, split, toasted

1) In 12-inch nonstick skillet, heat oil over medium-high heat. Add turkey and onion; cook 6 to 9 minutes, stirring occasionally, until turkey is no longer pink. Drain.

2) Meanwhile, spray 3½- to 4-quart slow cooker with cooking spray. In cooker, mix remaining ingredients except buns; stir in turkey mixture.

3) Cover and cook on Low heat setting for 4 to 5 hours.

4) Fill each bun with ⅓ cup of the turkey mixture.

Nutrition Information Per Serving	
Calories: 260	From Fat: 90
Total Fat	10g
Saturated Fat	2.5g
Trans Fat	0g
Cholesterol	45mg
Sodium	720mg
Total Carbohydrate	25g
Dietary Fiber	2g
Sugars	5g
Protein	18g

Tuscan Lentil Stew

PREP TIME: 15 MINUTES (READY IN 8 HOURS 20 MINUTES)
SERVINGS: 6 (1-1/2 CUPS EACH)

 EASY   LOW FAT

1¼ cups Progresso® chicken broth (from 32-oz carton) or vegetable broth

1 cup dried lentils, sorted, rinsed

1½ lb russet potatoes (3 large), cut into ¾-inch pieces

2 cups chopped onions

3 cloves garlic, finely chopped

2 cans (14.5 oz each) diced tomatoes, undrained

2 teaspoons Italian seasoning

1 teaspoon salt

¼ teaspoon crushed red pepper flakes

1 bag (5 or 6 oz) fresh baby spinach leaves, chopped

Shaved or shredded fresh Parmesan cheese

1) Spray 4- to 5-quart slow cooker with cooking spray. In cooker, mix all ingredients except spinach and cheese.

2) Cover; cook on Low heat setting 8 to 10 hours.

3) Stir in spinach. Cover and cook about 5 minutes longer or until the spinach is wilted. Sprinkle each serving with Parmesan cheese.

Nutrition Information Per Serving	
Calories: 290	From Fat: 30
Total Fat	3g
Saturated Fat	1.5g
Trans Fat	0g
Cholesterol	5mg
Sodium	940mg
Total Carbohydrate	50g
Dietary Fiber	11g
Sugars	8g
Protein	16g

Pizza-Stuffed Peppers

PREP TIME: 20 MINUTES (READY IN 4 HOURS 30 MINUTES)
SERVINGS: 6

 EASY

½ cup uncooked orzo or rosamarina pasta

4 cups boiling water

6 small bell peppers (about 5 oz each)

½ package (1¼-lb size) lean ground turkey (about 10 oz)

½ cup diced pepperoni (about 2½ oz)

1 can (15 oz) pizza sauce

1½ cups shredded pizza cheese blend (6 oz)

½ cup water

1) In 2-quart saucepan, cook pasta in 4 cups boiling water 3 minutes. Drain; rinse with cold water to cool. Drain well. Meanwhile, cut thin slice from stem end of each bell pepper to remove top; reserve tops. Remove seeds and membranes; rinse peppers. To make peppers stand upright, cut thin slice off bottom of each.

2) In 10-inch nonstick skillet, cook turkey and pepperoni over medium-high heat 4 to 6 minutes, stirring occasionally, until turkey is no longer pink. Drain if necessary. Stir in pizza sauce, 1 cup of the cheese and the cooked pasta. Divide turkey filling among peppers.

3) Spray 5- to 6-quart slow cooker with cooking spray. Pour ½ cup water into cooker. Stand peppers upright in cooker; replace pepper tops. Cover; cook on Low heat setting 4 to 5 hours.

4) Remove pepper tops; reserve. Top filling with remaining ½ cup cheese. Cover; cook 5 to 10 minutes longer or until cheese is melted. To remove peppers from cooker, lift out with large slotted spoon, using tongs to support peppers (do not squeeze). Garnish with pepper tops.

Nutrition Information Per Serving	
Calories: 330	From Fat: 160
Total Fat	17g
Saturated Fat	8g
Trans Fat	0g
Cholesterol	70mg
Sodium	530mg
Total Carbohydrate	19g
Dietary Fiber	3g
Sugars	6g
Protein	23g

Baked Beans with Smoked Sausage

2 cans (15 oz each) pork and beans, undrained

1 can (15 oz) great northern beans, drained, rinsed

1 can (15 oz) pinto beans, drained, rinsed

1 ring (14 to 16 oz) beef smoked sausage, cut into 1-inch pieces

½ cup chopped onion

½ cup ketchup

¼ cup packed brown sugar

2 tablespoons red wine vinegar

2½ teaspoons ground mustard

1½ teaspoons chili powder

Nutrition Information Per Serving	
Calories: 700	From Fat: 240
Total Fat	26g
Saturated Fat	10g
Trans Fat	1g
Cholesterol	55mg
Sodium	1930mg
Total Carbohydrate	86g
Dietary Fiber	19g
Sugars	30g
Protein	30g

1) Spray 3½- to 4-quart slow cooker with cooking spray. In cooker, mix all ingredients. Cover; cook on Low heat setting 5 to 7 hours.

Barbecued Pork Chops for Two

2 boneless pork loin chops, 1 inch thick (about ¾ lb), trimmed of fat

2 slices onion

1 clove garlic, finely chopped

½ cup barbecue sauce

1 tablespoon water

1 teaspoon cornstarch

Nutrition Information Per Serving	
Calories: 380	From Fat: 115
Total Fat	13g
Saturated Fat	5g
Trans Fat	105g
Cholesterol	690mg
Sodium	720mg
Total Carbohydrate	25g
Dietary Fiber	0g
Sugars	17g
Protein	37g

1) Spray 3- to 4-quart slow cooker with cooking spray. In cooker, place pork chops. Top each with onion slice. Sprinkle with garlic. Pour barbecue sauce over pork. Cover; cook on Low heat setting 5 to 6 hours.

2) About 5 minutes before serving, remove pork from cooker; place on serving platter. Top each pork chop with onion slice; cover to keep warm.

3) In 2-cup glass measuring cup or small microwavable bowl, stir water and cornstarch until smooth. Pour juices from cooker into cornstarch mixture; mix well. Microwave on High 1 to 2 minutes, stirring once halfway through cooking, until mixture boils and thickens slightly. Serve sauce with pork.

Hearty Steak and Tater Soup

PREP TIME: 20 MINUTES (READY IN 8 HOURS 50 MINUTES)
SERVINGS: 9 (1-1/2 CUPS EACH)

 LOW FAT

1 lb boneless beef round steak

1 lb small red potatoes, cut into ¼-inch slices (4 cups)

2 medium stalks celery, chopped (1 cup)

2 medium carrots, chopped (1 cup)

1 medium onion, chopped (½ cup)

2 cloves garlic, finely chopped

1 tablespoon beef bouillon granules

½ teaspoon pepper

1 jar (6 oz) Green Giant® sliced mushrooms, undrained

1 carton (32 oz) Progresso® beef flavored broth (4 cups)

½ cup water

½ cup all-purpose flour

1) Spray 5- to 6-quart slow cooker with cooking spray. Cut beef into 1x¼-inch pieces. In cooker, mix beef and remaining ingredients except water and flour.

2) Cover and cook on Low heat setting 8 to 9 hours.

3) In small bowl, mix water and flour; gradually stir into soup until blended. Increase heat setting to High; cover and cook about 30 minutes or until slightly thickened.

Nutrition Information Per Serving

Calories: 150	From Fat: 20
Total Fat	2.5g
Saturated Fat	1g
Trans Fat	0g
Cholesterol	25mg
Sodium	1200mg
Total Carbohydrate	18g
Dietary Fiber	3g
Sugars	2g
Protein	15g

Tuscan Turkey and Beans

PREP TIME: 30 MINUTES (READY IN 9 HOURS 30 MINUTES)
SERVINGS: 6

- 6 cups water
- 1 bag (16 oz) dried navy beans (2 cups), sorted, rinsed
- 3 cups Progresso® chicken broth (from 32-oz carton)
- ¼ cup olive oil
- ¾ cup chopped parsley
- 1 tablespoon Italian seasoning
- 2 tablespoons chopped garlic (from a jar)
- 1½ teaspoons salt
- ½ teaspoon pepper
- 1 package (1½ to 2¼ lb) turkey thighs, skin removed
- 1½ cups Green Giant® Valley Fresh Steamers™ frozen cut green beans, thawed

1) Spray 5-quart slow cooker with cooking spray. In 3-quart saucepan, heat water to boiling over medium-high heat. Add navy beans. Reduce heat to medium-low; simmer uncovered 10 minutes. Drain; rinse with cold water. Place beans in slow cooker; add broth.

2) Meanwhile, in medium bowl, stir together olive oil, ½ cup of the parsley, the Italian seasoning, garlic, ½ teaspoon of the salt and the pepper. Press mixture firmly onto turkey thighs. Place turkey on top of beans in slow cooker. Cover; cook on Low heat setting 7 to 9 hours or until beans are tender and turkey pulls apart easily with fork.

3) Remove turkey from slow cooker. Increase heat setting to High. Stir green beans and remaining 1 teaspoon salt into slow cooker. Cover; cook 15 to 20 minutes or until vegetables are hot. Meanwhile, remove turkey from bones. To serve, place bean mixture in shallow bowls; top with turkey, and sprinkle with remaining parsley.

Nutrition Information Per Serving	
Calories: 480	From Fat: 120
Total Fat	14g
Saturated Fat	2.5g
Trans Fat	0g
Cholesterol	90mg
Sodium	1080mg
Total Carbohydrate	49g
Dietary Fiber	19g
Sugars	2g
Protein	39g

Spanish Pork and Rice

PREP TIME: 15 MINUTES (READY IN 5 HOURS 45 MINUTES)
SERVINGS: 4

 EASY

2 tablespoons butter or margarine

½ cup chopped onion

1 small green bell pepper, chopped (¾ cup)

2 cloves garlic, finely chopped (1 teaspoon)

1 boneless pork loin (1 lb), cut into 1-inch cubes

1 can (14.5 oz) diced tomatoes, undrained

1 can (4.5 oz) Old El Paso® chopped green chiles

1 can (8 oz) tomato sauce

½ cup Progresso® chicken broth (from 32-oz carton)

¼ teaspoon salt

¼ teaspoon pepper

⅔ cup uncooked regular long-grain white rice

2 tablespoons finely chopped fresh cilantro

1) In 10-inch skillet, melt butter over medium heat. Add onion, bell pepper and garlic; cook 3 to 4 minutes, stirring occasionally, until tender.

2) Spray 3½ - to 4-quart slow cooker with cooking spray. In cooker, mix pepper mixture and remaining ingredients except rice and cilantro.

3) Cover; cook on Low heat setting 5 to 7 hours.

4) Stir in rice. Increase heat setting to High. Cover; cook 25 to 30 minutes longer or until rice is tender. Sprinkle with cilantro.

Nutrition Information Per Serving	
Calories: 420	From Fat: 140
Total Fat	15g
Saturated Fat	7g
Trans Fat	0g
Cholesterol	90mg
Sodium	940mg
Total Carbohydrate	40g
Dietary Fiber	3g
Sugars	8g
Protein	30g

Cuban Flank Steak

PREP TIME: 15 MINUTES (READY IN 8 HOURS 30 MINUTES)
SERVINGS: 8

 EASY   LOW FAT

1 large onion, thinly sliced

1 medium red bell pepper, cut into strips (1½ cups)

1 medium green bell pepper, cut into strips (1½ cups)

1 beef flank steak (2 lb), cut into 8 pieces

2 tablespoons chili powder

1 teaspoon dried oregano leaves

2 teaspoons dried minced garlic

1 teaspoon salt

2 tablespoons lime juice

1 cup Progresso® beef flavored broth (from 32-oz carton)

2 cups uncooked regular long-grain white rice

1 can (15 oz) Progresso® black beans, drained, rinsed

1) Spray 3½- to 4-quart slow cooker with cooking spray. In cooker, place onion and peppers. Top with beef. Sprinkle with chili powder, oregano, garlic and salt. Drizzle with lime juice. Add broth.

2) Cover; cook on Low heat setting 8 to 10 hours. About 20 minutes before serving, cook rice as directed on package.

3) Remove beef from cooker; place on cutting board. Shred beef with 2 forks; return to cooker and mix well. Stir in black beans. Increase heat setting to High. Cover; cook about 15 minutes longer or until thoroughly heated. Serve the beef and sauce over rice.

Nutrition Information Per Serving	
Calories: 420	From Fat: 50
Total Fat	6g
Saturated Fat	2g
Trans Fat	0g
Cholesterol	85mg
Sodium	640mg
Total Carbohydrate	53g
Dietary Fiber	4g
Sugars	2g
Protein	40g

Chicken Cacciatore

PREP TIME: 10 MINUTES (READY IN 7 HOURS 10 MINUTES)
SERVINGS: 6

 EASY

1 package (20 oz) boneless skinless chicken thighs (6 thighs)

1 jar (26 oz) tomato pasta sauce

1 cup white wine or Progresso® chicken broth (from 32-oz carton)

1 can (6 oz) tomato paste

2 teaspoons sugar

1 teaspoon dried basil leaves

1 package (8 oz) fresh whole mushrooms, quartered

1 medium red bell pepper, cut into 1-inch pieces

1 box (16 oz) penne pasta

⅓ cup shredded fresh Parmesan cheese

2 tablespoons chopped fresh basil leaves

1) Spray 4- to 5-quart slow cooker with cooking spray. In cooker, place chicken.

2) In medium bowl, mix pasta sauce, wine, tomato paste, sugar, dried basil, mushrooms and bell pepper; spoon over chicken.

3) Cover; cook on Low heat setting 7 to 9 hours.

4) About 15 minutes before serving, cook pasta as directed on package. Transfer chicken mixture to large serving bowl or deep platter. Serve with pasta. Garnish with cheese and fresh basil.

Nutrition Information Per Serving	
Calories: 680	From Fat: 140
Total Fat	16g
Saturated Fat	4.5g
Trans Fat	0g
Cholesterol	60mg
Sodium	1120mg
Total Carbohydrate	96g
Dietary Fiber	7g
Sugars	20g
Protein	39g

Tuscan Sausage and Bean Stew

PREP TIME: 15 MINUTES (READY IN 6 HOURS 30 MINUTES)
SERVINGS: 6 (1 CUP EACH)

 EASY

1 lb bulk mild or sweet Italian pork sausage

1 ⅓ cups chopped onion

2 medium stalks celery, sliced (1 cup)

1 medium carrot, chopped (1/2 cup)

1 jar (4.5 oz) Green Giant® sliced mushrooms, drained

1 can (14.5 oz) diced tomatoes with Italian herbs, undrained

2 teaspoons dried minced garlic

1 cup Progresso® chicken broth (from 32-oz carton)

1 can (15 oz) Progresso® cannellini beans, drained, rinsed

2 tablespoons chopped fresh basil leaves

1) In 10-inch skillet, cook sausage over medium-high heat 8 to 10 minutes, stirring occasionally, until no longer pink; drain.

2) Spray 3½- to 4-quart slow cooker with cooking spray. In cooker, mix sausage and remaining ingredients except beans and basil.

3) Cover; cook on Low heat setting 6 to 8 hours.

4) Stir in beans. Increase heat setting to High. Cover; cook 15 minutes longer. Garnish with basil.

Nutrition Information Per Serving

Calories: 240	From Fat: 90
Total Fat	11g
Saturated Fat	3.5g
Trans Fat	0g
Cholesterol	30mg
Sodium	780mg
Total Carbohydrate	22g
Dietary Fiber	6g
Sugars	5g
Protein	14g

Turkey Breast with Veggies

PREP TIME: 20 MINUTES (READY IN 7 HOURS 20 MINUTES)
SERVINGS: 8

 EASY

3 medium red potatoes,
cut into 1-inch pieces (about
4 cups)

8 medium carrots,
cut into 1-inch pieces (about
2 cups)

1 small onion, cut into wedges
(about ½ cup)

1 bone-in turkey breast with
gravy packet (5 to 6 lb)

Nutrition Information Per Serving	
Calories: 470	From Fat: 160
Total Fat	18g
Saturated Fat	5g
Cholesterol	150mg
Sodium	490mg
Total Carbohydrate	20g
Dietary Fiber	2g
Protein	57g

1) Spray 5- to 6-quart slow cooker with cooking spray. In cooker, mix potatoes, carrots, onion and gravy from turkey breast. Place turkey breast on top.

2) Cover; cook on Low heat setting 7 to 8 hours or until meat thermometer inserted in center of turkey reads 170°F.

Pork and Polenta with Chunky Tomato Sauce

PREP TIME: 30 MINUTES (READY IN 7 HOURS 30 MINUTES)
SERVINGS: 6

3 to 4 lb country-style pork loin ribs

½ cup chopped onion

2 medium carrots, chopped (1 cup)

2 medium stalks celery, chopped (1 cup)

1 jar (1 lb 10 oz) tomato pasta sauce

¼ teaspoon salt

⅛ teaspoon pepper

1 package (24 oz) cooked polenta

Nutrition Information Per Serving	
Calories: 1260	From Fat: 540
Total Fat	60g
Saturated Fat	21g
Trans Fat	0g
Cholesterol	215mg
Sodium	2150mg
Total Carbohydrate	116g
Dietary Fiber	8g
Sugars	17g
Protein	64g

1) Set oven control to broil. Place pork ribs on broiler pan. Broil with top about 6 inches from heat 12 to 14 minutes, turning once, until lightly browned.

2) Spray 3½- to 4-quart slow cooker with cooking spray. In cooker, place onion, carrots and celery. Place pork on vegetables. Pour pasta sauce over pork; sprinkle with salt and pepper. Cover; cook on Low heat setting 7 to 8 hours.

3) About 15 minutes before serving, make polenta as directed on package. Place polenta on individual serving plates; serve with pork and sauce.

Mediterranean Beef and Pasta

PREP TIME: 15 MINUTES (READY IN 7 HOURS 15 MINUTES)
SERVINGS: 4

 EASY

1 lb beef stew meat

½ cup chopped onion

1 can (14 oz) artichoke hearts, drained, chopped

1 jar (4.5 oz) Green Giant® sliced mushrooms, drained

1 can (14.5 oz) diced tomatoes, undrained

1 tablespoon balsamic vinegar

1 tablespoon drained capers

1 tablespoon dried minced garlic

1 teaspoon Italian seasoning

1 teaspoon salt

1 teaspoon sugar

1½ cups uncooked penne pasta

1 tablespoon olive oil

Fresh ground pepper, if desired

½ cup shredded Parmesan cheese

1) Spray 3½- to 4-quart slow cooker with cooking spray. In cooker, mix all ingredients except pasta, oil, pepper and cheese.

2) Cover; cook on Low heat setting 7 to 9 hours.

3) About 15 minutes before serving, make pasta as directed on package. Stir pasta, oil and pepper into beef mixture. Serve with cheese.

Nutrition Information Per Serving	
Calories: 560	From Fat: 190
Total Fat	21g
Saturated Fat	8g
Trans Fat	.5g
Cholesterol	70mg
Sodium	1470mg
Total Carbohydrate	58g
Dietary Fiber	13g
Sugars	8g
Protein	35g

Pork Chops with Mustard-Thyme Gravy

PREP TIME: 10 MINUTES (READY IN 6 HOURS 10 MINUTES)
SERVINGS: 6

 EASY

2 tablespoons spicy brown mustard

6 pork rib chops, about ¾ inch thick

½ teaspoon dried thyme leaves

1 jar (12 oz) pork gravy

½ cup cold water

3 tablespoons all-purpose flour

¼ teaspoon salt

Fresh thyme sprigs, if desired

1) Spray 4- to 5-quart slow cooker with cooking spray. Spread mustard on 1 side of each pork chop; sprinkle with dried thyme. Place pork in cooker. Pour gravy over pork.

2) Cover; cook on Low heat setting 6 to 7 hours.

3) Remove the pork to a platter; keep warm. Strain cooking liquid into 2-quart saucepan; heat to boiling. Meanwhile, in a small bowl, stir water, flour and salt until well blended, then stir into boiling liquid. Boil and stir 1 minute. Serve gravy with pork. Garnish with fresh thyme.

Nutrition Information Per Serving	
Calories: 260	From Fat: 110
Total Fat	12g
Saturated Fat	4g
Trans Fat	0g
Cholesterol	85mg
Sodium	530mg
Total Carbohydrate	6g
Dietary Fiber	0g
Sugars	0g
Protein	32g

Red and White Turkey Chili

PREP TIME: 30 MINUTES (READY IN 9 HOURS)
SERVINGS: 6 (1-1/2 CUPS EACH)

lf LOW FAT

- 1 medium onion, chopped (½ cup)
- 1 clove garlic, finely chopped
- 2 teaspoons ground cumin
- ⅛ teaspoon ground red pepper (cayenne)
- 1 can (15.5 oz) great northern beans, drained
- 1 can (15 oz) Progresso® dark red kidney beans, drained
- 2 cans (4.5 oz each) Old El Paso® chopped green chiles, undrained
- 3½ cups Progresso® chicken broth
- 2 lb turkey thighs, skin removed
- 1 cup Green Giant® frozen white shoepeg corn, thawed
- 2 tablespoons flour
- ¼ cup water
- 1 lime, cut into wedges, if desired

1) Spray 4- to 5-quart slow cooker with cooking spray. Mix all ingredients except turkey, corn, flour, water and lime in cooker. Place turkey on bean mixture. Cover and cook on Low heat setting for 8 to 10 hours.

2) Place turkey on cutting board. Remove meat from bones; discard bones. Cut turkey into bite-size pieces. Add turkey and corn to cooker. In small bowl, mix flour and water; stir into turkey mixture. Increase heat setting to High. Cover; cook 20 to 30 minutes or until thoroughly heated and slightly thickened.

Nutrition Information Per Serving

Calories: 370	From Fat: 45
Total Fat	5g
Saturated Fat	1.5g
Trans Fat	0g
Cholesterol	95mg
Sodium	970mg
Total Carbohydrate	40g
Dietary Fiber	9g
Sugars	20g
Protein	3g

German Red Cabbage and Pork Ribs

PREP TIME: 30 MINUTES (READY IN 5 HOURS 30 MINUTES)
SERVINGS: 6

4 slices bacon, chopped

6 boneless pork country-style ribs
(2 lb)

1½ teaspoons salt

½ teaspoon pepper

6 cups thinly sliced red cabbage
(about ½ head)

2 Granny Smith apples, peeled, thinly
sliced (3 cups)

1 medium onion, finely chopped
(½ cup)

½ cup cider vinegar

¼ cup apple juice

2 tablespoons sugar

1) In 12-inch skillet, cook bacon over medium-high heat, stirring occasionally, until crisp. Remove bacon from skillet to large bowl; reserve drippings in skillet. Sprinkle both sides of ribs with salt and pepper; cook in drippings until browned. Meanwhile, stir the cabbage, apples and onion into bacon in bowl.

2) Spray 4- to 5-quart slow cooker with cooking spray. Place ribs in cooker, reserving drippings in skillet. Spoon cabbage mixture over ribs.

3) Stir vinegar, apple juice and sugar into drippings in skillet; heat to boiling. Pour over the ribs and cabbage mixture.

4) Cover; cook on Low heat setting 5 to 6 hours. To serve, use slotted spoon to remove cabbage mixture and ribs from cooker.

Nutrition Information Per Serving	
Calories: 550	From Fat: 120
Total Fat	15g
Saturated Fat	4.5g
Trans Fat	0g
Cholesterol	50mg
Sodium	1280mg
Total Carbohydrate	22g
Dietary Fiber	3g
Sugars	17g
Protein	13g

Cioppino

PREP TIME: 20 MINUTES (READY IN 4 HOURS 5 MINUTES)
SERVINGS: 8

 EASY   LOW FAT

2 large onions, chopped (2 cups)

2 medium stalks celery, finely chopped (about 1 cup)

5 cloves garlic, finely chopped (about 2½ teaspoons)

1 can (28 oz) diced tomatoes, undrained

1 bottle (8 oz) clam juice

1 can (6 oz) tomato paste

½ cup Progresso® chicken broth (from 32-oz carton)

1 tablespoon Progresso® red wine vinegar

1 tablespoon olive or vegetable oil

2½ teaspoons Italian seasoning

¼ teaspoon sugar

¼ teaspoon crushed red pepper flakes

1 dried bay leaf

1 lb firm-textured white fish, cut into 1-inch pieces

¾ lb uncooked medium shrimp, peeled, deveined

1 can (6½ oz) chopped clams with juice, undrained

1 can (6 oz) crabmeat, drained

¼ cup chopped fresh parsley

1) Spray 5- to 6-quart slow cooker with cooking spray. Mix all ingredients except fish, shrimp, clams, crabmeat and parsley in cooker.

2) Cover; cook on High heat setting 3 to 4 hours.

3) Stir in fish, shrimp, clams and crabmeat. Reduce heat setting to Low. Cover; cook 30 to 45 minutes longer or until fish flakes easily with fork. Remove bay leaf. Stir in parsley.

Nutrition Information Per Serving	
Calories: 210	From Fat: 50
Total Fat	6g
Saturated Fat	1g
Trans Fat	0g
Cholesterol	95mg
Sodium	590mg
Total Carbohydrate	14g
Dietary Fiber	3g
Sugars	7g
Protein	24g

Shellfish, such as shrimp and clams, is a good source of vitamin B-12. Our bodies need B-12 to help break down foods to give us plenty of energy.

Spanish Chicken

PREP TIME: 15 MINUTES (READY IN 6 HOURS 15 MINUTES)
SERVINGS: 6

 EASY

1¾ lb boneless skinless chicken breasts, cut into 1-inch pieces

1 lb Italian turkey sausage links, cut into 1-inch pieces

1 large red bell pepper, chopped (1½ cups)

1 cup chopped onion

2 cloves garlic, finely chopped

1 teaspoon dried oregano leaves

½ to 1 teaspoon crushed red pepper flakes

1 can (28 oz) diced tomatoes, undrained

1 can (6 oz) tomato paste

1 cup uncooked regular long-grain white rice

2 cups water

1 can (14 oz) quartered artichoke hearts, drained

1 can (3.8 oz) sliced ripe olives, drained

1) Spray 3½ - to 4-quart slow cooker with cooking spray. In cooker, mix chicken, sausage, bell pepper, onion, garlic, oregano, pepper flakes, tomatoes and tomato paste.

2) Cover; cook on Low heat setting 6 to 8 hours.

3) About 25 minutes before serving, cook rice in 2 cups water as directed on package. Just before serving, stir artichoke hearts and olives into chicken mixture. Cover; cook until hot. Serve chicken mixture with rice.

Nutrition Information Per Serving	
Calories: 550	From Fat: 120
Total Fat	15g
Saturated Fat	3.5g
Trans Fat	0g
Cholesterol	120mg
Sodium	1280mg
Total Carbohydrate	49g
Dietary Fiber	7g
Sugars	10g
Protein	48g

CHUNKY TOMATO SOUP
PG. 262

Family Favorites

The tried-and-true classic dishes in this chapter are sure to please the ones you love.

HEARTLAND-STYLE SMOTHERED STEAK
PG. 268

HOT FUDGE BROWNIE DESSERT
PG. 272

CROWD-PLEASING SCRAMBLED EGGS
PG. 259

Sweet and Tangy Brisket

PREP TIME: 20 MINUTES (READY IN 9 HOURS 30 MINUTES)
SERVINGS: 12

 EASY   LOW FAT

1 teaspoon salt

½ teaspoon pepper

2 teaspoons ground ginger

1 teaspoon ground allspice

¼ teaspoon ground cinnamon

1 teaspoon dried minced garlic

1 beef brisket (3½ to 4 lb), trimmed of fat, cut into 3 pieces

1 cup chopped onion

⅔ cup cider vinegar

1 can (6 oz) tomato paste

½ cup packed brown sugar

1) Spray 4- to 5-quart slow cooker with cooking spray. In small bowl, mix salt, pepper, ginger, allspice, cinnamon and garlic. Rub seasoning mixture on beef pieces; set aside. Place onion in cooker; top with beef.

2) In medium bowl, mix vinegar, tomato paste and brown sugar. Pour mixture over beef. Cover; cook on Low heat setting 9 to 11 hours.

3) Remove beef from slow cooker. Transfer sauce to 2-quart saucepan; heat to boiling over medium-high heat, stirring occasionally. Reduce the heat; simmer 5 to 8 minutes, stirring occasionally until sauce is reduced to about half.

4) Cut the beef against the grain into slices; place on serving platter. Serve with sauce.

Nutrition Information Per Serving

Calories: 250	From Fat: 80
Total Fat	8g
Saturated Fat	3g
Trans Fat	0g
Cholesterol	55mg
Sodium	350mg
Total Carbohydrate	14g
Dietary Fiber	1g
Sugars	12g
Protein	29g

Tuna-Broccoli Casserole

PREP TIME: 20 MINUTES (READY IN 1 HOUR 10 MINUTES)
SERVINGS: 4

 EASY

1⅓ cups uncooked penne pasta (4 oz)

1 can (10¾ oz) condensed cream of mushroom soup

¼ cup milk

1 pouch (7.06 oz) chunk albacore (white) or light tuna in water, drained

1 jar (4.5 oz) Green Giant® sliced mushrooms, drained

1 bag (12 oz) Green Giant® Valley Fresh Steamers™ frozen broccoli cuts, thawed

1 tablespoon butter or margarine, melted

¼ cup Progresso® panko crispy bread crumbs

¼ cup slivered almonds

1) Heat oven to 350°F. Cook and drain pasta as directed on package, using minimum cook time. In ungreased 1½-quart casserole, stir together soup, milk, tuna, mushrooms and cooked pasta.

2) Cover; bake 20 minutes. Remove casserole from oven. Cut up large pieces of broccoli; gently stir broccoli into tuna mixture. In small bowl, mix butter, bread crumbs and almonds; sprinkle over casserole. Bake about 30 minutes longer or until bubbly around edges.

Nutrition Information Per Serving	
Calories: 370	From Fat: 110
Total Fat	13g
Saturated Fat	3.5g
Trans Fat	0g
Cholesterol	25mg
Sodium	850mg
Total Carbohydrate	42g
Dietary Fiber	5g
Sugars	4g
Protein	23g

Chicken Alfredo Biscuit Casserole

PREP TIME: 15 MINUTES (READY IN 35 MINUTES)
SERVINGS: 5

 EASY

1 tablespoon butter or margarine

2 cups sliced fresh mushrooms

½ cup chopped onion

1 jar (16 oz) Alfredo pasta sauce

¼ cup milk

2 cups chopped cooked chicken

2 cups Green Giant® Select® frozen broccoli florets, thawed

¼ teaspoon dried basil leaves

1 can (7.5 oz) Pillsbury® refrigerated buttermilk biscuits

1 tablespoon butter or margarine, melted

1 tablespoon grated Parmesan cheese

1) Heat oven to 375°F. Spray 8-inch square (2-quart) glass baking dish with cooking spray.

2) In 10-inch nonstick skillet, melt 1 tablespoon butter over medium heat. Cook mushrooms and onion in butter, stirring occasionally, about 5 minutes or until tender. Stir in Alfredo sauce, milk, chicken, broccoli and basil. Cook until mixture is hot and bubbly, stirring constantly. Spoon into baking dish.

3) Separate dough into 10 biscuits. Cut each biscuit in half crosswise. Arrange around edge of baking dish, overlapping slightly. Drizzle biscuits with melted butter; sprinkle with Parmesan cheese.

4) Bake 15 to 20 minutes or until biscuits are golden brown.

Nutrition Information Per Serving	
Calories: 590	From Fat: 340
Total Fat	38g
Saturated Fat	22g
Trans Fat	1.5g
Cholesterol	150mg
Sodium	850mg
Total Carbohydrate	32g
Dietary Fiber	3g
Sugars	6g
Protein	30g

Beer Cheese Soup

PREP TIME: 30 MINUTES (READY IN 30 MINUTES)
SERVINGS: 5 (1-1/2 CUPS EACH)

 EASY

½ cup butter or margarine

¾ cup finely chopped carrots

½ cup finely chopped celery

¼ cup finely chopped onion

1 cup quick-mixing flour

½ teaspoon paprika

⅛ teaspoon black pepper

⅛ teaspoon ground red pepper (cayenne)

3 cups Progresso® chicken broth (from 32-oz carton)

1 cup whipping cream

4 cups shredded sharp Cheddar cheese (16 oz)

1 can (12 oz) beer

1) In 4-quart Dutch oven, melt butter over medium heat. Add carrots, celery and onion; cook about 10 minutes, stirring occasionally, until celery and onions are transparent.

2) Stir in flour, paprika, black pepper and ground red pepper. Add broth; heat to boiling over medium heat. Boil and stir 1 minute.

3) Reduce heat; stir in whipping cream and cheese. Heat until cheese is melted, stirring occasionally. Stir in beer. If desired, serve with popcorn.

Nutrition Information Per Serving	
Calories: 790	From Fat: 570
Total Fat	64g
Saturated Fat	40g
Trans Fat	2g
Cholesterol	195mg
Sodium	1240mg
Total Carbohydrate	26g
Dietary Fiber	1g
Sugars	5g
Protein	28g

tip

Popped popcorn is the classic garnish for beer cheese soup. Croutons work well as a topping, too.

Burger 'n Fries Pot Pie

PREP TIME: 20 MINUTES (READY IN 45 MINUTES)
SERVINGS: 6

EASY

1½ lb lean (at least 80%) ground beef

1 large onion, chopped (about 1 cup)

2 tablespoons all-purpose flour

1 can (14.5 oz) diced tomatoes, undrained

1 cup shredded Cheddar cheese (4 oz)

2 cups frozen crispy French-fried potatoes (from 20-oz bag)

Nutrition Information Per Serving	
Calories: 340	From Fat: 180
Total Fat	20g
Saturated Fat	9g
Trans Fat	0g
Cholesterol	90mg
Sodium	340mg
Total Carbohydrate	13g
Dietary Fiber	2g
Sugars	0g
Protein	26g

1) Heat oven to 450°F. In 12-inch nonstick skillet, cook beef and onion over medium-high heat, about 8 minutes, stirring occasionally, until the beef is thoroughly cooked; drain well. Sprinkle flour over the beef mixture. Cook 1 minute, stirring constantly. Stir in tomatoes; heat to boiling. Remove from heat.

2) In ungreased 1½-quart casserole, spread beef mixture. Sprinkle with cheese. Arrange frozen potatoes evenly in single layer on top.

3) Bake uncovered about 20 minutes or until potatoes are golden brown. Let stand 5 minutes before serving.

Cincinnati Chili

PREP TIME: 30 MINUTES (READY IN 30 MINUTES)
SERVINGS: 5 (1 CUP CHILI AND 1 CUP SPAGHETTI EACH)

EASY

10 oz uncooked spaghetti

1 tablespoon vegetable oil

1 lb ground turkey breast

1 medium onion, chopped (½ cup)

1 clove garlic, finely chopped

1 jar (26 oz) chunky vegetable-style tomato pasta sauce

1 can (15 oz) Progresso® dark red kidney beans, drained, rinsed

2 tablespoons chili powder

Nutrition Information Per Serving	
Calories: 660	From Fat: 140
Total Fat	15g
Saturated Fat	3g
Trans Fat	0g
Cholesterol	60mg
Sodium	1030mg
Total Carbohydrate	94g
Dietary Fiber	10g
Sugars	17g
Protein	36g

1) Cook and drain spaghetti as directed on package. Meanwhile, in 10-inch skillet, heat oil over medium heat. Cook turkey, onion and garlic in oil 5 to 6 minutes, stirring occasionally, until turkey is no longer pink.

2) Stir pasta sauce, beans and chili powder into turkey mixture; reduce heat to low. Simmer uncovered 10 minutes, stirring occasionally. Serve sauce over spaghetti.

Individual Chicken Cobb Salads with Blue Cheese Dressing

PREP TIME: 15 MINUTES (READY IN 1 HOUR 15 MINUTES)
SERVINGS: 4

 EASY

DRESSING

- ⅓ cup mayonnaise or salad dressing
- 3 tablespoons plain low-fat yogurt
- 3 tablespoons red wine vinegar
- 1 clove garlic, finely chopped
- ½ cup crumbled blue cheese (2 oz)

SALADS

- 8 cups mixed salad greens
- 2 packages (5 oz each) sliced smoked chicken breast, chopped
- 4 hard-cooked eggs, quartered
- 1 medium ripe avocado, pitted, peeled and sliced
- 2 medium tomatoes, chopped
- ¼ cup bacon flavor bits or chips

1) In small bowl, beat mayonnaise, yogurt, vinegar and garlic with wire whisk. Stir in blue cheese. Cover and refrigerate at least 1 hour.

2) Just before serving, arrange greens on 4 salad plates. Top with remaining salad ingredients. Drizzle dressing over salads.

3) If desired, sprinkle with freshly ground black pepper.

Nutrition Information Per Serving

Calories: 460	From Fat: 300
Total Fat	33g
Saturated Fat	8g
Trans Fat	0g
Cholesterol	265mg
Sodium	1330mg
Total Carbohydrate	14g
Dietary Fiber	6g
Sugars	7g
Protein	27g

tip

Short time? Purchase hard-cooked eggs from the salad bar in your local supermarket.

Crescent Strawberry Shortcake

PREP TIME: 30 MINUTES (READY IN 1 HOUR 10 MINUTES)
SERVINGS: 4

3 tablespoons sugar

1 tablespoon cornstarch

2½ cups sliced fresh strawberries

½ cup water

2 tablespoons orange-flavored liqueur
   or orange juice

   Red food color, if desired

1 can (8 oz) Pillsbury® refrigerated
   crescent dinner rolls

1 egg white, slightly beaten

2 teaspoons sugar

1 cup frozen whipped topping, thawed

1) In small saucepan, combine 3 tablespoons sugar and cornstarch. In blender container or food processor bowl with metal blade, combine ½ cup of the strawberries and the water; puree until smooth. If desired, strain to remove seeds.

2) Stir pureed strawberries into sugar mixture in saucepan. Cook over medium heat for about 5 minutes or until thickened, stirring constantly. Stir in liqueur. Cool 10 minutes. Stir in remaining 2 cups strawberries and enough food color for desired red color. Refrigerate until serving time.

3) Heat oven to 325°F. Lightly grease cookie sheet. Separate dough into 8 triangles. For each roll, place 2 triangles together, one on top of the other; press all edges together to seal. Roll up, starting at shortest side of triangle and rolling to opposite point. Place point side down on greased cookie sheet. Brush each roll with egg white. Sprinkle evenly with 2 teaspoons sugar.

4) Bake at 325°F. for 20 to 25 minutes or until rolls are golden brown. Remove from cookie sheet; cool 15 minutes. Split rolls horizontally; place on individual dessert plates. Fill and top each with strawberry mixture and whipped topping.

Nutrition Information Per Serving	
Calories: 360	From Fat: 110
Total Fat	16g
Saturated Fat	3g
Trans Fat	0g
Cholesterol	0mg
Sodium	460mg
Total Carbohydrate	49g
Dietary Fiber	2g
Sugars	30g
Protein	6g

tip

To reduce the fat content in this recipe, use fat-free or light whipped topping in place of the regular frozen whipped topping.

Crowd-Pleasing Scrambled Eggs

PREP TIME: 15 MINUTES (READY IN 2 HOURS 10 MINUTES)
SERVINGS: 12

e EASY

2 dozen eggs

½ teaspoon salt

½ teaspoon pepper

1 cup half-and-half

2 cups diced cooked ham

1 tablespoon butter or margarine

8 green onions, chopped (½ cup)

1 small red bell pepper, chopped (½ cup)

1 cup shredded Cheddar cheese (4 oz)

1) Spray 4- to 5-quart slow cooker with cooking spray. In cooker, beat eggs, salt, pepper and half-and-half with electric mixer on medium speed until smooth. Sprinkle with ham. Cover; cook on High heat setting 1 hour, stirring after 30 minutes.

2) Continue cooking 40 to 50 minutes longer, stirring every 10 minutes, until eggs are moist and almost cooked through.

3) In 10-inch skillet, melt butter over medium heat. Add green onions and bell pepper; cook about 5 minutes, stirring occasionally, until pepper is tender. Stir pepper mixture and cheese into eggs. Serve immediately, or reduce to Low heat setting and hold up to 1 hour.

Nutrition Information Per Serving	
Calories: 280	From Fat: 180
Total Fat	20g
Saturated Fat	9g
Trans Fat	0g
Cholesterol	455mg
Sodium	1160mg
Total Carbohydrate	5g
Dietary Fiber	0g
Sugars	5g
Protein	20g

Chicken Muffuletta

PREP TIME: 15 MINUTES (READY IN 1 HOUR 15 MINUTES)
SERVINGS: 6

e EASY

OLIVE SALAD

- ½ cup pitted green and/or ripe olives, finely chopped

- 1 jar (4 oz) sliced pimientos, drained and finely chopped

- 1 clove garlic, finely chopped

- 2 tablespoons olive oil

- 1 tablespoon red wine vinegar

- ½ teaspoon crushed dried oregano leaves

SANDWICH

- 1 (8-inch) round Italian bread loaf (about 1¼ lb)

- 4 oz sliced provolone cheese

- 4 oz thinly sliced cooked chicken breast (from deli)

- 4 oz sliced Genoa salami

1) In small bowl, stir together olive salad ingredients. Cut loaf of bread horizontally in half. Scoop out soft center from top and bottom of loaf, making room for the filling and leaving a ¾-inch shell. Using tablespoon, scoop out or drain off 2 tablespoons liquid oil and vinegar dressing from olive salad, and drizzle over inside of bottom half of bread. Spread remaining olive salad mixture inside top half of bread.

2) Layer cheese, chicken and salami in bottom half. Cover with top of loaf; wrap well with plastic wrap. Place loaf on plate; cover with another plate and then a heavy weight, such as a large can. Refrigerate 1 to 6 hours.

3) To serve the muffuletta, cut sandwich into 6 wedges.

Nutrition Information Per Serving	
Calories: 480	From Fat: 190
Total Fat	21g
Saturated Fat	7g
Trans Fat	1g
Cholesterol	40mg
Sodium	1520mg
Total Carbohydrate	51g
Dietary Fiber	4g
Sugars	4g
Protein	21g

Beer-Can Chicken with Spicy Chili Rub

PREP TIME: 1 HOUR 45 MINUTES (READY IN 1 HOUR 45 MINUTES)
SERVINGS: 4

LOW FAT

1 whole chicken (3½ to 4 lb)

1 tablespoon packed brown sugar

1 tablespoon paprika

1 teaspoon seasoned salt

1 teaspoon chili powder

½ teaspoon garlic powder

½ teaspoon cumin

¼ teaspoon pepper

¼ teaspoon ground red pepper (cayenne)

1 can (12 oz) beer

1) If using charcoal grill, place drip pan directly under grilling area, and arrange coals around edge of firebox. Heat gas or charcoal grill for indirect cooking as directed by manufacturer. Remove and discard neck and giblets from chicken cavity. Rinse chicken with cold water; pat dry with paper towels. Fold wings of chicken across back with tips touching.

2) In small bowl, mix all remaining ingredients except beer. Sprinkle mixture inside cavity and all over outside of chicken; rub with fingers.

3) Open beer can; with can opener, make several other openings in top of can. Pour ⅔ cup beer from can; discard or reserve for another use. Spray outside of half-full can of beer with cooking spray. Holding chicken upright with larger opening of body cavity downward, insert beer can into larger cavity. Insert ovenproof meat thermometer so tip is in thickest part of inside thigh and does not touch bone.

4) Place chicken with beer can upright on grill rack over drip pan or over unheated side of gas grill. Cover grill; cook over medium heat 1 hour 15 minutes to 1 hour 30 minutes or until thermometer reads 180°F and leg moves easily when lifted or twisted.

5) Using tongs, carefully lift the chicken to 13x9-inch pan, holding large metal spatula under beer can for support. Let stand 15 minutes before carving. Twist the can to remove from the chicken; discard can.

Nutrition Information Per Serving	
Calories: 290	From Fat: 80
Total Fat	9g
Saturated Fat	2.5g
Trans Fat	0g
Cholesterol	110mg
Sodium	460mg
Total Carbohydrate	8g
Dietary Fiber	1g
Sugars	4g
Protein	36g

Chunky Tomato Soup

PREP TIME: 35 MINUTES (READY IN 1 HOUR 35 MINUTES)
SERVINGS: 8

 LOW FAT

- 2 tablespoons olive or vegetable oil
- 2 medium stalks celery, coarsely chopped (1 cup)
- 2 medium carrots, coarsely chopped (1 cup)
- 2 cloves garlic, finely chopped
- 2 cans (28 oz each) plum (Roma) tomatoes, undrained
- 2 cups water
- 1 teaspoon dried basil leaves
- ½ teaspoon pepper
- 3½ cups Progresso® chicken broth (from 32-oz carton)

1) In 5- to 6-quart Dutch oven, heat oil over medium-high heat. Add celery, carrots and garlic; cook 5 to 7 minutes, stirring frequently, until carrots are crisp-tender.

2) Stir in tomatoes, breaking up tomatoes coarsely. Stir in water, basil, pepper and broth. Heat to boiling. Reduce heat to low; cover and simmer 1 hour, stirring occasionally.

Nutrition Information Per Serving

Calories: 90	From Fat: 35
Total Fat	3.5g
Saturated Fat	.5g
Trans Fat	0g
Cholesterol	0mg
Sodium	680mg
Total Carbohydrate	11g
Dietary Fiber	2g
Sugars	6g
Protein	3g

Chicken Noodle Soup

PREP TIME: 10 MINUTES (READY IN 25 MINUTES)
SERVINGS: 4

   EASY   LOW FAT

1 tablespoon olive or vegetable oil

2 cloves garlic, finely chopped

8 medium green onions, sliced (½ cup)

2 medium carrots, chopped (1 cup)

2 cups cubed cooked chicken

2 cups uncooked egg noodles (4 oz)

1 tablespoon chopped fresh parsley or 1 teaspoon parsley flakes

¼ teaspoon pepper

1 dried bay leaf

5¼ cups Progresso® chicken broth (from two 32-oz cartons)

Nutrition Information Per Serving	
Calories: 300	From Fat: 90
Total Fat	10g
Saturated Fat	2g
Trans Fat	0g
Cholesterol	80mg
Sodium	1200mg
Total Carbohydrate	25g
Dietary Fiber	2g
Sugars	4g
Protein	27g

1) In 3-quart saucepan, heat oil over medium heat. Add garlic, onions and carrots; cook 4 minutes, stirring occasionally.

2) Stir in remaining ingredients. Heat to boiling; reduce heat. Cover; simmer about 10 minutes, stirring occasionally, until carrots and noodles are tender. Remove bay leaf.

Chicken BLT Wraps with Aioli

PREP TIME: 15 MINUTES (READY IN 15 MINUTES)
SERVINGS: 4 WRAPS

 EASY

AIOLI

⅓ cup mayonnaise or salad dressing

1 large clove garlic, finely chopped

1 tablespoon fresh lemon juice

WRAPS

4 flour tortillas (10 inch)

8 leaves green leaf lettuce

1 package (9 oz) thinly sliced oven-roasted chicken breast

2 medium tomatoes, chopped

¼ cup bacon flavor bits or chips

Nutrition Information Per Serving	
Calories: 390	From Fat: 190
Total Fat	21g
Saturated Fat	4g
Trans Fat	1g
Cholesterol	40mg
Sodium	1250mg
Total Carbohydrate	31g
Dietary Fiber	3g
Sugars	5g
Protein	18g

1) In small bowl, beat aioli ingredients with wire whisk. Spread on each tortilla, leaving 2-inch border at bottom of each.

2) Arrange 2 lettuce leaves on each tortilla, leaving 2-inch border at bottom. Evenly top each with chicken, tomatoes and bacon bits.

3) Fold bottom edge of each tortilla up, and roll tightly. Secure, if desired, with toothpick, foil or waxed paper.

Pork Diane Skillet Supper

PREP TIME:	30 MINUTES (READY IN 50 MINUTES)
SERVINGS:	4

2 tablespoons butter or margarine

1 lb pork tenderloins, cut crosswise into ¼-inch slices

1¾ cup Progresso® chicken broth (from 32-oz carton)

2 teaspoons Worcestershire sauce

¼ teaspoon salt

⅛ teaspoon pepper

8 small red potatoes, quartered

½ cup sliced green onions (8 medium)

1 cup sliced fresh mushrooms (3 oz)

2 tablespoons all-purpose flour

1) In 12-inch skillet or Dutch oven, melt butter over medium-high heat. Cook pork in butter 3 to 5 minutes or until browned on both sides. Remove pork from skillet; set aside.

2) In 1-cup measuring cup or small bowl, reserve ¼ cup of the broth. Add remaining 1½ cups broth, the Worcestershire sauce, salt, pepper and potatoes to skillet. Heat to boiling. Reduce heat; cover and simmer 13 to 17 minutes or until potatoes are tender.

3) Reserve 2 tablespoons onions for garnish. Stir remaining onions, mushrooms and pork slices into potatoes. Cover; simmer about 5 minutes longer or until pork is no longer pink in center.

4) Add flour to reserved broth in measuring cup; blend until smooth. Gradually stir into pork mixture. Cook over medium-high heat 2 to 3 minutes, stirring constantly, until mixture is bubbly and thickened. Sprinkle with reserved onions.

Nutrition Information Per Serving	
Calories: 460	From Fat: 90
Total Fat	11g
Saturated Fat	5g
Trans Fat	0g
Cholesterol	65mg
Sodium	660mg
Total Carbohydrate	63g
Dietary Fiber	8g
Sugars	5g
Protein	29g

Hearty Chicken Rice Soup

| PREP TIME: | 55 MINUTES (READY IN 55 MINUTES) |
| SERVINGS: | 4 (1-1/2 CUPS EACH) |

lf LOW FAT

½ cup sliced celery

2 frozen boneless skinless chicken breasts

5¾ cups Progresso® reduced-sodium chicken broth (from two 32-oz cartons)

2 cups Green Giant® frozen mixed vegetables (from 1-lb bag)

¾ cup uncooked instant white rice

1 tablespoon dried parsley flakes

2 teaspoons salt-free lemon and herb seasoning

1) Spray 4-quart saucepan or Dutch oven with cooking spray. Heat over medium-high heat until hot. Add celery; cook and stir 1½ to 2 minutes or until crisp-tender. Add frozen chicken breasts and broth. Heat to boiling. Reduce heat; cover and simmer 10 to 12 minutes, stirring occasionally, until juice of chicken is clear when center of thickest part is cut. Remove the chicken from saucepan and cool slightly. Cut chicken into bite-size pieces.

2) Heat broth mixture in saucepan to boiling over medium-high heat; stir in frozen vegetables. Return to boiling. Stir in rice, chicken, parsley and seasoning. Reduce heat; cover and simmer about 10 minutes or until rice and vegetables are tender.

Nutrition Information Per Serving	
Calories: 460	From Fat: 25
Total Fat	2.5g
Saturated Fat	0.5g
Trans Fat	0g
Cholesterol	40mg
Sodium	1670mg
Total Carbohydrate	25g
Dietary Fiber	2g
Sugars	4g
Protein	22g

Pork Chops with Apples and Stuffing

PREP TIME: 20 MINUTES (READY IN 1 HOUR 25 MINUTES)
SERVINGS: 4

 EASY

½ teaspoon butter or margarine, softened

2 unpeeled red baking apples, sliced

2 teaspoons all-purpose flour

1 teaspoon packed brown sugar

¼ teaspoon ground cinnamon

½ teaspoon seasoned salt

4 bone-in pork loin chops, ¾ inch thick (about 2 lb), trimmed

1 cup apple juice or apple cider

2 tablespoons butter or margarine

1½ cups stuffing mix for pork or chicken (from 12-oz box or 8- or 12-oz canister)

¼ cup sweetened dried cranberries

1 tablespoon chopped fresh parsley

1) Heat oven to 375°F. Brush ½ teaspoon butter in bottom of 13x9-inch (3-quart) glass baking dish. Spread apple slices in dish. In small bowl, mix flour, brown sugar and cinnamon; sprinkle over apples. Sprinkle seasoned salt on both sides of each pork chop; place pork chops over apples.

2) In 2-quart saucepan, heat apple juice and 2 tablespoons butter to boiling over medium-high heat. Stir in stuffing mix and cranberries. Cover; remove from heat. Let stand 5 minutes. Fluff mixture with fork. Scoop ½ cup stuffing onto each pork chop.

3) Spray sheet of foil with cooking spray; place sprayed side down over baking dish. Bake 40 to 50 minutes. Uncover; bake 5 to 10 minutes longer or until pork is no longer pink in center and meat thermometer inserted in center reads 160°F. Sprinkle with parsley. To serve, lift pork chops with stuffing to serving plates; serve apples on the side.

Nutrition Information Per Serving	
Calories: 420	From Fat: 180
Total Fat	20g
Saturated Fat	9g
Trans Fat	0g
Cholesterol	120mg
Sodium	680mg
Total Carbohydrate	48g
Dietary Fiber	3g
Sugars	23g
Protein	38g

Cordon Bleu Chicken Rolls

PREP TIME: 15 MINUTES (READY IN 3 HOURS 45 MINUTES)
SERVINGS: 6

 EASY

6 boneless skinless chicken breasts (about 5 oz each)

3 thin slices (¾ oz each) deli ham, cut in half

3 slices (1 oz each) Swiss cheese, cut in half

1 can (10¾ oz) condensed cream of celery soup

1 cup sour cream

1 teaspoon parsley flakes

1 teaspoon marinade for chicken (white Worcestershire sauce) or regular Worcestershire sauce

½ teaspoon onion powder

¼ teaspoon pepper

1) Spray 3- to 4-quart slow cooker with cooking spray. Between pieces of plastic wrap or waxed paper, place each chicken breast smooth side down; beginning in center of breast, gently pound with flat side of meat mallet or rolling pin until about ¼ inch thick.

2) Place ½ ham slice and ½ cheese slice on each breast. Roll up, folding in sides. Place rolls, seam sides down, in single layer in slow cooker. In medium bowl, mix remaining ingredients; spoon over chicken.

3) Cover; cook on Low heat setting 3 hours 30 minutes to 4 hours 30 minutes.

4) Remove rolls from cooker to cutting board. Beat sauce in cooker with wire whisk until smooth. Spoon about ⅓ cup sauce onto each of 6 plates. Cut each roll crosswise into thin slices; arrange on sauce.

Nutrition Information Per Serving	
Calories: 360	From Fat: 180
Total Fat	19g
Saturated Fat	9g
Trans Fat	.5g
Cholesterol	135mg
Sodium	630mg
Total Carbohydrate	6g
Dietary Fiber	0g
Sugars	3g
Protein	39g

Heartland-Style Smothered Steak

PREP TIME: 25 MINUTES (READY IN 7 HOURS 25 MINUTES)
SERVINGS: 8

If LOW FAT

2 lb boneless beef round steak, cut into 8 pieces

⅓ cup all-purpose flour

1 teaspoon salt

¾ teaspoon pepper

2 tablespoons vegetable oil

1 cup chopped onion

3 medium carrots, chopped (1½ cups)

2 medium stalks celery, sliced (1 cup)

1 cup Progresso® beef flavored broth (from 32-oz carton)

½ cup red wine or Progresso® beef flavored broth

1 can (15 oz) tomato sauce

1 teaspoon dried minced garlic

1) In 1-gallon resealable food-storage plastic bag, place beef, flour, salt and pepper; seal bag. Shake to coat beef evenly.

2) In 12-inch nonstick skillet, heat 1 tablespoon of the oil over medium-high heat. Add half of the beef; cook 4 to 5 minutes, turning once, until browned on all sides. Repeat with remaining oil and beef.

3) Spray 3½- to 4-quart slow cooker with cooking spray. In cooker, place onion, carrots and celery; place beef on top. In medium bowl, mix broth, wine, tomato sauce and garlic. Pour over beef.

4) Cover; cook on Low heat setting 7 to 9 hours.

Nutrition Information Per Serving	
Calories: 290	From Fat: 70
Total Fat	8g
Saturated Fat	2g
Trans Fat	0g
Cholesterol	85mg
Sodium	750mg
Total Carbohydrate	14g
Dietary Fiber	2g
Sugars	6g
Protein	35g

Deep-Dish Lasagna Pie

PREP TIME: 25 MINUTES (READY IN 1 HOUR)
SERVINGS: 8

1 lb bulk Italian pork sausage

1 large onion, chopped (about 1 cup)

2 cups tomato pasta sauce

½ teaspoon dried oregano leaves

1 egg

1 container (15 oz) part-skim ricotta cheese

½ cup grated Parmesan cheese

2 cups shredded mozzarella cheese (8 oz)

2 cans (13.8 oz each) Pillsbury® refrigerated classic pizza crust

1) Heat oven to 425°F. Spray 13x9-inch (3-quart) glass baking dish with cooking spray. In 12-inch nonstick skillet, cook sausage and onion over medium-high heat 5 to 7 minutes, stirring occasionally, until sausage is no longer pink; drain well. Stir in pasta sauce and oregano; cook until thoroughly heated.

2) In medium bowl, beat egg. Stir in ricotta cheese, Parmesan cheese and 1½ cups of the mozzarella cheese.

3) Unroll dough for 1 pizza crust. Press in bottom and 1 inch up sides of dish. Spread cheese mixture over dough in bottom of dish. Spread sausage mixture over cheese mixture. Unroll dough for second pizza crust; place over sausage mixture and press edges to seal. Cut 4 slits in top crust.

4) Bake uncovered 15 minutes. Cover dish with sheet of foil to prevent excessive browning. Bake 9 to 11 minutes longer or until crust is golden brown. Top with remaining ½ cup mozzarella cheese. Let stand 5 minutes before serving.

Nutrition Information Per Serving	
Calories: 600	From Fat: 230
Total Fat	25g
Saturated Fat	11g
Trans Fat	0g
Cholesterol	85mg
Sodium	1350mg
Total Carbohydrate	64g
Dietary Fiber	3g
Sugars	6g
Protein	30g

Deep-Dish Turkey Pot Pie

PREP TIME: 15 MINUTES (READY IN 5 HOURS 45 MINUTES)
SERVINGS: 6

 EASY

1½ lb boneless skinless turkey breast tenderloin, cut into ¾-inch cubes

½ cup chopped onion

1 medium carrot, chopped (½ cup)

1 medium stalk celery, chopped (½ cup)

1 jar (4.5 oz) Green Giant® sliced mushrooms, drained

1 teaspoon poultry seasoning

½ teaspoon salt

½ teaspoon pepper

2 tablespoons water

1 can (18.6 oz) Progresso® chicken pot pie style soup

1½ cups Green Giant® Valley Fresh Steamers™ frozen mixed vegetables, thawed, drained

1 Pillsbury® refrigerated pie crust, softened as directed on box

¼ cup shredded Parmesan cheese

1) Spray 3½- to 4-quart slow cooker with cooking spray. In cooker, mix turkey, onion, carrot, celery, mushrooms, poultry seasoning, salt, pepper and water. Cover; cook on Low heat setting 5 to 6 hours.

2) Stir in soup and mixed vegetables. Increase heat setting to High. Cover; cook about 20 minutes or until thoroughly heated.

3) Meanwhile, heat oven to 450°F. Remove pie crust from pouch; unroll on work surface. With 2¾- to 3-inch round cookie cutter, cut 12 rounds from crust, rerolling once; discard scraps. Place pie crust rounds on ungreased cookie sheet. Sprinkle each with about 1 teaspoon Parmesan cheese. Bake about 8 minutes or until pie crust rounds are golden brown and crisp. Immediately remove from cookie sheet to cooling rack.

4) Top each serving of pot pie with 2 baked crusts.

Nutrition Information Per Serving	
Calories: 380	From Fat: 130
Total Fat	15g
Saturated Fat	6g
Trans Fat	0g
Cholesterol	65mg
Sodium	2240mg
Total Carbohydrate	35g
Dietary Fiber	4g
Sugars	6g
Protein	26g

Old-Fashioned Oven Beef Stew

PREP TIME: 15 MINUTES (READY IN 4 HOURS 15 MINUTES)
SERVINGS: 6 (1-1/2 CUPS EACH)

 EASY

1½ lb beef stew meat

3 tablespoons all-purpose flour

2 bags (1 lb each) frozen vegetables for stew

1 can (14.5 oz) diced tomatoes, undrained

2½ cups Progresso® beef flavored broth (from 32-oz carton)

1 tablespoon sugar

⅛ teaspoon pepper

2 dried bay leaves

1) Heat oven to 325°F. In 5-quart Dutch oven or 13x9-inch (3-quart) glass baking dish, toss beef with flour. Add frozen vegetables.

2) In large bowl, mix remaining ingredients. Pour over beef and vegetables; gently stir until mixed.

3) Cover; bake 3 hours 30 minutes to 4 hours or until beef is tender. Remove bay leaves before serving.

Nutrition Information Per Serving	
Calories: 320	From Fat: 110
Total Fat	13g
Saturated Fat	4.5g
Trans Fat	.5g
Cholesterol	60mg
Sodium	550mg
Total Carbohydrate	29g
Dietary Fiber	4g
Sugars	7g
Protein	22g

Hot Fudge Brownie Dessert

RENA REED | LILY, KENTUCKY

BAKE-OFF® CONTEST 44, 2010

 EASY

PREP TIME:	15 MINUTES (READY IN 1 HOUR 30 MINUTES)
SERVINGS:	16

2 boxes (19.5 oz each) Pillsbury®
  Chocolate Fudge Brownie Mix

1 cup Land O Lakes® butter, melted

½ cup strong brewed coffee (room
  temperature)

4 Eggland's Best eggs

¾ cup Fisher® Chef's Naturals®
  chopped pecans

1 can (14 oz) Eagle Brand® sweetened
  condensed milk

1 jar (11.75 oz) Smucker's® hot fudge
  ice cream topping

1 container (8 oz) frozen whipped
  topping, thawed

1) Heat oven to 350°F. Spray 13x9-inch pan with Crisco® original no-stick cooking spray.

2) In large bowl, stir together brownie mixes, butter, coffee, eggs and pecans until well blended. Pour into pan.

3) Bake 30 to 40 minutes or until toothpick inserted 2 inches from side of pan comes out almost clean.

4) In 1-quart saucepan, heat milk and fudge topping over medium-low heat about 5 minutes, stirring constantly, until hot (mixture must be hot). Cool brownies 5 minutes; poke several times with long-tined fork, wiping fork with paper towel if necessary. Pour hot fudge mixture over brownies. Cool 35 minutes before serving. Serve warm with whipped topping.

Nutrition Information Per Serving	
Calories: 570	From Fat: 240
Total Fat	27g
Saturated Fat	12g
Trans Fat	.5g
Cholesterol	85mg
Sodium	280mg
Total Carbohydrate	75g
Dietary Fiber	1g
Sugars	55g
Protein	7g

So-Simple Tuna-Pasta Casserole

PREP TIME: 15 MINUTES (READY IN 45 MINUTES)
SERVINGS: 4

 EASY

CASSEROLE

- 1 bag (24 oz) Green Giant® frozen pasta, carrots, broccoli, sugar snap peas & garlic sauce
- 2 cans (5 oz each) tuna in water, drained, flaked
- 1 can (10¾ oz) condensed cream of potato soup
- ¼ cup milk

TOPPING

- 1 cup soft bread crumbs (about 2 slices white bread)
- 2 tablespoons butter or margarine, melted

1) Heat the oven to 350°F. Spray a 2-quart casserole dish with no-stick cooking spray.

2) In large microwavable bowl, place pasta-vegetable mixture. Cover with plastic wrap; microwave on High 9 to 11 minutes, stirring halfway through microwave time, until sauce chips are melted and vegetables are cooked. Stir in tuna, soup and milk. Pour into casserole.

3) In small bowl, toss topping ingredients. Sprinkle over tuna mixture. Bake 25 to 30 minutes or until hot and topping is golden brown.

Nutrition Information Per Serving	
Calories: 460	From Fat: 110
Total Fat	12g
Saturated Fat	6g
Trans Fat	0g
Cholesterol	40mg
Sodium	1350mg
Total Carbohydrate	58g
Dietary Fiber	4g
Sugars	7g
Protein	28g

tip

Stretch this casserole by stirring in 1 can (15.25 oz) of Green Giant® whole kernel sweet corn, drained, with the tuna. Bake 5 minutes longer than the recipe states.

Holiday Extravaganza

Celebrating Halloween, Thanksgiving and Christmas
is pure fun when these recipes are on the menu.

APPLE-SAGE BRINED TURKEY
BREAST
PG. 286

MAKE-AHEAD POTATO-ONION
GRATIN
PG. 296

SWEET POTATOES WITH CINNAMON
HONEY
PG. 285

CRANBERRY RIBBON
CHEESECAKE
PG. 284

Halloween Cookie Pizza

PREP TIME: 15 MINUTES (READY IN 1 HOUR 5 MINUTES)
SERVINGS: 16

e EASY

1 roll (16.5 oz) Pillsbury® refrigerated
  sugar cookies

½ cup creamy peanut butter

1 cup candy corn

½ cup raisins

¼ cup vanilla ready-to-spread frosting
  (from 1-lb can)

1) Heat oven to 350°F. Line 12-inch pizza
   pan with foil; grease foil with shortening.
   Cut cookie dough into ¼-inch-thick
   slices; arrange in pan. With floured
   fingers, press slices to form crust.

2) Bake 15 to 20 minutes or until deep
   golden brown. Cool completely, about
   30 minutes.

3) Use foil to lift crust from pan. Carefully
   remove foil from crust; place crust on
   serving platter or tray. Spread peanut
   butter over crust. Sprinkle candy corn
   and raisins evenly over top.

4) In small microwavable bowl, microwave
   frosting on High 10 to 15 seconds or
   until thin and drizzling consistency.
   Drizzle frosting over cookie pizza. Cut
   into wedges or squares.

Nutrition Information Per Serving

Calories: 270	From Fat: 100
Total Fat	11g
Saturated Fat	3g
Trans Fat	0g
Cholesterol	10mg
Sodium	125mg
Total Carbohydrate	39g
Dietary Fiber	0g
Sugars	27g
Protein	3g

Funny Face Taco Dip

| PREP TIME: | 10 MINUTES (READY IN 10 MINUTES) | EASY |
| SERVINGS: | 16 (2 TABLESPOONS DIP AND 3 CHIPS EACH) | |

1 package (8 oz) cream cheese, softened

½ cup sour cream

2 teaspoons Old El Paso® taco seasoning mix (from 1-oz package)

¼ cup red jalapeño pepper jelly

¼ cup Old El Paso® thick 'n chunky salsa

1 cup finely shredded Cheddar cheese (4 oz)

Small pieces assorted fresh vegetables

8 oz tortilla chips

1) In medium bowl, mix the cream cheese, sour cream and taco seasoning mix until smooth. Spread in 9-inch glass pie plate.

2) In a small bowl, stir the jelly until softened. Stir in the salsa. Spread the mixture evenly over cream cheese mixture. Sprinkle with shredded Cheddar cheese.

3) Decorate top of dip with vegetable pieces to resemble silly face. Serve dip with tortilla chips. Store in refrigerator.

Nutrition Information Per Serving

Calories: 180	From Fat: 110
Total Fat	12g
Saturated Fat	6g
Trans Fat	0g
Cholesterol	25mg
Sodium	220mg
Total Carbohydrate	14g
Dietary Fiber	0g
Sugars	0g
Protein	4g

Barbecued Worm Sandwiches

PREP TIME: 15 MINUTES (READY IN 15 MINUTES)
SERVINGS: 8 SANDWICHES

8 **hot dogs, each cut lengthwise into 6 strips**

½ **cup barbecue sauce**

8 **slices (¾ oz each) American cheese**

8 **sandwich buns, split, toasted**

1) In 10-inch nonstick skillet, heat hot dog strips over medium-high heat until strips begin to curl.

2) Gently stir in the barbecue sauce until hot dog strips are coated. Heat until bubbly.

3) Place slices of cheese on bottom halves of buns. Top with the hot dog mixture and cover with the top halves of buns.

Cut each hot dog in half lengthwise, then cut each half in thirds to make 6 strips. Strips will curl slightly when heated.

Nutrition Information Per Serving	
Calories: 370	From Fat: 200
Total Fat	22g
Saturated Fat	10g
Trans Fat	1g
Cholesterol	50mg
Sodium	1060mg
Total Carbohydrate	29g
Dietary Fiber	0g
Sugars	7g
Protein	14g

Cutie Bugs

PREP TIME: 1 HOUR (READY IN 1 HOUR)
SERVINGS: 32 COOKIES

12 oz chocolate-flavored candy coating, cut into pieces

1 package (1 lb) peanut-shaped peanut butter-filled sandwich cookies

64 small pretzel twists

4 teaspoons miniature candy-coated chocolate baking bits

1) Line cookie sheets with waxed paper. In 1-quart saucepan, melt the candy coating over low heat, stirring constantly, until smooth.

2) For each cookie bug, hold 1 cookie with tongs; dip entire top and sides of cookie into melted coating, letting excess drip off. Place cookie, coated side up, on cookie sheet.

3) Cut pretzels into curved pieces for legs. Dip 1 end of each curved piece in coating; place 3 "legs" on each side of each cookie.

4) Cut 2 short pretzel pieces for antennae. Dip 1 end of each pretzel piece in coating; place 2 "antennae" on top of each cookie. Place 2 baking bits near antennae for eyes. If desired, decorate bugs with additional candies. Let stand about 10 minutes until coating is set before storing.

Nutrition Information Per Serving	
Calories: 140	From Fat: 65
Total Fat	7g
Saturated Fat	3g
Trans Fat	0g
Cholesterol	0mg
Sodium	95mg
Total Carbohydrate	18g
Dietary Fiber	0g
Sugars	9g
Protein	1g

Spider Web Pumpkin Pancakes

PREP TIME: 1 HOUR (READY IN 1 HOUR)
SERVINGS: 8 (4 PANCAKES AND 2 TABLESPOONS SYRUP EACH)

lf LOW FAT

2 eggs, slightly beaten

¼ cup sugar

¾ cup milk

¼ cup vegetable oil

1 teaspoon vanilla

1 can (15 oz) pumpkin (not pumpkin pie mix)

2 cups all-purpose flour

2 teaspoons baking powder

1 teaspoon ground cinnamon

1 cup maple-flavored syrup

1) In large bowl, mix eggs, sugar, milk, oil and vanilla until well blended. Stir in remaining ingredients except syrup just until mixed.

2) Line 1-quart pitcher or bowl with gallon-size resealable food-storage plastic bag. Pour batter into bag; seal bag, pressing out air.

3) Heat large nonstick electric griddle to 375°F or heat 12-inch nonstick skillet over medium heat.

4) Grease hot griddle with oil. Cut ¼-inch hole in one bottom corner of bag. For each pancake, gently squeeze bag to pipe about 2 tablespoons batter onto hot griddle in 4-inch spider web shape. Cook 1 to 2 minutes or until pancakes are puffed and dry around edges. Turn pancakes; cook about 1 minute longer or until other side is golden brown. Serve with syrup.

Nutrition Information Per Serving	
Calories: 370	From Fat: 80
Total Fat	9g
Saturated Fat	1.5g
Trans Fat	0g
Cholesterol	55mg
Sodium	200mg
Total Carbohydrate	66g
Dietary Fiber	3g
Sugars	24g
Protein	6g

Bubbly Black Punch with Wormy Ice Ring

PREP TIME: 10 MINUTES (READY IN 6 HOURS 10 MINUTES)
SERVINGS: 14 (3/4 CUP EACH)

 EASY   LOW FAT

- 1 cup gummy candy worms
- 4 cups green berry rush kiwi-strawberry fruit punch (from 128-oz container)
- 3 cans (12 oz each) orange-flavored carbonated beverage
- 3 cans (12 oz each) grape-flavored carbonated beverage
- 1 can (11.5 oz) frozen grape juice concentrate, thawed

Nutrition Information Per Serving	
Calories: 190	From Fat: 0
Total Fat	0g
Saturated Fat	0g
Trans Fat	0g
Cholesterol	0mg
Sodium	40mg
Total Carbohydrate	48g
Dietary Fiber	0g
Sugars	44g
Protein	0g

1) In bottom of 6-cup ring mold, scatter most of candy worms. Pour fruit punch over candy, filling to within 1 inch of top (candy worms will float to top). Place remaining candy worms over edge of mold. Freeze 5 to 6 hours or until solid.

2) Just before serving, in 3-quart or larger punch bowl, mix both carbonated beverages and thawed juice concentrate.

3) Dip outside of ring mold in hot water until ice ring is loosened. Remove ice ring; place in punch so gummy worms are visible.

Chocolate Gremlins

PREP TIME: 15 MINUTES (READY IN 15 MINUTES)
SERVINGS: 24 COOKIES

 EASY

- 1 cup butterscotch chips
- 1 cup semisweet chocolate chips
- 2 cups Fiber One® original bran cereal
- 48 miniature candy-coated chocolate baking bits

Nutrition Information Per Serving	
Calories: 100	From Fat: 40
Total Fat	4.5g
Saturated Fat	3g
Trans Fat	0g
Cholesterol	0mg
Sodium	30mg
Total Carbohydrate	14g
Dietary Fiber	3g
Sugars	9g
Protein	0g

1) In 2-quart saucepan, heat butterscotch chips and chocolate chips over low heat, stirring constantly, until melted and smooth.

2) Gently stir in cereal until well coated. Onto waxed paper, drop mixture by teaspoonfuls to form 24 "gremlins." Press 2 baking bits onto each to resemble eyes. Refrigerate until set.

Moldy Bones with Ghoulish Dip

PREP TIME: 10 MINUTES (READY IN 25 MINUTES)
SERVINGS: 6 (2 TABLESPOONS DIP AND 1 BREADSTICK EACH)

 EASY

1 can (7 oz) Pillsbury® refrigerated original breadsticks (6 breadsticks)

1 egg white, beaten

1 tablespoon grated Parmesan cheese

½ teaspoon dried basil leaves

1 can (8 oz) pizza sauce, heated

1) Heat oven to 375°F. Spray cookie sheet with cooking spray. Unroll dough; separate at perforations into 6 breadsticks. Roll each until 12 inches long. Loosely tie knot in both ends of each breadstick; place on cookie sheet (do not twist).

2) Brush breadsticks with egg white. Sprinkle with cheese and basil.

3) Bake 12 to 14 minutes or until golden brown. Serve warm "bones" with warm pizza sauce for dipping.

Nutrition Information Per Serving	
Calories: 120	From Fat: 30
Total Fat	3.5g
Saturated Fat	0.5g
Trans Fat	0g
Cholesterol	0mg
Sodium	430mg
Total Carbohydrate	19g
Dietary Fiber	1g
Sugars	3g
Protein	4g

Baked Eyeball Eggs

PREP TIME: 15 MINUTES (READY IN 1 HOUR 20 MINUTES)
SERVINGS: 10

 EASY

1 bag (30 oz) frozen shredded hash brown potatoes, thawed

1 can (10¾ oz) condensed cream of potato soup

1 container (8 oz) sour cream (about 1 cup)

1½ cups shredded Cheddar cheese (6 oz)

2 teaspoons dried minced onion

½ teaspoon salt

¾ teaspoon pepper

10 slices Canadian bacon (about 6 oz)

10 eggs

Ketchup

1) Heat oven to 350°F. In large bowl, mix potatoes, soup, sour cream, cheese, onion, salt and pepper. Spoon mixture into ungreased 13x9-inch (3-quart) glass baking dish, spreading evenly.

2) Arrange bacon slices in pairs over top of potato mixture to resemble eyes. Press bacon into mixture to form deep cups (for eggs). Bake 40 minutes.

3) Remove baking dish from oven. If necessary, press bacon into mixture to reshape cups. Carefully break 1 egg into each bacon cup.

4) Bake 20 to 25 minutes longer or just until eggs are set. Decorate eggs with ketchup "veins" to resemble bloodshot eyeballs.

Nutrition Information Per Serving	
Calories: 350	From Fat: 160
Total Fat	18g
Saturated Fat	9g
Trans Fat	0g
Cholesterol	255mg
Sodium	780mg
Total Carbohydrate	30g
Dietary Fiber	3g
Sugars	0g
Protein	17g

Cranberry Ribbon Cheesecake

PREP TIME: 30 MINUTES (READY IN 8 HOURS 50 MINUTES)
SERVINGS: 16

CRUST

1½ cups finely crushed creme-filled chocolate sandwich cookies (15 cookies)

¼ cup butter or margarine, melted

CRANBERRY SAUCE

1¼ cups sugar

3 tablespoons cornstarch

1½ cups fresh or frozen (thawed) cranberries

¾ cup cranberry juice cocktail

FILLING

4 packages (8 oz each) cream cheese, softened

1 cup sugar

4 eggs

½ cup whipping cream

4 teaspoons grated orange peel

1) Heat oven to 350°F. Spray 9-inch springform pan with cooking spray. Mix crust ingredients; press in bottom of pan. Bake crust 7 to 9 minutes or until set. Cool. Reduce oven temperature to 300°F.

2) Meanwhile, in 2-quart saucepan, mix 1¼ cups sugar and the cornstarch. Add cranberries and cranberry juice. Heat to boiling over high heat. Reduce heat to medium. Cook 7 to 8 minutes, stirring frequently, until mixture is thick and all cranberries have popped open. In blender or food processor, place cranberry mixture. Cover; blend until smooth. Place strainer over medium bowl; pour cranberry mixture in strainer. Press mixture with back of spoon through strainer to remove skin; discard skin. Set aside to cool.

3) In large bowl, beat cream cheese and 1 cup sugar with electric mixer on medium speed until light and fluffy. Beat in eggs; one at a time, just until blended. Stir in whipping cream and orange peel.

4) Pour half of filling (about 3¼ cups) into cooled crust. Evenly spoon half of cranberry sauce (¾ cup). Carefully spoon remaining filling over cranberry sauce in pan. Cover and refrigerate remaining cranberry mixture for the topping.

5) To minimize cracking, place shallow pan half full of hot water on lower oven rack. Bake 1 hour 15 minutes to 1 hour 25 minutes or until edge of cheesecake is set at least 2 inches from edge of pan but center of cheesecake still jiggles slightly when moved. Run small metal spatula around edge of pan to loosen cheesecake. Turn oven off; open oven door at least 4 inches. Let cheesecake remain in oven 30 minutes. Cool in pan on cooling rack 30 minutes. Refrigerate at least 6 hours or overnight before serving. Run small metal spatula around edge of pan; remove side of pan. Spread reserved cranberry mixture over cheesecake.

tip

To crush cookies, place cookies in plastic bag or between sheets of waxed paper; crush with rolling pin. Or crush in blender or food processor.

Nutrition Information Per Serving	
Calories: 390	From Fat: 220
Total Fat	24g
Saturated Fat	14g
Trans Fat	0.5g
Cholesterol	115mg
Sodium	220mg
Total Carbohydrate	39g
Dietary Fiber	1g
Sugars	33g
Protein	6g

Sweet Potatoes with Cinnamon Honey

PREP TIME:	20 MINUTES (READY IN 1 HOUR 15 MINUTES)
SERVINGS:	8

 EASY

5 tablespoons butter or margarine, melted

1 teaspoon ground cinnamon

½ teaspoon salt

2 teaspoons grated fresh lemon peel

½ cup honey

4 lb medium sweet potatoes

1) Heat oven to 325°F. Brush 13x9-inch (3-quart) glass baking dish with melted butter. To remaining butter, stir in cinnamon, salt, lemon peel and honey; set aside.

2) Peel sweet potatoes; cut into 1-inch chunks. Place in baking dish. Drizzle with half of the honey mixture; stir to evenly coat potatoes.

3) Cover tightly with foil; bake 30 minutes. Remove foil; spoon remaining honey mixture on top. Recover; bake 20 to 30 minutes longer or until potatoes are tender.

Nutrition Information Per Serving	
Calories: 260	From Fat: 70
Total Fat	7g
Saturated Fat	4.5g
Trans Fat	0g
Cholesterol	20mg
Sodium	250mg
Total Carbohydrate	46g
Dietary Fiber	5g
Sugars	26g
Protein	3g

Apple-Sage Brined Turkey Breast

PREP TIME: 1 HOUR 25 MINUTES (READY IN 14 HOURS 25 MINUTES)
SERVINGS: 8

LOW FAT

BRINE AND TURKEY

½ gallon (64 oz) apple cider

1 cup packed brown sugar

½ cup kosher (coarse) salt

¼ cup chopped fresh sage or
1 tablespoon rubbed sage

1 tablespoon whole peppercorns

1 bone-in whole turkey breast
(5 to 6 lb), thawed if frozen

BASTING SAUCE AND GRAVY

¼ cup butter or margarine

1 tablespoon chopped fresh sage or
1 teaspoon rubbed sage

5 cloves garlic, finely chopped

¼ cup all-purpose flour

½ teaspoon salt

1) Reserve 1 cup apple cider for basting; cover and refrigerate. In 6-quart bowl or stockpot, stir remaining cider, the brown sugar, kosher salt, ¼ cup fresh sage and the peppercorns until salt is dissolved. Add turkey breast. Cover; refrigerate at least 12 hours but no longer than 24 hours.

2) Heat oven to 325°F. Remove turkey from brine; rinse thoroughly under cool running water, and pat dry. Discard brine.

3) Place turkey, skin side up, on rack in large shallow roasting pan. Insert ovenproof meat thermometer so tip is in the thickest part of breast and does not touch bone. Roast uncovered 1 hour.

4) In 1-quart saucepan, heat reserved apple cider, the butter, 1 tablespoon fresh sage and the garlic over medium heat until butter is melted and mixture is hot. Roast turkey about 1 hour longer or until thermometer reads 165°F and juice of turkey is clear when center of thickest part is cut, basting turkey generously with apple cider mixture and pan juices every 15 minutes. Remove the turkey from oven, and let stand 15 minutes for easier carving.

5) Meanwhile, pour pan drippings and scrapings into measuring cup; let stand 5 minutes. Skim 4 tablespoons fat from top of drippings, and place in 2-quart saucepan; skim and discard any remaining fat. Add enough water to remaining drippings to measure 2 cups; set aside.

6) Stir ¼ cup flour into fat in saucepan, using wire whisk. Cook over medium heat, stirring constantly, until mixture is smooth and bubbly; remove from heat. Gradually stir in reserved 2 cups drippings and the salt. Heat to boiling, stirring constantly. Boil and stir about 1 minute or until the gravy thickens.

Nutrition Information Per Serving	
Calories: 360	From Fat: 70
Total Fat	8g
Saturated Fat	4.5g
Trans Fat	0g
Cholesterol	160mg
Sodium	1000mg
Total Carbohydrate	21g
Dietary Fiber	0g
Sugars	16g
Protein	52g

Corn-Chorizo Stuffing

PREP TIME: 40 MINUTES (READY IN 1 HOUR 30 MINUTES)
SERVINGS: 20 (1/2 CUP EACH)

2 pouches (6.5 oz each) Betty Crocker® cornbread & muffin mix

⅔ cup milk

¼ cup butter or margarine, melted

2 eggs

1 lb chorizo sausage

1 large onion, chopped (1 cup)

¾ cup chopped celery

1 bag (12 oz) Green Giant® Valley Fresh Steamers™ Niblets® frozen corn, thawed

1 can (4.5 oz) Old El Paso® chopped green chiles

2 to 3 teaspoons poultry seasoning

1 teaspoon salt

½ teaspoon pepper

2½ to 3 cups Progresso® chicken broth (from 32-oz carton)

1) Heat oven to 400°F. Spray 15x10x1-inch pan with cooking spray. In large bowl, stir cornbread mixes, milk, butter and eggs just until moistened (batter will be lumpy). Spread batter in pan. Bake 10 to 12 minutes or until toothpick inserted in center comes out clean. Cool in pan 10 minutes.

2) Cut warm cornbread into ½-inch cubes, leaving in pan. Stir cubes. Bake 10 minutes. Stir cubes again; bake 10 to 15 minutes longer or until golden brown on top. Dump cubes into large bowl. Reduce oven temperature to 350°F.

3) Meanwhile, in 12-inch skillet, cook sausage, onion and celery over medium-high heat 7 to 10 minutes, stirring frequently, until sausage is no longer pink; drain if desired. Stir in corn, chiles, poultry seasoning, salt and pepper.

4) Stir sausage mixture into cornbread cubes. Gradually stir in just enough broth to moisten stuffing without making mixture mushy. Spoon mixture into ungreased 13x9-inch (3-quart) glass baking dish. Cover with foil; bake 25 minutes. Uncover and bake about 15 minutes longer or until hot in center (165°F).

Nutrition Information Per Serving	
Calories: 230	From Fat: 110
Total Fat	12g
Saturated Fat	5g
Trans Fat	0g
Cholesterol	50mg
Sodium	710mg
Total Carbohydrate	20g
Dietary Fiber	0g
Sugars	5g
Protein	8g

Sausage Cornbread Stuffing

PREP TIME: 25 MINUTES (READY IN 45 MINUTES)
SERVINGS: 12 (1/2 CUP EACH)

1 cup chopped onions

1 cup chopped celery

½ cup chopped green bell pepper

2 links sweet Italian turkey sausage (6 oz), casings removed, cut up

1 package (8 oz) cornbread stuffing mix (3 cups)

⅓ cup chopped pecans, toasted

¼ cup chopped fresh parsley

1 teaspoon dried sage leaves

1 teaspoon dried thyme leaves

1¾ cups Progresso® chicken broth (from 32-oz carton)

1) Heat oven to 325°F. Spray 10-inch ovenproof skillet with cooking spray. Heat over medium heat until hot. Add onions, celery, bell pepper and sausage; cook and stir 3 to 5 minutes or until sausage is no longer pink and vegetables are tender.

2) Add stuffing mix, pecans, parsley, sage and thyme to sausage mixture; mix well. Gradually stir in broth to moisten.

3) Bake, uncovered, at 325°F with turkey for last 20 minutes of roasting time.

Nutrition Information Per Serving

Calories: 120	From Fat: 40
Total Fat	4.5g
Saturated Fat	0.5g
Trans Fat	0g
Cholesterol	15mg
Sodium	390mg
Total Carbohydrate	13g
Dietary Fiber	1g
Sugars	2g
Protein	5g

tip Pecans can be toasted up to 1 day ahead. To toast pecans, heat oven to 350°F. Spread pecans on ungreased shallow pan. Bake uncovered 6 to 10 minutes, stirring occasionally, until golden brown. Cool; store in food-storage plastic bag or covered container.

Sherry-Shallot Sauce

PREP TIME:	25 MINUTES (READY IN 25 MINUTES)	EASY
SERVINGS:	8 (1/4 CUP EACH)	

¼ cup butter or margarine

½ cup thinly sliced shallots

¼ cup all-purpose flour

½ teaspoon salt

½ teaspoon dried thyme

¼ teaspoon pepper

⅓ cup medium or dry sherry or apple juice

1½ cups Progresso® reduced-sodium chicken broth (from 32-oz carton)

Nutrition Information Per Serving	
Calories: 90	From Fat: 50
Total Fat	6g
Saturated Fat	3.5g
Trans Fat	0g
Cholesterol	15mg
Sodium	590mg
Total Carbohydrate	6g
Dietary Fiber	0g
Sugars	0g
Protein	1g

1) In 2-quart heavy saucepan, melt butter over medium heat. Cook and stir shallots in butter 7 to 10 minutes or until butter and shallots are deep golden brown. Stir in flour, salt, thyme and pepper. Continue to cook and stir 1 minute.

2) Gradually stir in sherry and chicken broth. Heat to boiling, stirring constantly; reduce heat to low. Cook and stir about 5 minutes longer or until gravy is thickened and flavors are blended.

Ultimate Slow Cooker Mashed Potatoes

PREP TIME:	30 MINUTES (READY IN 5 HOURS)
SERVINGS:	20 (1/2 CUP EACH)

5 lb baking potatoes, peeled, cut into 1-inch chunks

1½ cups Progresso® chicken broth (from 32-oz carton)

¼ cup butter or margarine, cut into chunks

1 cup sour cream or plain yogurt

1 teaspoon garlic powder

1 teaspoon onion powder

½ teaspoon salt

¼ teaspoon ground black pepper

½ to 1 cup milk, warmed

Nutrition Information Per Serving	
Calories: 120	From Fat: 40
Total Fat	4.5g
Saturated Fat	3g
Trans Fat	0g
Cholesterol	15mg
Sodium	150mg
Total Carbohydrate	16g
Dietary Fiber	1g
Sugars	2g
Protein	2g

1) In 4- to 5-quart slow cooker, place potatoes, chicken broth and butter. Cover; cook on High heat setting 4 hours to 4 hours 30 minutes or until potatoes are tender.

2) Add remaining ingredients except milk. Mash, crush or smash potatoes using potato masher, or beat with electric mixer on low speed until well blended. Do not overmix. Stir in enough milk for desired creamy consistency. Cover and keep warm on Low or Warm heat setting until serving time, up to 2 hours. Stir before serving.

Broccoli and Squash Medley

PREP TIME: 30 MINUTES (READY IN 30 MINUTES)
SERVINGS: 14 (1/2 CUP EACH)

 EASY

2 bags (12 oz each) Green Giant® Valley Fresh Steamers™ frozen broccoli cuts

2 cups cubed (½ inch) seeded peeled butternut squash (1½ lb)

¾ cup orange juice

¼ cup butter or margarine, melted

½ cup sweetened dried cranberries

½ cup finely chopped pecans, toasted

1 tablespoon grated orange peel (from 1 orange)

1 teaspoon salt

1) Cook broccoli as directed on bag; set aside.

2) Meanwhile, in 12-inch skillet, place squash and orange juice. Cover; cook over medium-low heat 8 to 10 minutes, stirring frequently, until tender but firm.

3) Stir in broccoli and remaining ingredients; toss to coat. Serve immediately.

Nutrition Information Per Serving	
Calories: 100	From Fat: 60
Total Fat	6g
Saturated Fat	2.5g
Trans Fat	0g
Cholesterol	10mg
Sodium	200mg
Total Carbohydrate	10g
Dietary Fiber	2g
Sugars	6g
Protein	2g

Caramelized Pears and Gorgonzola Salad

PREP TIME: 25 MINUTES (READY IN 25 MINUTES)
SERVINGS: 8

 EASY

VINAIGRETTE

¼ cup extra-virgin olive oil

2 tablespoons white wine vinegar

½ teaspoon Dijon mustard

½ teaspoon salt

¼ teaspoon pepper

CARAMELIZED PEARS

2 tablespoons butter or margarine

4 firm ripe pears, peeled, quartered, cored and cut into eighths

1 teaspoon sugar

SALAD

8 cups mixed spring greens

½ cup thinly sliced red onion

½ cup coarsely chopped candied pecans (from 5-oz bag)

½ cup crumbled Gorgonzola cheese

1) In small bowl, beat vinaigrette ingredients with wire whisk. Cover and refrigerate up to 24 hours.

2) In 12-inch nonstick skillet, melt butter over high heat. Add pears and sugar; cook and stir 6 to 8 minutes or until fruit is tender and golden. Cool slightly.

3) In large salad bowl, toss greens, onion and half the vinaigrette. Transfer to large platter. Arrange pears, pecans and cheese over greens. Drizzle with remaining vinaigrette. Serve immediately.

Nutrition Information Per Serving	
Calories: 260	From Fat: 160
Total Fat	17g
Saturated Fat	5g
Trans Fat	0g
Cholesterol	15mg
Sodium	310mg
Total Carbohydrate	21g
Dietary Fiber	4g
Sugars	14g
Protein	3g

Beer and Rosemary Roasted Turkey

PREP TIME: 25 MINUTES (READY IN 4 HOURS)
SERVINGS: 12 TO 14

1 whole turkey (12 to 14 lb), thawed if frozen

¼ cup butter or margarine, melted

2 tablespoons Dijon mustard

1 tablespoon chopped fresh rosemary leaves or 1 teaspoon dried rosemary

1 teaspoon salt

½ teaspoon pepper

1 can or bottle (12 oz) dark beer

½ cup cold water

¼ cup all-purpose flour

Nutrition Information Per Serving	
Calories: 320	From Fat: 100
Total Fat	11g
Saturated Fat	4.5g
Trans Fat	0g
Cholesterol	170mg
Sodium	380mg
Total Carbohydrate	4g
Dietary Fiber	0g
Sugars	0g
Protein	49g

tip

Add 6 to 8 small peeled onions to roasting pan after 1 hour of roasting. Garnish platter with roasted onions, fresh rosemary sprigs and orange slices.

1) Move oven rack to lowest position. Heat oven to 325°F. Remove and discard neck and giblets from turkey. Rinse turkey inside and out with cold water; pat dry with paper towels. Fasten neck skin to back of turkey with skewer. Fold wings across back of turkey so tips are touching. In shallow roasting pan, place turkey, breast side up.

2) In medium microwavable bowl, stir together butter, mustard, rosemary, salt, pepper and beer. Microwave uncovered on High 1 to 1½ minutes, stirring after 30 seconds, until well mixed. Brush about ⅓ of mixture evenly over surface of turkey. Fasten drumsticks together with cotton string. Insert ovenproof meat thermometer so tip is in thickest part of inside thigh and does not touch the bone.

3) Roast uncovered 2½ to 3 hours, brushing with additional beer mixture and pan juices every 30 minutes. Turkey is done when thermometer reads 165°F and drumsticks move easily when lifted or twisted. If necessary, cover turkey breast with heavy-duty foil during the last 1 hour 30 minutes to 2 hours of baking to prevent excess browning.

4) Let turkey stand 15 to 20 minutes for easier carving. Remove the skewers before slicing.

5) Meanwhile, measure drippings and enough water to make 2 cups. In 2-quart saucepan, heat drippings to boiling. In small cup, stir together cold water and flour until smooth. Stir flour mixture into boiling drippings. Continue stirring 2 to 3 minutes longer or until gravy is thickened and bubbly.

Pumpkin-Ginger Pie with Gingersnap Streusel

PREP TIME: 30 MINUTES (READY IN 4 HOURS 30 MINUTES)
SERVINGS: 8

FILLING

- 1 can (15 oz) pumpkin (not pumpkin pie mix)
- 1 cup evaporated milk
- ½ cup packed light brown sugar
- 2 eggs, slightly beaten
- 2 teaspoons grated fresh ginger
- 1 teaspoon pumpkin pie spice
- ¼ teaspoon salt

CRUST

- 1 Pillsbury® Pet-Ritz® frozen deep dish pie crust

STREUSEL

- ½ cup crushed gingersnap cookies (9 cookies)
- 2 tablespoons packed brown sugar
- 2 tablespoons all-purpose flour
- 2 tablespoons butter or margarine, softened
- ¼ cup chopped pecans

1) Heat oven to 425°F. Place cookie sheet on oven rack. In large bowl, mix filling ingredients. Pour into pie crust.

2) Bake pie on cookie sheet 15 minutes. Reduce oven temperature to 350°F; bake 15 minutes longer. Meanwhile, in small bowl, mix streusel ingredients. Sprinkle streusel over filling. Bake at 350°F for 25 to 30 minutes longer or until knife inserted in center comes out clean.

3) Cool completely on cooling rack, about 3 hours. Cover and refrigerate any remaining pie.

Nutrition Information Per Serving	
Calories: 330	From Fat: 120
Total Fat	14g
Saturated Fat	5g
Trans Fat	0g
Cholesterol	70mg
Sodium	290mg
Total Carbohydrate	44g
Dietary Fiber	2g
Sugars	25g
Protein	6g

Cranberry-Pomegranate Sauce

PREP TIME: 10 MINUTES (READY IN 30 MINUTES)
SERVINGS: 10 (1/4 CUP EACH)

 EASY   LOW FAT

1½ cups sugar

1 cup pomegranate juice

1 tablespoon grated orange peel

½ teaspoon ground cinnamon

1 bag (12 oz) fresh cranberries

1) In nonreactive 2-quart saucepan, stir together all ingredients. Heat to boiling over high heat, stirring occasionally. Reduce heat to medium-low. Cook 20 to 25 minutes, stirring occasionally, until cranberries pop and sauce thickens slightly.

2) Pour into serving bowl; cover and refrigerate until ready to serve.

Nutrition Information Per Serving	
Calories: 150	From Fat: 0
Total Fat	0g
Saturated Fat	0g
Trans Fat	0g
Cholesterol	0mg
Sodium	0mg
Total Carbohydrate	38g
Dietary Fiber	2g
Sugars	34g
Protein	0g

tip

Give this cranberry sauce a kick by substituting lime peel for the orange and adding ½ teaspoon ground red pepper (cayenne) with the cinnamon.

Roasted Garlic Gravy

PREP TIME: 15 MINUTES (READY IN 1 HOUR 15 MINUTES)
SERVINGS: 14 (1/4 CUP EACH)

 EASY

1 medium bulb garlic

2 teaspoons olive oil

Drippings from roasted turkey

3 cups liquid (turkey juices, canned chicken broth or water)

½ cup all-purpose flour

¼ teaspoon salt

⅛ teaspoon pepper

1) Heat oven to 325°F. Carefully peel paper-like skin from around bulbs of garlic, leaving just enough to hold garlic cloves together. Cut ¼ to ½ inch from top of bulb to expose cloves. Place cut side up on 12-inch square of aluminum foil. Drizzle bulb with oil. Wrap securely in foil. Place in pie plate or shallow baking pan. Roast 45 to 60 minutes, or until garlic is tender when pierced with toothpick or fork. Cool slightly. Squeeze garlic into bowl; mash with fork.

2) After removing turkey from roasting pan, pour drippings (turkey juices and fat) into bowl or glass measuring cup, leaving brown bits in pan. Let drippings stand about 5 minutes to allow fat to rise. Skim 6 tablespoons fat from top of drippings, and return to pan; discard any remaining fat. Add enough broth or water to remaining drippings to measure 3 cups; reserve.

3) Stir mashed garlic and flour into fat in pan, using wire whisk. Cook over medium heat about 1 minute, stirring constantly and scraping up brown bits, until mixture is smooth and bubbly. Remove from heat.

4) Gradually stir in reserved 3 cups drippings; increase heat to medium-high. Heat to boiling, stirring constantly. Boil and stir about 1 minute or until gravy thickens. Stir in salt and pepper.

tip

For this recipe, if roasting a turkey at the same time at a higher temperature, check the garlic for doneness earlier.

Nutrition Information Per Serving	
Calories: 80	From Fat: 60
Total Fat	7g
Saturated Fat	2g
Trans Fat	0g
Cholesterol	5mg
Sodium	150mg
Total Carbohydrate	3g
Dietary Fiber	0g
Sugars	0g
Protein	0g

Make-Ahead Potato-Onion Gratin

PREP TIME: 20 MINUTES (READY IN 9 HOURS 40 MINUTES)
SERVINGS: 26 (1/2 CUP EACH)

 EASY

- 2 tablespoons plus ¼ cup butter or margarine
- 1 large onion, chopped (1 cup)
- 1 teaspoon kosher (coarse) salt
- ½ teaspoon ground black pepper
- 1½ cups Progresso® reduced-sodium chicken broth (from 32-oz carton)
- 1½ cups whipping cream
- 15 cups frozen shredded hash brown potatoes (from two 30-oz bags)
- 1 cup finely shredded Parmesan cheese
- 3 cups soft white bread crumbs (about 4 slices bread)

1) Spray 13x9-inch (3-quart) glass baking dish with cooking spray, set aside.

2) In 5-quart Dutch oven, melt 2 tablespoons of the butter over medium heat. Stir in onion, salt and pepper; cook, stirring occasionally, about 5 minutes or until softened and golden brown.

3) Stir in broth and cream; heat just to boiling over medium heat, stirring frequently. Remove from heat; fold in potatoes. Stir in Parmesan cheese. Spread in baking dish. Cover with foil; refrigerate up to 24 hours.

4) Heat oven to 350°F. Bake uncovered 30 minutes.

5) Meanwhile, in small microwavable bowl, microwave remaining ¼ cup butter uncovered on High 15 to 20 seconds or until melted. Stir bread crumbs into melted butter; set aside.

6) Remove potatoes from oven; sprinkle bread crumbs on top. Return to oven; bake 40 to 50 minutes longer or until topping is golden brown and edges are bubbly. Let stand 5 minutes before serving.

Nutrition Information Per Serving	
Calories: 240	From Fat: 80
Total Fat	9g
Saturated Fat	5g
Trans Fat	0g
Cholesterol	25mg
Sodium	320mg
Total Carbohydrate	34g
Dietary Fiber	3g
Sugars	3g
Protein	5g

Christmas Confetti Cookies

PREP TIME: 40 MINUTES (READY IN 40 MINUTES)
SERVINGS: 32 COOKIES

1 roll (16.5 oz) Pillsbury® refrigerated sugar cookies

2 tablespoons all-purpose flour

2 tablespoons red, green and white decors or candy sprinkles

1 container (12 oz) fluffy white whipped ready-to-spread frosting

Nutrition Information Per Serving	
Calories: 110	From Fat: 45
Total Fat	5g
Saturated Fat	1.5g
Trans Fat	1.5g
Cholesterol	0mg
Sodium	60mg
Total Carbohydrate	16g
Dietary Fiber	0g
Sugars	12g
Protein	0g

1) Heat oven to 350°F. In a large resealable food-storage plastic bag, place cookie dough, flour and decors. Seal bag; squeeze to mix.

2) Shape dough into 32 (1-inch) balls; place 2 inches apart on ungreased cookie sheets.

3) Bake 9 to 12 minutes or until edges are light golden brown. Cool 1 minute; remove from cookie sheets.

4) Serve cookies with bowl of frosting for dipping. If desired, sprinkle on additional decors.

Poinsettia Cookies

PREP TIME: 40 MINUTES (READY IN 50 MINUTES)
SERVINGS: 24 COOKIES

1 roll (16.5 oz) Pillsbury® refrigerated sugar cookies

¼ cup all-purpose flour

¼ teaspoon red food color

1/3 cup red sugar

24 yellow gumdrops (½ to 1 inch)

Nutrition Information Per Serving	
Calories: 110	From Fat: 30
Total Fat	3.5g
Saturated Fat	1g
Trans Fat	1g
Cholesterol	0mg
Sodium	65mg
Total Carbohydrate	20g
Dietary Fiber	0g
Sugars	13g
Protein	0g

1) Heat oven to 350°F. In large bowl, break up cookie dough. Stir or knead in flour and food color until blended and color is even. Remove half the dough, and refrigerate remaining dough until needed.

2) Shape dough into 12 (1¼-inch) balls; roll in red sugar, and place 2 inches apart on ungreased cookie sheets. With thin sharp knife dipped into flour, cut each ball into 6 wedges, cutting ¾ of the way down into ball but not through bottom. Spread wedges apart very slightly to form flower petals (cookies will separate and flatten as they bake). Repeat with remaining dough and red sugar.

3) Bake 10 to 12 minutes or until set and edges just begin to brown. Immediately press 1 gumdrop in center of each cookie. Cool 1 minute; carefully remove from cookie sheets to cooling racks. Cool completely, about 10 minutes. Store in tightly covered container.

Mrs. Claus' Mittens

PREP TIME: 50 MINUTES (READY IN 1 HOUR 20 MINUTES)
SERVINGS: 16 COOKIES

e EASY

1 roll (16.5 oz) Pillsbury® refrigerated holiday gingerbread cookies

1 container (12 oz) fluffy white whipped ready-to-spread frosting

½ to 1 teaspoon red paste icing color or 3 teaspoons red liquid food color

4 teaspoons white candy sprinkles

1) Heat oven to 350°F. Work with half of cookie dough at a time; refrigerate remaining dough until needed. Cut dough into 8 (½-inch) slices.

2) For each cookie, cut off ⅓ of 1 slice of dough. Place larger piece of dough lengthwise on ungreased cookie sheet. Place smaller piece of dough slightly at a diagonal next to larger piece; press dough into 4-inch mitten shape. Repeat with remaining dough, placing cookies 1 inch apart on cookie sheets.

3) Bake 7 to 10 minutes or until light golden brown and set. Cool 2 minutes; remove from cookie sheets. Cool completely, about 10 minutes.

4) In small bowl, place 1 cup of the frosting. Stir in red icing color until well blended. Frost mittens with red frosting.

5) Place remaining frosting in small resealable food-storage plastic bag; seal bag. Cut ⅛-inch hole in bottom corner of bag. Pipe white frosting at bottom of each mitten. Sprinkle each with ¼ teaspoon sprinkles. Let stand until frosting is set, about 30 minutes. Store between sheets of waxed paper in tightly covered container.

Nutrition Information Per Serving	
Calories: 220	From Fat: 100
Total Fat	11g
Saturated Fat	3g
Trans Fat	3g
Cholesterol	10mg
Sodium	120mg
Total Carbohydrate	31g
Dietary Fiber	0g
Sugars	20g
Protein	1g

Frosted Christmas Trees

PREP TIME: 1 HOUR 10 MINUTES (READY IN 1 HOUR 25 MINUTES)
SERVINGS: 4 DOZEN COOKIES

 LOW FAT

1 roll (16.5 oz) Pillsbury® refrigerated sugar cookies

3 tablespoons all-purpose flour

1 tablespoon grated orange peel

2 cups powdered sugar

2 to 3 tablespoons fresh orange juice

3 to 4 drops green food color

3 tablespoons candy sprinkles

1) Heat oven to 350°F. In large bowl, break up cookie dough. Stir or knead in flour and orange peel until well blended. Work with half of dough at a time; refrigerate remaining dough until needed.

2) On floured surface with rolling pin, roll dough to 1/8-inch thickness (about 11-inch round). Cut with floured 3- to 3½-inch tree-shaped cookie cutter; place 1 inch apart on ungreased cookie sheets. Repeat with remaining dough.

3) Bake 6 to 9 minutes or until cookies are set and edges just begin to brown. Cool 1 minute; remove from cookie sheets. Cool completely, about 10 minutes.

4) In small bowl, mix powdered sugar and enough orange juice until smooth and desired spreading consistency. Stir in green food color until well blended. Frost cooled cookies; sprinkle with sprinkles. Let stand until icing is set, about 15 minutes. Store between sheets of waxed paper in tightly covered container.

Nutrition Information Per Serving	
Calories: 60	From Fat: 15
Total Fat	1.5g
Saturated Fat	0.5g
Trans Fat	0.5g
Cholesterol	0mg
Sodium	30mg
Total Carbohydrate	12g
Dietary Fiber	0g
Sugars	9g
Protein	0g

MINI ICE CREAM COOKIE CUPS
PG. 306

Cookies & Bars

These scrumptious specialties are sure to satisfy
your sweet tooth...no matter what time of day!

COCONUT-FILLED CHOCOLATE
DELIGHTS
PG. 314

CHOCOLATE-ORANGE PASTRIES
PG. 305

FUDGY CHOCOLATE CHIP-TOFFEE
BARS
PG. 303

Spiced Mocha Chocolate Cookies

JENNIFER HUNTER | MARIETTA, GEORGIA

BAKE-OFF® CONTEST 44, 2010

PREP TIME: 45 MINUTES (READY IN 1 HOUR)
SERVINGS: 2 DOZEN COOKIES

1 roll (16.5 oz) Pillsbury® refrigerated chocolate chip cookies

¼ cup Smucker's® sweet orange marmalade

½ cup Fisher® Chef's Naturals® chopped pecans

½ cup Pillsbury Best® all-purpose unbleached or all purpose flour

¼ cup Hershey's® baking cocoa

2 tablespoons instant coffee granules

1 teaspoon ground cinnamon

¼ teaspoon ground cloves

¼ teaspoon ground allspice

¼ teaspoon ground red pepper (cayenne)

24 chocolate-covered espresso beans

½ cup powdered sugar

1 to 2 tablespoons milk

1 tablespoon Hershey's® baking cocoa

Let cookie dough stand at room temperature for 10 minutes to soften. Meanwhile, heat oven to 350°F. In large bowl, break up cookie dough; add marmalade and pecans. In small bowl, mix flour, ¼ cup cocoa, coffee granules, cinnamon, cloves, allspice and red pepper; stir into dough mixture with wooden spoon until well blended.

1) Shape dough into 24 (about 1½-inch) balls. On ungreased large cookie sheets, place balls 2 inches apart. Gently press 1 espresso bean into center of each cookie.

2) Bake 9 to 12 minutes or until tops are cracked and edges are set. Let stand on cookie sheet 1 minute; remove to cooling racks. Cool completely, about 30 minutes.

3) In small bowl, mix powdered sugar, milk and 1 tablespoon cocoa until smooth and well blended; drizzle over cookies. Let stand about 15 minutes until set.

Nutrition Information Per Serving	
Calories: 150	From Fat: 60
Total Fat	7g
Saturated Fat	2g
Trans Fat	1g
Cholesterol	0mg
Sodium	65mg
Total Carbohydrate	21g
Dietary Fiber	1g
Sugars	12g
Protein	1g

Fudgy Chocolate Chip-Toffee Bars

SARAH FUCHS | OZARK, MISSOURI

BAKE-OFF® CONTEST 44, 2010

e EASY

PREP TIME: 20 MINUTES (READY IN 2 HOURS 55 MINUTES)
SERVINGS: 32 BARS

½ cup Land O Lakes® butter, melted

2 cups graham cracker crumbs (32 squares)

1 bag (8 oz) Heath® Bits 'O Brickle® toffee bits (1½ cups)

1 roll (16.5 oz) Pillsbury® refrigerated chocolate chip cookies

1 bag (12 oz) Hershey's® semi-sweet chocolate baking chips (2 cups)

1 can (14 oz) Eagle Brand® Sweetened Condensed Milk

1 tablespoon Land O Lakes® butter

1 teaspoon vanilla

1) Heat oven to 350°F (325°F for dark or nonstick pan). Spray bottom only of 13x9-inch pan with Crisco® original no-stick cooking spray.

2) In medium bowl, stir ½ cup melted butter, 1½ cups of the cracker crumbs and ¾ cup of the toffee bits. Press mixture evenly in bottom of pan. Refrigerate about 15 minutes or until firm.

3) Meanwhile, let cookie dough stand at room temperature 10 minutes to soften. In 2-quart saucepan, heat chocolate chips, milk and 1 tablespoon butter over medium heat, stirring frequently, until chips are melted and mixture is smooth. Remove from heat; stir in vanilla. Spread mixture over cracker crust.

4) In medium bowl, break up cookie dough. Mix in remaining ½ cup cracker crumbs with wooden spoon until well blended. Crumble mixture evenly over chocolate layer. Sprinkle with remaining ¾ cup toffee bits.

5) Bake 25 to 35 minutes or until golden brown. Cool completely, about 2 hours. For a firmer bar, refrigerate 30 minutes longer. For bars, cut into 8 rows by 4 rows.

Nutrition Information Per Serving	
Calories: 270	From Fat: 130
Total Fat	14g
Saturated Fat	8g
Trans Fat	1g
Cholesterol	15mg
Sodium	130mg
Total Carbohydrate	32g
Dietary Fiber	1g
Sugars	24g
Protein	2g

Rocky Road S'more Bars

PREP TIME: 20 MINUTES (READY IN 1 HOUR 40 MINUTES)
SERVINGS: 32 BARS

 EASY

1½ cups all-purpose flour

⅔ cup packed brown sugar

½ teaspoon baking powder

½ teaspoon salt

¼ teaspoon baking soda

½ cup butter or margarine, softened

1 teaspoon vanilla

2 egg yolks

3 cups miniature marshmallows

1 cup milk chocolate chips

1 bag (11.5 oz) milk chocolate chips (2 cups)

⅔ cup light corn syrup

¼ cup butter or margarine

2 teaspoons vanilla

2 cups Golden Grahams® cereal

1 cup salted peanuts

1) Heat oven to 350°F. In large bowl, beat first 8 ingredients with electric mixer on low speed until crumbly. Press the mixture firmly in the bottom of an ungreased 13x9-inch pan. Bake 12 to 15 minutes or until light golden brown in color. Immediately sprinkle with marshmallows and 1 cup chocolate chips.

2) Bake 1 to 2 minutes longer or until marshmallows just begin to puff. Remove from oven; cool while preparing topping.

3) In 3-quart saucepan, cook 2 cups chocolate chips, light corn syrup, butter and vanilla over medium heat 2 to 3 minutes, stirring constantly, until butter and chocolate chips are melted. Stir in cereal and peanuts. Immediately spoon warm topping evenly over bars; spread gently to cover. Refrigerate about 1 hour or until firm. For bars, cut into 8 rows by 4 rows.

Nutrition Information Per Serving	
Calories: 110	From Fat: 45
Total Fat	5g
Saturated Fat	2.5g
Trans Fat	0.5g
Cholesterol	0mg
Sodium	50mg
Total Carbohydrate	14g
Dietary Fiber	0g
Sugars	11g
Protein	1g

tip

You can use any variety of salted nuts you like in this recipe.

Chocolate-Orange Pastries

PAM TAPIA | SUGAR HILL, GEORGIA

BAKE-OFF® CONTEST 44, 2010

PREP TIME: 15 MINUTES (READY IN 50 MINUTES)
SERVINGS: 16 PASTRIES

e EASY

1 package (3 oz) cream cheese, softened

2 to 3 teaspoons grated orange peel

1 Pillsbury® refrigerated pie crust, softened as directed on box

¼ cup Smucker's® sweet orange marmalade

½ cup Hershey's® Special Dark® chocolate baking chips

1 Eggland's Best egg, beaten

2 teaspoons sugar

1) Heat oven to 350°F. Line cookie sheet with cooking parchment paper or spray with Crisco® original no-stick cooking spray.

2) In small bowl, stir cream cheese and orange peel until blended. Unroll pie crust on work surface. Spread cream cheese mixture evenly over crust.

3) In small microwavable bowl, microwave marmalade uncovered on High 10 seconds. Brush marmalade evenly over cream cheese mixture. Cut crust into 16 wedges, using knife or pizza wheel. Sprinkle chocolate chips evenly over wedges.

4) Roll up each wedge, starting at shortest side and rolling to opposite point. Place pastries, point side down, on cookie sheet. Brush the egg on tops and sides of pastries. Sprinkle evenly with sugar.

5) Bake 20 to 25 minutes or until light golden brown. Remove from cookie sheet to cooling rack. Cool at least 10 minutes before serving.

Nutrition Information Per Serving	
Calories: 120	From Fat: 60
Total Fat	7g
Saturated Fat	3g
Trans Fat	0g
Cholesterol	20mg
Sodium	95mg
Total Carbohydrate	14g
Dietary Fiber	0g
Sugars	6g
Protein	1g

Mini Ice Cream Cookie Cups

SUE COMPTON | DELANCO, NEW JERSEY

BAKE-OFF® CONTEST 44, 2010

 EASY

| PREP TIME: | 20 MINUTES (READY IN 45 MINUTES) |
| SERVINGS: | 24 |

1 package (16 oz) Pillsbury® Ready to Bake!™ refrigerated sugar cookies (24 cookies)

4 teaspoons sugar

⅓ cup Fisher® Chef's Naturals® chopped walnuts, finely chopped

½ cup Hershey's® semi-sweet chocolate baking chips

¼ cup Smucker's® seedless red raspberry jam

1½ cups vanilla bean ice cream, softened

24 fresh raspberries

1) Heat oven to 350°F. Spray 24 mini muffin cups with Crisco® original no-stick cooking spray. Place 1 cookie dough round in each muffin cup. Bake 15 to 20 minutes or until golden brown.

2) Place 2 teaspoons of the sugar in small bowl. Dip end of wooden spoon handle in sugar; carefully press into center of each cookie to make 1-inch-wide indentation. Cool completely in pan, about 20 minutes.

3) Meanwhile, in a small bowl, mix walnuts and remaining 2 teaspoons sugar; set aside. In a small microwavable bowl, microwave the chocolate chips uncovered on High for 30 to 60 seconds, stirring after 30 seconds, until smooth.

4) Run knife around edges of cups to loosen; gently remove from pan. Dip rim of each cup into melted chocolate, then into walnut mixture. Place walnut side up on cookie sheet with sides.

5) In another small microwavable bowl, microwave jam uncovered on High about 15 seconds until melted. Spoon ½ teaspoon jam into each cup. Freeze cups about 5 minutes or until chocolate is set.

6) Spoon ice cream into cups, using small cookie scoop or measuring tablespoon. Top each cup with fresh raspberry; serve immediately.

Nutrition Information Per Serving	
Calories: 150	From Fat: 70
Total Fat	7g
Saturated Fat	2.5g
Trans Fat	1.5g
Cholesterol	0mg
Sodium	60mg
Total Carbohydrate	19g
Dietary Fiber	0g
Sugars	12g
Protein	1g

S'more Chippers

PREP TIME: 45 MINUTES (READY IN 1 HOUR 15 MINUTES)
SERVINGS: 36 COOKIES

 EASY

tip

For a s'more sandwich, top the s'more with another chocolate chip cookie.

1 roll (16.5 oz) Pillsbury® refrigerated chocolate chip cookies

18 large marshmallows

8 oz chocolate-flavored candy coating, chopped

1) Heat oven to 350°F. Shape cookie dough into 36 (1-inch) balls and on ungreased cookie sheets, place the balls about 2 inches apart.

2) Bake 9 to 13 minutes or until edges are light golden brown. Meanwhile, with kitchen scissors, cut each marshmallow in half crosswise. Immediately place 1 marshmallow half, cut side down, on top of each hot cookie.

3) Bake 1 to 2 minutes longer or just until marshmallows begin to puff. Cool 2 minutes; remove from cookie sheets. With fingers, gently flatten the marshmallows.

4) Melt candy coating as directed on package. Spoon about 1 teaspoon candy coating over marshmallow on each cookie, swirling with back of spoon to nearly cover marshmallow. Let stand until candy coating is set, about 30 minutes. Store between sheets of waxed paper in tightly covered container.

Nutrition Information Per Serving	
Calories: 110	From Fat: 45
Total Fat	5g
Saturated Fat	2.5g
Trans Fat	0.5g
Cholesterol	0mg
Sodium	50mg
Total Carbohydrate	14g
Dietary Fiber	0g
Sugars	11g
Protein	1g

Deluxe Triple-Chocolate Cookies

DENISE HOOPER | REISTERSTOWN, MARYLAND

BAKE-OFF® CONTEST 44, 2010

PREP TIME: 1 HOUR 10 MINUTES (READY IN 1 HOUR 10 MINUTES)
SERVINGS: 5 DOZEN COOKIES

1 cup Land O Lakes® unsalted or salted butter, softened

¾ cup packed brown sugar

¾ cup granulated sugar

2 Eggland's Best eggs

1 teaspoon vanilla

½ cup hazelnut spread with cocoa

½ cup Jif® creamy peanut butter

1 box (5 oz) Hershey's® goodnight kisses milk chocolate hot cocoa mix (four 1.25-oz envelopes) or 1 cup milk chocolate instant hot cocoa mix (dry)

2 cups Pillsbury Best® all-purpose flour

1 cup old-fashioned or quick-cooking oats

1 teaspoon salt

1 teaspoon baking soda

1 bag (12 oz) Hershey's® semi-sweet chocolate baking chips (2 cups)

1) Heat oven to 375°F. Line cookie sheets with cooking parchment paper or spray with Crisco® original no-stick cooking spray.

2) In large bowl, beat butter and sugars with electric mixer on medium speed until light and fluffy. Beat in eggs and vanilla. On low speed, beat in hazelnut spread, peanut butter and dry cocoa mix until well blended. Stir in flour, oats, salt and baking soda until well blended. Stir in chocolate chips.

3) Drop dough by rounded tablespoonfuls 2 inches apart onto cookie sheets. Bake 9 to 12 minutes or until edges are set. Cool 3 minutes; remove from cookie sheets to cooling racks. Store tightly covered.

Nutrition Information Per Serving	
Calories: 130	From Fat: 60
Total Fat	6g
Saturated Fat	3.5g
Trans Fat	0g
Cholesterol	15mg
Sodium	85mg
Total Carbohydrate	15g
Dietary Fiber	0g
Sugars	10g
Protein	2g

Apricot-Sour Cream Tea Cookies

MARGARET PARSONS | ROYERSFORD, PENNSYLVANIA

Bake-Off®   BAKE-OFF® CONTEST 44, 2010

PREP TIME:	40 MINUTES (READY IN 1 HOUR 10 MINUTES)
SERVINGS:	2 DOZEN COOKIES

COOKIES

1 roll (16.5 oz) Pillsbury® refrigerated sugar cookies

1 cup Fisher® Chef's Naturals® pecan halves

¾ cup dried apricots

¼ cup Smucker's® apricot preserves

¼ teaspoon ground cinnamon

¼ teaspoon ground cloves

¼ cup sour cream

¼ cup Pillsbury Best® all-purpose flour

GLAZE

2 cups powdered sugar

⅓ cup milk

1) Let cookie dough stand at room temperature 10 minutes to soften. Meanwhile, heat oven to 350°F. Spray cookie sheets with Crisco® original no-stick cooking spray.

2) In food processor, place pecans, apricots, preserves, cinnamon and cloves. Cover; process with on-and-off pulses 20 to 30 seconds or until pecans and apricots are finely chopped and mixture holds together.

3) In large bowl, mix pecan mixture and sour cream. Crumble cookie dough into pecan mixture, stir with wooden spoon until well blended. Stir in flour until well blended.

4) Drop the dough by 24 heaping tablespoonfuls 2 inches apart onto cookie sheets. Bake 12 to 15 minutes or until light golden brown. Cool on cookie sheets 2 minutes, then remove to cooling racks. Cool completely, about 20 minutes.

5) Place waxed paper under cooling racks. In medium bowl, stir powdered sugar and milk until smooth. Dip tops of cookies into glaze; place on racks and let stand 5 minutes. Dip cookies again; let stand 5 minutes longer or until glaze is set.

Nutrition Information Per Serving	
Calories: 180	From Fat: 60
Total Fat	7g
Saturated Fat	1.5g
Trans Fat	1g
Cholesterol	0mg
Sodium	65mg
Total Carbohydrate	29g
Dietary Fiber	0g
Sugars	21g
Protein	1g

Banana Nut Cheerios® Energy Bars

PREP TIME: 20 MINUTES (READY IN 50 MINUTES)
SERVINGS: 24 BARS

 EASY

4 cups Banana Nut Cheerios® cereal

1 cup sweetened dried cranberries

⅓ cup slivered almonds, toasted

⅓ cup roasted unsalted sunflower nuts

½ cup light corn syrup

¼ cup packed brown sugar

¼ cup creamy peanut butter

1 teaspoon vanilla

1) Spray 9-inch square pan with cooking spray. In large bowl, mix cereal, cranberries, almonds and sunflower nuts.

2) In 2-quart saucepan, heat corn syrup, brown sugar and peanut butter to boiling over medium-high heat, stirring constantly. Boil and stir 1 minute. Remove from heat; stir in vanilla.

3) Pour syrup mixture over cereal mixture; toss to coat. Press firmly in pan. Cool completely, about 30 minutes. For bars, cut into 6 rows by 4 rows.

Nutrition Information Per Serving	
Calories: 110	From Fat: 30
Total Fat	3.5g
Saturated Fat	0g
Trans Fat	0g
Cholesterol	0mg
Sodium	60mg
Total Carbohydrate	18g
Dietary Fiber	1g
Sugars	11g
Protein	1g

Maple-Walnut Shortbread Cookies

PREP TIME: 1 HOUR 40 MINUTES (READY IN 1 HOUR 40 MINUTES)
SERVINGS: 48 COOKIES

1 cup butter or margarine, softened

⅓ cup sugar

1½ cups finely chopped toasted walnuts

1 egg yolk

2 cups all-purpose flour

1 teaspoon baking powder

¼ teaspoon salt

1 teaspoon maple flavor

1 cup semisweet chocolate chips
(6 oz)

1) In large bowl, beat butter and sugar with electric mixer on medium speed about 30 seconds or until smooth. Beat in ½ cup of the walnuts and the egg yolk until blended. On low speed, beat in flour, baking powder, salt and maple flavor until stiff cookie dough forms. Shape dough into a ball. Wrap in plastic wrap; refrigerate 45 minutes.

2) Heat oven to 350°F. Divide dough into 8 equal parts. On lightly floured surface, shape each part into a rope 12 inches long and ¾ inch thick. Cut each rope into 6 (2-inch) pieces. On ungreased cookie sheets, place dough pieces about 2 inches apart; flatten slightly.

3) Bake 15 to 17 minutes or until edges begin to brown. Cool 2 minutes; remove from cookie sheets to cooling racks. Cool completely, about 30 minutes.

4) In small microwavable bowl, microwave chocolate chips uncovered on High about 1 minute 30 seconds, stirring every 30 seconds, until chips can be stirred smooth. In another small bowl, place remaining 1 cup walnuts.

5) For each cookie, dip ½ inch of 1 long side into chocolate, then coat chocolate edge with walnuts. Place on sheets of waxed paper; let stand about 2 hours or until chocolate is set.

Nutrition Information Per Serving	
Calories: 100	From Fat: 70
Total Fat	7g
Saturated Fat	3.5g
Trans Fat	0g
Cholesterol	15mg
Sodium	50mg
Total Carbohydrate	8g
Dietary Fiber	0g
Sugars	3g
Protein	1g

Cherry Winks

PREP TIME: 1 HOUR 20 MINUTES (READY IN 1 HOUR 20 MINUTES)
SERVINGS: 5 DOZEN COOKIES

1 cup sugar

¾ cup shortening

2 tablespoons milk

1 teaspoon vanilla

2 eggs

2¼ cups all-purpose flour

1 teaspoon baking powder

½ teaspoon baking soda

½ teaspoon salt

1 cup chopped pecans

1 cup chopped dates

⅓ cup chopped maraschino cherries, patted dry with paper towels

1½ cups coarsely crushed corn flakes cereal

15 maraschino cherries, quartered

1) In large bowl, beat sugar and shortening with electric mixer on medium speed, scraping bowl occasionally, until well blended. Beat in milk, vanilla and eggs. On low speed, beat in flour, baking powder, baking soda and salt, scraping bowl occasionally, until dough forms. Stir in pecans, dates and ⅓ cup chopped cherries. If necessary, cover with plastic wrap and refrigerate 15 minutes for easier handling.

2) Heat oven to 375°F. Spray cookie sheets with cooking spray. Drop dough by rounded teaspoonfuls into cereal; coat thoroughly. Shape into balls. Place 2 inches apart on cookie sheets. Lightly press maraschino cherry quarter into top of each ball.

3) Bake 10 to 15 minutes or until light golden brown. Cool 1 minute; remove from cookie sheets to cooling racks.

Nutrition Information Per Serving	
Calories: 80	From Fat: 35
Total Fat	4g
Saturated Fat	1g
Trans Fat	0g
Cholesterol	5mg
Sodium	45mg
Total Carbohydrate	11g
Dietary Fiber	0g
Sugars	6g
Protein	1g

Dulce de Leche Bars

PREP TIME:	20 MINUTES (READY IN 1 HOUR 35 MINUTES)	EASY
SERVINGS:	32 BARS	

1½ cups all-purpose flour

1½ cups quick-cooking or old-fashioned oats

1 cup packed brown sugar

¼ teaspoon salt

1 cup butter or margarine, softened

1 can (13.4 oz) dulce de leche (caramelized sweetened condensed milk)

1 cup toffee bits

1) Heat oven to 350°F. In large bowl, mix flour, oats, brown sugar and salt. With pastry blender or fork, cut in butter until mixture is crumbly. Press ¾ of mixture in ungreased 13x9-inch pan.

2) Bake 10 minutes. Meanwhile, in 1-quart saucepan, heat dulce de leche over low heat 2 to 4 minutes, stirring frequently, until slightly softened.

3) Spread dulce de leche over partially baked crust. Sprinkle evenly with toffee bits and remaining crumb mixture. Bake 20 to 25 minutes or until golden brown. Cool 15 minutes.

4) Run knife around sides of pan to loosen bars. Cool completely, about 30 minutes. For bars, cut into 8 rows by 4 rows.

Nutrition Information Per Serving	
Calories: 210	From Fat: 90
Total Fat	10g
Saturated Fat	6g
Trans Fat	0g
Cholesterol	30mg
Sodium	85mg
Total Carbohydrate	28g
Dietary Fiber	0g
Sugars	21g
Protein	2g

Coconut-Filled Chocolate Delights

ANITA VAN GUNDY | DES MOINES, IOWA

BAKE-OFF® CONTEST 44, 2010

PREP TIME: 30 MINUTES (READY IN 1 HOUR 40 MINUTES)
SERVINGS: 20 COOKIES

¾ cup Fisher® roasted and salted almonds

1½ cups coconut

½ cup Eagle Brand® sweetened condensed milk (from 14-oz can)

1 package (16 oz) Pillsbury® Ready to Bake!™ refrigerated sugar cookies (24 cookies)

⅓ cup Hershey's® baking cocoa

⅓ cup Hershey's® milk chocolate baking chips

tip

To refresh dried out coconut, sprinkle with a few drops of water, cover and microwave until warm.

1) Reserve 20 almonds; set aside. Chop remaining almonds. In medium bowl, stir chopped almonds, coconut and milk until well blended. Refrigerate mixture 25 minutes for easier handling. Let cookie dough stand at room temperature for 10 minutes to soften.

2) Meanwhile, heat oven to 350°F. In large bowl, knead cookie dough and cocoa with hands until well blended. Cover with plastic wrap; set aside.

3) For each cookie, press 1 rounded tablespoon dough into 3-inch round. Place 1 tablespoon coconut mixture on center of each round. Wrap dough around filling, pressing edges to seal; shape into a ball. Place balls 3 inches apart on ungreased cookie sheets. Press each ball with fingers into 2½-inch round. Press 1 whole almond on each cookie.

4) Bake 9 to 12 minutes or until puffed and edges are set. Immediately remove from cookie sheet to cooling rack. Cool completely, about 30 minutes.

5) In small microwavable bowl, microwave chocolate chips uncovered on High 10 to 20 second, stirring every 10 seconds, until smooth. Place in resealable food-storage plastic bag; cut small tip from corner of bag. Drizzle chocolate over cookies. Before storing, let cookies stand at room temperature until chocolate is set. Store in airtight container.

Nutrition Information Per Serving	
Calories: 220	From Fat: 110
Total Fat	12g
Saturated Fat	4.5g
Trans Fat	0g
Cholesterol	0mg
Sodium	110mg
Total Carbohydrate	24g
Dietary Fiber	1g
Sugars	16g
Protein	3g

Cup o' Joe Chocolate Cookies

HELEN FIELDS | SPRINGTOWN, TEXAS

BAKE-OFF® CONTEST 44, 2010

PREP TIME: 40 MINUTES (READY IN 1 HOUR 15 MINUTES)
SERVINGS: 2-1/2 DOZEN COOKIES

1 roll (16.5 oz) Pillsbury®
  refrigerated sugar cookies

⅓ cup Hershey's® baking cocoa

1½ tablespoons instant espresso
  coffee powder or granules

⅓ cup whipping cream

⅓ cup Hershey's® mini chips
  semisweet chocolate

Nutrition Information Per Serving	
Calories: 90	From Fat: 35
Total Fat	4g
Saturated Fat	1.5g
Trans Fat	1g
Cholesterol	0mg
Sodium	50mg
Total Carbohydrate	12g
Dietary Fiber	0g
Sugars	7g
Protein	1g

1) Let cookie dough stand at room temperature 10 minutes to soften. Meanwhile, heat oven to 350°F.

2) In large bowl, mix cocoa, espresso powder and cream with wooden spoon until well blended. Crumble cookie dough into cocoa mixture; stir until well blended.

3) Shape dough into 30 balls; place 2 inches apart on ungreased cookie sheets. Using bottom of drinking glass, flatten balls into 1½-inch rounds. Press thumb into center of each round to make indentation. Fill each indention with ½ teaspoon of the chocolate chips.

4) Bake 9 to 13 minutes or until edges of cookies are set. Cool on cookie sheets 2 minutes; remove to cooling racks. Cool completely, about 20 minutes.

Chunky Chocolate Cookies

PREP TIME: 25 MINUTES (READY IN 40 MINUTES)
SERVINGS: 24 COOKIES

1 roll (16.5 oz) Pillsbury®
  refrigerated sugar cookies

3 tablespoons unsweetened
  baking cocoa

1 cup semisweet chocolate chunks

½ cup miniature semisweet
  chocolate chips

½ cup chopped pecans

Nutrition Information Per Serving	
Calories: 160	From Fat: 80
Total Fat	9g
Saturated Fat	3g
Trans Fat	1g
Cholesterol	5mg
Sodium	250mg
Total Carbohydrate	19g
Dietary Fiber	1g
Sugars	12g
Protein	1g

1) Heat oven to 350°F. Into large bowl, break up cookie dough. Add remaining ingredients; mix well.

2) On ungreased cookie sheets, drop dough by well-rounded tablespoonfuls 2 inches apart.

3) Bake 8 to 11 minutes or just until set. Cool 2 minutes; remove from cookie sheets. Cool completely, about 15 minutes.

Peach-Pecan Thumbprint Cookies

KATHY LANGNEHS | LOUISVILLE, KENTUCKY

 BAKE-OFF® CONTEST 44, 2010

| PREP TIME: | 1 HOUR (READY IN 1 HOUR) |
| SERVINGS: | 32 COOKIES |

1 roll (16.5 oz) Pillsbury® refrigerated sugar cookies

½ cup Pillsbury Best® all-purpose flour

1 tablespoon granulated sugar

½ teaspoon ground cinnamon

¼ teaspoon ground ginger

2 Eggland's Best eggs

3 tablespoons water

1¼ cups Fisher® Chef's Naturals® chopped pecans, finely chopped

⅓ cup Smucker's® peach preserves

1 cup powdered sugar

2 tablespoons bourbon or water

1) Let cookie dough stand at room temperature for 10 minutes to soften. Meanwhile, heat oven to 350°F. Line cookie sheets with cooking parchment paper or spray with Crisco® original no-stick cooking spray.

2) In large bowl, break up cookie dough. Mix in flour, granulated sugar, cinnamon and ginger with wooden spoon until well blended. Shape dough into 1-inch balls.

3) In shallow dish, beat eggs and water until well blended. In another shallow dish, place pecans. Roll dough balls in egg mixture, then coat with pecans (press pecans into dough if necessary). Place 2 inches apart on cookie sheets. Make small indentation in each cookie, using handle of wooden spoon. Fill each indentation with about ½ teaspoon preserves.

4) Bake 11 to 15 minutes or until light golden brown. Meanwhile, in small bowl, mix powdered sugar and bourbon until smooth. If necessary, stir in small amount of water for desired drizzling consistency.

5) Remove cookies from cookie sheets to cooling racks. Cool 3 minutes. Drizzle bourbon mixture over warm cookies.

Nutrition Information Per Serving	
Calories: 130	From Fat: 50
Total Fat	6g
Saturated Fat	1g
Trans Fat	1g
Cholesterol	10mg
Sodium	50mg
Total Carbohydrate	18g
Dietary Fiber	0g
Sugars	11g
Protein	1g

Easy Oatmeal Caramel Bars

NIELA FRANTELLIZZI | BOCA RATON, FLORIDA

BAKE-OFF® CONTEST 37, 1996

PREP TIME: 35 MINUTES (READY IN 2 HOURS 40 MINUTES)
SERVINGS: 16 BARS

1 roll (16.5 oz) Pillsbury® refrigerated chocolate chip cookies

1 cup quick-cooking oats

Dash salt, if desired

⅔ cup caramel topping

5 tablespoons all-purpose flour

1 teaspoon vanilla

¾ cup chopped walnuts

1 cup semisweet chocolate chips (6 oz)

1) Heat oven to 350°F. In large bowl, break up cookie dough. Stir or knead in oats and salt. Reserve ½ cup dough for topping; press remaining dough in ungreased 9-inch square pan.

2) Bake 10 to 12 minutes or until dough puffs and appears dry. Meanwhile, in small bowl, mix caramel topping, flour and vanilla until well blended.

3) Sprinkle walnuts and chocolate chips evenly over crust; drizzle with caramel mixture. Crumble reserved ½ cup dough mixture over caramel.

4) Bake 20 to 25 minutes longer or until golden brown. Cool 10 minutes. Run knife around sides of pan to loosen. Cool completely, about 1½ hours. Cut into 4 rows by 4 rows.

Nutrition Information Per Serving	
Calories: 280	From Fat: 110
Total Fat	12g
Saturated Fat	4g
Trans Fat	1g
Cholesterol	5mg
Sodium	140mg
Total Carbohydrate	40g
Dietary Fiber	1g
Sugars	24g
Protein	4g

Quick Peanut Blossoms

PREP TIME: 1 HOUR (READY IN 1 HOUR)
SERVINGS: 3 DOZEN COOKIES

1 roll (16.5 oz) Pillsbury® refrigerated
  peanut butter cookies

3 tablespoons sugar

36 milk chocolate candy drops or
   pieces, unwrapped

1) Heat oven to 375°F. Shape the dough
   into 1-inch balls; roll in sugar. On
   ungreased cookie sheets, place balls
   2 inches apart.

2) Bake 10 to 12 minutes or until golden
   brown. Immediately top each cookie
   with 1 milk chocolate candy, pressing
   down firmly so cookie cracks around
   edge. Remove from cookie sheets to
   cooling racks. Cool completely
   before storing.

Nutrition Information Per Serving

Calories: 80	From Fat: 35
Total Fat	4g
Saturated Fat	1.5g
Trans Fat	0g
Cholesterol	0mg
Sodium	65mg
Total Carbohydrate	11g
Dietary Fiber	0g
Sugars	8g
Protein	1g

tip

If the cookie dough
becomes too soft,
refrigerate it or add
flour 1 tablespoon at a
time until it is stiff
enough to handle.

Soft Ginger-Pumpkin Cookies with Browned Butter Frosting

PREP TIME: 1 HOUR 15 MINUTES (READY IN 1 HOUR 15 MINUTES)
SERVINGS: 4 DOZEN COOKIES

COOKIES

1 cup packed brown sugar

¼ cup chopped crystallized ginger

¾ cup butter or margarine, softened

½ cup canned pumpkin (not pumpkin pie mix)

1 egg

2½ cups all-purpose flour

1 teaspoon baking soda

1 teaspoon ground ginger

¼ teaspoon salt

FROSTING

⅓ cup butter (do not use margarine)

2 cups powdered sugar

1 teaspoon vanilla

2 to 4 tablespoons milk

1) Heat oven to 375°F. In large bowl, beat brown sugar, crystallized ginger, ¾ cup softened butter, the pumpkin and egg with electric mixer on medium speed until well blended. Stir in remaining cookie ingredients to form soft dough. (If dough is too soft, refrigerate about 15 minutes.)

2) Shape dough into 1-inch balls; place about 2 inches apart on ungreased cookie sheets. Slightly flatten balls.

3) Bake 7 to 10 minutes or until light golden brown. Immediately remove from cookie sheets to cooling racks. Cool completely, about 15 minutes.

4) In 2-quart saucepan, heat ⅓ cup butter over medium heat, stirring constantly, until light golden brown. Remove from heat. Stir in remaining frosting ingredients until smooth and spreadable. Immediately spread frosting on cooled cookies.

Nutrition Information Per Serving	
Calories: 100	From Fat: 40
Total Fat	4.5g
Saturated Fat	2.5g
Trans Fat	0g
Cholesterol	15mg
Sodium	70mg
Total Carbohydrate	15g
Dietary Fiber	0g
Sugars	9g
Protein	1g

Decadent Desserts

There's always room for dessert with these simply sensational delights.

CARAMEL-PEAR PUDDING CAKE
PG. 329

"O MY GANACHE" CHERRY
MACAROON TORTE
PG. 325

CHOCOLATE-CHERRY-PISTACHIO
BROWNIES
PG. 330

PUMPKIN-APPLE GINGERBREAD
PG. 341

Mocha Mousse Puffs

PREP TIME: 35 MINUTES (READY IN 50 MINUTES)
SERVINGS: 12

- 1 cup whipping cream
- 1 teaspoon instant espresso coffee granules
- ¾ cup dark chocolate chips
- 1 teaspoon vanilla
- 1 can (8 oz) Pillsbury® refrigerated crescent dinner rolls
- 1 egg
- 2 tablespoons powdered sugar
- 12 chocolate-covered coffee beans or fresh strawberries
- 1 teaspoon cocoa or powdered sugar

1) In 1-quart saucepan, mix ¼ cup of the whipping cream and the coffee. Cook over low heat, stirring constantly, until mixture simmers; remove from heat. Using a wire whisk, stir in the chocolate chips until melted. Stir in vanilla.

2) Pour into medium bowl; cool until room temperature, about 10 minutes. In another medium bowl, beat remaining ¾ cup whipping cream with electric mixer on high speed until soft peaks form. Refrigerate half (about ¾ cup) whipped cream for garnish. Fold remaining whipped cream into chocolate mixture. Cover and refrigerate 30 minutes.

3) Heat oven to 375°F. Unroll dough on work surface; firmly press perforations to seal. Using ruler, push dough into 10x7-inch rectangle. Cut into 24 squares, 6 rows by 4 rows. Place 1 inch apart on ungreased cookie sheet. In small bowl, beat egg and 2 tablespoons powdered sugar with fork. Brush on tops of squares.

4) Bake 8 to 10 minutes or until puffed and golden brown. Cool completely, about 10 minutes.

5) Just before serving, spoon about 2 tablespoons chocolate mixture on 12 of the crescent squares. Place remaining crescent squares on top. Top each with about 1 tablespoon reserved whipped cream and 1 chocolate-covered coffee bean. Measure 1 teaspoon cocoa into fine mesh strainer. Sift cocoa over tops of puffs.

Nutrition Information Per Serving	
Calories: 210	From Fat: 130
Total Fat	14g
Saturated Fat	7g
Trans Fat	1g
Cholesterol	40mg
Sodium	160mg
Total Carbohydrate	17g
Dietary Fiber	0g
Sugars	20g
Protein	3g

Creamy Orange-Chocolate Truffle Bars

DEBBIE HUBER | PETERSBURG, NEW JERSEY

BAKE-OFF® CONTEST 44, 2010

PREP TIME: 25 MINUTES (READY IN 3 HOURS 15 MINUTES)
SERVINGS: 20 BARS

BASE

- 1 cup Land O Lakes® butter, softened
- ½ cup powdered sugar
- ¼ teaspoon salt
- 1¼ cups Pillsbury Best® all purpose flour
- ½ cup Fisher® Chef's Naturals® chopped pecans

TRUFFLE

- 1 can (14 oz) Eagle Brand® sweetened condensed milk
- 1 bag (12 oz) Hershey's® Special Dark® chocolate baking chips (2 cups)
- ⅔ cup Smucker's® sweet orange marmalade

TOPPING

- 1 container (8 oz) mascarpone cheese
- 1⅓ cups granulated sugar
- ⅔ cup whipping cream
- 1 tablespoon grated orange peel (from 1 large orange)

1) Heat oven to 350°F. Spray 13x9-inch pan with Crisco® original no-stick cooking spray.

2) In medium bowl, beat butter, powdered sugar and salt with electric mixer on medium speed until fluffy. On low speed, gradually beat in flour until dough forms. Stir in pecans. Spread mixture in pan. Bake 15 to 20 minutes or until golden brown. Cool completely, about 30 minutes.

3) In medium microwavable bowl, microwave milk and chocolate chips uncovered on High 1 minute; stir. Microwave up to 1 minute longer, stirring until smooth. Stir in marmalade; spread over base. Refrigerate 1 hour or until set.

4) In medium bowl, beat cheese, granulated sugar and cream on medium speed until smooth. Beat on high speed until mixture is thickened. Stir in orange peel. Spread over truffle layer. Refrigerate 1 hour or until chilled. For bars, cut into 5 rows by 4 rows, wiping knife after each cut. Store covered in refrigerator.

Nutrition Information Per Serving	
Calories: 330	From Fat: 210
Total Fat	18g
Saturated Fat	6g
Trans Fat	.5g
Cholesterol	50mg
Sodium	90mg
Total Carbohydrate	38g
Dietary Fiber	1g
Sugars	41g
Protein	2g

Orange-Coconut Tiramisu Tart

GAIL DEAN | ST. AUGUSTINE, FLORIDA

BAKE-OFF® CONTEST 44, 2010

PREP TIME: 35 MINUTES (READY IN 2 HOURS 30 MINUTES)
SERVINGS: 12

1 Pillsbury® refrigerated pie crust, softened as directed on box

1 container (16 oz) mascarpone cheese or 2 packages (8 oz each) cream cheese, softened

½ cup Fisher® Chef's Naturals® chopped pecans

⅓ cup powdered sugar

2 tablespoons instant espresso coffee powder or granules

1 container (12 oz) frozen whipped topping, thawed

1 cup Smucker's® sweet orange marmalade

2 teaspoons Hershey's® baking cocoa

¾ cup flaked coconut, toasted

12 whole strawberries with leaves, cut into fans, if desired

1) Heat oven to 450°F. In 10- or 9-inch springform pan, press pie crust evenly on bottom and 1 inch up side. Generously prick crust with fork. Bake 9 to 11 minutes or until golden brown. Cool completely, about 15 minutes.

2) Meanwhile, in medium bowl, mix cheese, pecans, powdered sugar and coffee granules. Gently fold in 1 cup of the whipped topping. Spread evenly over crust.

3) In another medium bowl, place remaining whipped topping; gently fold in marmalade until well mixed. Spread evenly over cheese mixture.

4) Using fine-mesh strainer, sprinkle cocoa over whipped topping mixture. Sprinkle with coconut. Refrigerate at least 1½ hours until chilled.

5) Remove side of pan; place tart on large round serving plate. Garnish with strawberry fans. Store loosely covered in refrigerator.

Nutrition Information Per Serving	
Calories: 340	From Fat: 170
Total Fat	19g
Saturated Fat	10g
Trans Fat	0g
Cholesterol	15mg
Sodium	125mg
Total Carbohydrate	41g
Dietary Fiber	2g
Sugars	23g
Protein	1g

"O My Ganache" Cherry Macaroon Torte

DENNIS DEEL | WOOSTER, OHIO

BAKE-OFF® CONTEST 44, 2010

PREP TIME: 30 MINUTES (READY IN 2 HOURS 15 MINUTES)
SERVINGS: 12

1 roll (16.5 oz) Pillsbury® refrigerated sugar cookies

1¼ cups whipping cream

⅔ cup Hershey's® Special Dark® chocolate baking chips

⅓ cup Fisher® Chef's Naturals® blanched slivered almonds

1 cup flaked coconut

1 jar (12 oz) Smucker's® cherry preserves (1 cup)

1 cup sweetened dried cherries

1 tablespoon orange juice

1) Let cookie dough stand at room temperature 10 minutes to soften. Meanwhile, heat oven to 350°F. In 1-quart saucepan, heat ½ cup of the whipping cream over low heat just until hot but not boiling; remove from heat. Stir in chocolate chips until smooth. Set aside.

2) In 8-inch skillet, cook almonds over medium heat 5 to 7 minutes, stirring frequently, until golden brown. Remove from heat; cool 5 minutes. Coarsely chop almonds.

3) In medium bowl, break up cookie dough. Mix in coconut with wooden spoon until well blended. Press dough evenly in bottom of 9-inch springform pan. Sprinkle with ¼ cup of the almonds; lightly press into dough. Bake 20 to 25 minutes or until light golden brown. Cool completely, about 1 hour.

4) Meanwhile, in blender or food processor, place the preserves, cherries and orange juice. Cover; process with on-and-off pulses until blended. Set aside.

5) Spread cherry mixture over crust to within ½ inch of edge. Stir chocolate mixture with wire whisk; pour over cherry mixture, spreading to cover cherry mixture. Sprinkle with remaining almonds. Freeze 30 minutes until chocolate is firm.

6) Meanwhile, in small bowl, beat remaining ¾ cup whipping cream with electric mixer on high speed until soft peaks form. Run sharp knife around edge of torte to loosen. Remove side of pan. To serve, cut into 12 wedges. Top each serving with dollop of whipped cream. Store covered in refrigerator.

Nutrition Information Per Serving	
Calories: 460	From Fat: 190
Total Fat	21g
Saturated Fat	11g
Trans Fat	2.5g
Cholesterol	30mg
Sodium	160mg
Total Carbohydrate	64g
Dietary Fiber	2g
Sugars	20g
Protein	3g

Almond Brownie-Cherry Mousse Torte

CATHERINE WHITE | WEST PALM BEACH, FLORIDA

BAKE-OFF® CONTEST 44, 2010

PREP TIME: 25 MINUTES (READY IN 1 HOUR 40 MINUTES)
SERVINGS: 10

- 1 box (19.5 oz) Pillsbury® classic milk chocolate brownie mix
- ½ cup Crisco® pure vegetable oil
- ¼ cup water
- 2 Eggland's Best eggs
- 1 teaspoon almond extract
- 1 jar (10 oz) maraschino cherries, drained, 2 teaspoons cherry juice reserved
- 1 package (8 oz) cream cheese, softened
- 1 cup powdered sugar
- 1 container (8 oz) frozen whipped topping, thawed
- ¼ cup Fisher® Chef's Naturals® natural sliced almonds, toasted

1) Heat oven to 350°F. Generously spray 2 (8-inch) round cake pans with Crisco® original no-stick cooking spray. Line bottoms of pans with cooking parchment paper; spray paper with cooking spray.

2) In large bowl, stir brownie mix, oil, water, eggs and almond extract 50 strokes with spoon. Divide batter evenly between pans.

3) Bake 20 to 25 minutes or until toothpick inserted 2 inches from edge of pan comes out almost clean. Cool in pans 10 minutes. Carefully invert brownie layers from pans onto cooling racks. Cool completely, about 1 hour.

4) Meanwhile, finely chop cherries. In large bowl, beat cream cheese, powdered sugar, cherries and 2 teaspoons cherry juice with electric mixer on medium speed until well blended. Fold in whipped topping. Refrigerate while brownies cool.

5) To assemble torte, place 1 brownie layer, bottom side up, on serving plate. Spread half of cherry mixture over top of brownie. Top with remaining brownie, top side up; spread or pipe remaining cherry mixture on top. Sprinkle almonds around edge of torte. Serve immediately, or refrigerate until ready to serve. Store covered in refrigerator.

Nutrition Information Per Serving	
Calories: 570	From Fat: 260
Total Fat	29g
Saturated Fat	10g
Trans Fat	0g
Cholesterol	60mg
Sodium	230mg
Total Carbohydrate	71g
Dietary Fiber	1g
Sugars	55g
Protein	5g

Mile-High Peanut Butter-Brownie Pie

DEBBI BRACKER | CARL JUNCTION, MISSOURI

BAKE-OFF® CONTEST 44, 2010

PREP TIME: 20 MINUTES (READY IN 2 HOURS 50 MINUTES)
SERVINGS: 10

e EASY

1 Pillsbury® refrigerated pie crust, softened as directed on box

1 box (15.5 oz) Pillsbury® chocolate chunk brownie mix

¼ cup Reese's® peanut butter chips

⅓ cup Crisco® pure vegetable oil

3 tablespoons water

1 Eggland's Best egg

1 package (8 oz) cream cheese, softened

½ cup Jif® creamy peanut butter

1 cup powdered sugar

1 container (8 oz) frozen whipped topping, thawed

2 tablespoons Fisher® party peanuts, chopped

2 tablespoons Hershey's® mini chips semi-sweet chocolate

1) Heat oven to 350°F. Unroll pie crust; place in ungreased 9-inch glass pie plate as directed on box for One-Crust Filled Pie; flute edge.

2) In medium bowl, stir brownie mix, peanut butter chips, oil, water and egg 50 strokes with spoon. Pour batter into crust-lined pie plate.

3) Bake 30 to 40 minutes, covering edge of crust with strips of foil after 15 to 20 minutes, until crust is golden brown and center of brownie is set. Cool slightly, about 20 minutes. Refrigerate 1 hour or until completely cooled.

4) In medium bowl, beat cream cheese, peanut butter and powdered sugar with electric mixer on medium speed until smooth. Fold in whipped topping. Spread mixture over brownie. Sprinkle with peanuts and chocolate chips. Refrigerate 30 minutes before serving. Store covered in refrigerator.

Nutrition Information Per Serving	
Calories: 620	From Fat: 350
Total Fat	39g
Saturated Fat	15g
Trans Fat	2g
Cholesterol	45mg
Sodium	380mg
Total Carbohydrate	60g
Dietary Fiber	1g
Sugars	37g
Protein	7g

Dulce de Leche Fondue

PREP TIME: 5 MINUTES (READY IN 1 HOUR 5 MINUTES)
SERVINGS: 8 (3 TABLESPOONS FONDUE AND 6 DIPPERS EACH)

 EASY

1 can (13.4 oz) dulce de leche
(caramelized sweetened
condensed milk)

1 tablespoon rum or milk

Dippers (pound cake cubes,
strawberries, pineapple chunks,
apple slices, marshmallows)

Nutrition Information Per Serving	
Calories: 260	From Fat: 80
Total Fat	8g
Saturated Fat	4g
Trans Fat	.5g
Cholesterol	35mg
Sodium	55mg
Total Carbohydrate	42g
Dietary Fiber	1g
Sugars	36g
Protein	4g

1) In 1-quart slow cooker, cover and
cook dulce de leche 30 minutes; stir.
Cook about 30 minutes longer or
until thoroughly heated.

2) Stir in rum until smooth. (Stir in additional rum or milk for a thinner
fondue.) Unplug slow cooker before serving. Serve with dippers.

Crescent Puff S'mores

PREP TIME: 15 MINUTES (READY IN 35 MINUTES)
SERVINGS: 16 SNACKS

EASY

2 cans (8 oz each) Pillsbury®
refrigerated crescent dinner rolls

16 large marshmallows

2 to 3 (1.2 oz each) milk chocolate
candy bars, broken into squares

½ cup butter or margarine, melted

1 cup graham cracker crumbs
(about 14 squares)

Nutrition Information Per Serving	
Calories: 230	From Fat: 120
Total Fat	14g
Saturated Fat	6g
Trans Fat	2g
Cholesterol	15mg
Sodium	290mg
Total Carbohydrate	23g
Dietary Fiber	0g
Sugars	11g
Protein	3g

1) Heat oven to 375°F. Spray 16 regular-size muffin cups with cooking spray.
Separate dough into 16 triangles.

2) For each snack, place 1 marshmallow on shortest side of triangle. Top with
2 squares of chocolate candy. Starting with shortest side of triangle, fold
corners of dough over marshmallow and chocolate, then roll to opposite
point, completely covering marshmallow and chocolate; pinch dough to
seal well.

3) Dip snacks in or brush with melted butter; roll in cracker crumbs to coat.
Place in muffin cups.

4) Place pans on sheet of foil or cookie sheet (to catch any spills); bake 15 to
20 minutes or until golden brown. Immediately remove from muffin cups;
serve warm.

Caramel-Pear Pudding Cake

PREP TIME: 15 MINUTES (READY IN 1 HOUR)
SERVINGS: 8

e EASY

1 cup all-purpose flour

⅔ cup granulated sugar

1½ teaspoons baking powder

½ teaspoon ground cinnamon

½ cup milk

2 tablespoons butter or margarine, melted

1 can (15 oz) pears, coarsely chopped, drained and liquid reserved

1 tablespoon grated orange peel

Water

¾ cup packed brown sugar

¼ cup butter or margarine, softened

1 quart vanilla ice cream

1) Heat oven to 375°F. In medium bowl, mix flour, granulated sugar, baking powder and cinnamon. Stir in milk and melted butter until mixture is smooth. Stir in pears and orange peel. Spread evenly in ungreased 12x8-inch (2-quart) glass baking dish.

2) Add enough water to reserved pear liquid to measure 1 cup; heat to boiling in 1-quart saucepan. Stir in brown sugar and softened butter until melted. Pour hot sugar mixture evenly over batter.

3) Bake 40 to 45 minutes or until top is deep golden brown. Cut into 8 squares; using spatula, place each square upside down on individual dessert plate. Serve warm with ice cream.

Nutrition Information Per Serving	
Calories: 470	From Fat: 150
Total Fat	16g
Saturated Fat	10g
Trans Fat	.5g
Cholesterol	55mg
Sodium	220mg
Total Carbohydrate	76g
Dietary Fiber	2g
Sugars	57g
Protein	4g

tip

Perfectly softened butter will still hold its shape but not be melted.

Chocolate-Cherry-Pistachio Brownies

YOLANDA SUE BOWSER | SOLON, OHIO

BAKE-OFF® CONTEST 44, 2010

⊖ EASY

| PREP TIME: | 20 MINUTES (READY IN 2 HOURS 50 MINUTES) |
| SERVINGS: | 20 BROWNIES |

1 box (19.5 oz) Pillsbury® chocolate fudge brownie mix

½ cup Crisco® pure vegetable oil

¼ cup water

3 Eggland's Best eggs

1 jar (10 oz) maraschino cherries, well drained, cut in half

1 box (4-serving size) pistachio instant pudding and pie filling mix

½ cup cold milk

1 container (8 oz) frozen whipped topping, thawed

½ cup pistachio nuts, chopped, toasted

½ cup Land O Lakes® unsalted or salted butter

1 bag (12 oz) Hershey's® semi-sweet chocolate baking chips (2 cups)

1) Heat oven to 350°F. Spray bottom only of 13x9-inch pan with Crisco® original no-stick cooking spray.

2) In large bowl, stir brownie mix, oil, water and eggs 50 strokes with spoon. Stir in cherries. Spread batter in pan. Bake 28 to 31 minutes or until toothpick inserted 2 inches from side of pan comes out almost clean. Cool completely, about 1 hour.

3) Meanwhile, in medium bowl, beat pudding mix and milk with wire whisk until well blended. Fold in whipped topping and nuts. Spread over brownie. Refrigerate 30 minutes.

4) In medium microwavable bowl, microwave butter and chocolate chips uncovered on High about 1 minute, stirring every 30 seconds, until melted and smooth. Cool 5 minutes; carefully spread over pudding mixture. Refrigerate 30 minutes or until chocolate is set. For brownies, cut into 5 rows by 4 rows. Store covered in refrigerator.

Nutrition Information Per Serving	
Calories: 370	From Fat: 190
Total Fat	21g
Saturated Fat	9g
Trans Fat	0g
Cholesterol	40mg
Sodium	160mg
Total Carbohydrate	42g
Dietary Fiber	2g
Sugars	32g
Protein	3g

Pecan-Date Pie

PREP TIME: 20 MINUTES (READY IN 3 HOURS 10 MINUTES)
SERVINGS: 10

 EASY

CRUST

1 Pillsbury® refrigerated pie crust, softened as directed on box

FILLING

¼ cup butter or margarine, softened

⅔ cup packed brown sugar

3 eggs

1 cup light corn syrup

2 tablespoons cornstarch

2 tablespoons lemon juice

1 teaspoon vanilla

¾ cup whole or chopped pecans

¾ cup whole pitted dates, chopped

TOPPING

½ cup whipping cream

⅛ teaspoon ground cinnamon

½ teaspoon grated lemon peel

1) Heat oven to 375°F. Place pie crust in 9-inch glass pie plate as directed on box for one-crust filled pie.

2) In large bowl, beat softened butter and brown sugar with electric mixer on low speed until well mixed, scraping bowl occasionally. Add eggs one at a time, beating well after each addition. Reduce speed to low; beat in corn syrup, cornstarch, lemon juice and vanilla until well blended.

3) Sprinkle pecans and dates in crust; carefully pour filling mixture in crust over pecans and dates. Cover crust edge with 2- to 3-inch-wide strips of foil to prevent excessive browning; remove foil during last 15 minutes of bake time.

4) Bake 45 to 55 minutes or until the center is set. Cool on cooling rack at least 2 hours before serving.

5) In chilled small bowl, beat whipping cream and cinnamon on high speed until stiff peaks form. Fold in lemon peel. Spoon a dollop of topping on each serving.

Nutrition Information Per Serving	
Calories: 450	From Fat: 190
Total Fat	21g
Saturated Fat	8g
Trans Fat	0g
Cholesterol	90mg
Sodium	190mg
Total Carbohydrate	62g
Dietary Fiber	1g
Sugars	35g
Protein	3g

Banana-Peanut Butter Cream Tart

LENORE KLASS | KOLOA, HAWAII

Pillsbury Bake-Off®

BAKE-OFF® CONTEST 44, 2010

e EASY

PREP TIME: 20 MINUTES (READY IN 1 HOUR 55 MINUTES)
SERVINGS: 8

1 Pillsbury® refrigerated pie crust, softened as directed on box

6 tablespoons Land O Lakes® butter, softened

1 package (3 oz) cream cheese, softened

⅓ cup Jif® creamy peanut butter

½ teaspoon vanilla

2 cups powdered sugar

1½ cups ¼-inch slices firm ripe bananas (about 2 medium)

1 cup whipping cream

¼ cup Fisher® party peanuts, finely chopped

1) Heat oven to 450°F. Unroll pie crust; place in ungreased 9- or 9½-inch tart pan with removable bottom. Press crust firmly against bottom and side of pan; fold excess crust over and gently press into side of pan to make double thickness. Prick bottom of crust with fork several times. Bake 9 to 11 minutes or until golden brown. Cool completely, about 25 minutes.

2) In medium bowl, beat butter, cream cheese, peanut butter and vanilla with electric mixer on medium speed until well blended. Gradually add powdered sugar, beating until smooth and creamy. Spread peanut butter filling in tart shell, building up side 1 inch and leaving shallow indentation in center of filling. Fill indentation with bananas; gently press into filling.

3) In small bowl, beat whipping cream on high speed until soft peaks form (do not overbeat). Spread whipped cream over filling and bananas. Sprinkle peanuts around edge of tart. Refrigerate 1 hour or until chilled. Store covered in refrigerator.

Nutrition Information Per Serving	
Calories: 550	From Fat: 320
Total Fat	35g
Saturated Fat	18g
Trans Fat	1g
Cholesterol	70mg
Sodium	300mg
Total Carbohydrate	52g
Dietary Fiber	2g
Sugars	35g
Protein	5g

Caramel Apple Pizza

| PREP TIME: | 10 MINUTES (READY IN 25 MINUTES) |
| SERVINGS: | 16 |

 EASY

1 can (11 oz) Pillsbury® refrigerated thin pizza crust

1 can (21 oz) apple pie filling

½ cup all-purpose flour

½ cup packed brown sugar

½ cup quick-cooking oats

1 teaspoon ground cinnamon

½ cup butter or margarine

1 cup shredded Cheddar cheese (4 oz)

½ cup chopped pecans

¼ cup caramel topping

1) Heat oven to 400°F. Spray a 15x10-inch or larger dark or nonstick cookie sheet with cooking spray. Unroll dough on cookie sheet; starting at center, press dough into 15x10-inch rectangle.

2) Spoon apple pie filling evenly on dough. In medium bowl, mix flour, brown sugar, oats and cinnamon. Cut in butter, using pastry blender (or pulling 2 table knives through mixture in opposite directions), until mixture looks like fine crumbs. Stir in the cheese and pecans. Sprinkle evenly over the apples.

3) Bake 13 to 16 minutes or until crust is golden brown. Drizzle with caramel topping. Serve immediately.

Nutrition Information Per Serving	
Calories: 270	From Fat: 110
Total Fat	12g
Saturated Fat	6g
Trans Fat	0g
Cholesterol	25mg
Sodium	330mg
Total Carbohydrate	35g
Dietary Fiber	1g
Sugars	19g
Protein	4g

Caribbean Panna Cotta Pie

DAVID DEMATTEO | BLUE BELL, PENNSYLVANIA

Bake-Off®

BAKE-OFF® CONTEST 44, 2010

PREP TIME: 30 MINUTES (READY IN 3 HOURS 25 MINUTES)
SERVINGS: 8

1 Pillsbury® refrigerated pie crust, softened as directed on box

1 envelope (1/4 oz) unflavored gelatin

2 tablespoons cold water

1¼ cups whipping cream

1¼ cups (from 16 oz can) cream of coconut (not coconut milk)

1 tablespoon grated lime peel

¼ cup lime juice

½ cup Land O Lakes® butter

½ cup packed light brown sugar

¾ cup Fisher® Chef's Naturals® chopped pecans

4 ripe firm medium bananas, cut into ¼-inch slices (about 2½ cups)

½ cup flaked coconut, toasted

1) Heat oven to 450°F. Make pie crust as directed on box for One-Crust Baked Shell using 9-inch glass pie plate—except do not prick crust. Carefully line pie crust with double thickness of foil, gently pressing foil to bottom and side of pastry. Fold in edges of foil to fit pie crust. Bake 9 to 11 minutes or until golden brown. Remove foil. Cool completely on cooling rack, about 15 minutes.

2) Meanwhile, in small bowl, sprinkle gelatin over cold water; set aside. In 2-quart saucepan, heat whipping cream, cream of coconut, lime peel and lime juice to boiling over medium heat, stirring occasionally. Remove from heat. Beat in gelatin mixture with wire whisk until well blended. Pour into crust. Refrigerate 2½ to 3 hours or until set.

3) When ready to serve, in 10-inch skillet, heat butter and brown sugar over medium-low heat, stirring occasionally, until smooth. Stir in pecans; cook 2 minutes, stirring frequently. Remove from heat; stir in bananas. Cool 10 minutes. Top each serving of pie with banana sauce and coconut. Store covered in refrigerator.

Nutrition Information Per Serving	
Calories: 710	From Fat: 500
Total Fat	56g
Saturated Fat	35g
Trans Fat	1g
Cholesterol	75mg
Sodium	260mg
Total Carbohydrate	48g
Dietary Fiber	4g
Sugars	27g
Protein	5g

Chai Brownie Cupcakes with Creamy Froth

CHRIS CASTON | JONESBORO, MAINE

BAKE-OFF® CONTEST 44, 2010

PREP TIME: 20 MINUTES (READY IN 1 HOUR 40 MINUTES)
SERVINGS: 12 CUPCAKES

e EASY

10 tea bags spiced chai-flavored black tea

1 cup boiling water

1 box (19.5 oz) Pillsbury® chocolate fudge brownie mix

¾ cup Crisco® pure canola oil

3 Eggland's Best eggs

¾ cup frozen (thawed) extra-creamy whipped topping

¾ cup marshmallow creme

⅛ teaspoon ground cinnamon

1) Heat oven to 350°F. Place paper baking cup in each of 12 regular-size muffin cups.

2) In 2-cup glass measuring cup, steep tea bags in boiling water 5 minutes. Using back of spoon, press tea bags against side of cup to make ¾ cup tea. Discard tea bags. If necessary, add enough water so tea measures ¾ cup.

3) In large bowl, stir brownie mix, oil, eggs and tea with wooden spoon until well blended. Divide batter evenly among cups (cups will be almost full).

4) Bake 25 to 30 minutes or until toothpick inserted comes out almost clean. Remove from pan to cooling rack. Cool about 45 minutes.

5) Meanwhile, in medium bowl, beat whipped topping and marshmallow creme on medium speed about 3 minutes or until fluffy. Refrigerate while cupcakes cool. Generously frost cupcakes with topping mixture; sprinkle with cinnamon.

Nutrition Information Per Serving	
Calories: 320	From Fat: 160
Total Fat	18g
Saturated Fat	1.5g
Trans Fat	0g
Cholesterol	45mg
Sodium	130mg
Total Carbohydrate	36g
Dietary Fiber	01g
Sugars	25g
Protein	3g

Black-Bottom Cranberry Cream Pie

PREP TIME: 50 MINUTES (READY IN 2 HOURS 20 MINUTES)
SERVINGS: 12

RUM PASTRY CREAM

- ⅓ cup sugar
- 3 tablespoons cornstarch
- ¼ teaspoon salt
- 1½ cups half-and-half
- 4 egg yolks
- 2 teaspoons vanilla
- ½ teaspoon rum extract

CRANBERRY TOPPING

- 1 cup sweetened dried cranberries
- 1 cup cranberry juice cocktail
- ¼ cup seedless raspberry jam
- 1 tablespoon plus 1 teaspoon cornstarch mixed with 1 tablespoon cold water
- ½ teaspoon grated orange peel

CRUST

- 1 Pillsbury® refrigerated pie crust, softened as directed on box

GANACHE

- ½ cup whipping cream
- 1 tablespoon unsalted or salted butter
- ¼ cup dark chocolate chips

1) In heavy 2-quart saucepan, mix ⅓ cup sugar, 3 tablespoons cornstarch and the salt with wire whisk. Gradually beat in half-and-half, then egg yolks. Cook over medium heat about 6 minutes, stirring constantly with wire whisk, until mixture just comes to a boil and begins to thicken. Remove from heat; stir in vanilla and rum extract. Pour into medium bowl; cover with plastic wrap, touching wrap directly on surface. Refrigerate at least 2 hours but no longer than 2 days.

2) In 1-quart saucepan, heat cranberries and cranberry juice to boiling over high heat, stirring occasionally. Reduce heat to medium-low; simmer 5 minutes stirring occasionally. Stir in jam; cook 2 minutes. Stir in cornstarch/water mixture. Increase heat to medium. Heat to boiling; boil 1 minute, stirring constantly. Remove from heat; stir in orange peel. Cool 5 minutes, stirring occasionally. Refrigerate about 15 minutes or until room temperature. Or place saucepan in bowl of ice and water, stirring frequently until cool.

3) Heat oven to 450°F. Bake pie crust as directed on box for one-crust baked shell, using 10-inch tart pan. Cool on cooling rack.

4) In 2-quart saucepan, heat cream and butter over medium-low heat until hot (do not boil). Remove from heat; add chocolate chips. Gently stir with wire whisk until smooth; pour evenly over crust. Refrigerate crust until ganache is firm, about 30 minutes. Spread rum pastry cream evenly over ganache; spread cranberry topping on top. Cover and refrigerate any remaining pie.

Nutrition Information Per Serving	
Calories: 320	From Fat: 150
Total Fat	16g
Saturated Fat	9g
Trans Fat	0g
Cholesterol	95mg
Sodium	170mg
Total Carbohydrate	40g
Dietary Fiber	1g
Sugars	26g
Protein	2g

Oatmeal Raisin Cheesecake Crumble

MAURICE CHINN | BRUNSWICK, GEORGIA

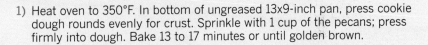

BAKE-OFF® CONTEST 44, 2010

e EASY

PREP TIME: 20 MINUTES (READY IN 3 HOURS 15 MINUTES)
SERVINGS: 16

1 package (16 oz) Pillsbury® Big Deluxe™ refrigerated oatmeal raisin cookies (12 cookies)

2 cups Fisher® Chef's Naturals® chopped pecans

2 packages (8 oz each) cream cheese, softened

1 can (14 oz) Eagle Brand® sweetened condensed milk

1 teaspoon vanilla

2 Eggland's Best eggs

1 cup Pillsbury Best® all purpose flour

¾ cup packed light brown sugar

½ cup cold Land O Lakes® unsalted or salted butter

¾ cup Hershey's® cinnamon chips

1 cup raisins

½ cup old-fashioned or quick-cooking oats

1) Heat oven to 350°F. In bottom of ungreased 13x9-inch pan, press cookie dough rounds evenly for crust. Sprinkle with 1 cup of the pecans; press firmly into dough. Bake 13 to 17 minutes or until golden brown.

2) Meanwhile, in large bowl, beat cream cheese with electric mixer on medium speed until smooth. Add milk, vanilla and eggs; beat until well blended. On low speed, beat in ½ cup of the flour. Pour over crust; spread evenly.

3) In medium bowl, mix brown sugar and remaining ½ cup flour. Cut in butter, using pastry blender or fork, until mixture looks like coarse crumbs. Stir in cinnamon chips, raisins, oats and remaining 1 cup pecans. Sprinkle over cheese mixture.

4) Bake 35 to 45 minutes longer or until set. Cool completely, about 2 hours. To serve, cut into 4 rows by 4 rows. Store in refrigerator.

Nutrition Information Per Serving	
Calories: 520	From Fat: 280
Total Fat	32g
Saturated Fat	14g
Trans Fat	.5g
Cholesterol	75mg
Sodium	180mg
Total Carbohydrate	50g
Dietary Fiber	2g
Sugars	38g
Protein	8g

Chocolate-Peanut Butter Layered Cupcakes

CARA SAPIDA | TURTLE CREEK, PENNSYLVANIA   BAKE-OFF® CONTEST 44, 2010

PREP TIME: 35 MINUTES (READY IN 1 HOUR 35 MINUTES)
SERVINGS: 18 CUPCAKES

1½ cups Pillsbury Best® all purpose flour

⅓ cup Hershey's® baking cocoa

1 cup packed brown sugar

1 teaspoon baking soda

¼ teaspoon salt

⅓ cup Crisco® pure vegetable oil

1 cup water

1 tablespoon white vinegar

½ teaspoon vanilla

1 Eggland's Best egg

1 package (8 oz) cream cheese, softened

¾ cup Jif® creamy peanut butter

⅓ cup granulated sugar

⅓ cup powdered sugar

¼ cup Reese's® peanut butter chips

¼ cup Hershey's® semi-sweet chocolate baking chips

1) Heat oven to 350°F. Place paper baking cup in each of 18 regular-size muffin cups.

2) In large bowl, mix flour, cocoa, brown sugar, baking soda and salt. Add oil, water, vinegar and vanilla to flour mixture, stirring just until smooth (do not overmix).

3) In another large bowl, beat egg, cream cheese, peanut butter and granulated sugar with electric mixer on medium speed until smooth. Add powdered sugar; beat until creamy.

4) Spoon 1 level tablespoon chocolate batter into each cup; evenly spread 1 level tablespoon peanut butter filling on top. Repeat layers. Sprinkle with peanut butter chips and chocolate chips.

5) Bake 25 to 30 minutes or until toothpick inserted in center comes out clean (do not overbake). Cool in pan 15 minutes. Remove from pan to cooling rack; cool 15 minutes. Serve warm or cool.

Nutrition Information Per Serving	
Calories: 260	From Fat: 110
Total Fat	13g
Saturated Fat	4.5g
Trans Fat	0g
Cholesterol	25mg
Sodium	180mg
Total Carbohydrate	31g
Dietary Fiber	1g
Sugars	21g
Protein	4g

Nutty Chocolate Hot Bites

SHEILA SUHAN | SCOTTDALE, PENNSYLVANIA

 BAKE-OFF® CONTEST 44, 2010

PREP TIME:	15 MINUTES (READY IN 1 HOUR)
SERVINGS:	24

 EASY

1 package (16 oz) Pillsbury® Ready to Bake!™ refrigerated chocolate chip cookies (24 cookies)

1¼ cups Fisher® mixed nuts with peanuts

1¼ cups Hershey's® Special Dark® chocolate baking chips

1¼ cups marshmallow creme

2 tablespoons half-and-half

⅛ teaspoon ground red pepper (cayenne)

1) Heat oven to 375°F. Place paper baking cup in each of 24 regular-size muffin cups. Place 1 cookie dough round in each cup. Using floured fingers, press dough to flatten slightly.

2) Bake 7 to 10 minutes or until golden brown. Cool in pans 15 minutes. Remove from pans to cooling rack. Cool completely, about 20 minutes.

3) Meanwhile, remove Brazil nuts from mixed nuts; coarsely chop Brazil nuts. In 2-quart saucepan, heat chocolate chips, marshmallow creme, half-and-half and red pepper over medium-high heat, stirring occasionally, until chips are melted and mixture is smooth. Stir in Brazil nuts and remaining mixed nuts.

4) Drop about 1 tablespoon nut mixture onto each cookie. Let stand about 15 minutes or until chocolate is set. To serve, remove bites from paper baking cups. If desired, place each bite into a new paper baking cup.

Nutrition Information Per Serving	
Calories: 200	From Fat: 100
Total Fat	11g
Saturated Fat	3.5g
Trans Fat	1g
Cholesterol	0mg
Sodium	80mg
Total Carbohydrate	23g
Dietary Fiber	1g
Sugars	16g
Protein	2g

Hot Fudge-Marshmallow Monkey Bread

BEBE WILLIAMS | HUNTSVILLE, ALABAMA   BAKE-OFF® CONTEST 44, 2010

PREP TIME: 25 MINUTES (READY IN 1 HOUR 10 MINUTES)
SERVINGS: 12

1 tablespoon Land O Lakes® butter, softened

1 can (16.3 oz) Pillsbury® Grands!® Homestyle refrigerated buttermilk biscuits (8 biscuits)

1 can (10.2 oz) Pillsbury® Grands!® Homestyle refrigerated buttermilk biscuits (5 biscuits)

13 large marshmallows

½ cup Land O Lakes® unsalted or salted butter

½ cup Smucker's® hot fudge ice cream topping

1 teaspoon vanilla

1 cup sugar

1 tablespoon Hershey's® Special Dark® baking cocoa

1) Heat oven to 350°F. Grease 12-cup fluted tube cake pan with 1 tablespoon butter. Cut all 13 biscuits into quarters; set aside.

2) In large microwavable bowl, place marshmallows, ½ cup butter, hot fudge topping and vanilla. Microwave uncovered on High 1 to 2 minutes, stirring once, until melted. Using wire whisk, stir until smooth.

3) In medium bowl, stir sugar and cocoa until blended.

4) Carefully place ¼ of the biscuit pieces into hot chocolate mixture, gently folding in to coat. Add another ¼ of the biscuits, gently folding in to coat. Using tongs, remove biscuits from chocolate, letting excess chocolate drip off. Drop 1 biscuit piece at a time into sugar mixture; spoon sugar over biscuit to coat. Layer biscuits in cake pan. Repeat with remaining biscuits. Sprinkle any remaining sugar mixture over biscuits.

5) Bake 30 to 40 minutes or until biscuits are deep golden and no longer doughy in center. Cool in pan 5 minutes. Place heatproof serving plate upside down over pan; carefully turn plate and pan over. Remove pan; immediately scrape any remaining topping in pan onto bread. Pull apart warm bread to serve.

Nutrition Information Per Serving	
Calories: 410	From Fat: 160
Total Fat	17g
Saturated Fat	8g
Trans Fat	4g
Cholesterol	25mg
Sodium	690mg
Total Carbohydrate	58g
Dietary Fiber	0g
Sugars	31g
Protein	4g

Pumpkin-Apple Gingerbread

PREP TIME: 15 MINUTES (READY IN 1 HOUR 40 MINUTES)
SERVINGS: 16

 EASY

4 cups all-purpose flour

3 teaspoons baking powder

2½ teaspoons ground ginger

½ teaspoon baking soda

½ teaspoon salt

½ teaspoon pumpkin pie spice

1 cup butter or margarine, softened

1 cup granulated sugar

½ cup packed brown sugar

4 eggs

1 can (15 oz) pumpkin (not pumpkin pie mix)

1 large green apple, peeled, shredded (1 cup)

½ cup molasses

Powdered sugar, if desired

1 cup whipping cream, beaten to stiff peaks

3 tablespoons finely chopped crystallized ginger

1) Heat oven to 350°F. Grease 12-cup fluted tube cake pan with shortening (do not use cooking spray); coat with flour. In medium bowl, mix flour, baking powder, ground ginger, baking soda, salt and pumpkin pie spice; set aside.

2) In large bowl, beat butter, granulated sugar and brown sugar with electric mixer on medium speed until creamy. Add eggs 2 at a time, beating well after each addition. Beat in pumpkin, apple and molasses. Gradually beat in flour mixture. Spoon into pan.

3) Bake 1 hour to 1 hour 10 minutes or until toothpick inserted in center of cake comes out clean. Cool in pan on cooling rack 15 minutes. Place cooling rack upside down on pan; turn rack and pan over. Remove pan. Cool completely, about 2 hours. Sprinkle with powdered sugar. Serve each slice on serving plate topped with about 2 tablespoons whipped cream and about ½ teaspoon crystallized ginger.

Nutrition Information Per Serving	
Calories: 410	From Fat: 160
Total Fat	18g
Saturated Fat	11g
Trans Fat	.5g
Cholesterol	100mg
Sodium	320mg
Total Carbohydrate	57g
Dietary Fiber	2g
Sugars	28g
Protein	5g

Cherry-Nut-Crescent Crisp

BETTY CHROMZACK | NORTHLAKE, ILLINOIS

BAKE-OFF® CONTEST 23, 1972

PREP TIME: 15 MINUTES (READY IN 55 MINUTES)
SERVINGS: 12

e EASY

- 1 cup all-purpose flour
- ¾ cup chopped pecans
- ½ cup granulated sugar
- ½ cup packed brown sugar
- 1 teaspoon ground cinnamon
- ½ cup butter or margarine, softened
- 2 cans (8 oz each) Pillsbury® refrigerated crescent dinner rolls
- 1 can (21 oz) cherry pie filling (2 cups)

  Powdered sugar, if desired

1) Heat oven to 375°F. In medium bowl, mix flour, pecans, granulated sugar, brown sugar, cinnamon and butter until crumbly. Sprinkle ⅓ of crumb mixture evenly in bottom of ungreased 13x9-inch pan.

2) Separate both cans of dough into 4 long rectangles. Place 3 rectangles over crumb mixture in pan; bring dough 1 inch up sides of pan to form crust. Sprinkle half of remaining crumb mixture over dough.

3) Spoon pie filling into crust. Sprinkle with remaining crumb mixture. Cut remaining dough rectangle into strips; place diagonally over pie filling to form a criss-cross pattern.

4) Bake 30 to 40 minutes or until golden brown. Sprinkle with powdered sugar; serve warm.

Nutrition Information Per Serving	
Calories: 420	From Fat: 190
Total Fat	21g
Saturated Fat	8g
Trans Fat	2.5g
Cholesterol	20mg
Sodium	350mg
Total Carbohydrate	53g
Dietary Fiber	2g
Sugars	31g
Protein	5g

White Chocolate-Banana Crème Brûlée Tarts

KRISTEN ABBOTT | HAVERTOWN, PENNSYLVANIA

BAKE-OFF® CONTEST 44, 2010

PREP TIME: 30 MINUTES (READY IN 1 HOUR 20 MINUTES)
SERVINGS: 12 TARTS

1 box Pillsbury® refrigerated pie crusts, softened as directed on box

2 Eggland's Best egg yolks

½ cup whipping cream

1 bag (12 oz) Hershey's® premier white baking chips (2 cups)

18 hard caramel or butterscotch candies, finely crushed (½ cup)

3 bananas, cut into ¼-inch slices

1) Heat oven to 450°F. Turn 12-cup muffin pan with regular-size cups upside down. Spray backs of muffin cups with Crisco® original no-stick cooking spray. Unroll 1 pie crust on work surface; roll into 12-inch round. Using 4-inch round cookie cutter, cut into 6 (4-inch) rounds. Repeat with the second crust.

2) Place dough rounds over backs of muffin cups, pleating dough to fit around cups. Prick dough several times with fork. Bake 5 to 10 minutes or until lightly browned. Cool 5 minutes. Carefully remove tart shells from muffin cups; place open sides up on cooling rack.

3) In small bowl, beat egg yolks; set aside. In 2-quart nonstick saucepan, heat cream and baking chips over medium heat, stirring constantly, until chips are melted. Stir about 1 cup of the hot cream mixture into egg yolks until well blended. Pour egg mixture back into saucepan; reduce heat to low. Cook 10 minutes, stirring constantly, until thickened.

4) Place tart shells on cookie sheet. Pour cream mixture into tart shells. Sprinkle each with 1 rounded teaspoon of the candies. Bake about 5 minutes or until candy is melted. Remove tarts from cookie sheet to cooling rack; cool 30 minutes. Top tarts with bananas; serve warm or cooled. Store covered in refrigerator.

Nutrition Information Per Serving	
Calories: 410	From Fat: 190
Total Fat	12g
Saturated Fat	12g
Trans Fat	0g
Cholesterol	45mg
Sodium	290mg
Total Carbohydrate	52g
Dietary Fiber	0g
Sugars	28g
Protein	4g

Alphabetical Index

General Recipe Index

This handy index lists every recipe by food category, major ingredient and/or cooking method, so you can easily locate recipes to suit your needs.

Nuts & Peanut Butter (continued)

Asian Chicken Salads with Peanuts, 111
Asian-Spiced Cashew-Chicken Piadinis, 55
Banana Nut Cheerios® Energy Bars, 310
Banana-Peanut Butter Cream Tart, 332
Blueberry-Almond Crème Muffins, 18
Cherry-Nut-Crescent Crisp, 342
Chocolate-Cherry-Pistachio Brownies, 330
Chocolate-Peanut Butter Layered
    Cupcakes, 338
Garlic Chicken over Baby Spinach with
    Toasted Pine Nuts, 115
Gorgonzola and Hazelnut-Stuffed
    Mushrooms, 42
Green Beans with Bacon-Walnut
    Vinaigrette, 112
Halloween Cookie Pizza, 276
Maple-Walnut Shortbread Cookies, 311
Mile-High Peanut Butter-Brownie Pie, 327
Nutty Chocolate Hot Bites, 339
Orange-Cherry-Almond Pinwheels, 108
Peach-Pecan Thumbprint Cookies, 316
Peanut Butter Cookie Granola, 10
Pecan Cookie Waffles with Honey-Cinnamon
    Butter, 15
Pecan-Date Pie, 331
Pecan-Sweet Potato Appetizers, 32
Quick Peanut Blossoms, 318
Rocky Road S'more Bars, 304
Salmon Pecan-Crusted Tartlets, 41
Spicy Cashew-Chicken Bundles, 77

Onions & Leeks

Caramelized Onion Beef Stew, 228
Greek Chicken Stew, 230
Italian Onion Soup, 93
Leek and Garlic Mashed Potatoes, 118
Make-Ahead Potato-Onion Gratin, 296
Onion and Oregano Beef Pot Roast, 227
Oregano Chicken Stir-Fry, 160
Pork Roast with Mushroom-Leek
    Compote, 229
Quick and Easy Onion Rolls, 118
Sautéed Sugar Snap Peas, Peppers and
    Onions, 98
Sizzling Chicken Fajitas, 161
White Chicken Pizza with Caramelized
    Sweet Onions, 169

Oranges

Chocolate-Orange Pastries, 305
Creamy Orange-Chocolate Truffle Bars, 323
Double Chocolate-Orange Scones, 22
Orange-Cherry-Almond Pinwheels, 108
Orange-Coconut Breakfast Rolls, 19
Orange-Coconut Tiramisu Tart, 324
Orange-Kissed Breakfast Bread Pudding, 28
Saucy Orange-Barbecued Chicken, 225

Pasta, Polenta & Gnocchi

Beef Tortellini Soup, 87
Chicken Alfredo with Sun-Dried Tomato
    Cream, 216
Chicken and Gnocchi Soup, 65
Chicken and Spinach Tortellini Soup, 80
Chicken Noodle Soup, 263
Chorizo and Pasta, 178
Chicken Cacciatore, 241
Cincinnati Chili, 256
Creamy Chicken Noodle Soup with Pesto
    Drizzle, 84
Easy Italian Wedding Soup, 76
Easy Pasta E Fagioli, 200
Family Favorite Lasagna,
Four Cheese-Veggie Lasagna
    Cups, 192
Garden Patch Minestrone, 204
Garden Vegetable Lasagna, 202
Italian Beef and Ravioli Stew, 139
Make-Ahead White Chicken
    Lasagna, 170
Mediterranean Beef and Pasta, 244
Not-Your-Mother's Tuna Pot Pie, 181
Pepperoni Pizza Chicken, 162
Pizza-Stuffed Peppers, 235
Pork and Polenta with Chunky Tomato
    Sauce, 243
Simple Hamburger Hot Dish, 133
So-Simple Tuna-Pasta Casserole, 273
Southwestern Corn Skillet, 205
Three Cheese-Sausage Lasagna, 210
Tuna Broccoli Casserole, 253
Tuna Florentine, 206
Turkey, Squash and Pasta Soup, 68

Pepperoni

Bubble Pizza, 129
Grilled Crisp-Crust Pizzas, 187
Italian Pepperoni-Vegetable Quiche, 213
Pepperoni-Pesto Popovers, 97
Pepperoni Pizza Chicken, 162
Pepperoni Pizza Snacks, 50
Pepperoni Quiche Squares, 14
Pizza-Stuffed Peppers, 235
Stuffed-Crust Pizza, 190

Peppers

Bacon-Chile Rellenos, 59
Chicken Mole Chili, 76
Chile and Cheese Empanaditas, 51
Chile Rellenos Bake, 143
Cuban Flank Steak, 240
Impossibly Easy Chiles Rellenos
    Pie, 214
Italian Sausage and Pepper Stew, 196
Oregano Chicken Stir-Fry, 160
Pineapple-Chicken Kabob Packets, 171
Pizza-Stuffed Peppers, 235
Raspberry-Chipotle Barbecue Chicken
    Pizza, 165
Sautéed Sugar Snap Peas, Peppers and
    Onions, 98
Sizzling Chicken Fajitas, 161
Snappy Joes on Texas Toast, 91
Thai-Style Chicken Curry Soup, 79

Pesto

Butternut Squash-Pesto Pizza, 184
Caprese Pesto Margherita Stackers, 39
Creamy Chicken Noodle Soup with Pesto
    Drizzle, 84
Parmesan Crostini with Spinach-Pesto
    Spread, 49
Pepperoni-Pesto Popovers, 97
Pesto-Parmesan Grilled Chicken, 153
Pesto-Quinoa-Spinach Quiche, 29
Tomato Pesto Pizza, 196

Pies & Tarts

Banana-Peanut Butter Cream Tart, 332
Black-Bottom Cranberry Cream Pie, 336
Caribbean Panna Cotta Pie, 334
Mile-High Peanut Butter-Brownie Pie, 327
Orange-Coconut Tiramisu Tart, 324
Pecan-Date Pie, 331
Pumpkin-Ginger Pie with Gingersnap
    Streusel, 293
White Chocolate-Banana Crème Brûlée
    Tarts, 343

Pineapple

Chicken-Coconut-Pineapple Curry, 226
Curry-Mustard Glazed Meatballs, 50
Pineapple-Chicken Kabob Packets, 171
Pineapple-Pork Tacos, 223
Sweet-and-Sour Pork, 231

Pizzas

Barbecue Pork and Veggie Pizza, 178
Broiled Buffalo Chicken Pizza, 157
Butternut Squash-Pesto Pizza, 184
Chicken and Spinach Dip Pizza, 157
Chutney Pizza with Turkey, Spinach and
    Gorgonzola, 163
Deep-Dish Sausage Patty Pizza, 193
Easy Gyro Pizza, 211
Easy Mexican Chicken Pizza, 164
Grilled Crisp-Crust Pizzas, 187
Mediterranean Three-Tomato Tart, 195
Philly Cheese Steak Pizza, 138
Raspberry-Chipotle Barbecue Chicken
    Pizza, 165
Shrimp and Veggie Appetizer Pizza, 43
Spicy Double-Mozzarella Pancetta Pizza, 179
Stuffed-Crust Pizza, 190
Tomato Pesto Pizza, 196
White Chicken Pizza with Caramelized
    Sweet Onions, 169
Wild West Pizza, 132

Pork

Barbecue Pork and Veggie Pizza, 178
Barbecued Pork Chops for Two, 236
Fajita Pulled Pork Sandwiches, 221
German Red Cabbage and Pork Ribs, 247
Honey Barbecue Pork Roast with
    Carrots, 224
Just-in-Time Pork Stew, 186
Pineapple-Pork Tacos, 223
Pork and Polenta with Chunky Tomato
    Sauce, 243
Pork and Sweet Potato Chili, 89
Pork Chops with Apples and Stuffing, 266
Pork Chops with Mustard-Thyme Gravy, 245
Pork Chops with Sauerkraut, 205
Pork Diane Skillet Supper, 264